THE ORIGINS OF RUSSIA

THE ORIGINS OF RUSSIA

BY

GEORGE VERNADSKY

OXFORD

AT THE CLARENDON PRESS

1959

Oxford University Press, Amen House, London E.C.4

GLASGOW   NEW YORK   TORONTO   MELBOURNE   WELLINGTON
BOMBAY   CALCUTTA   MADRAS   KARACHI   KUALA LUMPUR
CAPE TOWN   IBADAN   NAIROBI   ACCRA

PRINTED IN GREAT BRITAIN

PREFACE

THE purpose of this book is to reconsider the ancient background of Russia, as well as the basic trends in the formation and early development of the eastern Slavs and their civilization in the light of both previous and current historical research (including my own).

In my opinion, the growth of the Russian people cannot be properly understood without a careful examination of the position of the Slavs and the Russes (Rus, Ros) in the Ancient World and of their early civilization. It is clear, to me at least, that that civilization is historically connected with the central Asian cultural sphere in which the Alanic peoples for a long time played a major role. The Celts and the Teutons seem likewise to have had ancient ties with that background. In their migrations the Eurasian nomads—Scythians, Alans, Turks, and others—extended the elements of that culture westward where it mingled with Hellenism.

Various aspects of the Eurasian world—political and social ideology and organization, mythology, epics, and art—are examined in the first chapter of this book. The second and third chapters deal with the position of the early Slavs and the old Russes in the constantly changing conditions of successive waves of nomadic migrations and of the expansion and tribulations of the Alanic and Turkish empires which rose one after another in western Eurasia and eastern Europe.

Chapter 4 is devoted to the spiritual foundations of the old Russian culture, permeated as it was with religious notions and feelings. The old Slavic Paganism was not as primitive as it is often represented. It must have constituted a rather complex system of rites, myths, and ideas, in which different layers and aspects can be discerned, such as the clan cult and the more elaborate tribal religious systems. In origin the old Slavic religion resembled Mithraism in many respects. In its further development it absorbed various elements from Manichaeism and Gnosticism especially.

The last two chapters in the book (5 and 6) deal with the tremendous upheaval in the spiritual life of the Slavic world in the early Middle Ages.

The Slavs's close contacts with Byzantium resulted in their gradual conversion to Christianity. The decisive step in this direction was the mission of Constantine (St. Cyril) and Methodius to Moravia in 863 which led to the creation of the Christian Slavic Church and Slavic Letters.

Although many Russians were baptized in the second half of the ninth century, it was only as late as the end of the tenth century that Christianity became Russia's state religion. Even then the official victory of the new faith did not at once eradicate the ancient beliefs. Their remnants were clearly active not only in the period immediately following the conversion, but in the Muscovite era as well. The old beliefs receded but slowly under the impact of the Christian Church and in their turn affected the Russian religious mind in many ways. Even in the europeanized Russian empire of the eighteenth and nineteenth centuries traces of the ancient notions and rites could be observed, especially among the peasants in remote districts. It was the spread of industrialization and the rise of urban fashions in the late nineteenth and twentieth centuries which led to the final disintegration of the old folk-art and folk-beliefs. The Revolution of 1917 greatly undermined the influence of the Christian Church. Karl Marx's doctrine was made the basis of the official line of thought and behaviour in the Soviet state. The tortuous road of history thus led the Russians from Mithraism through Christianity to Marxism. Christianity is not dead in Russia, however, and Marxism is not as alive ideologically as it used to be in the first years of the Revolution.

The outcome of the present-day spiritual confusion can hardly be predicted as yet. Whatever it will be, it will affect the fate not of the Russians alone but of all mankind.

In my work on this book and the problems related to it I have received much stimulation from many interested friends and colleagues. With some of them I discussed, personally or through correspondence, a number of thorny problems. Some were kind enough to let me read their yet unpublished studies, or sections of them, in manuscript. (This is acknowledged in each case in the notes). Many sent me copies of their books or reprints of their articles. I wish to extend my warm thanks to all of them and especially to W. E. D. Allen, Yury Arbatsky, H. W.

Bailey, Dzambulat Dzanty, Michael de Ferdinandy, Ilya Gershevitch, János Harmatta, H. W. Haussig, Roman Jakobson, R. J. H. Jenkins, Jaap Kunst, Tadeusz Lewicki, Philip Lozinski, Manfred Mayrhofer, V. F. Minorsky, Gyula Moravcsik, Basile Nikitine, Johannes Rahder, N. A. Rast, George Roerich, Baron Michael de Taube, and Paul Tedesco, as well as to remember with gratitude the late Grace Faulkner Ward.

My sincere thanks are due to the staff of the Yale University Library for their kind co-operation. It is my pleasant duty to express my gratitude to the offices of the Clarendon Press for their advice and help in preparing the manuscript for the printers.

G. V.

New Haven, Conn.
6 *December* 1957

CONTENTS

ILLUSTRATIONS

Between pp. 310–11

ABBREVIATIONS

AAAH	*Acta Archaeologica Academiae Hungaricae* (Budapest).
AKM	*Abhandlungen für die Kunde des Morgenlandes.*
Annuaire	*Annuaire de l'Institut de Philologie et d'Histoire Orientales et Slaves* (Bruxelles).
ASEER	*American Slavic and East European Review.*
BGA	*Bibliotheca Geographorum Arabicorum,* De Goeje, M. J., ed.
BSOAS	*Bulletin of the School of Oriental and African Studies.*
EI	*Encyclopaedia of Islam.*
ESA	*Eurasia Septentrionalis Antiqua.*
FUF	*Finnisch-Ugrische Forschungen.*
GSU	*Godišnik na Sofiiskiia Universitet, Istorikofilologičeski Fakultet.*
IGAIMK	*Izvestiia Gosudarstvennoi Akademii Istorii Materialnoi Kultury.*
JAOS	*Journal of the American Oriental Society.*
KS	*Kratkie Soobshcheniia Instituta Istorii Materialnoi Kultury Akademii Nauk.*
MAS	*Mémoires de l'Académie Impériale des Sciences.*
MGH	*Monumenta Germaniae Historica.*
MGT	*Magyar-Görög Tanulmányok* (Budapest).
MIAS	*Materialy i issledovaniia po arkheologii SSSR.*
MVAG	*Mitteilungen der Vorderasiatisch-Ägyptischen Gesellschaft.*
OLDP	*Obshchestvo Liubitelei drevne-russkoi pismennosti, Pamiatniki.*
OSP	*Oxford Slavonic Papers.*
PG	Migne, *Patrologia Graeca.*
PSRL	*Polnoe Sobranie Russkikh Letopisei.*
PW	Pauly-Wissowa, *Realencyclopedie der Klassischen Altertumswissenschaft.*
RES	*Revue des Études Slaves.*
RIB	*Russkaia Istoricheskaia Biblioteka.*
SEER	*Slavonic and East European Review.*
SOF	*Südost-Forschungen.*
TPhS	*Transactions of the Philological Society.*
ZDMG	*Zeitschrift der Deutschen Morgenländischen Gesellschaft.*
ZMNP	*Zhurnal Ministerstva Narodnogo Prosveshcheniia.*

1

THE ANCIENT SLAVS AND THE WORLD OF THE STEPPES

1. *The historical background of the early Slavs*

'WHO are the Russians?' is a question no more or no less difficult to answer than the equivalent question about any other modern nation. On the other hand, the companion question, 'What is the origin of the Russians?' is perhaps more difficult to deal with than a similar query concerning the English, the French, or the Germans.

To take the first question first, the clearest characteristic of a nation is its language. We are on firm ground when we say that the Russians are those people who speak Russian, that is, for whom Russian is their mother tongue. This is, however, not a full answer to the question, since language is not the only determinant. Anthropological, psychological, and biological factors have to be taken into consideration if we are to know more about a people. And last, but not least, it is the great cultural traditions that build up a nation and make her conscious of her place in the world. Most of these factors, as well as their interrelation and the relative importance of each, change substantially in the course of history. The Russian people of the early Middle Ages differed from the present-day Russians in many respects. The Pagan Russian society of the ninth century was not the same as the Christian society of the eleventh century. The deeper we go into the past the more difficult it is for us to understand the spirit and the ways of life of the forefathers of any people. We have to evaluate carefully every bit of evidence on both the spiritual life and the material culture of the peoples and tribes of that remote era in order to try to understand the main trends in their development.

The Russian language is a Slavic tongue and thus, linguistically, the Russians belong to the Slavic group within the Indo-European family of peoples. Historically, ethnically, and

culturally the Russians had been, through the ages, closely connected with other Slavs. That connexion was even more evident
in the early periods of Slavic history when the difference between various Slavic dialects was not as great as it is now between modern Slavic languages, and when the religious and
cultural foundations of life of the Slavic tribes were common to
all of them. When speaking of remote antiquity it would be
hard to discern a 'proto-Russian' tongue. The linguistic ancestors of the Russians must have spoken a form of the 'ancient
Slavic' language. From this point of view it is obvious that the
problem of the origin of the Russians is only a part of a wider
problem—that of the origin of the Slavs.

In discussing the historical background of any nation we
must first discover the geographic location of the original ancestral group from which that nation eventually developed through
many vicissitudes. Few if any modern peoples can be considered
aborigines of the countries which they now occupy. Most
modern nations were formed through migrations, in some cases
through several successive waves of migrations which occurred
both in ancient times and in the early Middle Ages (and some
of them, in the modern age). In view of this, the problem of the
aboriginal home (in German *Urheimat*; in Russian *pra-rodina*) of
the Indo-European peoples is a moot one. Quite a number of
hypotheses (contradicting each other) were suggested and subsequently abandoned to be replaced by new ones. The search
for the original home of the Slavs is no exception in this respect.[1]
It is supposed that the Slavs lived in the area of present-day
western Ukraine and Poland since around 600 B.C. Many a
leading Slavist even considers that region the *pra-rodina* of the
Slavs. By some scholars the Slav *Urheimat* is located more
specifically in the Pripet marshes. From the archaeological point
of view western Ukraine and Poland, as well as Moravia,
northern Bohemia, and Lusatia, are the area of the 'fields of
funeral urns', as an ancient form of burial is called. The culture
of funeral urns lasted from the early part of the first millennium
B.C. until about A.D. 200. A number of scholars consider it
Slavic though there is no consensus of opinion on this problem.

The bulk of the Slavs were agriculturists for ages and most of
them still are. Archaeological research has shown that agriculture

[1] See note A, p. 317.

was practised in the area of Poland and the Ukraine since time immemorial. This seems to support the view that the Slavs were aborigines in this area. And yet such a conclusion would not be entirely convincing. Nothing is known of the language the original populations of the area spoke. They may have belonged to a non-Slavic, even to a non-Indo-European race. The Slavs may have been (even though in the remote past) new-comers in this part of the world who, after settling in this area, merged with the aborigines and kept agriculture going. Moreover, we do not need to think that all of the proto-Slavs were agriculturists. In the early Middle Ages we find a considerable variety of occupations among the eastern Slavs. While many of them tilled land, others were cattle-breeders, hunters, bee-keepers, or fishermen. Of the latter, the Brodniki in the lower Don region constituted an autonomous society with their own customs and habits.[1] We may think that the variety in the Slavic way of life was no less marked in late antiquity than in the Middle Ages.

The diversity of the customs of various groups of the east Slavic tribes and certain other tribes associated with them was keenly felt by the compilers of the early Russian 'Chronography' (*Povest' Vremennykh Let*), the bulk of which was written in the eleventh century and which was completed at the beginning of the twelfth century. According to this chronicle, each of the Russian (east Slavic) tribes 'kept their own customs, and the laws and traditions of their fathers, and each had their own character'. Together they formed a kind of federation ('they lived in peace' with each other) which was called 'Great Scythia' by the Greeks. Obviously, the chronicler considered the variety of customs among the east Slavic tribes a legacy of the remote ages. Besides—and this is highly significant—he connected the origins of the east Slavs with Scythia, that is, the world of the steppes.

The Eurasian steppes stretch from Mongolia in the east to the mouth of the Danube in the west. There is a steppe island in central Europe—present-day Hungary. The zone of the steppes is one of the latitudinal landscape zones which are characteristic of the physical face of Eurasia. North of the steppes proper extends the intermediary belt of the 'wooded

[1] On the Brodniki see G. Vernadsky, *Kievan Russia* (New Haven, 1948), p. 158.

steppe' (in French *steppe boisée*, in Russian *lesostep'*); beyond it
lies the zone of the forests; the arctic tundra is the northernmost
zone of the Eurasian landscape; the deserts constitute its
southernmost fringe.

From time immemorial the steppes presented a convenient
avenue for the inroads and migrations of the pastoral peoples.
Every time the nomads migrated to the west they either conquered and subordinated to themselves the populations of the
south Russian and Ukrainian sections of the steppe zone or
pushed the previous settlers west—to central, and then to
western Europe—or north to the wooded steppe and the forest
zones. As the process of migrations went on for centuries and
millenniums, peoples and tribes which originally had lived in
central Asia and south Russia had to look for new abodes in
north Russia, as well as in central and western Europe. Such
was the course taken by most of the Indo-European peoples
except for those—the Indo-Aryans—who went south from their
original abodes in central Asia to Iran and India. It seems
most likely that the Slavs were no exception to this pattern of
migrations and that the proto-Slavs, or in any case a branch of
them, originated in central Asia. Such is the opinion of V. I.
Lamansky, V. M. Florinsky, and K. Moszyński.[1] Of the authors
of recent publications on the early Slavs, Francis Dvornik is
inclined to place the original home of the ancient Slavs more
to the west than most of his predecessors, namely, in the area
of the Lusatian culture between the Baltic Sea in the north and
the Carpathian mountains in the south; and between the Elbe
River in the west and the Vistula River in the east. But even F.
Dvornik admits that the progenitors of some Slavic peoples,
such as the Antes, the Croats, and the Serbs, came from the
Iranian and Alanic milieu in the northern Caucasus and the
area beyond the Caspian Sea.

The deep affinity of the culture of the early Slavs with that
of Indo-Aryan, Alanic, and Turkish peoples is evidenced by
many traits in the folk-lore, art, and religion of the Slavs. More
will be said about this in the following chapters. As regards art,

[1] See V. I. Lamansky, 'O Slavianakh v Maloi Azii, Afrike i Ispanii', *Akademiia
Nauk, Uchenye Zapiski II otdeleniia*, 1859, v; V. M. Florinsky, *Pervobytnye Slaviane*
(Tomsk, 1895–8, 2 vols.); K. Moszyński, 'Badania nad pochodzieniem i pierwotną
kulturą Słowian', *Polska Akademja Umiejętnosci, Wydział Filologiczny, Rozprawy*, 62,
Nr. 2 (1925).

suffice it to say here that the basic motifs of Russian peasant embroideries date back to the Scythian and Sarmatian eras. Concerning the pagan cult of the old Slavs, a number of names of Slavic deities are similar to Iranian and Indic. The very word for 'God' in Slavic (*bog*) may be compared to the Old Indic *bhagas* and the Old Persian *baga*. From the descriptions of the temples of the western Slavs (of which we know more than of the sanctuaries of the eastern Slavs) it is obvious that emblems and amulets similar to those used by the Alans and the Turks played an important role in the old Slavic cult. The god Svantovit, whose idol stood in the temple of Arkona, held a bow in his left hand. In front of the idol was placed a huge sword as well as the bridle and the saddle of the sacred white horse which was kept in a stable near the temple. No one except the priest was allowed to ride this horse. In order better to understand the significance of these emblems we have to recall that the bow was used as a badge of authority by both the Huns and the Mongols; that the cult of the sword was widely spread among the Alans (furthermore, the sword was an emblem of royal power both in Attila's realm and in the khanates of the Mongol empire); and that white horses were considered sacred by both the Aryans and the Mongols. According to old Mongol custom, the chief minister of the clan cult (*beki*) was put on the white horse before his enthronement. It should be added that the cult of the horse, with bridle and saddle as its emblems, was practised not only in Arkona but in some other west Slavic sanctuaries as well, such as those of the god Triglav in Stettin and of god Svarozhich at Retra. As regards the architecture of the Slavic temples, that of Arkona had a square shape and in this respect, as the art historian Joseph Strzygovski has pointed out, closely resembled old Iranian temples and fire-altars. The recently discovered foundation of the sanctuary of the god Perun near Novgorod has a round shape, being enclosed in two concentric circular ramparts. This design is similar to that of the Koy-Krylgan Kala in Khorezm (which, however, was a castle, not a temple).

It is likewise significant that the military organization of the early Slavs shows certain traits reminding us of the armies of the steppe nomads. True, the latter consisted almost exclusively of cavalry, while most of the Slavs fought on foot. However, the Slavs had also cavalry squadrons. According to the Byzantine historian, Procopius of Caesaria, squadrons of 'Huns' (Bulgars), Sclaveni (Slovene), and Antes proved very useful to Belisarius in the Byzantine-Gothic war in the sixth century of our era. As will be explained later, the Sclaveni and the Antes represented two of the three major groups of Slavs mentioned by the sixth-century writers (the third group was known as the Venedi).

The armies of the Iranians and the Turks were organized on the decimal principle, consisting, as they were, of units of ten, of a hundred, and of a thousand. Such organization greatly simplified the task of mobilization, especially in an emergency. The decimal principle was likewise used by the eastern Slavs in the Kievan period. The city militia in major Russian towns of that age was known as the 'thousand'. In the border principalities close to the steppes, like Pereiaslav, the 'hundred' was the basic unit of the local military establishment. The highest army unit for which there existed a special numeral in the old Iranian language was the thousand. However, in the period between the fourth and the second centuries B.C., a larger unit came to the fore in central Asia, the 'ten thousand' (myriad). It existed in the Tokharian armies, and indeed there was a special numeral for it in the Tokharian language—*tmam* (dialect A) or *tumane* (dialect B).[1] This term was borrowed from the Tokharian into the Turkish language (*tümän*), as well as into the Mongol (*tümen*) and the Persian (*tuman*).

While the armies of the Slavs neither in the Roman era nor in the early Middle Ages were organized in the 'ten thousand' units, the Slavs had their own numeral for it—*t'ma*. The term may have been borrowed from the Tokharian, but it seems more likely that the Tokharian and the Slavic terms are cognate words, not borrowings from one of these two languages to another. It is likewise significant that the Tokharian word for 'army' (*ratäk*) corresponds to the Old Russian word *rat'* which means both 'army' and 'war'. The similarity of these Tokharian and Slavic terms seems to indicate in this case the identity of the Slavic military organization with the Tokharian in remote antiquity. It is only in central Asia that a contact between Slav and Tokhar armies could have taken place. On this basis we may surmise that at some remote period the Slavs, or in any case a branch of them, were a strong and warlike people. Why

[1] On the Tokharians see Chapter 2, section 1, below.

and when their organization broke down we do not know, but it may be assumed that they migrated partly westward and partly joined their more successful neighbours—the Alans and Turks. It will be recalled in this connexion that in the late Roman era many Slavic tribes were controlled by Alanic clans and that the Slavic element was strong in the Hunnish empire of the fifth century of our era.

If we assume that the Slavs might have represented a strong military factor in antiquity—either as an independent force or as auxiliaries of the Alans—then we may expect to find traces of their early expansion in the area overrun, at one time or another, by the Alans and the peoples and tribes associated with or controlled by the Alans. There are place-names both in Transcaucasia and in Asia Minor which sound Slavic and, in my opinion at least, they actually may be of Slavic origin. Such is, for example, Tiflis (now Tbilisi) in Georgia, known for its natural warm springs. The name seems to be an adaptation of the Slavic name Teplice (there is a town of that name in Czechoslovakia) derived from the Slavic adjective *teplyi* 'warm'. Consider also the name of the old castle in Mingrelia, Gordi, which W. E. D. Allen compares to that of Gordion in ancient Phrygia.[1] Both these names may derive from the Slavic *grad* (in Russian *gorod*, in Polish *gród*) 'castle' or 'town'. Place-names often move along the path of the migration of the tribe to whose language they belong. We may suppose that a Slavic group moved, around 800 B.C., from the north Caucasian plains, through the mountain pass of Daryal (*Dar-yal* 'the Gate of the Al', i.e. Alans) and stopped in Mingrelia, building a castle (Gordi) there. From there, later on, the same group, or a branch of it, moved to Phrygia and built another town of the same name (Gordion). The argument may seem hypothetical, but the possibility of the participation of the ancient Slavs in the Scythian and Alanic migrations in Hither Asia seems fairly certain.

Turning now from toponymics to vocabulary, it seems likely that a number of Slavic words were borrowed by the peoples of Hither Asia in remote antiquity. The late Czech orientalist, B. Hrozný, pointed out the striking similarity between the

[1] W. E. D. Allen, 'Two Georgian Maps of the First Half of the Eighteenth Century', *Imago Mundi*, x (1953), 104 and n. 6. W. E. D. Allen was kind enough to supplement the information contained in this article in a letter to me.

Babylonian word for 'road', *daragu*, and the Czech *dráha* (same meaning). The Russian word for 'road', *doroga*, is even closer to the Babylonian form than the Czech. The Sumerian term *urudu* 'copper', Hrozný likens to the Slavic *ruda* 'ore'.[1] He explains these parallels by suggesting the existence of early contacts between the Semites and the Indo-Europeans in Transcaucasia. The Indo-Europeans in question obviously were Slavs.

Of great significance is also the impact of the Slavic language on the Thracian and Phrygian. It is supposed that the migration of the Thracians and Phrygians to the Balkan peninsula and Asia Minor began around 1200 B.C. Only fragments of the Thracian and Phrygian languages are known to us. Both these languages belong to the Indo-European family and are closely interrelated. The vocabulary of both contains words strikingly similar to Slavic. Presumably a number of Slavic clans mixed with the Thraco-Phrygians either before the beginning of the latter's migrations or during their migrations.

The westward migration of the Slavs seems to have started in the Scythian era. By about 550 B.C. a number of Slavic tribes must have penetrated into the area of present-day Ukraine. Presumably, the tempo of their movement was slow, and their migration might have lasted for about a century. Other Slavic tribes apparently continued to stay east of the lower Volga for a few centuries more. They came to the Don region and the Pontic steppes in the wake of the Roxolani[2] and of the Alans in the course of the first century B.C. and the first century of our era. With their arrival, the second stage of the early Slavic migrations was set.

To sum up the preceding argument, our information on the history of the Slavs in the first millennium B.C. is so fragmentary that it is hardly possible, at the present stage of historical research, to draw a systematic picture of the Slavic way of life and culture in that early era. One thing seems certain, namely, that in that period the Slavs played a much greater role in the history of both central Asia and Hither Asia than has been admitted until recently. Indeed, the evidence available indicates that the Slavs had a strong army; that they built cities; and

---

[1] B. Hrozný, *Histoire de l'Asie Antérieure, de l'Inde et de la Crète depuis les origines jusqu'au début du second millénaire* (Paris, 1947), p. 86.

[2] On the Roxolani see Chapter 2, section 2, below.

that their language left traces in the languages of their neighbours. It should be added that the Slavic language was well
equipped already in that early era for expressing not only concrete terms of everyday life but abstract notions as well. This is
a clear indication of the level it had achieved. One of such
notions is 'liberty', in Slavic *svoboda*. As the philologist G. Bonfante has pointed out, the word *svoboda* is found in Slavic only
and has no cognates in other Indo-European languages. It is
from this Slavic word that the name of the Thraco-Phrygian
god Sabazios (Sabadios) derives.[1] Sabazios was venerated as
the 'liberating' God in Phrygia, Thrace, the Caucasus, and the
Crimea. Since his name is of Slavic background, it seems likely
that his cult originated in a mixed Phrygian-Slavic milieu.
Subsequently, the cult spread among the Greeks as well.

2. *Nomadic society: kinship and fraternity*

In view of the close affiliation of the early Slavs with the
peoples of the steppes, especially with the Alans, a study of the
social and political organization of the nomads, as well as of
their folk-lore and mythology, is indispensable for a better
understanding of the early history and culture of the Slavs.[2]

It would not be amiss to comment on the term 'nomad' itself.
It is, of course, of Greek origin. Webster defines it as 'one of a
race or tribe that has no fixed location, but wanders from place
to place'. The term is used in this sense in all modern languages.
As to its Greek background, in Homer we find *nomós* 'pasture'
and *nemo* 'to pasture', 'graze', i.e. 'drive to pasture'. It is obvious that the original meaning of the term 'nomads' in Greek
was 'pastoral peoples', not 'wandering' or 'roving' peoples.
Pastoral peoples do not wander aimlessly. They drive their
herds from one suitable pasture to another in each season, and
from summer pastures to winter pastures and vice versa, depending on the local conditions and following a well established
traditional pattern. Only in case of emergency, like drought,
the pattern has to be changed. A number of pastoral tribes live
in movable felt tents, but they usually pitch their tents for the
winter in the same locality every year. Others have houses in
which they stay permanently, at least for part of the year.

[1] G. Bonfante, 'Sabadios-Svoboda le Libérateur', *Annuaire*, vii (1944), 41–46.
[2] See note B, p. 317.

It is the duty of the clan elders, the 'wise men' or the 'notables' of the tribe, to distribute pastures among single clans and families, and to direct the course of the summer and winter movements of men and cattle. The notables are men of 'name', i.e. of prestige. In Alanic, *nom* means both 'name' and 'fame'. The Alanic suffix -*ad* is used to form abstract notions. Thus *nomad* in Alanic means 'namedom', i.e. 'notables' collectively. The 'name' in this case is not the 'personal name' but the 'clan name'. The 'nomads' in this sense are clan elders.[1]

Kinship was the main principle on which all of the ancient societies were built. The pastoral peoples of Eurasia were no exception to this rule. The clan was the main channel for the continuity of kinship. Through the clan the living considered themselves protected by the dead. On the other hand, the duty of the living was to produce offsprings in order to perpetuate the clan in the future. The eternal biological force which worked through the clan, its living matter, the sperm, was revered as the link between generations—past, present, and future. 'Clan' in Alanic is *mygkag*, from *myg* 'sperm'. *Mygkag* literally means 'belonging to the sperm', i.e. 'of the same sperm'. The continuity of kinship through the clan was also expressed by the notions of 'blood' and 'bone'. The sib referred to themselves as being 'of one blood' (*ju tug*) or 'of one bone' (*ju stæg*).

How strong was the feeling of responsibility towards their dead kinsmen among the descendants of the Alans—the Ossetians—even in the late nineteenth century is shown by some of their traditional habits. A characteristic feature of these was the dedication of a horse to the deceased. The purpose of this rite was to provide him with decent transportation to the place reserved for him in the Nether World. The rite, which in modern times was merely symbolic, is a survival of the ancient custom of the burying with the dead warrior of his horse or horses. The Ossetian funeral was followed by a lavish banquet to which not only the kin but neighbours and passers-by were invited. It was believed that the food consumed by the guests in the name of the deceased reached the latter in some mystic way. There was no greater offence to the Ossetian than to tell him that his dead starve. In many cases after the funeral banquet, horse-races and shooting competitions were held. The

[1] See note C, p. 317.

kinsmen of the deceased had to provide prizes for the victors. Expenses for the memorial rites often ran so high that the deceased's family would become completely destitute. But the custom could not be eradicated, not in any case until the Soviet Revolution.[1]

It would not be inappropriate to observe here that the funeral banquet was a solemn rite with the Slavs as well (the Old Slavic word for it is *strava*). It is also significant that burying the deceased prince with his favourite horse constituted an important part of the old Russian funeral ceremonies. The custom was kept for a long time even after Russia's conversion to Christianity.

Each Alanic clan had an emblem of its own. This was called *damyghæ* (*da-myg* 'thy sperm'). It is from this term that the word *tamga* (Turkic for 'clan emblem') derives.[2] In this latter form the term was used by the Turks and the Mongols and was later borrowed by the Russians. The clan had its ancestral abode, *mæsyg*. In Ossetian *mæsyg* means 'tower'. The typical Ossetian tower was built of stone and had a rectangular shape. It was a several-storied building and served as a fortress in the cases of an enemy attack. Many such towers stood in the mountains of Ossetia in the late nineteenth century and some of them presumably still stand.

In the wooded regions the mæsyg was built of timber; in the steppe and arid areas, of sun-hardened clay bricks. The Khorezmian archaeological expedition of the 1940's, led by S. P. Tolstov, discovered a number of ancient sites of huge clan dwellings in the region of the delta of the Amu-Darya River, south of Aral Sea. One of them, known as Kalaly-gyr I, has a rectangular shape, 1,100 metres by 700 metres. Another, Küzeli-gyr, is in the form of a triangle to fit the shape of the hill where it is located (one side 1,000 metres long, the other two about 400 metres each). In both these settlements the dwelling rooms were built in the thick wall which surrounded the site. The access to the rooms was from the inside. The whole enclosed space was empty; it was apparently intended to keep the clan's cattle safe in case of an enemy attack. In Kalaly-gyr there were

---

[1] I have no information about the present-day situation in Ossetia in this respect.
[2] See G. Vernadsky, 'Note on the Origin of the Word Tamga', *JAOS*, lxxvi (1956), 188–9.

two rows of rooms along the walls; in Küzeli-gyr, three rows. According to S. P. Tolstov, both these settlements must have been built in the middle of the first millennium B.C. Another, a less ancient type of clan abodes (400–200 B.C.) is that of two, or more, many-roomed houses with a broad street between them. Each of these houses could contain from 500 to 1,000 inhabitants. The whole settlement was enclosed within walls, but the houses were not built into the wall. In Janbas-kala, where the complex consists of two houses only, there are two different types of tamga impressed on the bricks of the wall. Obviously, this was a two-clan settlement.[1]

When the clan grew too large, it had to break into several branches. Part of the clan would migrate in such cases. An intermediary group between the clan and the family was the 'greater family', comparable to the Slavic *zadruga*. Several generations lived together under the authority of the great-grandfather or of the grandfather. In the old times the eldest woman—the wife or widow of the family elder—likewise enjoyed great prestige in the family commune. She was called *æxsin* 'the lady'. This word was borrowed from the Alanic into the Hungarian with the same meaning ('asszony').

The greater family commune was typical of the Ossetian way of life as late as the nineteenth century. The older generations lived in the main house; for the younger, new houses were built around. The main room in the main house constituted the centre of the community life. It served as a combination of kitchen, dining-room, and lounge. There was located the hearth on which food for the whole family group was prepared. Above the hearth an iron chain (*ræxys*) was fixed. This was the symbol of the hearth and the most sacred object in the house.

Hospitality was a sacred custom with the Alans and still is with the Ossetians. Anyone who was able to speak the words 'I am your guest' to the master of the house was received as a friend, even though before he had been an enemy of the family. To the guest the seat of honour was given. In case of an attack by brigands, the master of the house defended his guest even at the peril of his own life.

All of the members of the clan were bound to help each other

---

[1] S. P. Tolstov, *Drevnii Khorezm* (Moscow, 1948), pp. 77–80, 88–94; id. *Po sledam drevnekhorezmiiskoi tsivilizatsii* (Moscow, 1948), pp. 93–95, 112–16.

and to defend each other. In case of an offence by an outsider against any member of the clan, or a murder, vengeance was the sacred duty of kinsmen. If the murderer could not be found or reached, a kinsman of his had to be killed. 'Blood is washed off by blood' was the traditional rule of behaviour. The result of the custom was constant blood feuds. In nineteenth-century Ossetia the vengeance could be substituted by a demand for blood-money. In some cases the murderer was led to the grave of his victim and consecrated to the man he killed. The shameful name of *fældyst* ('consecrated [to the dead]') was then given to the murderer as well as to his whole clan. Under the burden of this name, the murderer was supposed to lose his 'self'; he was no longer regarded as a complete human being. He did not belong to himself any more, but was now the dead man's eternal slave.[1]

While the clan was the basis of the ancient society, the variety of human relations could not be forced into the rigid forms of clan behaviour, nor monopolized by kinship alone. Besides, clans and families could be broken by wars and migrations, or decimated by disease or famine. Remnants of a broken clan or family needed adjustment and protection as individuals. There were also numerous cases where men of one clan looked for association with those of another clan, or clans, for an adventure or undertaking of some kind, be this a trade caravan, a hunt, or a war raid. Warriors, merchants, artisans, ministers, and attendants of religious or magic cults could not be confined within the narrow limits of clan life. Furthermore, the natural desire for friendship, among the youth especially, similarly required new forms of association. As a result of all this the principle of blood kinship was to be supplemented by that of the symbolic kinship which may also be called the principle of fraternity.

Symbolic kinship could be of two kinds—individual and of a group. A man in need of protection could be adopted by a family or a clan. In Ossetia such a man would be allowed to touch the sacred hearth-chain. After that, he was considered one of the house. Another type of symbolic kinship was the association of two 'sworn brothers', a custom which was widely

---

[1] See H. Field, 'Contributions to the Anthropology of the Caucasus', *Papers of Peabody Museum of American Archaeology and Ethnography*, xlviii, No. 1 (1953), p. 24.

spread among both the Alans and the Mongols. It was chiefly the young and ambitious warriors in search of glorious adventures who concluded the pact of fraternity. In Lucian's dialogue 'Toxaris'—that mine of precious information about the customs of the Scythians and the Alans—a Scythian youth explains to his Greek friend the meaning of the pact in the following words:

When we see a brave man, capable of great achievement, we all make after him, and we think fit to behave in forming friendships as you do in seeking brides. . . . And when a man has singled out and is at last a friend, there ensues formal compact and the most solemn oaths that we will not only live with one another but die, if need be, for each other; and we do just that. For once we have cut our fingers, let the blood drip into a cup, dipped our sword-points into it, and then, both at once, have set it to our lips and drunk, there is nothing thereafter that can dissolve the bond between us.

(A. M. Harmon's translation here and hereafter.)

It should be noted that among the Scythian antiquities found in south Russia there is an exact representation of just such a ritual on a gold plaque from the tomb of Kul-Oba near Kerch in the Crimea.[1] Sacred friendship between two youthful heroes is a favourite theme in the epos of the Alans as well as in that of the Persians, the Turks, and the Mongols. We find it also in Russian byliny and fairy tales. One of the most poetic descriptions of it is the story of the sworn brotherhood of Avtandil and Tariel in the twelfth-century Georgian poem 'The Knight in the Tiger's Skin', by Shota Rustaveli.

How highly valued was the sworn brotherhood by its participants is shown by a story which we also find in Lucian's 'Toxaris'. The hero of the story, Arsakomas, fell in love with the daughter of Leucanor, king of the Bosporus.[2]

Leucanor was surprised, for he knew that Arsakomas was poor and just an ordinary Scythian, and he asked: 'How many cattle and how many wagons have you, Arsakomas, since they constitute the wealth

---

[1] See Ellis H. Minns, *Scythians and Greeks* (Cambridge, 1913), p. 203, fig. 98; M. Rostovtzeff, *Iranians and Greeks in South Russia* (Oxford, 1922), Plate XXIII, fig. 3.

[2] Cimmerian Bosporus, i.e. Panticapaeum (modern Kerch), is meant here. The name Arsakomas is a combination of two Alanic words *ars* 'bear' and *akomas* 'obeying': 'man to whom the bear obeys', i.e. a man who has magic power over the bear, a sorcerer.

of your people?' 'Why', said he, 'I own no wagons or herds, but I have two noble friends, such as no other Scythian has.'

Arsakomas' answer was found unsatisfactory, and he was insulted and rejected as a suitor. He then decided to avenge the offence and to kidnap his beloved girl. For such an undertaking he needed more assistance than that of his two friends. He solved his problem by gathering a band of followers (similar to the Teutonic *Gefolgschaft* and the Russian *druzhina*).

The story of how Arsakomas, supported by his two original friends, succeeded in collecting a private army of his own, is a remarkable example of the ritual of the group fraternity pact.

Arsakomas . . . held conferences with the comrades and armed a force recruited from his relatives; then at last he sat upon the hide. Our custom in the matter of the hide is as follows. When a man who has been wronged by another wishes to avenge himself but sees that by himself he is not strong enough, he sacrifices a bull, cuts up and cooks the meat, spreads the hide out on the ground, and sits on it with his hands held behind his back like a man bound by the elbows. That is our strongest appeal for aid. The meat of the bull is served up, and the man's kinsmen and all else who wish approach, each takes a portion of it, and then, setting his right foot upon the hide, makes a pledge according to his ability, one that he will furnish five horsemen to serve without rations or pay, another ten, another still more, another foot-soldiers, heavy armed or light armed, as many as he can, and another simply himself, if he is very poor. So a very large force is sometimes raised on the hide, and such an army is especially dependable as regards holding together and very hard for the enemy to conquer, since it is under oath; for setting foot on the hide is an oath.

It should be borne in mind in this connexion that the bull played an important role in the mythology of the Hittites as well as in that of the Alans and Teutons. Also, the bull was a sacred animal in Mithraic religion.

Besides the war fraternities, war sororities also existed in the Alanic world. They were the source of the legend of the Amazons—the women of the Sauromatae. According to Herodotus the Amazons said to their Scythian suitors who invited them to settle with the Scythians: 'We could not live with your women —our customs are quite different from theirs. To draw the bow, to hurl the javelin, to bestride the horse, these are our arts—of womanly employment we know nothing.' (Rawlinson's translation here and hereafter.) Herodotus also says that the marriage-law of the Amazons 'lays it down that no girl shall wed till she has killed a man in the battle. Sometimes it happens that a woman dies unmarried at an advanced age, having never been able in her whole lifetime to fulfil the condition.' Even after marriage the women of the Sauromatae, Herodotus says, 'have continued ... to observe their ancient customs, frequently hunting on horseback with their husbands, sometimes even un-accompanied; in war taking the field; and wearing the very same dress as the men'. Such sororities seem to have been spon-sored by Sarmatian queens. Legends about these warlike queens were told by several Greek authors. Later, women-warriors of the steppes (in Russian *polenitsy* from *pole* 'prairie') reappeared in Russian byliny and fairy tales.

Let us now turn to religious fraternities and associations of magicians. In *Iliad* (xiii. 3) Homer speaks of the Abii whom he calls 'the most righteous of men'. Poseidonius, commenting on Homer, states that the Abii were so called because they lived apart from women and therefore led only a half complete life (*a-bios*). Poseidonius also says that among the Thracians there are some who live apart from womankind: 'These are called Ctistae.' The Greek word *ctistes* means 'creator' or 'founder'. There seems to be no relation between 'abstaining from women' and 'creating'. Presumably, the name of this Thracian group as recorded by Poseidonius derived from the Thraco-Phrygian language, not from the Greek. As has been mentioned (see section 1 above), there were close connexions between Thraco-Phrygian and Slavic languages. Could not *ctistae* be interpreted as the Slavic *chistyi* 'pure'? In such a case we may consider the 'womenless' Thracians forerunners of the Manichaeans and of the medieval heretics—the Bogomils and the Cathari. 'Cathari' means 'the Pure' in Greek. The Bogomils centred in Bulgaria, i.e. ancient Thracia.[1]

According to Herodotus, Scythia had an abundance of sooth-sayers. From what Herodotus says about them it can be deduced that they belonged to different corporations. When the king

---

[1] Another possibility of explaining the term *ctistae* would be to derive it from the Iranian *čisti*, name of the Goddess of Light, of power of seeing: H. S. Nyberg, 'Die Religionen des Alten Iran', *MVAG*, xliii (1938), 81. In such a case the *ctistae* would mean 'seers'.

wanted to consult soothsayers and was not satisfied with the first three he had called, he summoned others—apparently from a different corporation, and in some cases, still others. If one group contradicted the other, spokesmen of the one first summoned were denounced as 'lying diviners' and burnt in a wagon loaded with brushwood. Membership in the corporation of the soothsayers seems to have been hereditary, and so was the punishment. 'When the king puts one of them to death, he takes care not to let any of his sons survive: all the male off-springs are slain with the father.'

Besides the soothsayers there were in the nomadic world other groups of magicians, including the medicine men, and they too must have been organized in associations of one kind or another. The blacksmith's art was also considered magic in antiquity. Corporations and secret societies of magicians of various kind existed in the Caucasus as well as in the Balkans from remote antiquity, and some of them survived until modern times.

3. *The man and the horse*

Most of the Eurasian pastoral peoples were horsemen. It would be difficult for them to tend their enormous herds of cattle afoot, even with the help of the watch-dogs. Besides, in the steppe warfare cavalry reigned supreme. Only some of the smaller tribes, especially in the mountainous regions like the Balkans, managed to do without horses, or with a minimum of them. These relied on dogs and used donkeys for transporting loads in the mountains. They raised sheep, not horned cattle, in most cases. It is, however, not these small tribes but the horse-men who controlled the steppes and shaped the main currents of political history.

For the Scythians, Alans, Turks, and Mongols alike the horse was not only a convenient means of transportation; it was man's best friend and companion. They shared both life and death. As has been mentioned, when a man died, his horse, or horses, were buried with him. According to Herodotus (iv. 71–72), one year after the death of the Scythian king fifty of the best of his young attendants—all native Scythians—and fifty of his most beautiful horses were strangled and their bodies placed, on supports, around the royal tomb, the youths being mounted severally on the horses. When some of these royal tombs in south Russia were excavated by the archaeologists, Herodotus' story was found true and his description of the method of burial exact.

The Scythian way of killing the sacrificed men and horses is significant. Strangling was chosen to avoid shedding of blood. It was believed that the horse, like the man, has a soul and that the soul abides in the blood. Improper slaying would ruin the soul. Another way of preserving the soul of the sacrificed was by breaking his spinal column. This was the method used in the horse sacrifice by the shamans of the Altaic Turks as late as the nineteenth century. It will be recalled in this connexion that among the Mongols of the thirteenth and fourteenth centuries, when a prince of the royal house was sentenced to death (for treason), his spine was broken and in that way letting of his blood was duly prevented: rather a doubtful privilege from our present point of view.[1]

Horses of the central Asian race were especially popular in antiquity among the Eurasian nomads. In the second century B.C. both the Chinese and the Huns became acquainted with them, and many of them were imported into China. According to an old legend the horses of this race were of heavenly origin. A Chinese traveller of about 140 B.C. reported that there was in central Asia a remarkable breed of blood-sweating horses which derived from a heavenly horse. In a later Chinese chronicle it is said that hoof-prints of these horses were seen on rocks. It was also reported that there is a certain mountain in central Asia where horses live which nobody can catch. The people of that region bring their mares to the mountain for breeding with heavenly stallions. The colts thus sired sweat blood. The mares, according to the reports, have to be of five different colours. Presumably the five cardinal colours are meant (of which more will be said in section 5). Legends of heavenly horses living high in the mountains left their traces in the Alanic (Ossetian) folklore. The designs of winged horses on Khorezmian bowls and coins reflect similar notions.[2]

---

[1] See G. Vernadsky, *The Mongols and Russia* (New Haven, 1953), pp. 26–27.

[2] J. J. M. de Groot, *Chinesische Urkunden zur Geschichte Asiens* (Berlin and Leipzig, 1921–6, 2 vols.), ii. 12; G. Vernadsky, 'Anent the Epic Poetry of the Alans', *Annuaire*, xii (1952), 522–3; S. P. Tolstov, *Drevnii Khorezm*, pp. 206–8; S. I. Rudenko, *Kultura naseleniia Gornoga Altaiia v Skifskoe vremiia* (Moscow, 1953), pp. 146–235.

The Ossetian scholar Dzambulat Dzanty (now living in France) informed me that remnants of the Alanic race of horses survived in the Eisk region (east of the sea of Azov) until the Russian Revolution of 1917, after which they were exterminated. The most valued among them were the roan ones. These were called *xalas* (pronounced *khalas*) in Ossetian, literally of 'hoar-frost' colour. They had a black stripe along the back; the mane and the tail likewise were black. Dzambulat Dzanty (who had owned one of them) described them as 'tall, lean, and swift like the tempest'.

In Russian, the horse of this combination of colours of coat is called *chalyi*. The Russian word obviously derives from the Ossetian *xalas*. W. E. D. Allen called my attention to the fact that the most valued breed of Kabardian horses is called *shaulokh* in Circassian and that there is a breed of Arabian horses called *shalua* in Arabic. The Circassian term, like the Russian, derives from the Alanic; and the Arabic possibly from the Circassian. An example of how highly prized were the shaulokh horses is given by W. E. D. Allen in his *History of the Georgian People*. For such a horse David Soslan, the Ossetian consort of Queen Thamar of Georgia, paid a village and a castle.[1]

There was a close connexion between the clan's horses and the clan. The design of the clan emblem (*tamga*) was represented on the horse brands. It was never used for the property marks of the horned cattle. This shows that the horses were considered part of the clan. It is significant that in the Old Turkic inscriptions of the seventh and eighth centuries after Christ in the cases when the booty seized by the victor in a successful war is described, horses are mentioned under the clan names of the conquered tribes.

On the other hand, the breed of the horses raised by the clan, or tribe, was often used as a clan or tribal name. Even the clan leaders were known under such names. As an example, an Alanic chieftain of the late fourth century who joined the Goths in the latter's drive to the Balkans was called Safrac. This is the Latin transliteration of the Alanic word *saurag* (literally 'black back') the name of a breed of horses somewhat resembling the *xalas* (*chalyi*) horses. The term was taken into the Russian language in the form *savrasyi*. In English both *chalyi* and *savrasyi*

[1] W. E. D. Allen, *A History of the Georgian People* (London, 1932), pp. 332-3.

are rendered as 'roan'. Not only clans but whole tribes were sometimes known under the name of their favourite breed of horses. Of such origin is the name of the Turkish people who controlled the south Russian steppes in the Kievan period—the Cumans (Qumans), in Russian Polovtsy. Both *qu* in Turkic and *polovyi* in Old Russian mean 'yellowish grey'. This undoubtedly refers to the colour of the horses preferred by the Cumans. In Russian sources of the sixteenth and the seventeenth centuries a 'Skewbald horde' (*Pegaia orda*) is mentioned in the middle Ob basin in western Siberia, in the vicinity of the Ostiaks and the Samoyeds. In Kazakh (Kirghiz) folk-lore a 'Skewbald people' is described. In that people's country 'all of the horses are skewbald and all of the hearths are of gold'.[1]

There are cases in the nomadic armies when a cavalry squadron was mounted on horses of special colour. Thus Chingis-Khan's famous guards, the Thousand Bagaturs, rode all on black horses. Horses were likewise selected by colour for religious purposes. As has been mentioned (section 1 above) white horses were considered sacred.

4. *Expanding society: tribal state*

The clan, as we know, was the basic cell of the nomadic society. A clan could not live in complete isolation, however. In the first place, many neighbouring clans descended from a common ancestor. The clan, it may be repeated, was based on the principle of blood kinship, of belonging to 'the same sperm' (*mygkak*). Originally, many lesser clans belonged to the same ancestral mygkak. In a wider and deeper sense all of the clans in the kinship society were bound together as descendants of the same primeval mygkak. As more clans branched off from the original clan tree, each of them became more self-sufficient, and the term mygkak assumed a narrower connotation. When a clan multiplied, new offshoots separated from it. Migrations and wars likewise resulted in breaking clan unity and in other cases in the merging of two or more smaller clans to form a suitable military unit. In Old Turkic a small army unit was called 'arrow' (*oq*). Such units apparently had the size of an

---

[1] N. A. Aristov, 'Zametki ob etnicheskom sostave tiurkskikh plemen i narodnostei', *Zhivaia Starina*, vi, 3/4 (1896), 381.

average clan, and the term eventually acquired the connotation of 'clan', which shows that the clans in this case were adjusted to fit the military needs.

Clans of different origin might migrate together and settle together and could be joined by members of fraternities not connected with any specific clan. Gradually, a new form of settlement would emerge—the neighbourhood commune or the township (in Alanic *qæu*). The communal affairs in such settlements were discussed and settled at the town meeting in which the heads of all of the households participated. The assembly of this type was called *nyxas* in Alanic, literally a place where people speak (about community affairs). It should be noted that the Russian term *veche*, as the city assembly in the Kievan period was known, has exactly the same meaning.

There were situations when several clans—even not of the same mygkak—had to form an alliance for the purpose of defence against an aggressive neighbour, for instance, or in order to control a trade route. Such an alliance more often than not resulted in the formation of a permanent unit of a larger significance than a clan—the tribe. The tribe can be called the first stage of the nomadic state.

The tribe did not constitute a nation in the modern sense of the word. It could consist of clans of heterogeneous origin, even of different languages. For example, the Magyar horde in the eighth and ninth centuries of our era consisted of Ugrian, Turkish, and probably Alanic and Slavic clans. The tribe could be known under the name of its leading clan or under a new name. In many cases the tribe was called by the number of clans which formed it. Among the names of the Turkish and Mongol tribes we find such as 'Ten Arrows' (*Onoq*), 'Ten Uigurs' (*On Uigur*, i.e. 'ten Uigur clans'), 'Four Oyirads' (*Dörben Oyirad*). In the Caucasus a combination of four Kas clans established itself: *Čahar Kas* (i.e. 'Four Kas'), hence Cherkas (Circassians).

When a tribe was formed, one of the most respected clan elders assumed the leadership over the whole tribe, and the town assembly was superseded by the Council of the Notables.

Among the Alans the chieftain of the tribe had the title of *ældar*. While this Alanic term sounds similar to the English 'elder', its origin is differnt. *Ældar* derives from *arm-dar*. 'Arm' in

Alanic has the connotation of the English 'hand', not that of
the English 'arm'. *Armdar* is one who extends his hand for protection of his dependants—a 'Lord Protector' so to say. In modern
Ossetian *ældar* means both 'town elder' and 'prince'.

The Council of Notables was known in Alanic as *Tærxon*. In
modern Ossetian this word has the connotations of 'court trial',
'court decision', and 'deliberation'. The latter connotation is
apparently the original one. It should be noted that there is a
similar word in Turkic, *tarxan*, which means 'chieftain' and
also 'a landowner granted tax immunity'. The similarity between the Alanic and Turkic words may be accidental, but in
my opinion there is a possibility that the Turkic term is somehow connected with the Alanic. In Old Russian the term corresponding, in its meaning, to the Alanic *tærxon* is *duma* (as in
'Boyar Duma'). The Council of Notables of a large tribe was
called the 'High Council' (*Bærzond-Tærxon*). In the Ossetian
historical tale *Iry Dada* (verse 143) the members of the council
are called 'the country's chief deliberators', *bæsty særmættæ*. This
latter Alanic word (a plural form) derives from *sær* ('head',
'chief') and *mæt* 'thought', 'deliberation'. The corresponding
medieval Russian term is *boyare dumaiushchie* ('the deliberating
boyars', i.e. 'the boyars, members of the council').

A tribe could remain in the same locality for a long period.
But there were cases when the tribe, or part of it, had to move
in search of more suitable lands. Such migrations could be
caused by changes of climate, droughts, and overpopulation.
It could also be a result of a military defeat or, on the contrary,
of a successful military campaign—the conquest of an adjacent
land. To keep the conquered neighbouring tribe in control, the
conquerors had to place at least some of their forces in strategic
positions in their new dominions. Usually, when a tribe migrated, most of the constituent clans participated in the migration. Some of the clans, however, might prefer to stay at home.
In other cases, one part of each clan would follow the tribe and
another part would stick to the clan's ancestral abodes (*mæsygtæ*, which is plural of *mæsyg*). Those who migrated would establish new mæsygtæ in their new lands, to symbolize the eternal
connexion with their kin. In that way a distinction between the
'inner' and 'outer' clans and tribes would develop. The 'outer'
clans, more often than not, had to mix with the clans they had

conquered in their abodes—either to form an alliance with alien clans or to dominate them.

In the Greek and Latin sources of the late Roman and the early Byzantine periods the 'outer' tribes of the Alans were called Antes (Antae). The name derives from the Alanic word *ændæ* 'outside'. It is from the same root that the name of a Gothic chieftain, Andag, and that of an Alanic king, Addac, should be derived. *Ændag* in the Digor dialect of the Ossetic language, as well as the corresponding *ædtag* in the Iron dialect, means 'outer'.

While separating themselves from the 'inner' clans, the 'outer' clans did not lose their feeling of kinship with the former and, wherever possible, kept in touch with them. In cases where an 'outer clan' was in trouble, the 'inner' clan was expected to come to the assistance of their sib. Thus, when around A.D. 374 the Antes of Bessarabia were conquered by the Goths, the Alans of the Don region intervened and defeated the Goths. When an 'outer' tribe was at too great a distance from the 'inner', or when the 'inner' tribe was not strong enough to offer assistance, the 'outer' tribe, if overwhelmed by enemies, would return to its former abode and rejoin the 'inner' clan. Thus, after the downfall of Attila's Hunnish empire (A.D. 454), the tribe of the Utiguri (subsequently to become known as the Bulgars), which had been an important component of the Hunnish horde, returned to the Azov-Kuban region in which it had been stationed prior to the beginning of the westward drive of the Huns.

While originally all of the clans were equal, war and migration could change the interrelations of clans and tribes, and in fact did so in many cases. When the forces of two conflicting clans or tribes were commensurable and further hostilities seemed to be aimless, the two parties would join their forces in an alliance rather than exhaust them in mutual struggle. Such unions of two clans, or two tribes, were reflected in the appearance of double names, like 'Gothalans' (Goths and Alans), 'Alanorsi' (Alans and Aorsi), 'Roxolani' (i.e. Ruxs-Alan, Ruxs and Alans).

On the other hand, when a clan or a tribe was overwhelmingly defeated by its opponent, it had to plead allegiance to the conqueror and to accept the status of a 'serf-clan' or 'serf-tribe'. The members of the subjugated tribe had to work for the conquerors or to pay them a tribute in kind. When an agricultural tribe was conquered by a pastoral tribe, it had to till land for the benefit of the conquerors. Of this pattern were the relations of an 'outer' Sarmatian tribe, Acaragantes (Acarag-Antes) and a Slavic tribe, Limigantes (Limig-Antes), both residing in the fourth century of our era in the basin of the middle Danube River. In the contemporary Latin sources the Acaragantes are called 'Free Sarmatians'; the Limigantes, their 'slaves' (*servi*).[1]

5. *Nomadic empires*

Tribal state proved but an intermediary stage in the political history of the nomads. Now and again, responding to the inner rhythm of hidden historical forces, several tribes would join their armies to form a strong khanate, and the ball of expansion would start rolling. More and more neighbouring and distant tribes would be engulfed, and a mighty empire would be created. Some of these empires lasted for centuries, others proved ephemeral. Quite a number of them rose and fell in Eurasia, one to be succeeded by another, almost without interruption. The characteristic trait of each of them was the feeling of universality which guided their builders. Each nomadic empire was a world state, potentially, nay more than that—a cosmic monarchy.

The urge to universal authority and universal order was a significant psychological factor in the growth of the nomadic empires. No less important was the urge to exhibit the prowess of the army leaders and armies—the motive of glory. On the more practical side, greediness for booty constituted a powerful incentive too. As regards the economic foundation of the nomadic empires, the desire to control the great transcontinental caravan trade routes and to link them with the main sea ports and maritime commerce was a factor of primary importance in the steppe empire-building.

The nomads were as much interested in commerce as they were in war. As patrons of trade they made useful contributions to the unity of the Old World; it is they who forged a link between China and Iran, as well as between Iran and the Greco-Roman world. In regard to both war and commerce the steppe may be likened to the sea. The mobile detachments of the

---

[1] More will be said about these tribes in Chapter 2, section 3, below.

nomad cavalry functioned as so many naval squadrons. Similarly it may be said that commercial caravans are the merchant marine of the steppes. There were enclaves in the steppe zone—islands of settled civilization as it were—Khorezm in central Asia being one of the most important. The late W. Barthold aptly explained the rise of Khorezm's commerce by its 'insular' position and compared Khorezm to the British Isles sociologically and historically.[1]

While the centre of their man- and horse-power was in the steppe zone, the great nomadic empires could not confine themselves to the domination of the steppes alone. For both strategic and economic reasons they had to extend their control to the forest zone in the north, as well as to the mountainous areas adjacent to the steppe zone, such as the Altai mountains, Tian-Shan, the Pamirs, the Ural mountains, and the Caucasus. W. E. D. Allen is even 'inclined to believe that the mountains have been rather the human reservoirs from which successive floods of men have poured down, like the spring waters, into the neighbouring lowlands'.[2]

From the economic angle, cattle-breeding was to be supplemented by agriculture, and the nomads had to allow—even to encourage—the tilling of at least parts of the steppe zone by agricultural tribes subjugated by them. In many cases the nomads themselves would gradually take to farming, establishing large landed estates of their own, as the Scythians in the Crimea did, using serf labour. The nomads likewise needed skilled artisans—smiths for the forging of their weapons and their armour; masons for building fortresses; engineers for constructing siege engines; jewellers, and so on. It was the smiths of the Altai mountains and of the Caucasus who provided the Alanic, Tokharian, and Turkish warriors with proper weapons. It should be noted in this connexion that many a mountainous area contained deposits of valuable minerals, such as iron, copper, gold, silver, as well as of precious stones.

The expansion of commerce and crafts is conducive to the growth of cities. And, indeed, cities played an important role in the life of the nomadic empires. The prosperity of the Golden horde in the Mongol period depended, to a considerable extent,

---

[1] W. Barthold, *Istoriia kulturnoi zhizni Turkestana* (Leningrad, 1927), p. 34.
[2] W. E. D. Allen, 'Ethiopian Highlands', *The Geographical Journal*, ci (1943), 12.

on its cities, such as Urgenj in Khorezm, Saray on the lower Volga (close to Astrakhan), and Solkhat in the Crimea (now known as Staryi Krym). Earlier, in the Khazar period, Itil on the lower Volga (close to Astrakhan) was one of the most important cities. To go back to the Scythian age, Neapolis in the Crimea (adjacent to present-day Simferopol) was for a long period (fourth century B.C. to third century of our era) the capital of a mighty Scythian state. Neapolis was, of course, its Greek name (meaning 'New Town' in Greek). In Alanic the city must have been known as Næuæg Qæu.[1]

Let us now turn to the cosmic idea of nomadic kingship. To the pastoral tribes who practised Sky-worship,[2] the Sky was the source of the monarchic power. The Huns of Mongolia in the fourth and the third centuries B.C. believed in the heavenly origin of their emperor (called Shan-yu, 'the Highest', in Chinese sources). Each morning the emperor went out of his tent to venerate the rising sun, and each evening, the rising moon. The emperor of the Altaic Turks was likewise referred to as 'the Heaven-like, Heaven-born, wise Kagan'. In an Orkhon inscription of the eighth century after Christ a Turkish ruler describes the origin of the Turkish kaganate in the following words: 'When the Blue Sky and the Dark Earth beneath it had originated, men were created between, and my forefather Bumyn-Istemi Kagan sat [on the throne].'[3] The kagan's second name, Istemi, may be likened to the name of the Hittite Sun-god, Istanu. In Magyar, *Isten* means 'God'. According to the Mongol concept of imperial power in the thirteenth century, the first kagan, Chingis-Khan, was given to the Mongols by the Eternal Blue Sky and was invested with imperial 'fortune'.[4] His successors ruled through the virtue of this fortune. The idea of the imperial fortune was widespread among the nomads.

While it is not possible clearly to differentiate the characteris-

---

[1] More will be said about it in Chapter 2, section 2, below.

[2] On the variety of the religious beliefs among the Eurasian nomads see section 6 below.

[3] See V. Thomsen, 'Alttürkische Inschriften aus der Mongolei', *ZDMG*, lxxviii (1924), 144–5; A. Bernshtam, *Sotsialnoekonomicheskii stroi orkhono-eniseiskikh Tiurok VI–VIII vekov* (Moscow and Leningrad, 1946), p. 106; G. Vernadsky, *The Mongols and Russia*, pp. 97–98.

[4] G. Vernadsky, *The Mongols and Russia*, pp. 96–97. On the ideological background of the nomadic empires see M. de Ferdinandy, 'Die nordeurasischen Reitervölker und der Westen', *Historia Mundi*, v (1956), 178–86.

tics of Sky-worship and Sun religion, it may be said that among the Sun-worshippers a more complicated system of ideas prevailed. The king was not considered given to men by the primordial element, the Sun, directly. The king was rather a descendant of the Sun-god. If he was not the Sun-god's direct descendant, he had to receive a mystic investiture for ruling, as, for example, through the mysteries of Mithraism. He then ruled by the authority of the god of Light, Mithra, the protector of the proper social order on Earth.

According to the shamanistic notions, the shaman was an intermediary between the king and the primeval elements—the Sky, the Sun, and the Moon. The Votiak shamans believed that the king's fate was the same as the sun's. The king's power rose with the sun in the spring. It was in full vigour at the same time as the sun. In the autumn, when the sun lost its strength, so did the king. The king was then killed by the tribe. Ritualistic execution of the king was also practised by the Khazars. According to the Arabic writer Ibn-Fadhlan, the term of the rule of the Khazar kagan was forty years. When the kagan had ruled that long, he was killed on the next day after the expiration of the term. Michael de Ferdinandy comments that the figure 40 is the basic 4 multiplied by 10 and that the period of 40 years was considered the accomplished cycle of the virile period of life.

In view of the sacred nature and the cosmic function of the kagan, he was, in some Eurasian empires, relieved of direct military and administrative duties. These were performed by a deputy kagan. The result was, as Andreas Alföldi and Michael de Ferdinandy have shown, the establishment of the system of dual kingship.[1] Such was the case with the Khazars and the Magyars in eastern Europe. In the Hunnish empire in Mongolia there were two deputy kagans subordinated to the supreme kagan. One of them ruled over the eastern portion of the empire, and the other over the western. The latter was subordinate to the former.

A striking manifestation of the cosmic character of the Eurasian empire is its orientation to the cardinal points, each being assigned a special colour. Black was the colour of the north;

---

[1] M. de Ferdinandy, *A kettőskirályság* (Budapest, 1941), pp. 6–9, with a reference to A. Alföldi's opinion.

white of the west; red of the south; and blue (replaced by green in China) of the east. The empire's centre was yellow—the colour of gold. The sections of the empire, or the tribes forming the empire, were known under these colours accordingly. Hence such names as the Golden horde, the Blue horde, the White horde.[1] The four cardinals (emanating from the centre) may be considered an expression of the basic notion of quaternity (fourfoldness) which C. G. Jung refers to the inorganic in man (carbon which is characterized by four valencies). Another application of the same notion is the ancient idea of the four elements, water, fire, earth, and air.

Four cardinal colours plus the central yellow make five. In Tibetan symbolism we find five elements (wood, fire, earth, iron, and water) instead of four. They are assigned the same colours as the cardinals and the centre. In that connotation blue is the symbol of wood; red of fire; yellow of earth; white of iron; and black of water.

Along the same lines of thought, special consideration was given to the planning of the empire's capital city. The founding of many an ancient city was accompanied by special ceremonies. As C. Kerényi says, 'Ceremonial is the translation of a mythological value into an act'.[2] According to Plutarch's account of the founding of Rome, a circle was drawn with a plough around the chosen centre of the new city. Other sources speak of the 'square Rome' (*Roma quadrata*). Apparently we have a square within a circle. In the Eurasian world the square plan and the circle plan were used separately in different cases. The square plan was preferred in Khorezm, although the circle plan also occurs there in certain cases (Koy-Krylgan-Kala). The circle is the natural plan for a nomadic camp in the prairie. In Mongolian such a camp is called *küriyen* (hence the Russian word *kuren'*—denoting, among other things, the barrack of a Cossack company). In such a camp the tents, which sometimes numbered over a thousand, were pitched in a huge circle.

The square plan was sanctioned by the sacred books of *Avesta*. We read in the story of the founding of the city Vara by the mythological king Yima (Vendidad, ii. 33): 'And Yima built

Vara as a square, each side of the length of the horse's run [around two miles according to Darmstetter]. And he brought there the seeds of bulls, men, dogs, birds, and glaring fires. He made Vara, of the length of the horse's run on all four sides, men's dwelling . . . and the cattle's pen.'[1] As we have seen (section 2 above), the ancient settlements in Khorezm were exactly of this shape and purpose.

In the Khazar kaganate, as we know from the letter of the Khazar king Joseph, there were three main cities. The smallest of them served as the winter headquarters of the king; it had the shape of the circle. In the largest, the dowager queen-mother lived; it was likewise of circular shape. The third city served as the settlement of the merchants (Jews, Christians, and Moslems) as well as of their slaves. This apparently was square. The circle pattern was used by the Avars for their camps. When the Avars established themselves in the middle Danube area in the late sixth century they placed nine such fortified circles in strategic locations to control the newly conquered countries.

As regards its social structure, the Eurasian empire was an association of clans and tribes on which the imperial authority and the imperial institutions were superimposed. The kagan's own clan occupied a position of honour in the whole system. The kagan, or his deputy, was the head of the army. The army constituted the backbone of the administration. The military organization was based on the decimal principle to which the contingents supplied by the clans and tribes were adjusted. Usually, the 'greater family' corresponded to the unit of ten; the clan to a hundred; and the tribe to a thousand. A guards regiment was formed for the protection of the kagan. In the Mongol empire of the thirteenth century the guards consisted of the best warriors selected from various army units. In other cases the kagan's own clansmen supplied the guards. Some-times, the guards consisted of mercenary troops. An alien hire-ling was called *iskæj* in Alanic; hence, the Russian term *izgoi* as the members of the princely druzhina from the Caucasus were known.

The kagan and the members of his family had vast domains to which their clansmen and all their dependants were assigned. Huge herds of horses and cattle, as well as landed

[1] S. P. Tolstov, *Drevnii Khorezm*, p. 81.

estates, were owned by the imperial family. From the population of these domains the kagan's own army was drafted. As a
result of these arrangements the empire, more often than not,
consisted of two parts—one under the immediate authority of
the kagan and the other an association of free clans, ruled as
far as their local affairs were concerned by the clan elders—
the 'notables'. To co-ordinate the clan activities with the imperial policies, an assembly of the princes of the imperial family,
the high army leaders, and the clan elders, was called in cases
of emergency. In Mongolian such an assembly was known as
kuriltay.

The armed forces were divided into two main groups—the
right and the left 'arms'. As the nomads always pitched their
tents facing the south, the left arm meant the eastern army
group and the right arm the western. In most cases an elaborate
hierarchy of the princes of the imperial house and the leading
army commanders was established to avoid any confusion in
the army organization and functioning. In the Persian historian
Rashid ad-Din's great work, *Collection of Chronicles*, a list of
seniority of the descendants of the six sons of the Turkish Khan
Oguz is given. To each a special *tamga* (emblem) is assigned,
and his spirit-protector (*ongon*) defined.[1] In addition, the precise
cut of meat to which he is entitled at the kagan's banquets is
laid down. In the Chinese sources, the hierarchy of the rulers
of the Hunnish empire in Mongolia is described. As has been
mentioned, it was divided into two parts, the eastern and the
western under the supreme authority of the 'heavenly kagan'.
In each portion there was a deputy kagan and eleven other
chieftains, each commanding a division of troops (larger or
smaller according to his rank). Each was assigned a section of
the country to rule. There were thus twenty-four viceroys under
the heavenly kagan. The eastern viceroys ranked higher than
the western. It should be noted that in the Mongol empire of
the thirteenth century where the army likewise was divided into
two 'arms', the commander of the right arm was considered
higher in rank than his counterpart of the left arm. Similarly,
in the Muscovy of the Mongol and post-Mongol period, the
voevoda (general) of the right army division (*polk*) had a higher

---

[1] Rashid ad-Din, *Sbornik letopisei*, A. A. Semenov, ed., i, Part 1 (Moscow and
Leningrad, 1952), 87–90. On 'ongon' see sec. 6 below.

rank than that of the left division. It may also be added that the general Muscovite system of 'place ranks' (*mestnichestvo*) is in many ways similar to the hierarchy of ranks in Eurasian empires.

In view of its universal and cosmic nature, the Eurasian empire cannot be called a national state. And, indeed, such an empire was, in most cases, multinational, consisting as it did of clans and tribes of diverse ethnic and linguistic background. Ethnic terms which are traditionally applied to those empires, like Scythian, Sarmatian, Hunnish, Gothic, and so on, have really no meaning, except as references to the origin of the royal clan, and even in this sense such terms have often been misused by both ancient and modern authors.

6. *Mythology and epos of the nomads*

'Myth as it exists in a savage community', Bronislaw Malinowski says, 'is not merely a story told but a reality lived. It is ... a living reality, believed to have once happened in primeval times and continuing ever since to influence the world and human destinies.'[1] In C. Kerényi's words, 'Mythology gives a ground, lays a foundation. It does not answer the question "why?" but "whence".' It deals not with 'causes' but with the beginnings or first principles, with primary states that never age, can never be surpassed, and produce everything always. The teller of myths steps back into primordiality in order to tell us what 'originally was'. Primordiality is the same thing for him as authenticity.[2]

Mythology may be likened to philosophy—that kind of philosophy which is in search of fundamental principles. But philosophy's main vehicle is thought, and mythology's the image. In the Christian world of the Middle Ages philosophy became the 'handmaid' of religion, and mythology followed suit, the remnants of the ancient myths being adjusted to Christian notions. Mythology did not perish, however, and myths of quite a different nature still play an important role in our society—in our science and literature, politics, and social habits, as well as in our prejudices, even though we do not always realize it.

[1] Bronislaw Malinowski, *Myth in Primitive Psychology* (New York, 1926), p. 18.
[2] C. G. Jung and C. Kerényi, *Essays on a Science of Mythology*, pp. 8–10.

Mythology is not religion but may be called religion's twin sister. Religious beliefs are permeated with mythologems, and, on the other hand, myths reflect in many cases the inner meaning of religious cults. At the basis of religion lies the notion of Infinite Being. That notion exists even in the so-called 'polytheistic' religions. Religious feeling is channelled through a system of rites—the cult. Strictly speaking, the cult is the basis of all religions, or at least of all ancient religions. The cult went through different stages—clan, tribal, universal. The wider the religious system became, the more elaborate was the ritual. This led to the growth of the class of the cult attendants—the shamans, the magi, the priests. In most cases, they were not only ministers of the cult, but exponents of myths, as well as the Ancient World's first scientists, well versed in astronomy, alchemy, and medicine.

The core of the Eurasian world, the area between the Altai mountains and the Caucasus, occupied a central position between the Far East, India, Hither Asia, eastern Europe, and the Mediterranean world. As we know, this central area served from time immemorial as a hub for the transcontinental trade routes. The exchange of goods was inevitably supplemented with the exchange of ideas. No wonder that a variety of religious notions and of religious systems found their way into the nomadic world, and indeed we find among the nomads adherents of almost all of the universal religions of antiquity: Shamanism; Sky-worship; Hinduism; Zoroastrianism and Mithraism; Buddhism; and, in later times, Judaism, Christianity, Manichaeism, and Islam.

The three main religious systems prevailing among the Eurasian nomads in antiquity were Shamanism, Sky-worship, and Sun-worship. Shamanism was originally the religion of the forest tribes of Siberia. Shamanism is a complex phenomenon in which several elements are integrated. Its basis is the faith in a God of Heaven. Shamanism has a cosmological theory of its own, the belief in the Tree of the World which serves as the World Axis, connecting three cosmic zones—Heaven, Earth, and Hell. The characteristic trait of Shamanism is the shaman's ecstatic trance technique which permits him to fly up to Heaven or to descend into hell. All shamans are healers of body and soul.

Sky-worship was the basic religion of the Altaic Turks and
the Mongols. There were shamans among both these pastoral
peoples, but the majority of the Turkish and Mongol clans
believed in the direct protection of the Eternal Blue Sky over
them and did not want any middleman between them and the
Sky. And, as has been said (section 5 above), the Turkish and
Mongol kagans derived their authority directly from Heaven.
'Heaven' in Old Turkic is *tangri*, and this word eventually
assumed the connotation of 'god' in Turkish. In modern Turkish the word is spelled *tanri*.

Sun-worship was widespread among the Aryans and the
Slavs. With the notion of 'Sun' (*xvar* in Avestan, *xur* in Alanic)
that of 'light' (*raoxša* in Avestan, *ruxs* in Alanic) was closely
connected. Both terms form the basis of many place, personal,
and tribal names, such as Khorezm (*Xvar-zem* 'the Land of the
Sun'), Rusa (a derivative of *ruxs*, name of a king of Uratru in
Transcaucasia), and Roxolani (*Ruxs-Alan*).

The most popular of the Sun religions in the last two centuries
B.C. and the first two centuries after Christ was Mithraism.
Mithra was an ancient Aryan deity (the name is spelt Mitra in
the *Vedas* and Mithra in the *Avesta*). He is the Light, not the
Sun; the latter is his vehicle. In Iran, under Zoroastrianism,
Mithra was at first removed from the upper rank of divinities.
He reappeared, however, in the later Avestan literature where
the Sun is represented as Mithra's close associate. Among the
masses, Mithra soon became the most beloved god. Mithra has
manifold emanations and functions. He is 'the Lord of Wide
Pastures' and 'the Lord of Fecundity'. He is the Lord of truth
and loyalty. He guarantees all contracts and promises and
punishes all the offenders. He is invoked whenever oaths are
taken. As Lord of Light he leads the hosts of Heaven against
the forces of Darkness. As such, he is the invincible Lord of
Battles.

The adherents of both Sky-worship and Sun-worship believed that certain localities, such as mountains, rivers, lakes,
and springs, were holy because they seemed to be convenient
for the presence of gods and spirits. Certain trees were considered sacred as well. Many a Hittite king was known by the
name of a sacred mountain. The cult of the goddess Anahita,
often represented as Mithra's associate, was connected with

holy rivers. The very name of this goddess means 'moist'. In the Caucasus, the highest mountain of the range, Elbrus, was considered holy. Its old name is Shat. The name of the Eternal Wise Woman of the Ossetian legends, Shatana, presumably derives from the name of this mountain. It was also believed that Shat was the throne of the divine bird Simurg. With one eye Simurg contemplates the present, the other being fixed on the future. When he beats his mighty wings, the earth trembles, a terrible storm arises in the mountains, and the foaming waves of the sea rise and tumble over each other.[1]

Of the sacred trees, the birch symbolized the Tree of the World which the shaman climbed in his ascent to Heaven. Among the Alans, the oak tree was especially revered. From the life of St. Cyril we know that to complete the conversion to Christianity of the Crimean Alans he had to cut their sacred oak. When they saw that this could be done without immediate retaliation on the part of the spirit of the tree, they abandoned their old faith.

Let us now examine the family and clan cults. In the Kuban area a golden amulet having the shape of a bead attached to a chain was found with a name of the God Uatafarn on it. The name (in Greek letters) is in filigree technique. The name is Alanic. *Uat* means 'bed' (also 'room'), *farn* 'peace', 'fortune'. Obviously this god (or spirit) was the protector of marriage and of the homestead. The chain to which the bead is fixed apparently symbolizes the sacred-hearth chain (*ræxys*).

Each clan had its spirit protector—*ongon*, as it was called among the Altai Turks and Mongols. Both animals and birds could serve as ongons. According to D. K. Zelenin the cult of ongons developed from primitive totemism.[2] In the totemistic cult, a live animal or bird was venerated. In the ongon cult, the spirit (*ongon*) was revered through its symbolic representation—a figure of the proper animal or bird. Such representation was called a *lekan*. Among some of the Turkish tribes of central Asia, a bird—the eagle or the falcon—was a preferred ongon. Other Turkish tribes, as well as the Finno-Ugrians, considered the swan, or the goose, their spirit-protector. According to the

[1] See H. Field, 'Contributions to the Anthropology of the Caucasus', op. cit., p. 33.
[2] D. K. Zelenin, *Kult ongonov v Sibiri* (Moscow and Leningrad, 1936), p. 128.

notions of the Altaic and Siberian Turks, the meat of the animal or bird representing the ongon of a given clan should not be eaten by the members of the clan.[1]

The deer was universally revered by the Alans as well as by their eastern branch—the Saka. It may be said that the deer was the main ongon of the Alans and of the Saka. According to V. I. Abaev the very name Saka derives from the Alanic word *sag* 'deer'.[2] In the Ossetian folk-lore, brave warriors are called 'deer' (*sagtæ*, which is the plural form). There had been, apparently, an older word for 'deer' in the Alanic language, related to the name 'Alan' itself, *yæ* (its cognate survived in the Old Slavic *yelen'* 'deer'; the Russian form is *olen'*). It seems probable that the Old Alanic word for 'deer' became taboo and was eventually replaced by its synonym *sag*. Representations of the deer abound in the art of the Alans and the tribes affiliated with them (see section 7 below).

Stories of the sacred deer occur frequently in the Alanic and Saka folk-lore. We find them even in the Indo-Buddhic literature. According to the Buddhist tradition, the Saka of Kapilavastu, being converted to Buddhism, refused to take arms against the king Kosala when the latter attacked them, since it would be contrary to Buddha's law. (*Kosa* means 'beardless' in Ossetian.) Only one Saka, called Çambaka, killed a great number of enemies, but he was exiled for this by his kinsmen. He then moved to the country of Bakuda of which he became a king and where he taught his new subjects not to kill the deer. This means that he considered the deer his ongon. In other Buddhist texts the legend of the Golden Deer is told. 'It is an animal which moves in the air spreading light which illumines the mountain valleys.'[3] In the Ossetian legends in the story of the marriage of Atsamaz, it is related that, after the nuptial banquet, Agunda—the beautiful bride of Atsamaz—travelled to the groom's home in a chariot drawn by seven deer given to her on that occasion by Afsati, the spirit-ruler of noble animals and protector of hunters. Agunda is connected with deer in another Ossetian tale, that of the death of Sozryko. Sozryko

---

[1] *Castrén's Reiseberichte und Briefe aus den Jahren 1845* (St. Petersburg, 1856), p. 318.

[2] V. I. Abaev, *Osetinskii iazyk i folklor*, p. 179.

[3] J. Przyluski, 'Nouveaux aspects de l'histoire des Scythes', *Revue de l'Université de Bruxelles*, xlii (1936–7), 214–19; G. Vernadsky, 'Anent the Epic Poetry of the Alans', *Annuaire*, xii (1952), 520–1.

chased a white deer who turned into a beautiful princess with golden braid and golden wings. This happened to be Agunda.[1]

Among the Alanic antiquities of the north Caucasian area in addition to figures of deer, those of the ram were found. These presumably were lekans, evidence of the existence of the ram cult among certain Alanic clans, or clans associated with the Alans.

Herodotus mentions the names of several Scythian gods and goddesses. These may be considered tribal deities. Among them are Tabiti whom Herodotus likens to the Greek Hestia (goddess of the family hearth); Papaios identified as Zeus; Api, explained as Ge (Earth); Goitosyros, Apollo; and the god of war, Ares, for whom no Scythian name is given by Herodotus. The name Tabiti should be connected with the Alanic *tavyn* 'to warm'. This fits well with Herodotus' Hestia. 'Papaios' is explained by Max Vasmer from the Iranian *papa* 'protecting'.[2] In Ossetian there is the word *papi* which means both 'wealth' and 'cattle'. As regards the goddess Api, in Avestan *api* means 'water', not 'earth'. Water (moisture) is essential for the earth's productiveness. Api may be likened to the Iranian deity of moisture, Anahita. Api-Anahita was the 'Great Goddess' of the Scythians and the precursor of the Russian 'Mother Moist Earth'.[3] Anahita was considered the protector of semen, child-bearing, and sheep-breeding. It should be recalled that Mithra and Anahita were often worshipped as a pair. Herzfeld explains the name Goitosyros as Mithra's epithet *gavyutisura* 'Lord of Pastures'.[4] Herodotus' Scythian Apollo is Mithra.

As has been said, Mithra was not only the 'Lord of Wide Pastures', he was also the 'Lord of Battles'. The Scythians apparently worshipped these two emanations of Mithra separately. According to Herodotus (iv. 62), there is a sanctuary of Ares in each Scythian district, at the seat of government. Herodotus describes such a 'temple' as a 'pile of brushwood' of square shape the length of each side being three stadia (a stadium equals about 600 feet). It is somewhat less in height, having a square

---

[1] V. Dynnik, *Skazaniia o Nartakh* (Moscow, 1944), p. 76; V. F. Miller, 'Osetinskie Etiudy', Part III, *Moscow, Universitet, Uchenye Zapiski, Otdel Istoriko-filologicheskii*, viii (1887), iii. 10–11.

[2] M. Vasmer, *Iranier in Südrussland* (Leipzig, 1923), p. 15.

[3] See Chapter 4, section 2, below.

[4] E. Herzfeld, *Zoroaster and His World* (Princeton, 1947), ii. 423.

platform upon the top, three sides of which are precipitous while the fourth slopes so that men may walk up it. An antique iron sword is planted on the top of every such mound, and serves as the image of Ares. As N. P. Kondakov remarked, the edifice must actually have been an earthen tumulus the walls of which were reinforced with wattled twigs. Kondakov likens the shape of the edifice to the ancient Mesopotamian temples. Its square plan obviously corresponds to that of Vara as well as to the Iranian fire-altars.

According to Herodotus, yearly sacrifices of cattle and horses were made to the sword planted on the platform at the top of the temple. 'When prisoners are taken in war, out of every hundred men they [the Scythians] sacrifice one. . . . Libations of wine are first poured upon their heads, after which they are slaughtered over a vessel; the vessel is then carried up to the top of the pile, and the blood poured upon the sword.' The sword was venerated by the Alans as well. Ammianus Marcellinus (xxxi. 2. 23) says that among the Alans 'a naked sword is fixed in the ground and they reverently worship it as their god of war'. (John C. Rolfe's translation here and hereafter.) It should be borne in mind that the sword was not a 'god'; it was the lekan of the god.

The sword was also used for confirming the oath. Herodotus (iv. 70) describes the ritual of the oath in the following words:

A large earthen bowl is filled with wine, and the parties to the oath, wounding themselves slightly with a knife or an awl, drop some of their blood into the wine; then they plunge into the mixture a sword, some arrows, a battle-axe, and a javelin, all the while repeating prayers; lastly, the two contracting parties drink each a draught from the bowl, as do also the chief men among their followers.

As we know (see section 2 above), the ritual of the oath of sworn brotherhood was of the same type.

It will be recalled that one of Mithra's functions was to guarantee the pacts and contracts. Thus the use of the sword in the oath ritual seems to be another evidence of the spread of Mithraic notions among the Scythians and Alans. However, we cannot be sure that the Scythian god of war was actually called Mithra. As has been said, while Herodotus gives both Greek and Scythian names for most of the Scythian deities, he calls the

Scythian god of war by the Greek name, Ares, only. The question arises whether the omission of the Scythian name is accidendental or not, and in the latter case, what was the reason for the omission. It is possible that the Scythians were reluctant to reveal the name of this god to foreigners. But it seems more probable that the Scythian name of the god was identical with the Greek or was very close to the Greek. Such a name could have been Ar (Arya, Aryans) of which the name Al (Alan) is but a variation.[1]

Mythology is an important source of epos. For a long time the only medium for the spread of epic poetry among the nomads was oral tradition. Even when some of these peoples began to use a script of some kind, it served mainly for the needs of the state chancery, not for epos. Only on rare occasions were themes of epic poetry recorded in script. Because of this situation our information on the ancient nomadic epos is fragmentary in contrast with our knowledge of the Homeric epos of the Greeks, which became available in written form in the sixth century B.C. if not earlier. Among our sources of information about the old epos of the nomads are stories bearing on the life of the steppe society written down by Greek authors. A number of epic themes may be inferred from paintings and sculptures. In a few cases, inscriptions, either records of the military exploits of princes or memorial eulogies of the dead heroes, throw light on the development of epic poetry. Much insight into the ancient epos may be obtained from the later epic tradition preserved in the folk-lore of various tribes almost down to the present day and but recently recorded in writing.

Both the rhythmic form and the contents of the epic tale had a powerful appeal to the minds and hearts of listeners. The folk-poet was always a popular figure among the nomads and still is in remote localities of central Asia. It is, however, not solely the artistic urge which led to the creation of epos. Poetry served practical purposes as well; it was needed for the encouragement of military valour as well as for the promotion and dissemination of religious feelings and myths.

The poetic form of diplomatic messages of the nomadic rulers was an application of mnemonics to inter-tribal communications in an illiterate society. Clement of Alexandria recorded

[1] See Chapter 2, section 1, below.

the following message—an ultimatum—of the Scythian king
Ateas to the city of Byzantium: 'Do no harm to my revenues lest
my mares drink your water' (meaning that his horsemen will
attack the Byzantians if they refuse to satisfy his demands).[1]
An illiterate messenger could easily memorize a message of this
kind. The same devices of mnemonics were applied by the
Mongols in the twelfth and the early thirteenth centuries. Before the organization of imperial chancery by Chingis-khan, his
messages to the neighbouring rulers, as well as his orders to his
generals, were always oral and always in rhythmic form. They
were longer and more complicated than Ateas's message, and
yet were duly memorized.

Rhythmic forms of appeals to warriors were used by chieftains in exhortation for battles. In the Ossetian historical tale
Iry Dada, Prince Alamat addresses his retinue in the following
words: 'A misfortune fell on our heads. To avenge shame let us
dip our radiant garments in the enemy's blood, O warriors!
A misfortune fell upon us. . . . From this day that people are
our blood enemies.' (*Iry Dada*, verses 88 and 90.)

Funeral dirges were another form of oral rhythmic art. In the
same Ossetian tale we find the lament for Iry Dada (who had
been killed in battle): 'O our honorable ancient, our cherished
serene leader! For whom didst thou exist? For whom didst thou
cease to exist?' (meaning—for us, Ossetians).

These two elements, lament for the dead and exhortation of
the living to battle, are two embryonic motifs out of which the
heroic and the historical tale developed. *Iry Dada* is the only
Ossetian historical tale so far published. It was written down by
Dzambulat Dzanty in 1910 in a steppe village near Mozdok,
northern Caucasus, from an old Ossetian reciter, Khulyx. The
tale describes the conflict between the Alans and the Russians
which occurred in A.D. 1022 and led to a duel between the
Ossetian hero Iry Dada (called Rededia in Russian chronicles)
and the Russian prince Mstislav of Tmutorokan'. The image of
Iry Dada himself is obviously much older than the episode. *Iry
Dada* means 'Father of the Iron (Ossetians)'. He is a legendary
figure, superhuman rather than human. In this respect he

---

[1] Clement of Alexandria, *Stromateis*, 5. 5. 31; V. V. Latyshev, *Scythica et Caucasica*
(St. Petersburg, 1890–1904, 2 vols.), i. 598; G. Vernadsky, 'Anent the Epic Poetry
of the Alans', *Annuaire*, xii (1952), 532, 537–8.

closely resembles the heroes of the Ossetian cycle of legends
concerning the Narts.

The Narts are giants, akin to the Nordic Æsir. 'At the time
when Heaven and Earth were not yet completely separated
from one another, I was already living as a man of mature
years', says the Nart Sozryko. The Narts are not immortal,
however. They are in constant war with the vicious race of one-
eyed Cyclops called Uaigs in Ossetian. Each of the Narts has
his own personality and character. Most of them are brave
warriors, but some are wicked and crafty, as, for example,
Syrdon whom Georges Dumézil likens to the Nordic Loki.[1]

The legends of the Narts are permeated with mythological
notions, and there is no doubt that their basis is very old. Of
deities mentioned in the legends, Donbettyr is the Lord of Sea
and Water, and Barastyr the Lord of the Nether World. The
Heavenly Smith, Kurdalagon, is the protector of all smiths and
armourers. The Nart Batradz once asked Kurdalagon to temper
his body in the heavenly forge. Kurdalagon agreed although he
did not believe Batradz could survive the ordeal. But so strong
was Batradz that charcoal could not produce enough heat for
the work. Only coal made of dragons' bodies did it. Kurdalagon
then picked Batradz with his smith's tongs and threw him into
the sea. The whole sea boiled to the bottom, and Batradz's
body was then duly tempered except for his liver, for the tem-
pering of which no steam was left.

Apart from the Nartian cycle stands the Prometheus legend.
According to the Ossetian story, a poor shepherd went alone
into the mountains and heard a moaning. He entered the
mountain through an opening and saw a Titan bound to a
rock. The Titan asked the shepherd to give him his sword,
which was beside him, so that he might free himself. But the
sword was too heavy for the shepherd to lift. The Titan then
asked the shepherd to bring him the hearth-chain from his (the
shepherd's) house. 'But thou must not speak a single word on
thy way; otherwise thy help will be in vain.' The shepherd ran
to his house, took the chain, and went back to the mountain.
His wife ran after him and kept asking him what he was going
to do with the chain in the mountains. The shepherd kept
silence for a long time, but finally, exasperated by his wife's

[1] G. Dumézil, *Loki* (Paris, 1948).

curiosity, exclaimed: 'Thou shalt know later.' By uttering these words he broke the magic spell, and when he came to the place there was no opening in the mountain any more. Prometheus thus remained fettered. When he tries, from time to time, to free himself from the bonds, the mountain trembles, and the rocks fall down into the valley.[1]

Another Ossetian legend, which seems to constitute a link between the Ossetian and the Nordic epos, is that of Odin. So far only a French paraphrase of it, by Dzambulat Dzanty, has been published.[2] According to the legend, a boy was born in the mountains to a woman stunned by a thunderbolt through the magic of the giant Nalat. The woman died as soon as she gave birth to the boy. Neighbours took care of the boy and called him Ud-dæn (which means 'I am the soul' in Ossetian). When the boy grew up, he discovered the secret of smelting bronze and forging weapons from it. He then killed the wicked giant, assembled a host of followers, and departed northward in search of women with long golden hair. He finally arrived in Scandinavia where he was recognized as god and where he married the king's daughter. Feeling the approach of old age, Ud-dæn (Odin) returned to the Caucasus leaving in Scandinavia his son Votan. Ud-dæn was buried on a hill on the banks of the river Tarma-Don. This hill, according to Dzambulat Dzanty, was at first known as 'Odin's Hill' but later renamed 'Christ's Hill'.

Both mythology and epos played an important role in the spiritual life of the nomad. They strengthened his basic religious and moral values, his concepts of good and evil; they helped him better to realize his innate idea of truth. The nomad's whole life was dedicated to the defence of the integrity and honour of his clan as well as of his own. Behind this, there lay a wider notion of the cosmic struggle between the forces of Light and Darkness. The nomad felt himself a warrior in the Host of Light. His guiding ideal was that of valour (in Alanic *æxsar*) which was similar to the Greek *arete*. The original notion of arete encompasses both nobility of spirit and physical courage. Loyalty to one's clan, to one's friends, and chieftains is another important aspect of the nomad's concept of life. Hospitality is likewise considered one of the basic virtues.

---

[1] H. Field, 'Contributions to the Anthropology of the Caucasus', op. cit., pp. 32–33.   [2] D. Dzanty, 'Odin l'Ossète', *Oss-Alanes*, ii (1953), 11–13.

The nomad tried to live and to die in accordance with his ideals. Of the Alans Ammianus Marcellinus (xxxi. 2. 22) says that among them 'the man is judged happy who has sacrificed his life in battle'. Of Iry Dada it is said that once Barastyr, the Lord of the Nether World, let him know that he could come to the Nether City whenever he wanted and would be well received. 'One who heard these heavenly words from Barastyr's messengers, clad in black, is not afraid of the realm of the dead. And indeed, Iry Dada in his earthly life did not know cowardice, therefore he did not spare his soul or his body.' (*Iry Dada*, verses 23–24.)

7. *Art of the nomads*

The art of the nomads represents a mighty current in the stream of the aesthetic culture of mankind. The main patterns of that art were created in central Asia and were cherished by the peoples of Eurasia for more than a millennium. The patterns spread east, south, and west—to China, India, and Europe, deeply affecting the artistic culture of the whole Old World. On the other hand, the nomadic art, in its turn, reflected certain themes and notions of the art of China, Mesopotamia, Egypt, and Greece.[1]

The two characteristic expressions of the art of the Eurasian nomads are the animal style and the geometric style. An abundance of art objects of both these styles were found in the barrows of the Altai region, Mongolia, Turkestan, northern Caucasus, the Pontic steppes, Romania, Hungary, and the Balkans. As a result of the so-called Great Migration of Peoples of the fourth and fifth centuries, jewellery and various artifacts of the geometric style found their way to Italy, Germany, the British Isles, France, Spain, and North Africa. A blending of both styles is represented in the Scandinavian art. Beautiful creations of Eurasian art are preserved in the museums of many countries, including the Hermitage in Leningrad, the National Museum in Budapest, and the Metropolitan Museum of Arts in New York.

To take up the animal style first, representations of animals and birds, real or fantastic, are found on objects of almost any category and purpose. The nomad's armour, his headgear and

[1] See note D, p. 318.

garments, his belt, his horse's harness, his jewels, vessels, rugs—
everything about him was ornamented with figures of animals.
Most of this ornamentation was on metal—gold and silver
bowls and drinking cups, plaques, brooches, bracelets. The
shaman's wand, like that of the prince, usually had a statuette
of an animal or a bird on its top. Lion, tiger, deer, boar, horse,
and snake were the favourite animals of the artist, and the eagle
his favourite bird. In addition, fantastic creatures such as the
dragon and the gryphon were also preferred. Sometimes single
animals are represented, but mostly we have groups of two or
more of them. The scene of combat of two animals occurs very
frequently, especially on the belt plaques. A deer, male or
female, attacked by a glutton, a lion, or a tiger is a favourite
subject in nomadic art.

The existence of different schools is noticeable in the artist's
approach to the animal theme. One of these schools may be
called classic, reminding us of the Greek and Persian art. In this
manner the horses on the Chertomlyk vase are treated;[1] also,
the horses on a silver bowl found in the Perm region.[2] In the
works of another school, in some of the scenes of combat of
animals, the violence of the attacking animal and the agony of
the victim is accentuated to the utmost by over-emphasizing the
details against the artistic balance of the scene as a whole.[3]
This exaggerated naturalistic approach perhaps may be dubbed
impressionistic in a sense. In some cases we find a tendency
toward stylization of forms and the use of the end parts of the
animal form, especially the limbs and the tail, for decorative
purpose. As a result, the entire surface of the plaque, or other
groundwork of the scene, is filled with ornamental design based
on distorted animal forms. This may be called an ornamenta-
lized trend in the animal style. In the Krasnokutsk barrow,
among horse harness and trappings, a horse's cheek ornament
was found representing two figures of standing horses back to
back with the end parts curved and twisted in a decorative
way, showing remarkable resemblance to the northern 'beast
style' of the early Middle Ages.[4]

[1] See illustrations in Minns, op. cit., figs. 47 and 48, pp. 160–1; Rostovtzeff *Iranians and Greeks*, Plate XXI, figs. 2 and 3.

[2] Iakov I. Smirnov, *Vostochnoe serebro* (St. Petersburg, 1905), Plate XL, No. 69.

[3] Minns, op. cit., fig. 196, p. 275; fig. 198, p. 276; Rostovtzeff, op. cit., Plate XXV, fig. 2.   [4] Minns, op. cit., fig. 56, p. 167.

In the representation of some of the animal combat scenes of the 'impressionistic' style the artist used inlaid incrustation of precious stone or paste, often of variegated colours; a polychromic effect was thus achieved.[1] Here we have examples of a peculiar interpenetration of the animal style and the geometric style. This might have been a result of the mixture of two different ethnic groups. Most of the objects of this kind were found in Siberia.

The 'geometric' style (in that specific sense) is known indeed mainly from inlaid objects. M. I. Rostovtzeff used to call it the 'polychrome' style. The origin of the geometric style has been recently analysed in detail by B. Philip Lozinski.[2]

Jewelled objects in *cloisonné* inlay representing the geometric style are often made primarily of gold. The inlays are of garnet, emerald, lapis lazuli, mastic, or glass. Items of various kind and purpose were ornamented in this manner: belt-plaques, fibulae, signets, bracelets, torques, pendants, ear-rings, amulets, bowls, and crowns. Jewellery and other specimens of the geometric style were found in barrows and treasure hoards all over Europe from the Caucasus to Spain and North Africa. They were called Sarmatian, Gothic, Vandal, Frankish, Alamannic, and so on, mostly on the basis of the location of the find. An important group of *cloisonné* jewellery found in various places and now scattered in a number of museums in several countries is characterized by a special design—that of interlocked circles. This apparently is the emblem (*tamga*) of the royal clan to which these jewels originally belonged. B. P. Lozinski believes that all of these objects had originally belonged to one set and were made in the same workshop which he tentatively places in western Siberia.

With all its aesthetic appeal, the art of the nomads was not 'an art for art's sake'. It was deeply connected with the mythology and epos of the nomads, and corresponded to their philosophy of life, their notion of valour. Basically, the nomadic art was a religious and magic art.

As we have seen (section 6 above), there were several different

---

[1] Minns, op. cit., fig. 200, p. 277.

[2] B. Philip Lozinski's remarkable work, *A Workshop of Mediaeval Jewelry*, is being prepared for publication. I am grateful to Mr. Lozinski for allowing me to read part of his manuscript.

religious currents among the Eurasian nomads and a variety of magic notions and devices. Most of them were reflected in the nomadic art. A large proportion of the objects of animal style, especially those devoted to the theme of the combat of two animals, must be primarily connected, as both N. P. Kondakov and A. Alföldi have shown, with the animistic and totemistic notions of the nomads as well as with the magic of Shamanism.[1] More specifically, this current in the nomadic art must be considered an expression of certain fundamental concepts in the clan and tribal cults (see section 6 above). The attack on a cervoid by a carnivorous animal could symbolize the prowess of the clan's progenitor and, if a cervoid male was the victim of his attack, his victory over his enemies. But it could also symbolize, if his victim was a female cervoid, the conquest of the bride and the mystic foundation of the clan. In a general way, the theme of combat represented the idea of the eternal conflict between the hosts of Darkness and those of Light, the inexorable grip of Death, the constant interference of the cosmic forces in the course of earthly life. The skin of the animal was used by the shaman in his magic acts. The skin had thus a magic significance in itself. It may be added that objects of the Shamanistic cult, such as wands, bells, spoons, are frequent in the furniture of the Scythian and other Eurasian barrows. As regards statuettes of animals and birds found in abundance in both barrows and sites of settlements, made of metal, wood, or clay, they must have been amulets or representations (*lekans*) of the spirit-protector (*ongon*) of a given clan.

The Sky-worship, which prevailed among many a pastoral tribe, had likewise its symbolism; this had been elaborated in Babylonian and Tibetan cosmology and astronomy. The Tibetan chronology (adopted by the Turks and Mongols) was based on the twelve-year cycle, each year known under the name of an animal. In astrology, certain animals symbolized zodiacal signs; in alchemy each metal depended on one of the signs of the zodiac. In view of this, we have in most cases to attribute a special symbolic meaning to the animals represented in various

---

[1] N. P. Kondakov, *Ocherki i zametki po istorii srednevekovogo iskusstva i kultury* (Prague, 1929); A. Alföldi, 'Theriomorphe Weltbetrachtung in den hochasiatischen Kulturen', *Jahrbuch des Deutschen Archaeologischen Instituts*, xlvi (1931), 393–418.

combinations on many artifacts. Consider especially the scenes of royal hunts which often ornament silver dishes and bowls possessed by Eurasian rulers. Quite a number of these objects was found in north-east Russia in the basin of the Kama River. They might have been brought there from Khorezm. They are identified differently by different scholars as belonging to the Sassanid, the Parthian, or the Khoresmian art.

Animals also played an important role in Sun-worship. With the Mithraic cult the bull, the dog, the raven, the scorpion, and the snake were intimately connected.

The cult of the Great Goddess likewise was reflected in the art of the nomads. On the golden plaque of the tiara found in the Karagodeuashkh barrow in the northern Caucasus (upper Kuban River basin),[1] the goddess, wearing heavy ritual vestments, is represented in a solemn sitting position; in her right hand she holds a drinking horn (*rhyton*). Two women stand behind her and a man approaches her from her left side. On another gold plaque, found in the Dnieper River basin,[2] the goddess is accompanied by two sacred animals—the raven and the dog. In other cases the goddess stands between two horses, or two deer, or two panthers. It is known that the Great Goddess was known as the 'mistress of the animals' (in Greek *potnia theron*). This motif entered the early Slavic art and was preserved in Russian peasant embroidery.

Besides the gods and goddesses, kings and heroes also could serve as subject-themes of Eurasian art. As has been said, a favourite theme of central Asian art was that of the king engaged in the ritual hunt. The king in this case probably represents a god. Equestrian statues of gods or kings occur also on bas-reliefs found in the Crimea, south Russia, and Thrace. That representing the Scythian king Palak (found at the site of Neapolis in the Crimea) may be mentioned here.[3] The urge to monumental expression of the theme of the equestrian god or king led to hewing huge reliefs on rocks. Such are the well-known Sassanian reliefs in Iran. This iconographic theme was also represented on many metal and ceramic objects which

---

[1] E. H. Minns, op. cit., fig. 120, p. 218; M. Rostovtzeff, *Iranians and Greeks*, Plate XXIII, fig. 1.

[2] Ibid., fig. 5.

[3] B. B. Piotrovsky, P. N. Schultz et V. A. Golovkina, S. P. Tolstov, *Ourartou, Neapolis des Scythes, Kharezm* (Paris, n.d.), fig. 18, p. 77.

were carried by the migrating nomads from their original home-
lands westward to their new abodes in Europe. It is possible
that the relief of the so-called 'Madara Horseman' in the
Madara rocks, ten miles east of Šumen, Bulgaria,[1] was modelled
on a design of some such object of minor arts.

[1] G. I. Kacarov (Katsarov), 'Skalniiat relief pri Madara', *Madarskiiat konnik*
(Sofia, 1925), pp. 27–38; V. Beševliev, 'Les inscriptions au relief de Madara',
Byzantinoslavica, xvi, Part 2 (1955), 212–54. 'Madarskiiat konnik', *Bŭlgarska Akade-
miia na naukite, Arkheologicheski Institut, Epigrafska poreditsa*, No. 3 (Sofia, 1956).

2

THE ALANS, THE ANTES, AND THE RUS'

1. *The Alanic-Tokharian sphere*

THE heartland of Eurasia—the area between the Altai mountains and the Caucasus—was controlled by Indo-European peoples from time immemorial. After the migration of the Aryans to Iran and India and of most of the western branches of the Indo-Europeans to Europe, there still remained in the central Eurasian area two large groups of Indo-Europeans—the Alanic and the Tokharian. The Alanic language has survived in the Ossetian. After the investigations of the Russian philologist V. F. Miller in the 1880's, there prevails the opinion among the scholars that the Ossetian language belongs to the north-Iranian branch of the Indo-European family. There are, however, a few dissenting voices. Nicholas Marr emphasized the importance of pre-Iranian (Japhetic) elements in the Ossetian. Recently, Dzambulat Dzanty has expressed his belief that the Ossetian should not be called an Iranian language at all. Irrespective of what place we assign to the Ossetian (and, consequently, the Alanic) language in the Indo-European linguistic system, we must recognize it as an old language containing rich elements of its own in its vocabulary.

A great number of geographic and personal names connected with south Russia and her history derive from the Alanic. Consider, for example, the Ossetian word *don* 'river', 'water' (in Avestan *danu* 'river') which lies at the basis of the names Tanais (Greek transcription of the old name of the Don River), Danapris (Dnieper River), and Danubius (Danube River). With the westward migration of the Alans the name penetrated into France (Le Don, name of a river, also known as Uldon, i.e. Ulændon, which means 'Wavy River' in Alanic) and to Britain (Doncaster on the Don, Yorkshire, England).

In view of the fact that the Alans played a role of great importance in the early Slavic and Russian history, it is essential to examine here briefly the basic elements of their historical background as well as their relations with the Tokhars and some other Indo-European peoples. It is also necessary to analyse here the origin and the basic forms of the name 'Alan' itself. While I have tried, in the following discussion, to avoid unnecessary details, I am afraid that the argument may still seem too technical for those readers who are not sufficiently interested in the deeper background of Russian history. I beg the indulgence of these readers and suggest that they skip the details and note only the conclusions. Be this as it may, here is my argument.

According to Nicholas A. Rast, the name Alan derives from the root *yal* (the final *-an* is the plural suffix), a parallel form to *yar*.[1] Among the derivatives of that latter form are the names Arya (Aryans), Aran (a region in Transcaucasia), Iran (Persia), and Iron (self-appellation of the Ossetians). The stem *yal* also served for forming the words denoting 'deer' in certain Indo-European languages. Consider the Slavic *yelen'* ('deer') and the French *élan* ('moose'). Presumably *yal* also denoted 'deer' in the Old Alanic language but the word did not survive in Ossetian. We find, however, a trace of it in the Persian *yal* which means 'a hero', 'a valiant knight'. It will be recalled in this connexion that in Ossetian the word for 'deer' (*sag*) is used as an epithet of 'brave warrior'.[2]

The Alans were often referred to under another name, that of As (Asii). It seems probable that the Alans and the Asii had been originally two separate tribes but that later they merged together. In my opinion the name Asii is of religious origin. In Avestan the stem *yaz* expresses the notion of 'worship'. *Yazata* means 'who must be worshipped', hence 'deity', 'divine power' (in Ossetian *izæd* means 'angel', 'spirit'). A demon named Az is occasionally mentioned in the *Avesta*. In Manichaean texts Az is called 'the evil mother of all demons' and also a 'death demon'.[3] For the Manichaeans, naturally, former deities became evil spirits.

Let us now turn to the Tokharian group of peoples. The

---

[1] Nicholas A. Rast, *Les Alains dans la littérature, la poésie et la langue persane* (being prepared for publication). I am grateful to N. A. Rast for allowing me to read the Russian manuscript of his work.

[2] See Chapter 1, section 6, above.

[3] See R. C. Zaehner, *Zurvan: a Zoroastrian Dilemma* (Oxford, 1955), pp. 166–9.

Tokharian problem has become extremely involved. There is no consensus of opinion among the philologists about the origin of the Tokharian language, and even the name 'Tokharian' in its linguistic connotation is now considered a misnomer by some scholars. Suffice it to say here that certain elements of the 'Tokharian' language are very close to the Thraco-Phrygian. Besides, a number of words in the Tokharian are akin to the vocabularies of the Sanscrit, Iranian, Hittite, Greek, Latin, Celtic, Germanic, Baltic, and Slavic languages. A great number of manuscripts containing 'Tokharian' texts has been found in the area of Chinese Turkestan (Sinkiang).

'Tokhars' (*Tochari*) as the name of a people has been recorded by Strabo and a number of other Greek authors (as well as by some Latin writers). In the Chinese sources we find a name transcribed as Ue-tsi which refers to the 'Tokhars' in Sinkiang. It is supposed that the Chinese pronunciation of the name in the second century B.C. (the age of the western migration of the Ue-tsi) was something like Gwo-ti which some scholars explain as Getae (name of a Thracian tribe) or Gothi (Goths).

In my opinion the name 'Tokhar' was not an ethnic name but was applied to a conglomeration of tribes of various ethnic origin. I derive the name 'Tokhar' (*Tocharos* in Greek) from the Alanic word *toxar* (pronounced *tokhar*) which means 'warrior' (*tox* means 'war' in Alanic).[1] It is known that in the second and the first centuries B.C. a group of the Tokhars was controlled by the Asii (i.e. Alans). The Latin author Justinus mentions 'the Asian kings of the Tokhars' (*reges Tocharorum Asiani*).[2] I believe that 'Tokhars' is used, in this case, not as a name of a specific people, but as a military term. The Tokhars were the 'warriors' of the armies of the Alanic kings. These warriors must have belonged to various clans and tribes. This may explain the variety of linguistic elements in the 'Tokharian' language and dialects. The appearance of the term 'Tokhar' might have been the result of the important reform in the organization of the Alanic armies in the period from the fourth to the first centuries B.C. The essence of the reform consisted in the formation of

[1] G. Vernadsky, 'Toxar, T'ma, T'mutorokan', *For Roman Jakobson* (The Hague, 1956), pp. 588–9.
[2] P. Trogus, *M. Iuniani Iustini Epitoma Historiarum*, ed. O. Seel (Leipzig, 1935), Prologus Libri XLII.

special units of heavy cavalry. In these units horseman and horse were covered with corslets of scale or ring armour. A long spear and a sword were the main weapons of such a cavalry man. This type of armour seems to have originated in central Asia and then to have spread both eastward and westward. Cavalry units of this type must have constituted the backbone of the 'Tokhar' armies.

The vast area controlled by the Alans and the Tokhars may be conveniently called the Alanic-Tokharian sphere. During the first millennium B.C. this area played a role of paramount importance as the base for both eastward and westward migrations as well as for the radiation of artistic and mythological notions and patterns all over the Old World.

The ethno-musicologist Jaap Kunst—an outstanding authority on Indonesian music—has recently pointed out that there exist a number of striking parallels between the folk-music and art of Yugoslavia and of Indonesia. As regards music, he discovered the similarities at the time he attended the great National Yugoslav Folk-dance Festival at Opatija (previously Abbazzia) in September 1951.

As I sat in the great hall at the Kvarner Hotel [Dr. Kunst says], with all this beauty sweeping over me, I closed my eyes for an instant and suddenly I felt as if I were back in East Flores [Indonesia] near the remote Béléng Lake, and some moments later I seemed to be in the land of the Nagé in West Flores. It was the same music to which I was listening here, in the most literal sense of the word: it seemed to me that in several cases it was not only a matter of a certain similarity or parallelism but now and then of complete identity.[1]

In his study 'Cultural Relations between the Balkans and Indonesia' (1954) Dr. Kunst discussed the similarities in melody as well as those in musical instruments of these two distant areas and also collected a great deal of illustrations of artistic patterns and designs which show parallelisms in folk-art. The best way to explain those parallels is to assume that all these patterns—musical and artistic—spread east and west from a central area. That central area was the Alanic-Tokharian sphere.

Let us consider from this point of view the expansion of the

---

[1] Jaap Kunst, 'Cultural relations between the Balkans and Indonesia', *Royal Tropical Institute, Mededeling CVII, Afdeling Culturele en Physische Anthropologie*, No. 47 (Amsterdam, 1954), p. 3.

so-called pentatonic scale in folk-music. Its importance for the understanding of the early Russian cultural background was emphasized by the late Prince N. S. Trubetzkoy.[1] A considerable part of the Russian folk-songs, including some of the oldest ritual and wedding songs, is based on that scale. The scale is widespread in Indo-China, as well as among the Turkish peoples of central Asia, Siberia, and Volga basin, including the Chuvashians in that latter region.[2] In western Europe the pentatonic appears only among the Celtic peoples, the Irish, the Scots, and the Bretons. It seems probable, on that ground, that the Celts, in remote antiquity, had been in contact with the peoples of the Alanic-Tokharian sphere. Linguistic evidence of such a contact is the identity of the stem of the Ossetian word for 'hero' (Nart) with the Irish *nert* (strength) established by H. W. Bailey.[3] As regards art, it has been said that 'the Celts were the westernmost outpost of the vast Eurasian belt, stretching east to China'.[4]

All this dovetails well with the occurrence in the Celtic west of geographical and personal names with Alanic connotations deriving ultimately from the Ponto-Danubian area. In this connexion W. E. D. Allen, who has been pursuing some researches into the history of Ulster, writes me:

I have come across the name Ros (or Ross) and Allan (Gaelic, Alein) used as personal names in Ulster as early as the fourth century A.D. The subject is rather complex since the modern anglicised forms have diverse origins. For instance, in Ireland, Hill of Allen, Bog of Allen, derive from an original *Almha* (gen. *Almhain*). Lough Allen (*Loch Ailienne* of which nom. form is *Ailenn*) has a different origin. Professor Gerard Murphy, leading Celtic scholar, informs me that 'no scientific etymology has yet been proposed for either Almha or Ailenn'. According to O'Rahilly (*Early Irish History and Mythology*, Dublin, 1946, pp. 279–81), 'the hill of Almu (Allen) was a hill or *sid* within which the Otherworld, ruled by Nuadu, was believed to be located'. In Scotland, the place-name, generally in the anglicised form Allan, is widespread. Watson (p. 467) gives a list. He seeks a derivation from Old Irish *ail*, a rock, but has his doubts (p. 468, note 1). There was *Alauna* of the Damnonians, identified with the

---

[1] Prince N. S. Trubetzkoy, *K probleme Russkogo samopoznaniia* (Paris, 1927), p. 29.

[2] On the forefathers of the Chuvashians—the Volga Bulgars—see Chapter 3, section 2, below.

[3] H. W. Bailey, 'Analecta Indo-Scythica', I, *Journal of the Royal Asiatic Society*, October 1953, p. 107.   [4] P. Jacobsthal, *Early Celtic Art* (Oxford, 1944), p. 162.

Rock of Dumbarton and in later centuries the seat of the Brythonic kings of Strathclyde. This is to be distinguished from the *Alauna* of the Votadini of the Firth of Forth. The name occurs again, in Gaul and Bavaria. The Damnonians, migrants from west Britain, in the first century B.C. were within the cultural sphere of the Venets of Armorica. The common personal name Alan (Alain, Alanus) is of Breton origin and became fashionable in Britain after the Norman conquest. The founder of the Scottish royal house of Stewart was Alain, a Breton noble, and his immediate descendants adopted the name Fitzalan. The name Alain, Alanus, may well have had a 'national' origin (cf. Scot, Fleming, Barton, &c.). There were settlements of Alans in Armorica in the fifth century A.D. (cf. Vernadsky, *Ancient Russia*, p. 140). The name Alanus, 'the Alan', must have been common from that time. A couple of centuries earlier, in the last quarter of the third century A.D., large settlements (calculated at 5,500 men) of time-expired legionaries, Sarmatian Yazygi, had been established in the valley of the Ribble in Lancashire (cf. *Journal of Roman Studies*, 35, 1945, art. by I. A. Richmond, 'The Sarmatae, Bremetennacum Veteranum and the Regio Bremetennacensis'). In this connection it is notable that the name Allan can be verified as common in Lancashire since mediaeval times. The celebrated Cardinal William Allen (1532–94), a leader of the Roman Catholic resistance to Queen Elizabeth, came of an old gentry family established at *Rossall* in Lancashire. In the Scottish Highlands and Islands the name Allan, used as a personal and family name, was persistent and widespread, particularly among the MacDonalds, Camerons and MacDougalls. The Chief of Clanranald, a powerful branch of Clan Donald, was traditionally hailed by his bard as 'Mac 'ic Ailen'—'son of the line of Allen'. Although it has been noted that the forms *Alain, Alanus*, were fashionable among the Normans, the names *Ailen* or *Ailinn*, and also *Domnaill* (Donald), perhaps a servant of the goddess Domnua of the Damnonians (*Clann Domnann*), were current in Celtic Britain and Ireland long before the Norman conquest.[1]

It has been suggested that the 'outer clans' or 'outer tribes' of the Alans were called Antes. This latter name was widespread as a compound among the Celts of Britain: Brigantes, Decantes, Novantes, Setantes, Trinovantes. There was a tribe of Antes in association with the Venets and Pictones in the region of the Armorican peninsula. Their name has survived in 'Nantes'. It has been proposed that 'Trinovantes' has the significance of 'Three New Outer Clans'.

[1] See also W. E. D. Allen, *David Allens: the History of a Family Firm, 1857–1957* (London, 1957), pp. 7–8 and 23–25.

All this is evidence of Picto-Venetic and Alano-Antic elements among the peoples in movement from the continent to the British Isles during the period of disruption which followed the expansion of the Roman frontier to Gaul and the Rhine and into Britain. But all these shiftings promoted by the Roman advance had followed in the wake of earlier migrations—those of the first half of the first millennium B.C. The earlier movements corresponded with the disruption of the Cimmerian cultural world in Eastern Europe by the Scythians about the end of the 7th century B.C.

The Cimmerians must have been in close contact with the peoples of the Alanic-Tokharian sphere even before the beginning of the Scythian offensive. There is no consensus of scholarly opinion on the ethnic background of the Cimmerians. Some scholars relate them to the Thracians; others, to the Celts. In any case, as J. Harmatta has pointed out, the names of their rulers which we know are Iranian.[1] This indicates that the Cimmerians, or part of them, were controlled by the Iranians. It seems that here we have a key to understanding the dynamics of the early migrations, including the migrations of the Celts. Some of those peoples migrated westward because of the pressure from the east of the Scythians and Alans. Others were led by the Alans; still others associated with the Alans.

The Teutonic peoples likewise must have migrated westward in several waves. The bulk of them might have settled in Germany and Scandinavia in the first half of the first millennium B.C. Other tribes and groups trekked westward much later. The first settlers in the forest area of Germany were apparently not a nation of horsemen. Tacitus (*Germania*, 6) says of the Germans at large that 'There is more strength in their infantry [than in cavalry], and accordingly cavalry and infantry fight in one body'. Only one German tribe, according to Tacitus (ibid. 30), that of the Tencteri, 'excel in the accomplishments of trained horsemen'. Presumably, the Tencteri came to the Rhine from the steppe area much later than most of the other tribes.

It is through their connexion with the steppe world that another branch of the Teutons—the Goths—mastered the technique of cavalry warfare. In the great migrations of the fifth century the Goths and the Vandals acted in close co-opera-

---

[1] J. Harmatta, 'Le problème Cimmérien', reprint from *Archaeologiai Ertesitő* (c. 1948).

tion with the Alans, past masters of cavalry tactics. The beginnings of the association of the Goths with the Alans might be referred to a much earlier date. It takes several generations to form experienced horsemen. Consider also the practice of deformation of skulls widespread among both the Alans and the Goths.[1] The head of the male child (with the Goths, also of the girl in some cases) was tightly bound with a horizontal band, as a result of which the skull grew in the vertical direction and assumed an oblong shape. This, presumably, was done to the children of noble birth. The habit must have had some magic meaning. It is supposed that it had been originally an Alanic rite which later was borrowed by the Goths. Such habits are not accepted overnight. The spread of the ritual among the Goths must have been the result of a long process of cultural adaptation. We must, therefore, surmise that the Goths, or in any case a group of them, lived for centuries in the Alanic-Tokharian sphere.

To this it may be added that, as Franz Altheim has shown, the vestments and the ornaments of the royal robe of the Gothic kings of the fifth century after Christ were of central Asian pattern.[2] Besides, it will be recalled that there are common traits in Alanic and Teutonic mythology.[3] It also seems significant that the Goths called their victorious leaders 'not mere men, but demigods, that is *Ansis*' (Jordanes, *Gethica*, section 78). This name may be connected with Az and Asii.

A new way toward exploring ancient associations of peoples and tribes has been recently suggested by Nicholas A. Rast.[4] In his opinion the personal pronoun, first person nominative, had originally expressed the notion (name) of the god-protector of the clan or tribe. On that ground Rast refers the origin of the said pronouns to the beginnings of the historical era—the period of formation of primary empires which comprised heterogeneous

---

[1] See Max Ebert in *Reallexikon der Vorgeschichte*, xiii. 108; M. A. Miller, *Studii z istorii Prioziv'ia* (Geneva, 1947), Part VII: 'Sarmatska materialna kultura'; G. Vernadsky, 'Der sarmatische Hintergrund der germanischen Völkerwanderung', *Saeculum*, ii (1951), 366–7; Tadeusz Lewicki, 'Zagadnienie Gotów na Krymie', *Przegląd Zachodni*, 5/6 (1951), 97.

[2] Franz Altheim, *Die Krise der Alten Welt*, i (Berlin, 1943), 102.

[3] See Chapter 1, section 6, above.

[4] Nicholas A. Rast, *Origin of Persian Personal Pronouns* (Tehran, 1955) (in Persian).

peoples and tribes, often speaking different languages and dialects.

Of the various stems of personal pronouns discussed by Rast, the following one is of special interest to us: *yaz*. We have *æz* in Ossetian; *az* in Old Slavic, and *asz* in Lithuanian (denoting the pronoun 'I' in all cases). This stem may be connected with the name of the demon Az as well as with that of the people Asii.

Irrespective of the question of the origin of the personal pronouns, the similarity of these pronouns in certain languages is in itself an indication of old ties between the peoples speaking these languages. These data, dovetailed with other kinds of evidence, may help us to discern old groupings of various tribes. On the basis of the stem *yaz* it seems likely that the ancient Slavs and the Balts (Lithuanians) had been intimately associated with the Asii in a very remote period.

In Russian the pronoun 'I' has the form *ya* (similar forms we have in Polish, Czech, and Serbian). Rast likens it to *ye* in the ancient Urartu language. He derives both the Russian and the Urartu forms not from the stem *yaz* but from another stem (*yag*). Such derivation is contrary to the well-established opinion according to which *ya* derives from *yaz*.[1] Nevertheless, the similarity between the Slavic (Russian) and the Urartu forms noted by Rast seems significant, especially if we recall[2] that 'Rusa' was a royal name in the kingdom of Urartu.

2. *The Slavs and the Rus' in the Scythian-Sarmatian era*

During the Scythian-Sarmatian era, which lasted from around 700 B.C. to around 200 after Christ, western Eurasia was ruled by Iranian (Alanic) speaking peoples. The Scythians controlled the area for half a millennium until about 200 B.C., and then the Sarmatians took over.

Like all of the other Eurasian empires, the Scythian and Sarmatian kingdoms were multi-national states. Foreign observers—Greek and Latin writers in this case—mentioned quite a number of names of peoples and tribes in this area but gave no explicit information about the ethnic composition of the population. The first definite evidence about the Slavs appears

[1] See L. P. Iakubinsky, *Istoriia drevnerusskogo iazyka* (Moscow, 1953), p. 200.
[2] See Chapter 1, section 6, above.

in the written sources of the first and the second centuries after Christ, and that evidence is brief and incomplete. It is only the sixth-century writers who provide us with more adequate information concerning the Slavs. And yet, on the basis of what we know about the general historical background of the Slavs,[1] there cannot be any doubt that several groups of Slavs lived in western Eurasia, including the Pontic steppes, in the Scytho-Sarmatian era.

It should be borne in mind that neither the name 'Scythians' nor that of the 'Sarmatae' was the self-appellation of the peoples known under these names. As regards the Scythians, Herodotus (iv. 6) says that while the Greeks so call them, 'they are named Skoloti, after one of their kings'. The origin of either the name 'Scyth', or that of 'Skolot', has not been so far satisfactorily explained.

The name 'Sarmatae' is usually considered a contraction of 'Sauromatae', name of a tribe mentioned by Herodotus. (In Iranian *Sau-rom* means 'Black Hair'.) The Sauromatae lived in the Azov area and it is with them that the legend of Amazons was connected.[2] It is doubtful that the name 'Sarmatae' has any inner connexion with 'Sauromatae'; the similarity must be accidental. 'Sarmatae' was used by Greek and Latin writers to denote the whole group of tribes controlling the area of the Pontic steppes in the Hellenistic and the Roman periods and not a particular tribe. In my opinion 'Sarmatae' is not an ethnic name. It will be recalled that *særmæt* in Alanic means 'a member of the council'.[3] The term corresponds to the Russian *boyar*. It may be supposed that most of the Sarmatian tribes had an aristocratic constitution, the Council of the Boyars being in charge of all important affairs. Diplomatic negotiations were apparently led by the boyars, and treaties with foreign powers approved by them. This may explain why the Greeks and the Romans called the 'Sarmatian' tribes 'Sarmatae', i.e. boyars.[4]

---

[1] See Chapter 1, section 1, above.   [2] See Chapter 1, section 2, above.

[3] See Chapter 1, section 4, above.

[4] In a parallel way the Arabic writer Masudi calls the Slavic (Alano-Slavic) realm, centring around Galicia, 'Al-dajr', i.e. Ældar as Tadeusz Lewicki interprets it; see T. Lewicki, 'Państwo Wiślan-Chorwatów w opisie al-Masudiego', *Sprawozdania Polskiej Akademii Umiejętnosci*, xlix (1948), No. 1, 24–34. In Ossetic, as we know (see Chapter 1, section 4, above), *ældar* means 'prince', 'tribal chief'. Thus, 'Aldaria' means 'Land of the Princes'. 'Sarmatia', i.e. (as I think) 'Land of the Boyars', seems to be a name of the same type.

Cavalry was the main arm of both the Scythian and the Sarmatian military organization, but there was an important difference between the two.[1] The Scythian cavalry may be called 'light horse'. It seems that the Scythians used no stirrups. A short bow (around 2·5 feet) with a double curve was the most dangerous weapon of the Scythian horseman. Typical Scythian tactics consisted in attacking the foe at different places simultaneously with small cavalry detachments. After the first skirmish the Scythian horsemen took to flight in order to lure the enemy army deep into their country, where it was easy to encircle and destroy it.

As a contrast, heavy cavalry constituted the mainstay of the military might of the Alans who were the strongest of the Sarmatian tribes. This was recruited from the flower of nobility. The Alanic horseman wore a helmet and a coat of mail.[2] He used stirrups. His horse was likewise protected by a corslet. The Alan's weapons were a long spear and a long iron sword. We may call him a precursor of the medieval knight. Tacitus (*Historiae*, i. 79) comments that hardly any army could withstand the charge of Sarmatian cavalry unless the latter were handicapped by terrain and weather. On a rainy day or on swampy ground Sarmatian horses would slip and fall under the burden of their heavily armoured riders.

Herodotus mentions four main groups among the Scythians: the Royal Scythians, the Scythian Nomads, the Scythian Georgoi (agriculturists), and the Scythian Aroteres (ploughmen). The last two groups were apparently agricultural peoples subject to the Scythian rule, but not Scythians in the ethnic sense of the name. The Royal Scythians must have constituted the ruling clan of the empire. They were under the immediate authority of the king. The area restricted for them may be called the imperial domain of Scythia. The king's herds grazed there. As regards the Scythian Nomads it will be recalled[3] that the term 'nomad' had different connotations in Greek and in Alanic. If we understand the term in its Alanic sense, we must interpret the name 'Scythian Nomads' as the 'Scythian Notables', i.e. those autonomous Scythian clans which did not

---

[1] See G. Vernadsky, 'Der sarmatische Hintergrund der germanischen Völkerwanderung', *Saeculum*, ii. 367–8.

[2] See Chapter 2, section 1, above.   [3] See Chapter 1, section 2, above.

belong to the imperial household and were only under the political suzerainty of the king.

The Scythian kings amassed great treasures of jewellery and gold and silver vessels. After the death of the king, part of his treasure was buried with him. Many of these hoards were excavated by the archaeologists. Precious objects of art and jewellery from the funeral barrows of the Scythian kings have been preserved and are now kept at the Hermitage in Leningrad as well as in a number of other Russian and western museums. The main area of the Royal Scythians was in northern Tauria, that is, in the steppe section between the bend of the Dnieper River (below the cataracts) and the north-western shore of the sea of Azov. It is there that a number of big barrows with rich burial furniture was found. The Scythian empire may be described sociologically as a domination of the nomadic horde over neighbouring agricultural tribes as well as over a number of cities with artisan population. The Khazar horde (seventh to tenth centuries after Christ),[1] as well as the Golden horde, were to be built on the same pattern.

The Scythian domination secured peace for western Eurasia for several centuries. The *Pax Scythica* had great importance in promoting trade and bringing prosperity to both the Scythians themselves and the Greek cities which sprang up on the northern shore of the Black Sea like so many mushrooms. Prominent among these cities were Olbia, at the mouth of the Bug; Chersonese (Cherson) in the Crimea, near present-day Sevastopol; Panticapaeum, modern Kerch, on the western side of the Cimmerian Bosporus (strait of Kerch); Phanagoria (later known as Tmutorokan, present-day Taman), on the eastern side of the Cimmerian Bosporus; and Tanais, at the mouth of the Don, near present-day Azov. Cities grew in the Scythian hinterland as well, Neapolis (close to present-day Simferopol) being the most important. The Greeks bought slaves, cattle, hide, furs, fish, timber, wax, honey, and grain in Scythia; they sold to the Scythians textiles, wine, olive oil, and sundry items of art and luxury.

The Greek cities in the north Pontic area were not mere trading posts, however. They were part of the Hellenic world representing the material and spiritual wealth of the Hellenic

---

[1] See Chapter 3, section 3, below.

civilization in south Russia and spreading it north. In their
turn, the Greek inhabitants of those cities became well acquainted with the Eurasian culture. Gradually, reciprocal
acculturation took place.

The first of the Sarmatian tribes to appear in the Pontic area
were the Yazygi. Their name obviously derives from the stem
Yaz (Az). After crossing the steppes of south Russia in their
movement westward the Yazygi settled for about two centuries
in the region of present-day Bessarabia and then moved to the
middle Danube region, the present-day Hungary. The Roxolani followed in their wake. The Alans proper were the last-
comers to the Pontic area. Around 110 B.C. the Scythian king of
Neapolis in the Crimea, Palak, asked his suzerain, the king of
the Roxolani, Tasius, for help against the invasion of the
Crimea by the Greek troops of the king of Pontus, Mithradates
VI, who entertained far-reaching plans of creating a huge
west Asian monarchy to oppose the Roman expansion. Mithradates intended to make Bosporus in the Crimea his main base.
The Roxolani hurried to Palak's assistance, but the war was
fought in the hilly region of the Crimea where the Roxolani
had no room to deploy their cavalry. Their attack was beaten
off by Mithradates' hoplites. Mithradates became king of the
Bosporus.

The economic prosperity of the Bosporan kingdom was based
on the grain trade. Wheat was the staple product. It was both
raised locally and imported from the steppes beyond the sea of
Azov. Grain constituted the chief item of export to Greece at
that time. The king himself was the biggest dealer in grain. A
number of lesser dealers had their offices in Panticapaeum.
Members of the native aristocracy had large landed estates in
the neighbourhood of the city where they usually spent their
summers living in the traditional tents of nomads, supervising
their field workers and ready to protect them in case of any raid
from the north. There was a considerable artisan population in
the cities, engaged in various handicrafts. Hellenic civilization
was gradually losing ground with the people. Greek was still
spoken but chiefly as an official language. Greek costume likewise gave way to Iranian fashions. As to religious life, the cult
of the Heavenly Aphrodite, representing the Great Goddess of
the Scythians, was especially popular. The whole political

structure of the Bosporan kingdom underwent profound changes. Former Greek democratic institutions disappeared leaving few traces. The government became known as the 'Sublime Porte' and assumed a bureaucratic character not unlike that of the Persian kingdom or the Byzantine empire. It is significant that the emblem (*tamga*) of the Bosporan kings (in some cases, two-pronged spear-head, in others a trident) is close to the Khorezmian tamgas. Incidentally, the emblems of the Kievan Rurikids were of the same type. The Bosporan army was headed by the 'commander of the thousand' (*chiliarch*). It should be noted that later on there was a similar official in the Russian principalities of the Kievan period (in Russian *tysiatskii*).

Of other Greek cities of this area, Cherson in the Crimea recognized at first the suzerainty of the Bosporan kings but later became a Roman protectorate. The city kept its Greek character and institutions. Olbia, on the mouth of the Bug, was plundered by the Getae (a Thracian tribe) around 50 B.C. but later was restored and annexed to the Roman empire. The Goths sacked it again in the third century after Christ. A number of cities arose in south Russia in the Roman period. Among them Ptolemy (who wrote in the second half of the second century after Christ) mentions Metropolis and Azagarion, both on the Dnieper River. The name 'Metropolis' seems to indicate that this was rather a large town. Concerning the name 'Azagarion', in Iranian *gara* means 'mountain', 'hill'. The name may be interpreted as 'The Hill of Az'.

As has been said, the Sarmatae migrated by single tribes. However, as J. Harmatta has pointed out, they had a royal dynasty whose authority most of the tribes recognized.[1] Strabo (who wrote around 20 A.D.) mentions the 'Royal Sarmatae'. These must have represented the ruling Alanic clan, or rather a branch of it, which controlled the western group of the Sarmatae in the territory between the Dnieper and the Danube. Another branch of the Alanic clan established itself in the Don and Volga basins. A third—the Asii—reigned in eastern Iran and north-western India. Their empire is usually called Indo-Scythian. They were the 'kings of the Tokhars' mentioned by Justinus (see the preceding section 1). All of the three branches

---

[1] J. Harmatta, 'Studies on the History of the Sarmatians', *MGT*, xxx (1950), 20–26.

of the Alanic royal clan were apparently in close contact with each other, and entertained lively commercial relations. As both M. I. Rostovtzeff and J. Harmatta have shown, there are many similarities between the Indo-Scythian and Sarmatian art.[1] Richly adorned horse-trappings (*phalarae*) are among the characteristic items of the artistic patterns common to India and south Russia in the Sarmatian period.

Let us now turn to the Slavs. As has been said, evidence on them in the works of the classical authors is very scant. In fact, for the Scythian period there is no direct evidence at all. We may only surmise that some of the tribes subject to the Scythian kings were Slavic. The Neuri, who may be tentatively located in northern Podolia and Volynia, are considered Slavs by a number of scholars including Šafarik, Niederle, and Minns.[2] As regards another tribe mentioned by Herodotus, the Budini, Niederle remarks that their very name sounds Slavic. Herodotus (iv. 108) calls them 'a large and powerful nation' and says that 'they have all deep blue eyes and bright red hair'. Various opinions have been expressed as to the geographic location of the Budini. Niederle would place them in the middle Dnieper region, while Minns allows them the middle Volga area. I am inclined to think that they lived in the upper Don and the upper Donets region. It is probable that there were other Slavic tribes among the Scythian Agriculturists and the Scythian Ploughmen. Besides, Slavs might have been used as labourers by Scythian landowners in the northern Tauria. If there had been Slavs in northern Tauria, they must have called in their language the Scythian capital (Neapolis) Novgorod. In the story of a miracle of St. Stephen of Surozh (Sugdaea in the Crimea) of the late eighth century it is said that the Russian prince who attacked Surozh had come from Novgorod. This is usually understood as a reference to Novgorod the Great in north Russia, but Novgorod in the Crimea (Neapolis) might have been meant by the writer. In such a case we may suppose that Novgorod was an old name for Neapolis and that the name was still in use in the eighth century after Christ when nothing more than a small settlement might have remained at the site of the old city.

[1] M. Rostovtzeff, 'Sarmatskie i indo-skifskie drevnosti', *Recueil Kondakov* (Prague, 1926), pp. 239–58; J. Harmatta, op. cit., pp. 29–35.
[2] See also K. Moszyński, 'O Neurach Herodota', *Lud*, xli (1954), 134–52.

All of the preceding argument is hypothetical. It is only in the Sarmatian period that we feel ourselves on firmer ground. In his famous book on Germany, written in A.D. 98, Tacitus mentions the tribe of Venedi as located 'between the Germans and the Sarmatae'. The Venedi, remarks Tacitus, build houses, use shields, move about on foot; all this is different from the habits of the Sarmatae who live in tents and on horseback. The Venedi are likewise mentioned by Pliny (who died in A.D. 79) and Ptolemy. Ptolemy locates the Venedi in the area of the present-day Poland. In the Middle Ages the Venedi were called Wends by the Germans.

The Venedi were the forefathers of the western Slavs. The ancestors of the southern and the eastern Slavs lived in the Roman period in the area controlled by the Sarmatae and therefore the Greek and Latin writers of the period were not able clearly to differentiate them from the Sarmatian tribes. Of the future south Slavic tribes Ptolemy mentions the Serbs (Serbi) locating them west of the lower Volga. As to the Croats (Khorvats), the name occurs, as a personal name in two Tanais inscriptions of the late second and the early third centuries (*Chorouathos* in Greek transcription).

The sixth-century writers know the eastern Slavs under the name Antes. The name is mentioned, in the form 'Anti', by both Pomponius Mela (who wrote around 44 A.D.) and Pliny. Mela also has in his list of tribes of Transcaucasia (*Chorographia*, 13) three names which the copyists of his work were unable properly to divide: Mati, Anti, Barani (in some editions 'Mati-ani, Tibarani'; in others 'Mati, Antibarani'). The Barani became very active in the Gothic period (see section 3 below). The name is spelt 'Borani' by the fifth-century author Zosimos. The name is Slavic. *Boran*, spelt *baran* in Modern Russian, means 'ram'. Presumably ram was the ongon of this tribe.

In the later times (by around A.D. 800) the Antes merged with the Rus' and assumed the latter's name. In the Sarmatian period the Rus' were closely associated with the Alans. Hence the double name Rus-Alan (Roxolani). As has been mentioned,[1] *ruxs* in Alanic means 'radiant light'. The name 'Ruxs-Alan' may be understood in two ways: either as the 'Radiant Alans' or as the 'Rus' and Alans', that is a combination

[1] Chapter 1, section 6.

of two clans or two tribes.[1] That the Roxolani were actually a combination of these two clans may be seen from the fact that the name Rus (or Ros) was on many occasions used separately from that of the Alans. Besides, the armour of the Roxolani differed from that of the Alans. According to Strabo (7. 3. 17) the Roxolani wore helmets and corslets made of raw ox-hides —not metal helmets or coats of mail.

A strong group of the Roxolani had their abodes in the Volga basin. This explains the fact that the Volga was called Ros by a Greek geographer of the fifth century after Christ.[2] Other groups of the Roxolani moved westward. As has been mentioned, one of them penetrated into the Crimea in the late second century B.C. Around A.D. 62 the Roxolani reached the lower Danube region. It should be noted that, according to Strabo, a branch of the Roxolani penetrated into the Baltic area. Strabo (2. 5. 7) states that the Roxolani live 'above' (i.e. north of) the Dnieper River but south of the countries which are 'above' Britain (he probably means south of Scandinavia). His statement is rather confusing but seems to fit well the Nieman River basin. It surely is not a mere coincidence that the middle section of the Nieman was in old times known as Ros; also, the right channel of the lower Nieman. A tributary of the Narev (which is an eastern tributary of the western Bug) is also called Ros.[3] The occurrence of the name Ros in the toponymics of this region must be considered a trace of the old settlements of the Roxolani.

3. *The Slavs and the Rus' in the Alano-Gothic epoch*

Throughout the Sarmatian era, as we have seen, the royal clan of the Alans controlled the vast arc of lands stretching from India to Hungary. By A.D. 200 a new dynamic element came to the fore in the Pontic steppes—the Goths.

---

[1] A seventeenth-century scholar says that the Rossi (Rhos) 'Alanis permixti Rhoxalanorum gentem constituerunt', see Georgius Horn, *Arca Noae sive Historia imperiorum et regnorum a condito orbe ad nostra tempora* (Lugdunum Batavorum, 1666), p. 182.

[2] 'Hypotyposis Geographiae' (name of the author unknown), x. 29, see K. Müller, *Geographi Graeci Minores*, ii (Paris, 1882), 502. Reprinted in Latyshev, *Scythica et Caucasica*, ii. 295. Müller emended the name Rhōs to Rhās; in a note he explained, however, that in the manuscripts and previous editions the name always reads Rhos. Latyshev reprinted the name as in Müller's text (Rhās) and omitted the note. G. Horn, *Arca Noae*, p. 182, has correctly 'Rhos'.

[3] See G. Vernadsky, *Ancient Russia*, p. 97.

The origin of the Goths presents yet another controversial problem in the confused historical background of early Russia. In the classical sources the Goths are mentioned in turn by Pliny, Tacitus, and Ptolemy. Tacitus (*Germania*, 43) calls them Gotones, Ptolemy (3. 5. 8) Gythones. Ptolemy locates them in the Vistula River basin. Many scholars, including Friedrich Braun, considered this region the aboriginal home of the Goths. Recently, however, the opinion prevailed that the Goths had come to the Vistula basin from Scandinavia and that Scandinavia was the land of their origin. In view of what we know about the dynamics of the early migrations,[1] it may be doubted that either the Vistula region or Scandinavia was the *Urheimat* of the Goths. It seems more likely that they had originated in the east and that a group of them reached the southern Baltic shore in a remote period. From there some of them may have penetrated into Scandinavia. Other groups of them might have remained in central Asia and migrated westward much later.

It is supposed that the Goths trekked south from the Vistula River basin and reached the Dnieper near Kiev around A.D. 180. On the other hand, according to Franz Altheim, two Gothic names appear among the inscriptions of a Buddhic crypt at Junnar, Poona, India. The inscriptions date around A.D. 150.[2] In view of this discrepancy of dates we have either to surmise that the Goths had come to south Russia from the Baltic area much earlier than A.D. 180, or to assume that in the early second century there had existed another group of Goths in central Asia from where some of them penetrated into India by A.D. 150. I am inclined to give preference to this latter hypothesis. It will be recalled[3] that there are reasons to suppose that the Goths had been intimately associated with the Alans since ancient times. Most likely, it is through their connexion with the Alans (Asii) that a number of Goths had had the opportunity to reach India.

In the middle of the third century the Goths associated themselves with a Slavic tribe, the Borani.[4] According to the historian Zosimus (who wrote in the late fifth or in the beginning

---

[1] See Chapter 1, section 1, and Chapter 2, section 1, above.

[2] Franz Altheim, *Die Krise der Alten Welt*, i (Berlin, 1943), 96 and 194, n. 141; id., *Literatur und Gesellschaft im ausgehenden Altertum*, ii (Halle a. d. Saale, 1950), 87–88.

[3] See Chapter 2, section 1, above.

[4] On the latter see Chapter 2, section 2, above.

of the sixth century but used some earlier sources), around A.D. 250 the 'Scythians' (the Goths, the Borani, and two other tribes), coming from the Azov region, crossed the Danube River, invaded Thrace and started looting that country. Emperor Decius set forth against them but his army was surrounded by enemy forces and he himself perished in battle. The Goths and the Borani immediately resumed their depredations and penetrated to Illyria and even to northern Italy.

Simultaneously, another group of the Borani decided to raid the towns on the Caucasian shore of the Black Sea. From northern Tauria the Borani marched through the Crimea to Bosporus (ancient Panticapaeum) on the strait of Kerch and compelled the townspeople to ferry them in Bosporan boats to the Taman peninsula. The Borani then descended south along the shore and attacked Pityus (modern Pitsunda, south of Gagry). The attack was a failure (A.D. 255). In the next year the Borani repeated their venture. This time they seized the Bosporan boats and sailed to Pityus which they now stormed and sacked. They seized more boats in this region and collecting a large flotilla made straight for the rich city of Trebizond on the southern shore of the Black Sea. The unfortunate city was thoroughly looted, and the Borani returned home with their boats heavily laden with booty and prisoners.[1]

The success of the Borani encouraged the Goths, whose attention was attracted to the western shores of the Black Sea. About A.D. 258 the Goths dashed south through Thrace. The bulk of them marched overland, but part of them seized boats from local fishermen and sailed along the coast. They reached Gallipoli, attacked the town of Nicomedia in Asia Minor, and returned to the Balkans with rich booty. A few years later the Goths organized a major maritime expedition for which they built boats at the mouth of the Dniester River. Zosimus gives the number of boats as 6,000 and the number of men as 320,000. These figures seem greatly exaggerated unless we suppose that the boats were small and that the bulk of the army operated overland. The Gothic flotilla went through the Bosporus and

---

[1] Zosimus, *Historia nova*, ed. Mendelssohn (Bonn, 1887), i. 31–33 and 42; Ludwig Schmidt, *Geschichte der deutschen Stämme. Die Ostgermanen* (2nd edn., München, 1934), pp. 214–16; Tadeusz Lewicki, 'Zagadnienie Gotów na Krymie', *Przegląd Zachodni*, 5/6 (1951), 80 and 93.

the Dardanelles and reached Salonika. The Goths almost succeeded in taking it but lifted the siege when they heard of the
approaching Roman army. Most of the Goths abandoned their
boats and retreated overland north through Macedonia. They
were, however, attacked and defeated by the Romans. From
Zosimus' account of these and other Gothic invasions of this
period it is clear that the Goths fought on foot. It is cavalry
which turned the scale in favour of the Romans. In the next
few years the Roman empire regained strength and the Gothic
danger was averted, temporarily at least. For a long period the
Goths undertook no major attacks on Roman possessions and
turned their attention to consolidating their control of the
Pontic steppes. Some of the Goths entered Roman service.

The Goths were divided into several tribes, the most important two being known as the Ostrogoths and the Wisigoths.
Each of these two names was interpreted in different ways.
Concerning the former, the most plausible explanation of the
name is the 'Radiant Goths' (*Austr-Goth*). The name seems to
follow the pattern of Ruxs-Alan (the 'Radiant Alans'). The
Ostrogothic empire in south Russia reached its zenith in the
reign of King Ermanarich (who reigned from around 350 to
around 370). After consolidating his authority over the east
Gothic tribes Ermanarich began to subdue the neighbouring
non-Gothic peoples. Ammianus Marcellinus (31. 3. 1) charac-
terizes Ermanarich in the following words: ' . . . a most warlike
monarch, dreaded by the neighbouring nations because of his
many and varied deeds of valour.' Around A.D. 362 the Goths
conquered a considerable part of the Crimea, including Bosporus. Ermanarich then turned his attention to the Slavic tribes.
Among them were the Sclaveni (Slovene), a name which becomes familiar in the works of the sixth-century writers. One of
these, the Gothic historian Jordanes (an Alan by origin), says
that both the Sclaveni and the Antes recognized Ermanarich's
authority. The group of Antes he means occupied at that time
the southern Bug region; the Sclaveni were settled in the area
between the Carpathian mountains and the middle Dnieper.
Under Ermanarich's pressure a group of the Slovene migrated
north and settled around Lake Ilmen where they founded a
new city—Novgorod (literally 'New Town'). The bulk of the
Slovene remained, however, in their old abodes, being subject

to the Goths and later to the Huns. By the end of the fifth century they started their migration to the lower Danube.

After subduing the Slovene, Ermanarich attacked the Venedi in the region of the upper Vistula River. The Venedi were poorly armed and could rely only upon their numerical superiority. They were conquered without much difficulty, whereupon the Aestii (Balts) likewise recognized Ermanarich as their suzerain. The list of other tribes conquered by the Ostrogoths, as compiled by Jordanes, contains the names of several Finnish tribes as well as those of various tribes in the lower Volga and the Don regions.[1] Among them the Rogas (in some manuscripts Rocas) are mentioned. I interpret this name as Roc-As (Ruxs-As). One more tribal name is mentioned by Jordanes in a different connexion, the Rosomoni. In Ossetic *mojnæ* means 'man', 'husband'. The name Rosomoni is to be explained as the 'Ros men'.

At the basis of the expansion of the Ostrogoths lay the re-organization of their army in the first half of the fourth century. It will be recalled that in the third century the Goths had no cavalry, which enabled the Romans to repulse them. The Wisi-goths had no good cavalry even in the late fourth century. The battle of Adrianople (A.D. 378)—a catastrophe for the Roman army—was won by the Ostrogothic and Alanic cavalry. It is the consensus of opinion that the Ostrogothic cavalry was built up on the Alanic pattern. The Goths used weapons and armour of the Alanic type. A number of Alanic squadrons were incorpo-rated into the Ostrogothic army. Among the Alanic chieftains who joined the Goths, Safrac (Saurag) may be mentioned here.[2]

Even if we bear in mind that the Gothic cavalry was organ-ized with the help of the Alans, it seems hardly possible that the Goths could have mastered the art of cavalry warfare in the period of a few decades. It seems much more probable that a group of them had consisted of trained horsemen for a long period of time. There is no evidence of the presence of such a Gothic group in the Pontic steppes in the third century. Con-sequently we may think that this Gothic group appeared in the

---

[1] Jordanes, 'Romana et Getica', ed. Th. Mommsen, *MGH, Auctores Antiquissimi*, 5 (Berlin, 1882), 'Getica', section 116; J. J. Mikkola, 'Die Namen der Völker Her-manarichs, *FUF*, xv (1922), 56–66; G. Vernadsky, *Ancient Russia*, p. 120.

[2] See Chapter 1, section 3, above.

Black Sea region in the fourth century and that it had come from the east. It might have represented the last wave of the westward migration of the Goths. The group was probably small (the bulk of the Goths never became horsemen). That group constituted the flower of the Gothic aristocracy. The Gothic royal clan was known under the name of Amali. In Avestan *ama* means 'strong'. A Mithraic deity—the goddess of strength—was called Ama.[1] She might have been the protectress of the Amali.

Little is known of the system of administration established by the Goths in the Slavic areas conquered by them. By analogy with the practices of the rule of the Khazars and the Norsemen over the same areas in the later periods, it may be assumed that the Slavs had to pay a regular tribute to their conquerors. While the Slavic peasants were kept in a subordinated position, the Slavic tribal chieftains or princes might have been considered vassals of the Gothic king, and in this capacity admitted to his court where they could freely intermingle with the Gothic aristocracy. This may explain the fact that a number of the Gothic rulers had Slavic names such as Vithimir and Valamir.[2] Close interrelation between the Goths and the Slavs resulted in the penetration of a number of Gothic words into Slavic and of some Slavic words into the Gothic. Among the Gothic loan-words in Slavic we find certain terms bearing on administration, armour, and finance, like *kniaz'* 'prince' (Gothic *kunnigs*), *šlem* 'helmet' (Gothic *hilms*), *peniazi* 'money' (Gothic *pannings*), and *šeliag* 'coin' (Gothic *skillings*). The Slavic word for 'sword' (*meč*) was long considered a Gothic loan-word (*meki* in Gothic). It is now believed, however, that both these words derive from the same source—the language of the north Caucasian Andi. Of the Slavic loan-words in Gothic, *plinsjan* 'to dance' (Old Bulgarian *plęsati*), and *plat* 'patch' (Old Bulgarian *plat*; *platno* 'linen') may be mentioned here (cf. Polish *plasac*, *plótno*; Russian *pljasat'*, *polotno*).[3]

Two strong groups of the Antes lived in the fourth century in the middle Danube region, outside of the Gothic control and close to the boundary of the Roman empire. Their names are

---

[1] H. S. Nyberg, 'Die Religionen des Alten Iran', *MVAG*, xliii (1938), 70 and 74.
[2] On the Slavic names of this type see Chapter 4, section 3, below.
[3] See note E, p. 318.

given in the sources as the Acaragantes (Acarag-Antes) and
Limigantes (Limig-Antes). The former are also called 'Free
Sarmatians'. The latter were serfs of the formers. In Ossetic
æqæræg means 'voiceless', and *læmæg* 'weak', 'meek'. The Limig-
Antes were obviously Slavs. Their houses were thatched with
light straw, and they used river boats, each made of a single
tree-trunk (in Greek *monoxylon*). Such boats were also used by
the Slavs in the lower Danube region (see section 5 below) as
well as in Russia. The name Læmæg, survives in that of the
Lemki (singular Lemak), a tribe in the Carpathian Ukraine.[1]

The Acarag-Antes were Iranians. The name 'Voiceless' was
given to them after their defeat by the Romans A.D. 358, when
they pleaded for mercy. Their young prince Zizais, as Ammianus Marcellinus relates, 'on seeing the emperor . . . threw aside
his weapons and fell flat on his breast, as if lying lifeless. And
since the use of his voice failed him from fear at the very time
he should have made his plea, he excited all the greater com-
passion. . . . Upon this the throng [of the Sarmatians] was admitted to make its entreaties, but mute terror closed their lips'
(17. 12. 9–10). It seems likely that the Ossetian curse *æqæræg
fæu* ('be voiceless') originated from this episode. As to the name
of the prince, Zizais in Ossetic *dzizi* means 'teat'; *dzidzidaj*
'suckling'. Zizais was apparently a mock-name.

Zizais and his tribe had to recognize the suzerainty of the
emperor. Their serfs, the Slavic Limig-Antes, took advantage
of their masters' humiliation and revolted against them. The
Slavs proved not as 'meek' as their name implied. According to
Ammianus Marcellinus (17. 12. 18), the Slavs 'vanquished their
masters, being their equals in courage and far superior in number'. The defeated Sarmatians fled to the Roman boundary and
asked their suzerain the emperor for assistance.

The emperor ordered that the Limig-Antes leave the region
and migrate north. This they refused to do. 'They believed mad
license to be freedom', as Ammianus remarks (17. 13. 22). They
resisted the Romans 'with invincible stubborness' (*insuperabili
contumacia*, 17. 13. 10); 'not a single man asked for pardon'.
Most of them were killed in battle, after which the Roman soldiers burned their houses and seized their families. Other

---

[1] On the Lemki see Jan Czekanovski, 'Les Alains et les reliquats karpatiques des
migrations', *Rocznik Orientalistyczny*, xviii (1953), 378.

groups succeeded in escaping beyond the Tisa (Theiss). The Romans had to ask the co-operation of the 'Free Sarmatians' and the Taifali (a Gothic tribe) to break the resistance of the Limig-Antes. Finally, the assembly of their older men decided that further struggle was hopeless, and the Limig-Antes surrendered. With the help of the Romans Zizais was restored to the throne.

4. *The Alans and the Slavs in the Hunnic age*

Ermanarich's empire proved short-lived. It broke to pieces when the political equilibrium of the Alano-Gothic world was upset by the migration of the Huns from inner Asia to Europe. As has been said (section 3 above), in Ermanarich's time a number of the Alanic clans had joined the Ostrogothic army. The main body of the Alans resided at that time in the lower Volga basin, the Azov region, and in the northern Caucasus. The Huns penetrated into the Volga basin around A.D. 360. According to Ammianus Marcellinus (31. 2. 7) the Huns at that time had no king, and were 'content with the disorderly government of their important men'. From this it may be assumed that the Hunnic horde represented a rather loose association of clans. Some of the clan leaders must have been descendants of the former kings, and the monarchic tradition was later restored under the leadership of Attila.

The core of the Hunnic horde consisted of Turkish clans which were later to be known as the Bulgars. But there must have been in the horde a number of clans of different ethnic origin—Tokharian, Alanic (Asii), and Slavic. When the Huns entered the lower Volga–Azov area they clashed with the Alans and inflicted heavy losses on the latter. Instead of continuing the struggle the Alans decided to join the Hunnic horde and concluded a treaty of alliance with the Huns. Then the combined forces of the Huns and Alans invaded the confines of the Ostrogothic empire. Ermanarich's army was defeated and Ermanarich himself committed suicide. After their initial success the victors did not, at first, undertake any further sustained offensive. Since there was no cohesion in the conglomeration of the Huns and Alans at that time, each clan acted by itself and for its own advantage. A number of Huns were hired by Ermanarich's successor Vithimir in the latter's attempt to strengthen the badly shaken Gothic army. The Ostrogoths had to retreat west, nevertheless. When they reached the Dnieper River they found that the farther way westward was barred by the Antes of the Bug region. The Ostrogoths attacked the Antes and succeeded in crushing the latter's resistance. The captured Antian king Boz (Bus) was crucified together with his sons and seventy Antian notables. The Alans now hastened to the rescue of their kin, the Antes. The decisive battle between the Alans and the Ostrogoths took place at the river Erak (now called Tiligul), around A.D. 375. The Ostrogoths were defeated and had to move farther west. Before long they reached the shores of the lower Danube.

While Ammianus Marcellinus speaks of the war between the Alans and the Ostrogoths, Jordanes calls it a war between the Huns and the Ostrogoths.[1] Since Ammianus was a contemporary of the events and Jordanes wrote two centuries later, preference should be given to Ammianus' testimony. Besides, as we know, the name 'Huns' could have been—and was on many occasions—used not in the ethnic sense but in the political, being applied to the peoples of the Hunnic confederation at large. Using probably some old saga, Jordanes describes the battle of Erak as an archery duel between the king of the Huns and the king of the Ostrogoths. The former kills the latter with his arrow. According to Jordanes the name of this king of the Huns was Balamber. A similar name was later borne by a Gothic chieftain (grandson of Vithimir) Balamer (in Greek transcription, by Priscus) or Valamir (Jordanes' transcription). The latter name sounds Slavic (Velemir).

It is characteristic of the intermingling of clans of various ethnic origin in the Eurasian kingdoms of this period that at the time of the Alanic–Gothic war a number of the Alanic clans sided with the Goths. After the death of the Ostrogothic king Vithimir (who perished in the battle of Erac), his little son Viderich was proclaimed king. In his name the management of affairs was undertaken by two experienced generals, Alatheus and Safrac (Ammianus, 31. 3. 3). As we know, 'Safrac' is an Alanic name (*Saurag*). The name 'Alatheus' is to be compared to the 'Sarmatian' name in one of the Olbian inscriptions—

---

[1] Ammianus Marcellinus, xxxi. 2. 3; Jordanes, op. cit., 'Getica', sections 248–9; G. Vernadsky, *Ancient Russia*, pp. 130–1.

Alouthagos, 'Brewer' (*ælut* means 'beer' in Ossetian). We may think that of these two chieftains, one was famous for his horses (of the *saurag* breed) and the other for his beer. Beer was the national drink of the Alans (and still is, of the Ossetians) and was served at all the banquets—state and private.

After the withdrawal of the Goths, the Alans established themselves in Moldavia, and the river Pruth became known as the 'Alanic River'. Undoubtedly, the Bug region Antes were in close association with the Alans. In the sixth century the Antes themselves settled in Bessarabia and Moldavia. In the early fifth century, presumably because of the Hunnish pressure, the Alans, as well as some of the German tribes, the Vandals among others, migrated to Gaul and to Spain where the Alans united with the Vandals and later moved to North Africa. We may think that certain Slavic tribes followed the Alans and Vandals in their campaigns. Procopius (*Anecdota*, 18. 6) mentions the 'servants' of the Vandals who accompanied their masters to Spain. These were probably a Slavic 'serf-tribe' controlled by the Vandals. Besides, some of the Antes, who had been closely associated with the Alans after the Alano-Gothic war, might have now joined the Alans either as their associates or as their serfs. In this way a number of Slavs—and of Russes —might have penetrated into France, Spain, and North Africa.

By 420 the main horde of the Huns established itself in the steppes of the middle Danubian area (in the region which later became known as Hungary). From there they kept the Roman world in terror for about thirty years. Attila's empire (A.D. 434–53) was a confederation of the Huns and the peoples subordinated to them—the Germans, the Alans, and the Slavs.[1] While the latter are not mentioned as a separate group in the written sources available to us, there is no doubt that they constituted an important element in the Hunnic empire. Slavic was one of the languages used both in some regions controlled by the Huns and at the khan's court. Priscus, who was secretary of the east Roman embassy to Attila in 448, relates that when the embassy crossed the Danube, the local people treated the Greeks with the beverage called *medos* which is certainly the Slavic *med* (honey 'mead'). The embassy servants were offered another kind of beverage, made of barley, which Priscus calls

[1] See note F, p. 318.

kamos (the Slavic *kvas*).[1] Even more significant is the fact that, according to Jordanes, when Attila died, the ritual funeral banquet, in which all of the Hunnic notables participated, was called *strava* by the Huns.[2] This is a Slavic term and its use is an indication of the important role the Slavic ritual played at Attila's court.

A few years after Attila's death the Hunnic empire dis-integrated, and the bulk of the Hunnic horde retreated eastward to the Pontic steppes and the Azov and north Caucasian area where the horde broke into several tribes which eventually be-came known under a new name—that of the Bulgars. From time to time, in co-operation with the Slavs, they undertook devastating raids on Thrace and other Byzantine possessions. Presumably, some of the Slavic chieftains were closely asso-ciated with the Hunno-Bulgar khans. In central Europe the Sarmatian and German tribes, formerly subordinated to Attila, now became independent. A group of those Alans who had not migrated west earlier, moved to Dobrudja. A group of the Acarag-Antes settled in Illyricum. It was the German tribes which now remained in control of most of the middle Danube region with the Slavs (the Limig-Antes) in a subordinated position. The situation was different in the north. As the Anglo-Saxons moved to Britain and the Franks completed their migration to Gaul, a vacuum was formed in Germany which was filled by several Slavic tribes. The lower Elbe basin was occupied by the Obodrites and that of the middle Elbe by the Serbs. East of the Obodrites the Veleti established themselves, and on the Baltic shores between the Oder and the Vistula, the Pomorane (Pomeranians).

5. *The Slavs and the Russes in the sixth century*

The migrations and wars of the Hunnic age changed the political and ethnic map of Europe. They also affected in many ways the position of the Slavs. In the post-Hunnic period the Slavs came into the open and were able to form a number of

[1] Priscus, 'Fragmenta', L. Dindorf, ed., *Historici Graeci Minores*, i (Leipzig, 1870), fragment 8. For the English translation of this 'Fragment' see J. B. Bury, *History of the Later Roman Empire*, i (London, 1923), 279–88. See also G. Vernadsky, *Ancient Russia*, pp. 142–3.

[2] Jordanes, op. cit., 'Gethica', section 258.

their own tribal states. Among the reasons which brought about this change, the withdrawal of the Goths from south Russia westward was of considerable importance. Only two small Gothic groups remained on the northern shores of the Black Sea—the Crimean Goths and the Circassian Goths (Gothi Tetraxitae, i.e. Tetra-Kasitae).[1] Neither group presented any menace to the Slavs. Of no lesser significance was the westward exodus of several strong groups of Alans. Other groups of Alans continued to stay in the Caucasus and the Don–Donets basin; their relations with the Slavs were mostly friendly. Many of the 'Outer tribes' (Antes) in which formerly the Alanic element had predominated now became completely Slavicized even though some of their clan leaders still bore Alanic names.

It is in this period that the name 'Slavs' was for the first time noticed by foreign observers and appeared in Greek and Latin historical and geographical works (in the form *Sclabeni* in Greek, *Sclaveni* in Latin). The Old Slavic (and the Old Russian) form of the name was *Slovene* (in Modern Russian *Slaviane*). There is no consensus of opinion concerning the origin of the name. The derivation from the Slavic *slovo* 'word' seems the most plausible solution. The Slavs so called themselves because they spoke the same language and could understand each other. In contrast 'foreigners' were called *Nemtsy*, i.e. 'mute', from *nem* 'mute', 'dumb'. Later on, the name *Nemtsy* acquired a narrower connotation, that of the 'Germans'.[2]

The name 'Slovene' was used in two senses. As a generic name it was applied to all Slavic-speaking peoples and tribes. In the more restricted sense it denoted a specific tribe. In the Russian Chronography (*Povest' Vremennykh Let*) the name is used in both connotations. In the generic sense the Slavic people is said to derive from Noah's son Japhet and to represent one of the seventy-two languages scattered over the face of the earth after the destruction of the Tower of Bable. In the specific sense,

[1] On the Crimean Goths see A. A. Vasiliev, *The Goths in the Crimea* (Cambridge, Mass., 1936). On the 'Tetraxitae Goths' see T. Lewicki, 'Zagadnienie Gotów na Krymie', *Przegląd Zachodni*, 5/6 (1951); G. Vernadsky, 'The Riddle of the Gothi Tetraxitae', *SOF*, xi (1952), 281–3.

[2] Max Vasmer, *Russisches etymologisches Wörterbuch*. ii. 211, gives the above interpretation of the name 'Nemtsy', but refuses to accept the derivation of 'Slovene' from *slovo* (ii. 656–7). In my opinion these two names—Slovene and Nemtsy—form a natural pair of contrasting concepts.

the tribe settled around Novgorod in north-west Russia is called
'Slovene' in the Chronography. The two sixth-century authorities on the Slavs, the Byzantine historian Procopius of Caesarea
and the Gothic historian Jordanes, employ the name 'Slavs' in
the sense of a specific tribe. Procopius mentions two major
Slavic tribes: the Sclabeni (Slovene) and the Antes. He remarks
that these two peoples 'have had from ancient times the same
institutions and customs' and that they 'have also the same
language, an utterly barbarous tongue' (7. 14. 23 and 26).
According to Jordanes, the people formerly known as the Venethi (Tacitus' Venedi) 'have now three names, that is Venethi,
Antes, and Sclaveni'.

It should be noted that there was a tribe called 'Slovene' in
each of the three divisions of the Slavs in the later age: the
Slovenians among the southern Slavs; the Slovaks, among the
western Slavs; and the Slovene of Novgorod among the eastern
Slavs in old Russia. This must have been the result of the dispersion of the original Slovene in three different directions. As
we know, the Antes had been originally closely associated with
the Alans (and so were the Russes). The Venedi, in all probability, had had, in the remote past, intimate ties with the Celts and
the Illyrians. Consider the similarity of the name 'Venedi' to
that of 'Veneti' in Armorica, ancient Gaul, and to 'Veneti' in
northern Italy (hence Venice). The Slovene might have originally represented the purest stock of the Slavs.

In Ermanarich's time, as we know, Slovene were settled in
Galicia, Volynia, and the Kiev region, and a strong group of
the Antes resided in the Bug region. Following the disintegration of the Hunnic empire both the Slovene and the Antes
moved to the lower Danube region. In 517 huge bands of them
(called 'Getae' in our sources) invaded Illyricum and Macedonia, devastating the country, holding wealthy burghers for ransom, and demanding huge indemnities from the cities they
besieged. From then on, the Slavic pressure steadily increased.
According to Procopius:

Illyricum and Thrace in its entirety, comprising the whole ex-
panse of country from the Ionian Gulf to the outskirts of Byzantium,
including Greece and the Thracian Chersonese, was overrun practically every year by Huns (Bulgars), Sclabeni, and Antes, from the
time when Justinian took over the Roman empire, and they wrought

frightful havoc among the inhabitants of that region. For in each invasion more than twenty myriads of Romans, I think, were destroyed or enslaved there, so that a veritable 'Scythian wilderness' came to exist everywhere in this land. (*Anecdota*, 18. 20–21).

In Justinian's time the Slovene lived north of the lower Danube River in the region later to be known as Walachia, and the Antes in Moldavia and Bessarabia. These, however, represented only a branch of the Antes—the western one. The 'countless tribes' of their eastern branch Procopius locates 'above' the sea of Azov, that is in the middle Dnieper region and the Donets River basin.

Among the Antes of the sixth century with whom the Byzantines had to deal, the Slavic element definitely prevailed upon the Iranian.[1] Some of their chieftains, however, still bore names of Iranian origin, such as Ardagast and Peiragast; others had Slavic names formed along the same pattern (Dobrogast). In 531 Justinian decided to take energetic measures to protect Thrace from the inroads of the Antes and the Sclaveni. The general he appointed commander-in-chief for operations against the Slavs, Chilbudius, had been, prior to his appointment, a member of the emperor's private guards, and such units were usually at this time composed of foreign soldiers. Chilbudius might have been an Antas by origin. His first operations were successful, but in 534 he was killed in a battle. The Byzantine army retreated, and the Slavs were able to raid Moesia and Thrace once more. Further threat to imperial interests was averted by the skill of Byzantine diplomacy which succeeded in sowing seeds of discord between the Slovene and the Antes. A war started between these two peoples during which a rumour spread that Chilbudius had not been killed but that he went over to the Slavic side. A pretender appeared whom the Antes recognized as their leader. Before long, however, Pseudo-Chilbudius was seized by the Byzantines and detained in Constantinople. The result of all these events was that the Antes recognized Justinian as their suzerain and agreed to garrison the fortress of Tyras at the mouth of the Dniester River (Akkerman) to guard the frontier against the Bulgars (around 544).

[1] On the Antes and the Slovene in the sixth and seventh centuries and their relations with Byzantium see B. A. Rybakov, 'Anty i Kievskaia Rus', *Vestnik Drevnei Istorll*, 1939, 1, 319–37; G. Vernadsky, *Ancient Russia*, pp. 166–74 and 184–9.

Justinian now added the epithet 'Anticus' to his title. No agreement was reached between the Byzantines and the Slovene, and the latter resumed their raids on Thrace in 547. It should be mentioned that during this period auxiliary troops consisting of both Antes and Slovene were used by the Byzantine generals in Italy against the Goths (in 537 and again in 547).

While the Danubian Antes, as well as the Danubian Slovene, became part of the Byzantine world, politically in any case, other groups of the Slavs remained outside of it. Indeed, the Danubian Antes represented but a southern outpost of the Antian nation at large. The bulk of that nation lived in the middle Dnieper and upper Donets regions, on the northern fringe of the steppes and in the 'forest-steppe' ('wooded steppe') zone. There resided the mightiest chieftains of the Antes who did not consider themselves bound by any agreements between their Danubian kin and Byzantium. On many occasions they participated in the Bulgar and Slavic campaigns in the Balkans, and some of them enriched themselves with war booty seized during these raids. It is probably to such successful Antian leaders that a number of the treasure hoards found in the Russo-Ukrainian forest steppe zone should be attributed.

While the Danubian Antes recognized the authority of the Byzantine emperor, the Russo-Ukrainian Antes apparently concluded an agreement with the Bulgars. In 558 a huge horde of both Bulgars and Slavs crossed the Danube, looted Thrace and Macedonia, and appeared at the neck of the Thracian Chersonese (Gallipoli). The invaders' attempts to storm Constantinople failed and they agreed to lift the siege for a ransom. Following that the Bulgars returned to the Pontic steppes where they had soon to face the onslaught of the Avars from the east.

We turn now to the evidence concerning the Russes in the post-Hunnic period. In the Syriac compilation of the middle of the sixth century, the so-called 'Church History' of Zacharias Rhetor, a people called Hros is mentioned as living in the Don region. According to A. P. Diakonov this is an exact Syriac transliteration of the Greek 'Rhos'. In N. V. Pigulevskaia's opinion the Syriac name may also be read as Hrus (Rus).[1] The

---

[1] A. P. Diakonov, 'Izvestiia Psevdo-Zakharii o drevnich Slavianakh', *Vestnik Drevnei Istorii*, 1939, 4, 86–87; N. V. Pigulevskaia, 'Imia Rus v siriiskom istochnike VI veka', *Akademiku Grekovu* (Moscow, 1952), p. 47.

list of peoples of the north Caucasian and Don areas (to which Hros belongs) was inserted into Zacharias' *History* on the basis of the reports of the Amidans who had been captured by the Persians in A.D. 503 and then sold into slavery to the Huns (Bulgars). They returned home after a sojourn of about fifty years in the northern Caucasus and Azov region. Their reports may be considered basically sound. According to them the Hros were people with such large limbs that horses could not carry them. It may be concluded, as Pigulevskaia has done quite plausibly, that the Hros were not horsemen. This seems to indicate that by that time the Alanic element in the tribe had faded out and the Slavic prevailed.

This group of the Ros is called by the ancient name of 'Roxolani' in Ravennas Anonymus' geographic manual of the seventh century. The compiler of the manual places the 'Roxolani' in the Don area. In the same geographical treatise (iv. 3) a town by the name of Malorosa is mentioned among the Bosporan towns (of the Cimmerian Bosporus, i.e. strait of Kerch). In my opinion the name should be explained as Mal-Ros, the 'Swamp of the Ros' (*mal* means 'bog', 'swamp' in Ossetic). The Kuban River delta might have been meant.

6. *The Slavs and the Avars*

The invasion of the Avars, like that of the Huns, changed the whole political system of central-eastern Europe. It caused a new wave of migrations of a number of German and Sarmatian tribes, though of a more limited range than the general *Völkerwanderung* brought about by the Huns. The Avars seriously threatened the security of the Byzantine empire and of the Frankish realm in the west, and indirectly contributed to important political changes in Italy. But it is the Slavs who had to bear the brunt of the Avar onslaught and whose historical destinies were most affected by the new invaders.

The Avars rushed westward from central Asia to escape from the pressure of the Altaic Turks.[1] Having first defeated the

---

[1] On the Avars see Gyula Moravcsik, *Byzantinoturcica*, i (Budapest, 1942), 41–42; H. W. Haussig, 'Theophylakts Exkurs über die Skytischen Volker', reprint from *Byzantion*, xxiii (1954); id., 'Indogermanische und altaische Nomadenvölker im Grenzgebiete Irans', *Historia Mundi*, v (1956), 240–2 and map on p. 241; id., 'Die Quellen über die zentralasiatische Herkunft der europäischen Awaren', *Central Asiatic Journal*, ii (1956), 21–43.

Bulgars in the Pontic steppes, the Avars attacked the Antes in Bessarabia (A.D. 561). The latter at first offered a furious resistance but later entered into negotiations with the invaders. The negotiations were soon broken since the Avars were irritated by the haughty and independent behaviour of the Antian envoy Mezamer and put him to death. Following that, the war continued and the Antes suffered great losses; part of their country was thoroughly devastated. However, their resistance was not broken. In 562 the Avars succeeded in seizing Dobrudja but not for long. Six years later, being pressed by both the Byzantines and the Antes, the Avars decided to migrate to the middle Danube region. Part of them proceeded up the Danube River, while others went up the course of the rivers Pruth and Dniester to Galicia whence they could use several mountain passes to emerge upon the Tisza River valley. On their way through Galicia they conquered the Slavic tribe of the Dulebi. Part of the latter were compelled to follow the conquerors and settled in the Tisza valley. Before long, the Avars seized the whole middle Danube area where they were to stay for over two centuries.

The Avar conquest of this area put an end to the German and Sarmatian control there. While part of the Germans and the Sarmatae merged with the invaders, most of them preferred to migrate. The Langobardi moved to Italy accompanied by several German groups as well as by the Acarag-Antes. That part of the Slavic Antes (Limig-Antes) which were serfs ('aldii') of the Langobardi likewise followed their masters. In the long run the political revolution in central Europe caused by the appearance of the Avars proved beneficial to the Slavs. As the Germans moved out the Slavs came in. The Avar horde was not numerous and centred around the prairie region (the Hungarian *Alföld*). There was ample room left for Slavic colonization in the peripheral regions. While the Avar rule over the Slavs was harsh, especially during the first years after the conquest, the Slavs derived some profit from the mere fact of being included in a comparatively vast empire. Like the Huns and the Sarmatae in the earlier periods, the Avars were interested in controlling international trade routes, and the Slavs could not but take advantage of the growth of the Avar commerce. As the Slavs were compelled to supply auxiliary troops to the Avars, they must have had their share of war-booty as well (except during the first years after the conquest). Most important was the fact that the Slavs of central Europe were now able to establish direct relations with their kin both in the north—the Elbe and the Baltic Slavs—and in the south—the Balkan Slavs, and also with the Slavs in Galicia. Thus an opportunity for the slavs to acquire greater unity arose, and a new avenue was opened for the Slavic colonization of the Balkans through the middle Danube region.

The Avar kaganate was similar in purpose and its methods of government to other nomadic empires of inner Asia.[1] The Avars were a nation of horsemen who needed a strong central base for their far-reaching raids on the neighbouring peoples and states. The immediate motive of these raids was to obtain the immediate spoils of war and then to secure a permanent income through tribute and commerce. The core of the Avar empire was the Tisza River and the middle Danube basin. To ensure the subordination of the Slavic tribes around, Avar troops were placed in nine fortified camps strategically located to command the whole area of the future Hungary. Each such camp was protected by a ring of earthen ramparts. Stores of grain and other foodstuffs supplied by the Slavic peasants, as well as military booty and treasures, were kept by the Avars in these camps. Slavic tribes in that central area of the Avar empire were directly subordinated to the Avars and had no princes of their own. When the Czechs revolted against the Avars, A.D. 623, their leader was a merchant, not a prince. On the other hand, the peripheral Slavs, like the Antes and the Slovene in the lower Danube basin, were ruled by their own chieftains and princes, some of whom became vassals of the Avar khan.

In 581 the Avars seized Sirmium (now Sremska Mitrovica) on the lower Sava, an important Byzantine fortress which in fact was the key to the whole Byzantine defence line in northern Illyricum. The Byzantines hastened to conclude peace with the Avars, promising to pay yearly tribute ('presents'). As the tribute was not paid regularly, the Avars and the Slavs

---

[1] On the Avar kaganate see L. Hauptmann, 'Les rapports des Byzantins avec les Slaves et les Avars', *Byzantion*, iv (1929), 137–70; G. Vernadsky, *Ancient Russia*, pp. 178–91; M. de Ferdinandy, 'Die nordeurasischen Reitervölker und der Westen bis zum Mongolensturm', *Historia Mundi*, v (1956), 200–1.

continued their steady pressure on the empire. The Byzantine emperor Mauricius (582–602) at first avoided clashing with the Avars but decided to push the Slavs back north. The Byzantine army crossed the Danube and attacked the Slavic encampment in the dead of night. The Slavs were caught unawares and took to flight. Before long, however, the Slavs received reinforcements from their kin living farther north. The name of the Slavic prince who led the new army is given in Byzantine sources as Musokius. He came either from Galicia or from the Kiev region.[1] The Byzantines succeeded in defeating the new Slavic army, using again the stratagem of night attack. Musokius himself was taken prisoner. Upon receiving news of the defeat of Musokius' army the Avar kagan protested against the Byzantine invasion of the Slav country, which he considered his dominion. In order to avert a conflict with the Avars, the Byzantine commander offered to split the booty, and the kagan accepted. Accordingly, 5,000 Slav prisoners were turned over to the Avars despite the indignation of the Byzantine soldiery, thus deprived of part of their spoils.

A few years after the Slavs rallied, crossed the Danube, and raided lower Moesia. The Byzantines pushed them back beyond the Danube. A strong Byzantine army then entered the Slav country but was defeated by the Slavs. The Byzantines suffered great losses and had hastily to retreat. At that juncture the Avars renewed their attacks on the Byzantine dominions in the Balkans. The war lasted for several years with intermittent success. Finally, Emperor Heraclius (610–41) attempted to organize a vast coalition against the Avar kagan, urging both the Bulgars and the Franks to unite against the common enemy. Moreover, Byzantine agents established contacts with the Czechs in Bohemia, the Serbs in the Elbe region, and the Croats in Galicia in order to arouse these tribes against the Avars. The Avars, in their turn, entered into contact with the Persians, urging them to send their army against Constantinople through Asia Minor.

---

[1] Tadeusz Lewicki likens the name 'Musokius' to that of 'Majak' mentioned by the Arabic writer Masudi. In Lewicki's opinion 'majak' derives from the Slavic *mąż* (*muzh*) 'man'; see T. Lewicki, 'Jeszcze o Wieletach w opisie Słowiańszyzhy arabskiego pisarza z X w. al-Masudiego', *Pamiętnik Słowański*, ii (Kraków, 1951), 113–16. I believe that the name 'Musokius' may derive from the Alanic language. In Ossetic *mysæg* means 'schemer'.

In 623 (the date as given in Fredegar's chronicle), the Czechs revolted against the Avars under the leadership of a merchant by the name of Samo. According to Fredegar he was a Frank.[1] The uprising was successful. 'A great number of the Huns [Avars] were killed by Vinidian [Czech] swords.' Apparently the Czechs were able to break one of the nine Avar 'rings', that which was closest to them. Following that, they elected Samo their ruler. The Avars were not in a position immediately to organize a punitive expedition against the Czechs since at that time they were making final preparations for their grand campaign against Constantinople which was to be co-ordinated with the Persian expedition.

The Avaro-Slav army appeared before the walls of Constantinople in July 626. The Persians were already camped on the Asiatic shore of the Bosporus. As the Persians had no boats and the Byzantine fleet was still in command of the Straits, they had to wait while the Avars and the Slavs attempted to storm the Imperial City. According to their plan of campaign the invaders were to attack Constantinople simultaneously from land and sea. The Slavs succeeded in bringing boats to the Golden Horn. Their flotilla was, however, destroyed by the Byzantine fleet. The land attack likewise failed. Lack of food and the spread of epidemics compelled the Avar kagan to lift the siege and to return to Pannonia. When the Persians became aware of the failure of their allies, they retreated as well.

The disastrous result of the campaign of 626 greatly undermined the prestige of the kagan among his Slavic subjects and allies. The Czechs were able to maintain their independence.

Another blow to the integrity of the Avar kaganate was the migration, at the invitation of Emperor Heraclius, of groups of the Serbs of the Elbe region and of the Croats of Galicia to the Balkan peninsula (between 625 and 629). The Croats (Hrvat, Khorvats) must have come to Galicia from the Azov area either before the appearance of the Avars or soon after. Several different interpretations of the origin of the name Hrvat have been offered with none winning general recognition so far. In my opinion Paul Tedesco's explanation (communicated in a letter to me) is the only convincing one. He interprets 'Horvat' as the

---

[1] Fredegar, iv. 48 and 68; G. Vernadsky, 'The Beginnings of the Czech State', *Byzantion*, xvii (1944-5), 315-28.

Iranian *xvarvant* (Sanskrit *svarvant*) 'sun-like'. The Croats, then, may be identified with the Hvari (Khorezmians). The name is of the same type as 'Rukhs' (*Ruxs*) and approximately of the same meaning.

It should be noted that in the Old Persian inscriptions the province of Arachosia (in south-eastern Iran) is called Harah-vati.[1] This is obviously a variant of the name Hrvat. Presumably, part of the original Horvats migrated from Khorezm to Iran, and part to the Azov region and then westward. Like the Antes and the Serbs, the Croats were Slavicized in the course of time. That group of the Croats which remained in Galicia is called 'White Croats' by Constantine Porphyrogenitus. Those who migrated to the Balkans he calls just 'Croats'. Apparently both the Croats and the Serbs moved south through Samo's dominions. From Constantine Porphyrogenitus's story of their migration it may be deduced that the Croat new-comers were more numerous than the Serbs. Together they were able to vanquish the Avar troops in Illyricum, following which Heraclius allowed the Croats to settle there. The Serbs were established north of Mount Olympus. Encouraged by the success of the Serbs and Croats, the Macedonian Slavs in the Salonika region likewise refused to recognize the kagan's authority.[2]

It will be recalled that the westward migration of the Avars had been caused by the expansion of the Altaic Turks. Around A.D. 568 the Turks crossed the Volga River and invaded the north Caucasian area. The Bulgar tribe of the Utiguri recognized the suzerainty of the Turkish kagan. A Turkish division (*tuman*) reached the Black Sea at the mouth of the Kuban River. The commander of the division (*tuman-tarkhan*) established his headquarters there. Thus, a new town was founded, Tuman-Tarkhan (in Russian *Tmutorokan*).[3] In A.D. 576 the Turks crossed the strait of Kerch and seized the city of Bosporus (old Panticapaeum, modern Kerch). Five years later they appeared

[1] R. G. Kent, *Old Persian* (New Haven, 1950), p. 213; F. Dvornik, *The Slavs: Their Early History and Civilization* (Boston, 1956), p. 26, note.

[2] L. Hauptmann, 'Kroaten, Goten und Sarmaten', *Germano-Slavica*, iii (1935); F. Dvornik, *The Making of Central and Eastern Europe* (London, 1949), pp. 283–94; F. Dvornik, *The Slavs: Their Early History and Civilization* (Boston, 1956), pp. 62–64; T. Lewicki, 'Litzike Konstantyna Porfirogenety i Biale Srbove w pólnocnej Polsce', *Roczniki Historiczne*, xxii (1956), 9–32.

[3] G. Vernadsky, *Ancient Russia*, pp. 184, 215, 216; id., 'Toxar, T'ma, T'mutorokan', *For Roman Jakobson* (The Hague, 1956), pp. 590–1.

before the walls of Cherson. Though the Byzantine garrison had no hope of withstanding the onslaught, the Turks unexpectedly lifted the siege and retreated. The reason for their withdrawal was the news received by their commanding officers of internal strife at the court of the kagan in Turkestan. A protracted civil war now weakened the Turkish state for about two decades, during which period the Turks abandoned any further offensive plans in the Pontic area.

While the Altaic-Turkish invasion of the northern Caucasus proved short-lived, it had a certain influence on events that followed in that area. A number of the Turkish new-comers from the east remained in the area and thus reinforced the Turkish elements already present there—the Bulgars.

3

THE EASTERN SLAVS IN THE BULGAR-KHAZAR ERA

1. *Great Bulgaria*

ABOUT A.D. 600 northern Tauria, the Azov region, and the north Caucasian area were the home of a variety of clans and tribes of diverse ethnic origin. Besides the old settlers, like the Alans, the Kasogi (Circassians), and the Slavs, a number of Turkish and Ugrian (proto-Magyar) new-comer tribes established themselves in the area. Throughout the sixth century there had been no unity among the various ethnic groups. Each tribe pursued its own policies. There were times when one of the Turkish clans would make an alliance with the Avars, and another with Byzantium. Eventually, however, the Turkish tribes rallied around the princes of the Dulo clan—descendants of Attila's youngest son Irnik—and formed the backbone of a powerful federation known as Great Bulgaria. Its creator was Khan Kurt who reigned from 605 to 665.[1]

Like many other Eurasian empires, Great Bulgaria was a multi-national state. While the Turks constituted the strongest element, Alans and Slavs also played an important role in state affairs. A number of Alanic and Slavic clans were closely associated with the Turkish ruling group. Culturally, the Turks were influenced by Iranian and Slavic notions in many ways. To sum up, Great Bulgaria, like its successor the Khazar kaganate, came into being in an Alano-Slavic milieu, and represented a symbiosis of several ethnic groups.

Historical evidence for the study of Great Bulgaria is scant and fragmentary. We have, however, at our disposal a number of clan names and personal names, an analysis of which may enable us better to understand the complex social and cultural interrelations of diverse ethnic elements in the old Bulgar state.

[1] On the Bulgars see Guyla Moravcsik, *Byzantinoturcica*, i (1942), 50–58. See also p. 88, n. 3, and p. 89, n. 1.

To begin with the name 'Bulgar' itself, it is usually considered Turkic. In my opinion it is much more likely that the name is of Alanic origin. In Ossetic *bylgæron* means 'shore', 'bank' (of a river); also 'edge' (of a bluff, or a hill). On this basis the name 'Bulgar' might be interpreted as 'Shore People'. The name seems to be of the same type as that of the Slavic tribe Pomorane ('Sea Shore' tribe). It should be noted that in Byzantine sources the area of the origin of Great Bulgaria is defined as stretching from Maeotis (i.e. sea of Azov) to the Kouphis (i.e. Kuban) River. The 'shore' (of a sea and of a river) was obviously an important element in the landscape of the original country of the Bulgars.

Furthermore, we find a number of Alanic and Slavic names among the names of Bulgar khans. It should be noted that many a Bulgar khan had two names. One of them was usually Turkic, the other Alanic or Slavic. Thus, Khan Kurt (Turkic name) was also known as Kobratos (Khorvat—a Khorezmian–Slavic name). Kurt's successor, Bezmer (a Slavic name), was also known as Bat-Bayan (a Turkic name). In contrast to the rulers of Great Bulgaria, the first khan of the Danubian Bulgars had but one name (in any case, we know of only one of his names)—Esperikh (as in the Bulgarian princely list) or Asparukh (as in Byzantine sources), who reigned from 679 to 691. The name 'Asparukh' is undoubtedly of Alanic origin, to be compared to 'Aspar', name of the well-known Alan in Byzantine service (in the fifth century) who almost succeeded in seizing imperial power.[1]

We have now to examine the case of Kurt's predecessor, the regent (*namestnik* 'lieutenant') Gostun who ruled for two years from 603 to 605. The name is Slavic (in Old Slavic and Old Russian *gost* means 'guest' and also 'merchant'). Gostun's second name, according to Byzantine sources, is Organas. In Ossetic *ragon* means 'ancient', 'old'. Thus, Ragon-As 'the old As'. Apparently Gostun had a Slavic and an Alanic name but no Turkic name.

In this connexion the interrelation between Kurt's clan and Gostun's clan is of considerable interest. Kurt belonged to the old Turkish clan of Dulo, Gostun to a clan called Ärmi. According to O. Pritsak the Ärmi was a cognate clan

[1] See G. Vernadsky, *Ancient Russia*, pp. 150–2.

('Schwagerstamm') of the Dulo,[1] which means that Gostun was a member of the clan of Kurt's mother, perhaps her brother. The name 'Ärmi' seems to be Alanic. In Ossetic *arm* means 'hand' and, figuratively, 'protection'.[2] On this basis we may think that Kurt's mother was an Alanic princess. Her clan was probably half Slavicized through intermarriages, which explains the appearance in the family of the Slavic names Gostun, Khorvat, and Bezmer.

2. *The divided Bulgars*

After Khan Kurt's death Great Bulgaria was dismembered between his five sons just as the Hunnish empire had been partitioned after Attila's death among the latter's sons. Each of Kurt's sons was now at the head of his own horde, and none of them had forces large enough to cope with a rapidly growing rival centre of power, the incipient Khazar kaganate (see pp. 92–93). One Bulgar horde, led by Khan Bezmer (Bat-Bayan), went north and finally settled in the area of the middle Volga and Kama rivers. This group became known as the Volga Bulgars. Three hordes went west. One of them reached Pannonia and joined the Avars. Another penetrated into Italy. The Langobardi, who at that time controlled most of Italy, let the Bulgars in as their vassals and allowed them lands for settlement around Benevento. The third of those groups which went west, led by Asparukh, stopped in the region of the lower Danube. The fifth Bulgar horde, predominantly Ugrian, remained in the Azov region and recognized the suzerainty of the Khazars.

Of the divided Bulgars, two groups were destined to play a role of considerable importance in the political and economic history of the eastern Slavs—the Volga Bulgars and the Danubian Bulgars.

The Volga Bulgars established a prosperous trading state.[3] Their capital, Bulgar (or Great Bulgar), was situated on the

---

[1] O. Pritsak, *Die Bulgarische Fürstenliste* (Wiesbaden, 1955), p. 38.

[2] See Chapter 1, section 4, above.

[3] On the Volga Bulgars see Iu. V. Gotie, *Zheleznyi vek v Vostochnoi Evrope* (Moscow and Leningrad, 1930), pp. 156–85; W. Barthold, 'Bulgar', *EI*, i (1930), 786–91; I. N. Smirnov, 'Volzhskie Bolgary', in M. V. Dovnar-Zapolsky, ed., *Russkaia Istoriia*, i (Moscow, 1910); G. Vernadsky, *Ancient Russia*, pp. 222–8; B. D. Grekov, 'Volzhskie Bolgary v IX–X vekakh', *Istoricheskie Zapiski*, 14 (1945); A. P. Smirnov, *Volzhskie Bulgary* (Moscow, 1951: inaccessible to me); B. D. Grekov, ed., *Ocherki istorii SSSR. Period feodalisma*, i (Moscow, 1953), 717–23.

left (eastern) bank of the middle Volga, below the influx of the Kama River. Both the Volga and its tributaries provided the merchants with excellent riverways during the summer. The Bulgars traded mainly in furs which they obtained from the Finns and Slavs in north Russia and exported south. Since the region of the lower Volga formed part of the Khazar state, Bulgar commerce depended upon good relations with the Khazars. The Bulgars, however, established a direct route to Khorezm through the Iaik River (at present known as the Ural River) basin. According to the Persian geographical treatise of the tenth century, *Hudud al-Alam*, the Volga Bulgar army consisted of 20,000 horsemen. The Volga Bulgars controlled a number of neighbouring Finnish and Slavic tribes. The Alans of the upper Donets and Oskol river regions likewise recognized the suzerainty of the khan of the Volga Bulgars. The Arabic writer Ibn-Fadhlan called these Alans the Askal. The Slavs must have played an important role at the Bulgar khan's court, and Ibn-Fadhlan even calls the khan 'king of the Slavs'. In 922 the Volga Bulgars accepted Islam.

Let us now turn to the Danubian Bulgars.[1] Several years after Asparukh's horde reached the region of the lower Danube, it began preparations for invading the Byzantine provinces of Scythia (Dobrudja) and lower Moesia. The population of Scythia was predominantly Alanic; that of lower Moesia, Antian. The Byzantine historian Theophanes Confessor (who wrote in 810–15) mentions two Antian tribes in the lower Moesia—the Severi and the 'Seven Clans'.[2] These tribes had branches in south Russia. The Severi is one of the major east Slavic tribes listed in the old Russian Chronography. Theophanes' 'Seven Clans' are to be likened to the east Slavic tribes of the Radimichi and the Viatichi each of whom consisted of seven clans.[3] In view of the previous affiliation of a number of

---

[1] On the Danubian Bulgars see V. N. Zlatarski, *Istoriia na Bŭlgarskata Dr̄zava*, i (Sofia, 1918); S. Runciman, *A History of the First Bulgarian Empire* (London, 1930); I. Dujčev, 'Protobulgares et Slaves', *Annales de l'Institut Kondakov*, x (1938), 145–54; P. Mutafčiev, *Istoriia na Bŭlgarskiia narod*, i (Sofia, 1943); I. Dujčev, 'Slaviano-Bolgarskie drevnosti IX veka', *Byzantinoslavica*, xi (1950), 6–31; id., 'Eshche o Slaviano-Bolgarskikh drevnostiakh', *Byzantinoslavica*, xii (1951), 75–83; O. Pritsak, *Die bulgarische Fürstenliste* (Wiesbaden, 1955).

[2] Theophanes Confessor, *Cronographia*, ed. de Boor (2 vols., Leipzig, 1883–5), i. 547.

[3] See Chapter 4, section 7, below.

Alanic and Slavic clans with the Bulgars in great Bulgaria it seems quite probable that prior to his attack on Byzantium, Asparukh had sent Alanic and Slavic emissaries to Dobrudja and lower Moesia. In any case the people of these provinces surrendered to the Bulgars without fighting.

There ensued a protracted struggle between the Greeks and the Bulgars for the control of the Slavic population of the eastern part of the Balkan peninsula. Periods of war alternated with periods of peace and lively commerce between Byzantium and the Bulgars. On the whole, the Bulgars not only held their own but steadily expanded their state at the expense of the empire. Under Khan Krum (*c.* 803–14) the Bulgars controlled not only Moesia but parts of Thrace and Macedonia as well. In 803 Krum waged a war against the Avars who were simultaneously attacked by Charlemagne from the west. The war ended with the complete destruction of the Avar kaganate, its possessions being divided between the Franks and the Bulgars. The latter occupied both banks of the Danube up to the mouth of the Tisza. This resulted in the emancipation of the Slavs of the middle Danube region, and before long a new Slavic state emerged there, known as Great Moravia which also included White Horvatia. To the north the Polish state was in process of formation. Transylvania, the southern part of Bessarabia, and Moldavia were controlled by the Bulgars. The population of Bulgaria was predominantly Slav, and Slavic support was an important factor favouring the Bulgars in their struggle with both the Byzantines and the Avars. As the Bulgars constituted but a national minority in their own state, it is natural that they were gradually Slavicized. Conversion to Christianity (A.D. 864) finally bridged the gulf between the Bulgars and the Slavs. The new Slavic nation thus formed retained the name 'Bulgar'.

At the time of his conquest of the eastern part of the Balkan peninsula Asparukh's Bulgar horde consisted of several clans centring around the royal clan of Dulo. The khan was protected by guardsmen (*bagatur,* cf. the Russian *bogatyr'* 'valiant knight'). Prominent clan elders were known as *boyilar* (singular *boyila*). It is from this title that the Slavic term *boyare* (old form *bolyare*; singular *bolyarin, boyarin*) originated. Provincial administration was at first controlled exclusively by military commanders of various ranks, such as *tarkhan* and *bagain*. The former title belonged to the provincial governors; the latter was applied to the officers of lesser importance who eventually constituted the lower layer of Bulgar aristocracy. The religion of the old Bulgars was based on Sky-worship intermingled with belief in various spirits and other elements of Shamanism. Each clan venerated its ancestors, and the elders of the clan cult presided at communal religious sacrifices. Even after the conversion of the Bulgars to Christianity traces of their old religious beliefs, merged with remnants of Slavic paganism, were long preserved in Bulgarian folk-lore.[1]

Because of their close interrelations with the Byzantine empire the Bulgars, even before their conversion to Christianity, could not but be influenced by the Byzantine ways of life. As regards their state and administration, when the Bulgars became masters of a settled population of agriculturists and craftsmen—Slavs and Greeks—the old form of military control proved inadequate. It was but natural that the Bulgars now had to follow Byzantine patterns on many occasions. One of the new features was the appointment of civil officials to assist the military commanders in local administration. Those officials received the Byzantine title of *comes* ('count'), in Old Bulgarian *komit*. In the ninth and tenth centuries they were usually selected from among Slavic notables. The term entered several Slavic languages (in the form of *kmet*), changing its connotation in the course of time owing to varying social conditions. In later Bulgarian it meant 'village elder'; in Old Serbian 'a nobleman' or 'vassal'; in Modern Serbian 'a peasant notable'. As to the Russian language, the term occurs in the *Igor Tale* of the twelfth century in the sense of 'horseman'. In west Russia, in the period of the Grand Duchy of Lithuania, *kmet* denoted 'a peasant'. It had the same meaning in medieval Poland as well. In the higher political sphere the Bulgars gradually familiarized themselves with the Byzantine notions of imperial authority and the ranks of the imperial administration. As early as 705 Emperor Justinian II deemed it proper to confer on Khan Tervel the title of 'Caesar'. After the Bulgars' conversion to Christianity, the Byzantine idea of the Christian state could be better appreciated by them, and in the early tenth century Khan Simeon assumed the title of 'Tsar', which was used in the sense of the Byzantine

[1] V. Beševliev, 'Verata na prvobŭlgarite', *GSU*, xxxv, No. 1 (1939).

basileus. Generally speaking, because of her position in the core of the Byzantine-Slavic world, Bulgaria became a convenient base for the fusion of the Byzantine and Slavic civilizations and served as an intermediary link between Byzantium and the Slavs at large.

3. *The Alans and the Slavs under the Khazar suzerainty*

The Khazar kaganate, which replaced Great Bulgaria in the Azov and north Caucasian region, proved a much more stable organization.[1] It lasted over three centuries, from around 650 to 965. The title of the rulers of the Khazars—*kagan* (a Turkish title equivalent to the western 'emperor')—was in itself an indication of their imperial claims. The Khazars controlled a vast area. They were in close contact with Khorezm, and their dynasty was, apparently, of Khorezmian extraction. Economically, the Khazar kaganate was based on the control of two international trade routes, Khorezm and the lower Volga–Azov region. It may be said that the Khazars succeeded in uniting a considerable part of the former Alanic-Tokharian sphere.

The Alanic element was still strong in the western part of the Khazar empire. In central Asia, however, the process of Turkization of the Tokharian and Alanic peoples, which had been the result of the constant influx of new Turkish tribes from the east, went ahead rapidly. From the anthropological point of view, traits of Indo-European physical appearance were preserved in many Turkish people who came to the fore in this period. Consider, for example, evidence about the appearance of the Pechenegi ('hairy Pechenegi'). Some of the pre-Turkish clan and tribal names survived through the Turkish deluge. Thus, in the Oghuz Turkish federation we find a tribe named Duker (Tokhar); another bearing the name Yazyr (Yaz, As); and still another known as Yati (Antes). A Karakalpak clan was called Alan until recently.

As regards the political organization of the Khazar kaganate, its peculiar feature was the duality of the supreme power (dual kingship).[2] The first king, called *kagan*, represented the divine aspect of kingship. He may be called the king-priest. The second

[1] See note G, p. 318.   [2] See Chapter 1, section 5, above.

king commanded the army and was in charge of administration. His title, according to both Constantine Porphyrogenitus and Masudi, was *beg* (Turkic for 'prince'). Other writers call him *malik* (Arabic for 'king'). It should be noted that there was a certain similarity in this respect between the Khazar kaganate and its contemporary, the Merovingian kingdom of the Franks. Like the kagan, the Merovingian king was a sacred person. He was considered a healer. In a sense he can be called a king-priest. Eventually, he became the *roi fainéant*, and the mayor of the palace assumed the command of both the army and administration.

From the administrative point of view western Khazaria was divided into nine districts (*climata*, as Constantine Porphyrogenitus calls them). Eastern Khazaria (east of the Volga River) likewise must have consisted of nine districts. King Joseph in his letter speaks of 'nine peoples' in that area.[1] The number 'nine' indicates the Far Eastern origin of the principle of the administrative division of the Khazar kaganate. Nine was a sacred number to the Mongols. With the Alans, the western Turks, and the Magyars, the holy number was seven, not nine.

The core of the Khazar army consisted of a division of heavy cavalry 10,000 strong. The Alans, the Slavs, and the Magyars supplied auxiliary troops. The commander of the Alanic troops was known as the *As-tarkhan*. A detachment of the Alanic army must have been stationed in a fort at the mouth of the Volga. This fort eventually became a city which still stands—Astrakhan (i.e. As-Tarkhan). No special commander of the Slavic auxiliary troops is mentioned in our sources. Presumably, the Slavs served with the Alanic troops as well as in the Magyar army. The chieftain of the Magyar army unit was called *voevoda* ('army leader', cf. the German *Herzog*), which is a Slavic term. In the late eighth century one of the Slavic tribes, the Rus, succeeded in creating a strong military unit of its own, apparently with the help of the Norsemen.[2]

The position of the Slavs in the Khazar kaganate was twofold. Some of the Slavic tribes were under the direct Khazar (or Magyar) administration. Ibn-Fadhlan says that 'the Slavs and

---

[1] P. K. Kokovtsov, *Evreisko-Khazarskaia perepiska v X veke* (Leningrad, 1932), p. 91.
[2] Of this more will be said in Chapter 5, section 2, below.

their neighbours are in obedience to him [the Khazar king], and he addresses them as Slaves, and they obey him'. This was, apparently, the case of a number of peripheral Slavic tribes. We know from the Russian Chronography (entry under A.D. 859) that the Khazars imposed tribute upon the Poliane, the Severi, and the Viatichi, and collected one silver coin and a squirrel skin from each hearth. In another entry of the Chronography (A.D. 885) it is said that the Radimichi paid a shilling (apparently from each hearth). In A.D. 964 the Viatichi paid the Khazars one shilling from each plough. In contrast to the tributary Slavic tribes, certain Slavic clans might have occupied a much higher position in the Khazar state. Slavic undoubtedly was one of the languages spoken both at the Khazar court and in the army. Hence, the use in the Khazar state of such Slavic terms as *zakon* ('law') and the above-mentioned *voevoda*. It should be noted that in al-Bakri's description of Slavic lands based on the report of the Jewish merchant from Spain, Ibrahim ben-Jakub (965/966), among the 'northern' peoples who speak Slavic the Khazars (as well as the Russes) are mentioned.[1]

Quite a number of Slavic and Rus merchants and craftsmen must have resided in the Khazar cities. According to Masudi (ii. 11) there were seven judges in Khazaria's largest city Itil (on the lower Volga): two for the Moslems, two for the Jews, two for the Christians, 'and one for the Slavs, the Rus, and other heathen: he tries them in accordance with the Natural Law, that is with reason'.[2] It should be added that beside the heathen Slavs there must have been Christian Slavs in Khazaria in the eighth and the ninth centuries; these, obviously, were under the jurisdiction of the Christian judges. Many of the Alans likewise had been converted to Christianity by that time.

Tribute from the conquered tribes constituted an important source of the revenue of the Khazar treasury. Even more important were the custom duties collected from foreign merchants. The rate was 10 per cent. of the value of goods imported or in transit. The upper classes of the Khazar society thrived on trade. Both merchants and craftsmen of various kind lived in

[1] Tadeusz Kowalski, *Relacja Ibrahima ibn Jakuba z podróży do krajów słowiańskich w przekazie al-Bekrego* (Krakow, 1946), p. 52; T. Lewicki, 'Ze studiów nad źródłami arabskimi', Part II, *Slavia Antiqua*, v (1954), 166.

[2] Maçoudi (Masudi), *Les Prairies d'or*, Arabic text and French translation by C. Barbier de Meynard et Pavet de Courteille (9 vols., Paris, 1861–77), ii. 11.

the cities. Among the cities, besides Itil and Semender (in the northern Caucasus), Khorezm (Urgenj) was under Khazar control for a long period. In the letter of the Khazar king Joseph to Hasday ibn-Shaprut (about A.D. 960) Urgenj is called Jurjan.[1]

From Masudi's report on the judges in Itil it may be seen that there were three major religions in the Khazar state: Islam, Judaism, and Christianity. And there were, apparently, three stages in the development of Judaism in Khazaria. According to S. P. Tolstov, the Judaic tendencies at first came to the fore in Khorezm. Tolstov dubs this stage a Judaic syncretism.[2] In A.D. 712 the Arabs appeared in Khorezm. Under the pressure of militant Islam, the Khorezmian Judaizers fled to Khazaria. Syncretic Judaism was then accepted at the kagan's court (around A.D. 720). The next stage (about A.D. 760) was that of 'modified Judaism', as D. M. Dunlop calls it. The third stage was that of 'Rabbinic Judaism', which was introduced at the kagan's court about A.D. 800, according to Dunlop.[3] However, from the Life of Constantine (St. Cyril) it is plain that the final choice of religion had not been made by the kagan until Constantine and Methodius's mission to Khazaria (A.D. 860–1). That mission was a failure from the Christian point of view.

Both Islam and Christianity had many faithful in Khazaria. In A.D. 737 the kagan himself, being defeated by the Arabs, accepted Islam but his successors rejected it. Islam must have been especially popular among the Khazar merchants dealing with Islamic countries. An interesting piece of evidence of the spread of Christianity in Khazaria is the list of bishoprics of the Gothic eparchy compiled either in the middle of the eighth or in the middle of the ninth century.[4] In my opinion the list, in

---

[1] P. K. Kokovtsov, *Evreisko-Khazarskaia perepiska v X veke*, pp. 81, 99–100; D. M. Dunlop, *The History of the Jewish Khazars* (Princeton, 1954), pp. 150, 246, 247.

[2] S. P. Tolstov, *Po sledam drevnekhorezmiiskoi tsivilizatsii* (Moscow and Leningrad, 1948), pp. 225–6.

[3] D. M. Dunlop, *The History of the Jewish Khazars* (Princeton, 1954), p. 170.

[4] On the list of bishoprics of the Gothic eparchy see A. A. Vasiliev, *The Goths in the Crimea* (Cambridge, Mass., 1936), pp. 97–101; G. Vernadsky, 'The Eparchy of Gothia', *Byzantion*, xv (1941), 67–76; Gy. Moravcsik, 'Byzantine Christianity and the Magyars in the Period of their Migration', *ASEER*, v (1946), 39–41; S. P. Tolstov, *Po sledam drevnekhorezmiiskoi tsivilizatsii* (Moscow and Leningrad, 1948), pp. 227–9; T. Lewicki, 'Zagadnienie Gotów na Krymie', *Przegląd Zachodni*, 5/6 (1954), 86–87.

the form we know it, should be dated in the ninth century, but most of the bishoprics mentioned in it must have existed already in the eighth century. According to the list, the see of the metropolitan was in Doras, Crimean Gothia. The list includes the names of the following bishoprics: Khotzeron ('of the Khazars', at Phullae in the Crimea), Astel (Itil), Khouales (Khvalis, i.e. Khorezm), Onoguron ('of the Onoguri', east of the sea of Azov), Reteg (Terek), Ounnon ('of the Huns'), and Tymatarkha (Tmutorokan). Of these bishoprics, two (Phullae and Tmutorokan) could hardly have been created before the 860's. All of the others originated earlier. The list shows that in the late eighth and the early ninth centuries there were Christian communities, under the authority of the Patriarch of Constantinople, not only in the Azov and the northern Caucasus, but in Khorezm as well.

The Khazar kaganate played an important role in the international politics of the period. With the rise of Islam and the rapid expansion of the caliphate the Arab armies presented a menace to the countries of the Middle East, the Near East, and the Mediterranean world alike. The Arabs invaded both central Asia and Transcaucasia; attacked the Byzantine empire; and, following their westward march along the African shore of the Mediterranean and their conquest of Spain, appeared in France. In the resistance of the non-Moslem world against the Arabs three powers had to bear the brunt of the struggle: the Khazars, the Byzantines, and the Franks. In 717–18 the Byzantine emperor Leo the Isaurian beat off the attacks of the Arabian army and fleet on Constantinople. In 730 the Khazars undertook a successful offensive in Transcaucasia. In 732 Charles-Martel defeated the Arabs at Poitiers.

Of the three anti-Arabian powers, the Khazar kaganate was closest to the centre of the caliphate and most vulnerable to the Arabian attacks. The struggle between the Khazars and the Arabs was a protracted one. In 737 the Arabs broke the line of Khazar defences, raided the north Caucasian area, and reached the 'Slavonic River' (Don). Twenty thousand Slavs were taken prisoner in this area and sent to Transcaucasia where they were settled not far from the Byzantine frontier to protect the integrity of the caliphate.[1] The Khazar military organization was

[1] See note H, p. 319.

severely shaken by the defeat. It was on that occasion that a Khazar khan accepted Islam. Only after a period of almost thirty years had the Khazars recovered enough from the shock to resume their campaigns in Transcaucasia (764). Around 825 the Khazars were defeated again and, according to Muqaddasi, the Khazar kagan again accepted Islam (see p. 184).

The relations between the Khazar kaganate and the Byzantine empire were mostly friendly, which is natural in view of the fact that both countries were harassed by the same enemy and had to co-operate with each other on many occasions. On the other hand, there was a divergence of interests between the Khazars and Byzantium in the Taurida. The Khazar control of both sides of Kerch Strait endangered the Byzantine possessions in south-western Crimea. Both sides, however, preferred to settle their differences by negotiations rather than by war.

4. *The Magyars and Slavs in south Russia*

According to Constantine Porphyrogenitus (*De Administrando Imperio*, ch. xxxvii), the Magyars (whom Constantine calls 'the Turks') 'lived together with the Khazars for three years, and fought in alliance with the Khazars in all their wars'. The figure 'three years' is obviously a copyist's mistake. The figure has been emended by Dankovszky, Marczali, and Zichy, and finally by Henri Grégoire to 'three hundred years'. Undoubtedly the Magyars were under the Khazar suzerainty for a long period even if not exactly for three centuries.[1]

The Magyars consisted of seven clans, each being ruled by a voevoda. Constantine says that the Magyars 'had of old their dwelling next to Khazaria in the place called Lebedia after the name of their voevoda', whom Constantine calls Lebedias. The Khazar kagan gave in marriage to Lebedias a noble Khazar lady 'because of the fame of his valour and the illustriousness of his clan'. The name 'Lebedia' left numerous traces in the toponymics of south Russia. Several Russian and Ukrainian towns were called 'Lebedin' or 'Lebedian'. Three small rivers were known as 'Lybed' (in the Kiev, Chernigov, and Riazan regions, respectively). On the basis of these place-names and other considerations we may think that the area of Lebedia stretched

[1] See note I, p. 319.

from the Don–Donets basin westward to the middle Dnieper and beyond it, to the Bug basin and Podolia.

Constantine's derivation of the name 'Lebedia' from the name of the voevoda Lebedias is unacceptable. Lebedias was undoubtedly not a personal name but a clan name. Constantine himself states that the voevoda belonged to an 'illustrious' clan. 'Lebedias' is the Greek transcription of the Slavic word *lebed'* which means 'swan'. The Swan must have been the ongon of Lebedias' clan. Veneration of the swan was noticed by the ethnographers among many a Turkish clan in Siberia. In the Altai region, in the basin of the river Lebed', there exists a small Turkic-speaking tribe known in Turkic as *Ku-kiši*, i.e. 'the Swan People'. In Russian they are called the Lebed' Tatars, or Lebedintsy.[1] In my opinion that region must be considered the original Lebedia, and the present-day Lebedintsy (Ku-kiši) a fragment of the old and much larger tribe which, led by the Lebed' clan, had migrated to south Russia some time in the late seventh or in the eighth century. It should be mentioned in this connexion that the Russian chroniclers of the early twelfth century knew a tribe called Koui in the Chernigov region. The name derives from the Turkic *ku* 'swan',[2] and is identical with the Altaic Kukiši (Lebedintsy).

The relations between the Magyars and the Slavs apparently followed the same dual pattern as those between the Khazars and the Slavs. We have to differentiate between the tributary Slavic tribes and the Slavic clans of the higher social level.

Let us first deal with the lower stratum of the Slavs. Two oriental writers, Ibn-Rusta and Gardizi, described the interrelations between the Magyars and the Slavic tribes subjected to them. Ibn-Rusta wrote, in Arabic, around A.D. 920. Gardizi's work is in Persian; it was compiled in the middle of the eleventh century. At the time they wrote the Magyars were establishing themselves in their present abodes in Hungary, where they had subjugated the Slavs. Therefore the statements of both Ibn-Rusta and Gardizi may refer to the Magyar-Slavic relations in Hungary and not only to south Russia. Both Ibn-Rusta and

[1] W. Radlow, *Aus Sibirien* (2nd edn., 2 vols., Leipzig, 1912), i. 212; *Akademiia Nauk, Trudy Komissii po izucheniiu plemennogo sostava naseleniia SSSR*, No. 17 (Leningrad, 1929), pp. 54–55.

[2] K. H. Menges, *The Oriental Elements in the Vocabulary of the Oldest Russian Epos, the Igor Tale*, Supplement to *Word*, No. 7 (December 1951), p. 1.

Gardizi used earlier sources, however, and their picture must have been a composite one, dealing with two subsequent phases of the Magyar state. The pattern of the Magyar control over the Slavs must have remained essentially the same before and after the occupation of their new home (the *Landnahme*) by the Magyars. On the basis of these considerations we may think that Ibn-Rusta's and Gardizi's evidence reflects the Magyar attitude towards the tributary Slavic tribes both before and after the *Landnahme*. The evidence is as follows: the Magyars 'exercise dominion over all the Saqlab [Slavs] who are adjacent to them and they put upon them heavy burdens, and they are in their hands in the position of captives' (Ibn-Rusta). 'They have completely subjugated the Slavs and they always order them to provide food for them and consider them as their slaves' (Gardizi).[1] From these statements we may conclude that the Slavs had to work for the Magyars and to supply them with agricultural products.

It is interesting to note in this connexion the interrelation of some words in Magyar and Old Russian languages. For example, the Magyar word *rab* 'slave' (in which *a* is pronounced like the English *a* in 'tall'; in Russian transliteration it would be *rob*) corresponds to the Russian 'a slave'. Note that the Old Russian form was not *rab* but *rob*. It was more commonly used in the feminine, *roba*.

Another noteworthy word for comparison is the Magyar *dolog* 'work', 'labour', 'thing'. We have the Russian word *dolg* 'debt', 'duty'. The correspondence of these two words seems to be well adapted to the social conditions in Lebedia. The 'duty' of the Slavic agriculturists in Lebedia was to supply 'work' or 'things' for their Magyar masters; or, to put it in a different way, the Slavs had to supply 'work' to pay their 'debts'. It might well refer to an early stage in the development of the institution of the indentured labourers, known as *zakupy* in the Kiev period of Russian history. Furthermore, we have the Magyar *járom* 'yoke', to which the Russian *iarmo* (in Old Russian *iarŭm*) corresponds exactly. Both in Russian and in Hungarian the word *iarmo* means the yoke for oxen and the yoke in the sense of slavery. There are a number of Magyar words bearing on agricultural husbandry which are obviously borrowed from

[1] C. A. Macartney, *The Magyars in the Ninth Century* (Cambridge, 1930), p. 208.

the Slavic; this is quite natural since it was the Slavs who tilled
the land for the Magyars and supplied the latter with agricultural products. We may assume that in many cases the
borrowing took place before the *Landnahme*.

We now turn to the upper level of the Slavic element in the
old Magyar state and society. It will be recalled that the early
title of the Magyar chieftains was *voevoda*, a Slavic term. In the
later Magyar language the word was contracted to *vajda*. Of
great significance is likewise the fact that the first Magyar voevoda's clan had a Slavic name—Lebed'. There may be two
explanations of it. The Slavic form of the name could have
originated in the Altai region prior to the migration of Lebedias' clan to south Russia. In such a case we would have to surmise that a group of Slavs had lived in the Altai region until
the late seventh century. The other way to explain the use of
the Slavic form for the name Lebedias' clan is to suppose that
when the Ku-kiši (Lebedintsy) came to south Russia, they
merged with a Slavic clan there and fell under Slavic cultural
influence.

A close association at the top level between the Magyars and
the Slavs in the field of religion and magic may also be pre-
supposed. The word for 'miracle' is identical in Russian and
Magyar (*csoda* or *csuda* in Magyar; *chudo* in Russian). The
Magyar word *varázs* ('charm', 'spell', 'magic') corresponds to
the Russian *vorozhba* 'soothsaying' (the Russian verb form is
vorozhiti 'to soothsay'). Presumably we have in both cases a
borrowing from the Slavic into the Magyar.

As regards the ties between the old Magyar and the old
Russian princely clans, there are numerous traditions in Russian folk-lore concerning marriages of the Russian princes and
knights (*bogatyri*) to the princesses of the Lebed' clan. In the
fairy-tale of *Vasilisa the Sage*, Tsarevich Ivan has to choose his
fiancée from among twelve Swan-maidens. In another tale,
that of the *Seven Simeons*, Princess Helen the Beautiful turns into
a swan. In a variant of the bylina of the Bogatyr Ivan Godinovich, the Chernigovan princess whom he wooed is called White
Swan. In the bylina of Potok Bogatyr the following story is told.
Potok was sent by Prince Vladimir the Saint to the sea-shore to
shoot wild geese and swans for the Prince's table; taking pity on
a white swan with golden feathering, he spared it. The swan

turned into a beautiful girl whom Potok immediately fell in love with and married. In the Russian heroic poem of the late twelve century, the *Igor Tale* (*Slovo o polku Igoreve*), Violence is personified as a maiden with swan's wings.

It may be added that a swan-princess is likewise mentioned in the old Russian chronicle: namely Lybed', the sister of Kiy, Shchok, and Khoriv, the three legendary founders of the city of Kiev. It will be recalled that there was a river of the same name in Kiev and another in Chernigov; Lybed' is obviously a variation of *lebed'*, representing a different dialect or a different local pronunciation.

An 'Ugrian Settlement' (Ugorskoe) near Kiev is mentioned in the Russian Chronography, and there is enough evidence to suppose that from about A.D. 850 to about 878 Kiev was under the authority of the Magyar voevoda Almos (called Almoutzios in Constantine Porphyrogenitus' *De Administrando Imperio*, and Olma in the Russian Chronography). Almos belonged not to the Lebed' clan, but to another Magyar clan whose ongon was the falcon. The Hungarian chronicle by the Anonymous Notary of King Béla mentions a war between Almos and the chieftains of Kiev as a result of which the Kievans recognized Almos as their suzerain. The Anonymous's chronicle was compiled in the thirteenth century but was based partly on the earlier annals. The Russian Chronography mentions 'Almos' palace' (*Olmin dvor*) in Ugorskoe at Kiev.

Almos himself was under the suzerainty of the Khazar kagan and was apparently authorized by the kagan to collect tribute from the Slavs of the Kiev region (the Poliane). Around A.D. 858 two Norse chieftains, Askold and Dir, appeared in Kiev with a band of their followers.[1] According to the Russian Chronography they were noblemen (*boyare*), not princes. They must have ruled Kiev as Almos's lieutenants. When they were killed by order of another Norse ruler, Oleg (around 878), their bodies were carried to Almos's palace and then buried near it at Ugorskoe.

5. *Social and economic development of the eastern Slavs*

In the Kievan period (tenth to thirteenth centuries) the eastern Slavs became known under the name of Rus. In our

[1] See Chapter 5, section 5, below.

days the Rus are divided into three branches—the Russians
(formerly known as Great Russians), the Ukrainians (formerly
known as Little Russians), and the Belorussians (White Russians). Each of these three peoples now speak their own
language, the three languages being, of course, basically related
to each other. In the pre-Kievan period the eastern Slavs likewise consisted of three main groups but that division had had
no relation to the present one. The three ancient groups were
the Antes, the Slovene (of Novgorod), and the Rus. It is the
latter name which eventually became the generic name of the
eastern Slavs.

The Rus in the pre-Kievan period constituted a tribe by itself.
The Antes were divided into a number of tribes—the Tivertsy,
the Ulichi, the Poliane, the Severi, the Radimichi, and the Viatichi. The generic name Antes ceased to be used in the Khazar
period. The Slovene of Novgorod, like the Rus, were a separate
tribe. Besides these three groups, there were other Slavic tribes,
in the western part of the east Slavic area, whose affiliation is
not clear. The strongest among them were the Krivichi (forefathers of the Belorussians). They were probably akin to the
Slovene. The Khorvaty of Galicia (Constantine Porphyrogenitus' 'White Croats') were, of course, a branch of the Croats
who settled in the western part of the Balkan peninsula. As has
been said,[1] the Khorvaty seem to have originated in Khorezm.
I am inclined to think that the Volyniane, neighbours of the
Galician Khorvats, likewise came from Khorezm. In Old Russian the name Khvari (Khorezm) was pronounced Khvali. The
Caspian Sea was known in Old Russian as 'More Khvalynskoe'
(the Sea of the Khvali, i.e. of Khorezm). In Russian folk-lore it
is called 'More Volynskoe'. On this basis I submit that the
name Volyn (Volynia) derives from Khvari.[2]

It would be not amiss in this connexion to comment on the
origin of the name 'Severi', one of the above-mentioned Antian
tribes. It also occurs in the chronicles in the form 'Sever'.[3] In

[1] See Chapter 2, section 2, above.

[2] Max Vasmer, *Russisches etymologisches Wörterbuch*, i. 224, mentions several interpretations of the origin of the name Volyn so far given (the one I now suggest is not
among them), but rejects all of them.

[3] Max Vasmer, *REW*, ii. 600, derives the name 'Severiane' (Severi) from the
Slavic word *sever* 'north'. However, the Severi lived in south Russia not in north
Russia. Besides, the Severian land was called 'Severskaia Zemlia', and the adjective
form from *sever* 'north' is *severnyi* not 'severskii.'

my opinion the name should be derived from the Old Indic *svar* (Vedic *suvar*) 'sun', 'light', 'sky'. I interpret the name Sever as 'Sun-people'. The Avestan parallel to *svar* is *hvar*. The name is of the same pattern as Rus and Khorvat.

The early Slavic society was based on clans.[1] Many of the clan names, even in the later periods, were of the patronymic type, each clan being identified by the name of his forefather. Many of the names of the Slavic settlements are of similar type, which indicates that originally each clan settled separately, not mixing with the others. The clan community centred around the cult of its ancestors;[2] this entailed the mutual responsibility of all the members for the integrity of the clan, hence the mutual obligation of blood vengeance for the murder, by an outsider, of any member of the clan. It is in the clan, presumably, that the rights of land were originally vested. When a clan became too numerous, it would break into branches. Eventually, a smaller unit, the so-called 'greater family' commune (later to become known in the Balkans as *zadruga*), assumed much importance. Several clans could enter in an agreement or association, and out of such associations tribes came into existence. Each tribe was primarily a military organization centring around a fortified town (*grad*). Spiritually, the tribe must have depended on a common cult. In any case some of the sanctuaries of the Baltic Slavs were tribal temples.[3]

As a result of migrations and wars on the one hand, and of the growth of commerce on the other, the pattern of Slavic social organization underwent important changes. The towns, especially among the eastern Slavs, became so many outposts of commerce. Enriched by war booty and commerce, certain tribal and clan leaders rose above the clan community and formed the foundation of an aristocratic upper class. That rising aristocracy depended on slave labour. War was the primary source of such labour since the prisoners who could not redeem themselves were turned into slaves. The slaves were known, collectively, as *čeliad'*. The original connotation of the root *čel* is 'clan'; therefore we may assume that in the earlier period the slaves belonged to the clan as a whole and only later did individual households receive rights over them. Freemen not belonging

---

[1] See note J, p. 319. [2] See Chapter 4, section 1, below.
[3] See Chapter 4, section 2, below.

to the upper class were organized in communes based on kinship (*verv'*). Eventually, outsiders were admitted to membership and the commune was transformed into an association of neighbours, that is, a territorial unit (*mir*).

According to Procopius, the Danubian Slovene and Antes 'are not ruled by one man, but they have lived from of old under a democracy, and consequently everything which involves their welfare, whether for good or for ill, is referred to the people'. It seems that the Danubian Antes constituted a society of frontiersmen not unlike the Brodniki of the Kievan period and the Cossacks of the fifteenth, sixteenth, and seventeenth centuries. Therefore their form of political organization should not be considered typical of all of the early Slavs. In some other sources, Slavic 'archontes' are mentioned. These were presumably tribal and army leaders. Some of them had the title of 'prince' (*knjaz'*), others that of 'tysiatsky' (*chiliarch*) or voevoda. The old Slavic prince was not an autocratic ruler. He had to consult the Council of Elders (later called *boyars*). The large towns were ruled by the town assembly (*veche*). The important political role of the old Russian towns was based on the growth of commerce and of a powerful merchant class. The old Russian town was in many respects similar to the Greek *polis*, and we may think that the pattern of the old Russian municipal government developed partly under the influence of the constitution of the Greek towns in the north Pontic area, such as Cherson and Olbia. Besides, it should be recalled that the chiliarch (in Russian *tysiatsky*) was an important official in the Bosporan kingdom in the Crimea.

The eastern Slavs were scattered over a vast territory stretching from the Baltic shores and Lake Ilmen in the north to the Black Sea and sea of Azov in the south. They had, therefore, in their economic activities, to adapt themselves to a diverse geographic background. In the forest zone, hunting and apiculture were of considerable importance; by the seas, lakes, and rivers, fishing constituted a source of food supplies. In the wooded steppe zone and in the stretches of the steppe zone occupied by the eastern Slavs, cattle breeding was widespread. Horned cattle, horses, hogs, sheep, and goats were kept. This branch of husbandry provided the Slavs with both meat and dairy products such as milk and curd (*syr* or *tvorog*). Among the by-products of cattle breeding were the hides and bristles. As to metals, surface and near-surface deposits of iron ore were abundant in the swamps and at the lake shores in west and north Russia. Agriculture had been practised by the Slavs since time immemorial. Millet, rye, spelt (and later, wheat) were sown, as well as flax and hemp. As to agricultural tools, plough, harrow, sickle, and scythe were used. On the produce of various branches of Slavic husbandry, Slavic handicrafts were based, such as carpentry, textile arts, ceramics, tanning, and the dressing of furs. Most of these crafts in the early period belonged to the category of domestic industries. Later, with the growth of the towns and the rise of the aristocracy, groups of professional craftsmen came into existence.

Owing to their geographic background, the Slavs were early involved in the trade with both the East and the West. As has been mentioned, all of the nomadic empires, including their western extensions, thrived on commerce, and to the extent that the Slavs were a part of the Hunnic state, and later of the Avar and the Khazar kaganates, they were included in a vast system of international trade, some of the routes of which they later inherited. From the regional angle, the Baltic Slavs took an active part in the Baltic commerce; the Balkan Slavs traded with Byzantium; the Czechs with the Frankish empire; Great Moravia became a hub of central European trade; eastern Slavs were connected with the Baltic and the Black Sea areas and the oriental markets. The growth of commerce among the eastern Slavs was conducive to the rise of cities and to the beginnings of money economy. Hoards of Roman, Byzantine, and Oriental coins were found in many places in Russia. In the ninth century several east Slavic tribes paid tribute to the Khazars in silver money, called *bela* ('white money', cf. the Byzantine *aspron*) or 'shillings'.[1]

The houses of the eastern Slavs were of two basic types. In the forest zone the house was made of logs (*izba*). In the steppe zone, the Slavic domicile of the early periods was dug in the ground with a low framework over the ground built of wooden pillars and twigs cemented with clay. The roof was of wood or thatch. It is out of this type of building that the Ukrainian

[1] See Chapter 5, section 3, below.

khata developed. In addition to these primitive structures the Slavs had more elaborate buildings for their religious sanctuaries.[1]

Archaeological researches by Russian and Ukrainian scholars brought to light much evidence on the life of the eastern Slavs in the pre-Khazar and Khazar age (even more, of course, is known of the east Slavic civilization of the Kievan period). In the Novgorod area, besides the funeral mounds (called *sopki*), several sites of old agricultural settlements have been discovered of which one, the Old Ladoga on the Volkhov River, has been systematically studied in recent years. The sopki are referred to the period from the fourth to the tenth centuries. The earliest layer in Old Ladoga is dated in the seventh century. Remnants of large log houses indicate that each building housed a 'greater family'. The whole settlement was of the type of a large commune (the *verv'*). Iron tools, wooden vessels and furniture, animal-traps, and bones of cattle were found.[2]

In the upper Volga region, the site of a large settlement of the period from the third to the fifth centuries was excavated by P. N. Tretiakov, near the village of Berezniaki in the Iaroslavl region.[3] In this site, remnants of six small log dwellings centre around a large community house. Near the latter there are the foundations of a forge, of a barn, and of a building which apparently served for spinning and weaving. Close to the settlement is a small funeral house, a depository for the ashes of the cremated bodies of the deceased members of the community. The settlement was apparently that of a zadruga consisting of fifty or sixty people.

Sites of old Slavic settlements were also found in the upper Don and Donets basin, in the upper Oka region, in the middle Dnieper area, and in the lower Dniester region. Near the village Borshevo, situated on the right bank of the river Don south of the present-day city of Voronezh, two Slavic settlements existed from at least the eighth century. The houses were built in dug-out basements 1 metre deep. The framework was of

---

[1] See Chapter 4, section 7, below.

[2] *Po sledam drevnikh kultur: Drevniaia Rus'* (Moscow, 1953), p. 19.

[3] *Po sledam drevnikh kultur: Drevniaia Rus'*, pp. 20–21; I. Grabar, *Istoriia Russkogo Iskusstva*, i (1953), 82.

thick oak pillars, the walls being made of boards or twigs cemented with clay. The hearth was made of stones.[1]

Slavic houses of similar type have been described by Ibn-Rusta. He says:

In this country [i.e. the country of the Slavs] the cold is very severe, and it reaches such severity that a man there digs himself in like a wild animal, under the earth and then makes himself a roof of wood like that of church. Then he heaps earth on it, and the man enters it with his family and brings some firewood and stones, and kindles a fire there until it gets warm and becomes red, and when it becomes very hot, he sprinkles water on it, so that the vapour rises in that place and the house is warmed, and they remain in the house until the spring.[2]

It seems that Ibn-Rusta confused here some features of the arrangements of the Slavic bath-house with those of the dwelling-house. It is quite probable that bath-houses existed in the settlements of the Borshevo type. Single dwellings were connected by covered corridors. There were also larger buildings, apparently barns, and pits for storing grain.

Of similar type was the Gochevo settlement of the sixth and seventh centuries on the banks of the river Vorskla, a tributary of the middle Dnieper. Each such settlement was provided with many exits. This fits the description of Slavic and Antian settlements in Mauricius's 'Strategicon'.[3] According to this source, the existence of many exits helped the Slavs and the Antes to escape in case of a sudden enemy attack. Three sites of Slavic settlements near Kiev are attributed to the period from the eighth to the tenth centuries. The settlements of the tribe of Tivertsy in the lower Dniester basin, recently excavated, present a picture of the continuity of Antian culture from the sixth to the eleventh centuries.

---

[1] P. P. Efimenko and P. N. Tretiakov, 'Drevnerusskie poseleniia na Donu', *MIAS*, viii (1948), 18–26; *Po Sledam drevnikh kultur: Drevniaia Rus'*, pp. 22–23; I. Grabar, *Istoriia Russkogo Iskusstva*, i (1953), 80, 83.

[2] C. A. Macartney, *The Magyars in the Ninth Century*, p. 212.

[3] Mauricius, *Strategicon*, ed. J. Scheffer, xi. 5; Russian translation of excerpts from Mauricius on Slavs by S. A. Zhebelev and S. P. Kondratiev, *Vestnik Drevnei Istorii*, 1941, pp. 253–7; G. Vernadsky, *Ancient Russia*, p. 158.

4

RELIGIOUS FOUNDATIONS OF THE OLD RUSSIAN CULTURE

1. *Sun-worship and clan cult*

SUN-WORSHIP constituted the core of the old Slavic religion. It expressed the essence of the world-philosophy of the Ancient Slavs. As we know, the names of three old Slavic tribes—Rus, Khorvat, and Sever (and possibly four, if we include the Volynians in this list)—reflect the notion of Sun. With the Sun, the concepts of Light, of Fire, and of the generating forces of man were associated. In the Arabic treatise of the middle of the ninth century, known as the *Abregé des Merveilles* (formerly ascribed to Masudi), it is said that the Slavs adore the Sun and also the Fire.[1]

The Sun was the symbol of Good as contrasted to Evil. An old Russian name for Sun-god was Khors, and this was also the Old Russian word for the 'sun' itself. In Ossetic, 'sun' is *xur* (pronounced 'khoor'). This word corresponds to the Avestan *hvar* 'sun', 'sunlight' (hence, as has been mentioned, Khorezm, 'Land of the Sun'). Even closer to the name Khors is another Ossetic word *xorz* (pronounced 'khorz'), 'good', in the sense of both noun and adjective. The two Ossetic words presumably represent two different stages in the branching off of derivative notions from the stem *hvar*. It is to the Ossetic *xorz* that the Russian adjective *khoroshii* ('good') apparently corresponds.[2]

Beside 'Khors' the ancient Slavs had another word for 'sun', *solntse*, which is still in use and is in fact the only one now used. According to Max Vasmer[3] *solnce* is linguistically related to the Old Indic *svar* 'sun', 'light', 'sky'. As has been said,[4] to the Old Indic *svar* the Avestan *hvar* corresponds. On this ground it seems that there is a basic affinity between the two Old Russian

---

[1] C. A. Macartney, *The Magyars in the Ninth Century* (Cambridge, 1930), p. 216.
[2] See V. I. Abaev, *Osetinskii iazyk i folklor*, i (Moscow and Leningrad, 1949), 595.
[3] Max Vasmer, *Russisches etymologisches Wörterbuch*, ii. 690.
[4] See Chapter 3, section 5, above.

words for 'sun'—*khors* and *solnce*—even though the two sound differently.

The sun played an important role in the old Russian folk-lore. It should be noted that while the word *khors* is a masculine noun, *solnce* in Modern Russian as well as in other Slavic languages is neuter. In Slavic folk-lore, however, the word is often treated as if it were of either feminine or masculine gender. Beneath the variety of genders in the concept of 'sun' lies the idea of the original all-embracing creative force revealing itself through different emanations. In Indic mythology, likewise, there are cases where a divinity was represented sometimes as male and sometimes as female.

The sun is assigned an important position in the so-called *Book of Deep Wisdom (Glubinnaia Kniga)* which was very popular in Russia in the late Middle Ages and the early modern period.[1] This poem represents a blend of pre-Christian and Christian notions. The poem is in the form of a dialogue between Prince Vladimir and King David. Among questions the former asks are the following two: 'How did the White Light [*Belyi Svet*] originate?' 'How did the Sun originate?' It should be noted that the Russian word *svet* 'light' has also the connotation of 'world'. In the *Book of Wisdom* the word is used now in one sense, now in the other. In this particular case it is used in the original sense—that of 'light'.

King David's answers to the questions are: 'The White Light originated from God's heart; the Sun, from God's face.' Here, the pre-Christian idea of the divine nature of the sun, and of the sun's aboriginal affinity with light, is clearly expressed in terms somewhat adapted to Christian notions.

In Russian folk-lore the sun has the epithet *krasnoe*. In the Russian byliny, Prince Vladimir of Kiev is called 'Krasnoe Solntse'.[2] In modern Russian the adjective *krasnyi* (which is the masculine form) means 'red'. In Old Russian it usually meant

---

[1] *Glubinnaia Kniga* is also known as *Golubinaia Kniga*, 'Book of the Dove'. The Dove is an ancient religious symbol, both in Paganism and Christianity. For the text of the 'Book' (or rather of variants of fragments of the 'Book') see V. Varentsov, *Sbornik Russkikh dukhovnykh stikhov* (St. Petersburg, 1860), pp. 11–39; P. A. Bezsonov, *Kaliki Perekhozhie*, i (Moscow, 1860), 269–378. See also A. Kirpichnikov, 'Golubi-naia Kniga', Brockhaus-Efron's *Entsiklopedicheskii slovar*, half-volume xvii. 116–17; M. N. Speransky, *Russkaia ustnaia slovesnost'* (Moscow, 1917, pp. 371–3. Hrushevsky, M., *Istoriia Ukrainskoi literatury*, IV (Kiev, 1925), pp. 247–59.

[2] Or 'Krasnoe Solnyshko', which is the diminutive (caressing) form.

'beautiful'. The noun, *krasa*, means 'beauty' both in Old Russian and in Modern Russian. According to Afanasiev[1] the original connotations of *krasnyi* were 'radiant', 'bright', 'ardent'. On that basis Vladimir's epithet 'Krasnoe Solntse' may be understood in the sense of 'Ardent Sun' or 'Radiant Sun'. The concept of the sun's radiance is often expressed in terms of the sun's 'crown'.[2] In an old Russian tale it is said that the sun is wearing the tsar's crown.[3] In Serbian folk-songs the sun is called 'king with a golden crown'. Here we have a Mithraic conception. According to Hrozný, the original meaning of the name Mithra (in Old Indic *Mitra*) was 'diadem', 'crown' ('mitre').[4]

The cosmic nature of the sun is often reflected in Slavic folklore. According to Serbian tales Tsar-Sun is sitting on the radiant throne. Around him are two maidens, the dawn and the evening glow; seven judges (planets); seven messengers (comets); and the old man Month. According to some Russian fairy-tales, Tsar-Sun rules over twelve kingdoms, that is the twelve signs of the zodiac. The Tsar abides in the sun and the tsar's sons in the stars. They are all assisted by the sun's maidens.[5]

The Slavs believed that the course of the sun affected the fortunes of mankind. Masudi relates that among the Slavic temples there was one situated on a high mountain, so built that it was easy, through special openings, to observe the points of sunrise. Precious stones were inserted in various parts of the building and magic signs carved in stone. By co-ordinating the data on the course of the sun and the magic meaning of the precious stones and of the signs, Slavic high priests prophesied future events.[6]

Among the illustrations to the story of the events of the year A.D. 1092 in the Königsberg (Radziwill) Codex of the Russian Chronography there is one showing the signs of omens on the eve of a Polovtsian attack on Russia. There the darkened sun is

[1] A. N. Afanasiev, *Poeticheskie vozzreniia Slavian na prirodu* (Moscow, 1866–9, 3 vols.), i. 97.

[2] Ibid., i. 219.

[3] Ibid., iii. 781.

[4] B. Hrozný, *Histoire de l'Azie Antérieure, de l'Inde et de la Crète depuis les origines jusqu'au début de second millénaire* (Paris, 1947), p. 265.

[5] A. N. Afanasiev, *Poeticheskie vozzreniia Slavian*, i, p. 82.

[6] See F. B. Charmoy, 'Relation de Maçoudi et d'autres auteurs musulmans sur les anciens Slaves', *MAS*, 6ᵐᵉ série, ii (1834), 319–20; Maçoudi, *Les Prairies d'Or*, ed. and translated by C. Barbier de Meynard, iv (Paris, 1865), 58–59.

represented as a disk with a face on it within a ring of rays.[1]
The Königsberg Codex was written in the fifteenth century but
the illustrations are supposed to reproduce much earlier origi-
nals. In Russian folk-lore the rising sun is likened to a golden
ring. Another symbol of sun in Russian folk-lore and folk-art is
the wheel ('fire-wheel' in folk-lore). Representations of the sun-
wheel abound in Russian peasant art. This symbol is found on a
variety of tools, vessels, and pieces of furniture, as well as on
children's toys.

Fire was associated with both light and sun. In 'Hudud al-
Alam' it is stated that all of the Slavs were fire-worshippers.[2]
Long after Russia's conversion to Christianity, Christian writers
complained that the Russians still prayed to Fire 'whom they
call Svarozhich'. Svarozhich means 'son of Svarog'. The god
Svarog was the highest divinity in the Slavic pantheon (see
section 2 below). His name derives from the Old Indic *svar*
'light', 'sun', 'sky'. In Indic epic mythology the Sky-god was
called Svarga.[3] In old Russia Svarog seems to have been considered the god of Light (of 'the White Light' of the *Books of
Wisdom*) and the father of Fire. Fire-worship was reflected in
Slavic funeral customs. Many of the Slavs cremated the bodies
of their deceased.

Let us now turn to the generating functions of the sun. Sun
was considered the source of life on earth. The yearly course of
the sun, through the four seasons, was understood as a cosmic
drama—the death and the new birth of the Sun-god. The day
of the winter solstice was celebrated as the birth of the god.
After Russia's conversion to Christianity this festival merged
with the Nativity. In the Russian and Ukrainian customs associated with Christmas as well as in Russian and Ukrainian
carols, many pre-Christian traits were preserved. 'Carol' in
Russian (and Ukrainian) is *koliada*. This term derives from the
Latin word *calendae* which penetrated into Russia through
Byzantium. Presumably this word was substituted, in the
Middle Ages, for the original Slavic term *kolo* 'wheel', 'round
dance'. Incidentally, the original meaning of the English 'carol'

---

[1] The Radziwill or Königsberg Chronicle, photomechanical reproduction of the
manuscript, *OLDP*, cxviii (St. Petersburg, 1902), 124*b*.
[2] V. F. Minorsky, *Hudud al-Alam* (London, 1937), p. 158.
[3] George N. Roerich has let me know, in a letter of his, that the concept of
'Svarga's son' (corresponding to Slavic 'Svarozhich') also exists in Old Indic.

is 'round dance accompanied by song' (Webster). The main theme of the koliady (this is the plural form) is prayer for a good harvest for the next summer. There are remnants of ancient magical incantations in the koliady as well as hints of the sacrifices to the Sun-god in the old times. A sacrifice of a young goat is specifically mentioned in some of the old koliady.

The next solar festival was that of the vernal equinox. Some of the customs connected with it survived in Russian habits of the so-called 'Butter Week' (*Maslianitsa*), also known as the 'Curd Week' (*Syrnaia Nedelia*). This is the last week before Lent (a kind of Russian equivalent of the 'Mardi-Gras'). The special dish in the fare of the Butter-Week is the pancake (*bliny*). The round form of a *blin* (the singular form) symbolizes the sun-disk. In old Russia the Butter Week was the proper time for various entertainments, such as boxing, wrestling, and tobogganing. Companies of itinerant actors and musicians (*skomorokhi*) performed short plays, some of them remnants of the old sacred drama of the heathen times (see section 5 below). An outgrowth of these shows was the puppet-theatre (*Petrushka*). The vernal equinox signified the approaching spring thaw. With this, the tale of the melting of the Snow-Maiden (*Snegurka*) was associated. The legend served as a theme for Ostrovsky's poetical drama *Snegurochka* (this is the diminutive form) and for Rimsky-Korsakov's opera of the same name based on Ostrovsky's play.

The thaw tide is the period of the rapid rise of the sun's ardency and of the awakening of the forces of procreation. 'Ardent' (*iaryi*) is the special epithet of the sun at this stage of its course. In Russian folk-lore the creative ardency of the sun was personified in the image of the God Iarilo ('the Ardent God'). Iarilo was the god of Spring. The western Slavs called him Iarovit. It is likely that, for the old Slavs, the new year began on the day of the vernal equinox. In Kievan Russia the new year began on 1 March. It was only in the Mongol period that the Byzantine date for the beginning of the new year (1 September) was introduced in Russia. Peter the Great moved it to 1 January to comply with Western habits. In Russian folk-lore the beginning of the spring (that is, the beginning of the new year) is often invoked under the name of *ovsen* (*ovesen* from *vesna* 'spring'). In many Russian songs alongside of *ovsen* another word, *tavsen*, is used. This should be likened to the

Ossetic stem *tav* expressing the notion of 'warmth' (in Ossetic *tavyn* means 'to render warm').

Iarilo was in full power between the vernal equinox and the summer solstice. There were two ancient festivals around the summer solstice, one preceding it (the so-called Semik), and the other following it (the so-called Kupala). After Russia's conversion to Christianity, Semik, although not a church holiday, was assigned to the seventh Thursday after Easter, hence its name (*semik* from *sem'* 'seven'). The Semik, thus, preceded the Pentecost. Semik was celebrated in the forests and on the shores of lakes and rivers. Water, water-nymphs (*rusalki*), and trees (especially the birch tree) played an important role in the festivities. It was dedicated to the souls of the dead, but actually it was mainly a festival of youth and of pre-matrimonial love.

The Kupala festival took place on the day of St. John the Baptist (24 June). It was dedicated to the 'ardent god', Iarilo. Yury Arbatsky informs me that this festival is called *Jāņu Nakts* (John's Night) among the Letts and 'Ion Night' in northern Albania. There it is celebrated as the night of fecundation. A huge bonfire was built at these festivals, often on the bank of a river, or of a lake. A large wooden wheel was kindled at the top of a hill and pushed to roll downhill. Men, women, and maidens danced and sang round the bonfire. Men, young and old, jumped over the fire. This was done because of the belief in the purifying function of the fire. Two effigies, one male and one female, were made of straw that night. The male was called Iarilo, the female Kupala. These figures were burned together.

There is a brief description of the Kupala festival in the old Russian Chronography. According to the chronicler, among the Radimichi, the Viatichi, and the Severi:

there were no marriages . . . but simply festivals [which took place] in between the villages. When the people gathered together for games, for dancing, and for all other devilish amusements, the men on these occasions carried off wives for themselves, and each took any woman with whom he had arrived at an understanding. In fact, they even had two or three wives apiece.[1]

The rolling of the fire-wheel at the Kupala festival symbolized the impending turn of the sun after the solstice and the

---

[1] S. H. Cross and O. P. Sherbowitz's translation, p. 56 (slightly revised).

shorter days to come. This meant the waning of Iarilo's power.
And, indeed, a few days after the Kupala festival the rite of
Iarilo's burial was performed. The rite was observed in some
places in Russia and the Ukraine as late as the nineteenth century. In Kostroma (in the first half of the nineteenth century)
people gathered in the main square and elected an old man to
act as Iarilo's proxy. He was clad in a sackcloth and had to
carry an open coffin containing an effigy representing Iarilo.
The effigy's main feature was an enormous phallus. The procession went outside the city into the open fields. Women wailers
sang dirges and expressed their grief with gestures of desolation.
A grave was dug in the field, and Iarilo's effigy was buried
amidst general wailings. Immediately after, ritual games and
dances took place. At similar rites in the Ukraine women approached the coffin before the burial and wept, repeating 'He is
dead, dead'. The men then lifted and shook the effigy as if trying
to wake the sleeping Iarilo. They then agreed with the women
that Iarilo was dead and explained in a pretty candid way the
reason why Iarilo was so cherished by women. The women continued their laments.[1]

Special rites were performed at the time of the harvest.
According to Ibn Rusta: 'When the time of harvest comes, they
[the Slavs] take a handful of the millet grain, then throw it up
to the heavens and say: O Lord, thou art he who hast provided
our sustenance, complete thy favour toward us.'[2] Women wore
festive dresses when they started reaping. The first sheaf was
dedicated to the gods and brought to the village.

When the crops had been harvested, thanksgiving was celebrated. Saxo Grammaticus in his *Gesta Danorum* described such
a festival at the god Svantovit's sanctuary in Arkona on the
island of Rügen.[3] The whole tribe of the Rugi (Rani) gathered
in front of Svantovit's temple, driving herds of cattle to be
sacrificed. The high priest took the sacred horn with mead,
which had been fixed in the right hand of Svantovit's statue,
examined the quantity and state of the liquor, and prophesied
accordingly. The liquor was sprinkled as a libation to the god,

[1] A. N. Afanasiev, *Poeticheskie vozzreniia Slavian*, iii. 726–7.
[2] C. A. Macartney, *The Magyars in the Ninth Century*, p. 211.
[3] Saxo Grammaticus, *Gesta Danorum*, xiv (ed. Holder), 564. Conveniently reprinted in C. H. Meyer, ed., *Fontes Religionis Slavicae* (Berlin, 1931), pp. 49–50.

after which the priest refilled the horn, drank the mead, then refilled the horn once more, and restored it to the statue. It should be noted that, according to Yury Arbatsky, ritual horns of this type are still used (or in any case were used until recently) in the vicinity of Elbasan, Albania. After such a horn had been emptied, a lengthy note was sounded through it to announce the spirit's victory over matter.[1] In northern Albania such a horn is known as *kheran* (cf. the Hebrew *keren*).

To return to the Arkona festival, after the emptying of the sacred horn, an enormous round cake sweetened with honey, almost the height of a man, was brought in as the symbol of the harvest and placed between the priest and the people. The priest asked the people if they could see him, and if they answered that they still could, he expressed the hope that next year they would not be able to. After that, the general feast started; cattle and other viands which had been offered as sacrifice to the god were now consumed by the rejoicing crowd. On that occasion, as Saxo remarks: 'it is considered pious to violate sobriety, and sinful to observe it.' There is no doubt that Russian Slavs held similar festivals.

The harvest season was not the same in different parts of Russia. In south Russia it occurred late in June and early in July. In central and north Russia it was in July and August. The thanksgiving services in north Russia were performed around 1 September. It seems that no special festivities marked the equinox itself.

With Sun-worship the cult of certain plants and animals was connected. The birch tree, as has been mentioned, was venerated during the Semik. On the eve of the festival, houses in towns and villages were decorated with freshly cut birch trees and boughs. On the day of the festival young people went to the woods and made wreaths of birch branches. They then chose a nice birch tree to serve as 'the Semik tree', and decorated it with ribbons, after which they danced and sang songs around it. After that they tore a limb, or cut the whole tree if it was small, clothed it in woman's dress, and brought it to the village, placing the 'Semik tree' in a house selected by common agreement. There it spent three days as the villagers' guest. On the Pentecost Sunday it was carried to a nearby river or lake and

[1] See Y. Arbatsky, *Etiudy po istorii russkoi muzyki* (New York, 1956), pp. 43–44.

thrown in. It will be recalled that the birch tree was considered the Tree of Life by the shamans.[1] For music-lovers it may be of interest that the melody of one of the ritual Semik songs concerning the birch tree was used by Tchaikovsky as the main theme of the third and the fourth parts of his Fourth Symphony.

Of the animals, the horse, the deer, the bull or cow, and the goat were those most closely connected with Sun-worship. In a Russian fairy-tale the sun takes the shape of the red horseman riding a red horse.[2] In an old carol it is said that the Koliada rides on a black horse.[3] As has been said, the old word for *koliada* was *kolo* 'wheel'. The wheel is the sun's symbol, and here Koliada represents the sun. The horse is black because the sun is at the lowest point before revival. In a description of the Koliada festivities in Muscovy (1648) it is said that the participants in the ritual procession wore the *skomorokhi* masks and garments and led along with them a 'devilish mare'.[3] This is again the sun-horse. In Russian folk-lore the golden horse (or a horse with golden mane or golden tail) is a symbol of the sun. In Serbian folk-songs a winged horse appears with the image of the sun on his forehead.[4] The sun-horse is a Mithraic concept. Mithra had white horses dedicated to him.

The deer likewise was a sun-animal. The deer with golden antlers is a favourite character in Slavic folk-lore. Both in Russian and Serbian folk-songs the golden antlers represent the sun's radiance.[5]

The white bull (or a white cow) is likened in Slavic folk-lore to the Sun or to the Daylight, whereas the black bull or black cow personify the Night. A Bulgarian riddle reads: 'What divine cow filled the whole world?' The answer is—the Sun.[6] It has been mentioned that according to Hudud al-Alam the Slavs were fire-worshippers. In the parallel section of Ibn-Rusta the reading is 'bull-worshippers'. Gardizi says that the Slavs worshipped the cow.[7] Here we have a connexion between Fire and Bull (or Cow), and Fire was an element related to the Sun. As regards the connexion between Sun and Goat, the goat sacrifice to the Sun-god has been already mentioned.

[1] See Chapter 1, section 6, above.
[2] A. N. Afanasiev, *Poeticheskie vozzreniia Slavian*, i, 597.
[3] Ibid., p. 607.   [4] Ibid., p. 612.
[5] Ibid., pp. 638–9.   [6] Ibid., p. 659.
[7] C. A. Macartney, *The Magyars in the Ninth Century*, p. 211.

Through Iarilo, Sun-worship was connected with clan cult. 'Clan' in Russian is *rod*, to be associated with the verb *roditi* 'to beget'. In Old Russian 'rod' also had the connotation of 'genitor' ('procreator') and hence, that of the genius of procreation. Long after Russia's conversion to Christianity, Christian writers and preachers noted with indignation that many Russians still sacrificed to Rod and Rozhanitsy. Rozhanitsa (this is the singular form) 'genetrix', is the feminine counterpart of Rod. The name usually occurs in the plural, which is an indication of the existence of polygamy among the Slavs in ancient times. In concrete terms, *rod* might have denoted the phallus and *rozhanitsa* the vulva. The phallic cult was widespread in the Ancient World, including ancient Russia. According to L. Sternberg,[1] at the base of the phallic cult lays the ancient philosophical concept (of so-called 'animism') that each of the organs of the human body, and especially the organ of procreation, has its own 'soul', subordinated to man's main soul but capable of acting on its own. Hence the notion of the phallus as an active personified factor. In Sanskrit the emblem of phallus is called *liṅga*. In the worship of Śiva it is represented in the form of a stone or marble column. The veneration of linga is usually combined with that of *yoni* (emblem of vulva). Yoni is symbolized by a horizontal flat stone. In the combined cult the linga pillar is placed on the yoni stone piercing it.[2]

It would not be amiss to mention the combination of two apparently similar terms in a refrain in the Lettish songs during the celebration of 'John's Night' (corresponding to the Russian festival of Ivan Kupala), to which Yuri Arbatsky called my attention. The refrain is 'Ligo Iani'. While Ian is usually explained as 'John', the form of the word originally used on such occasions might have corresponded to the Indic *yoni*. 'Ligo' seems to be an equivalent of the Indic *linga*.[3]

The Russian festival of Ivan Kupala belongs to the same

[1] *Entsiklopedicheskii Slovar*, published by Brockhaus-Efron, half-volume lxix. 267.

[2] S. Bulich, 'Linga', *Entsiklopedicheskii Slovar*, published by Brockhaus-Efron, half-volume xxxiv. 698. See also Monier Monier-Williams, *A Sanskrit-English Dictionary* (Oxford, 1899), pp. 858 and 901; C. C. Uhlenbeck, *Kurzgefasstes etymologisches Wörterbuch der altindischen Sprache* (Amsterdam, 1898/9), p. 241.

[3] According to Arbatsky 'Jāṇu nakts' is also known among the Letts as 'Ligo nakts' (the *Ligo* Night). In the *Latyshsko–Russkii Slovar* (Moscow, 1942), p. 110, the meaning of *ligo* is given, without any explanation, as 'a refrain in the Lettish folksongs of the John's Day' (I am indebted to Yury Arbatsky for this reference).

cycle of phallic cult. As has been said, the phallus was the main trait of Iarilo's funeral effigy. It also will be recalled that at the Kupala festival two effigies—male (Iarilo) and female (Kupala) —were burned. Presumably, representations not only of the phallus but of the vulva as well played an important role in the symbolism of the Kupala festival in old Russia. 'Kupala' might have denoted the vulva.

The Slavs believed that a man's fate was predestined at his birth. There is a Russian saying *tak na rodu napisano* 'so has been written down at (his or her) birth'. A Russian proverb says: *ot rodu ne v vodu* 'you can't escape your prenatal destiny even if you plunge into water'. There is a Croatian tradition of a *Book of Nativity* (*Rozhdenik*) where all events in the life of every man have been written down in advance.[1] Through these beliefs the notion of destiny was associated with the cult of Rod and Rozhanitsy. In Afanasiev's opinion one of the functions of the Rozhanitsy was to assign his (or her) lot to every child at his (or her) birth.[2] According to Arbatsky,[3] the cult of the Rod and Rozhanitsy survived until recently in many remote localities in the Balkan peninsula. Among the rites of the cult is that of communion by drinking wine from the sacred horns. Arbatsky took part several times in this rite as performed near Elbasan in Albania (in the 1930's). Two horns were used, one for men and the other for women. Not only local Slavs but pilgrims of various origins visiting the monastery of St. Ion Vladimir (among them were Albanians, Aromuns, and Greeks) participated in the mysteries.

2. *Slavic mythology*

The central position occupied by the sun in Slavic religion is evidence of the affinity of Slavic beliefs with Mithraism as well as with the cult of Helios (Apollo) in Greece.

The basic religious notion, 'god', is expressed in Slavic by the word *bog*. In Old Slavic this word had also the connotation of 'wealth', hence the Modern Russian word *bogatstvo* 'wealth'. The Slavic *bog* is akin to the Old Indic *bhagas* and the Avestan

---

[1] A. N. Afanasiev, *Poeticheskie vozzreniia Slavian*, iii. 368. See also M. de Ferdi-nandy, *Ahnen und Schicksal* (München, 1955), p. 7.

[2] A. N. Afanasiev, op. cit., iii. 388.

[3] Y. Arbatsky, *Etiudy po istorii russkoi muzyki*, p. 68.

baga. Presumably, these Slavic and Aryan terms are cognate words, not borrowings from the Aryan to the Slavic.

Besides the names denoting the Sun-god mentioned before (Khors, Dazhbog, Iarilo), a number of names of other deities were invoked in Slavic cults. However, behind the variety of emanations of the divine power, there was a notion of the basic universality of godhood. In the sixth century the Byzantine historian Procopius, describing the Danubian Slavs, wrote that 'they believe that one god, the maker of the lightning, is alone lord of all things' (7. 14. 23). In the twelfth century the Roman Catholic priest Helmold, writing on the Baltic Slavs, said that

they do not deny that there is among the multiform godheads to whom they attribute field and woods, sorrows and joys, one god in the heavens ruling over the others. They hold that he, the all powerful one, looks only after heavenly matters; that the others, discharging the duties assigned to them in obedience to him, proceed from his blood; and that one excels another in the measure that he is nearer to this god of gods.[1]

There is a certain analogy between this concept and the cosmic outlook of the Mithraic religious beliefs. According to these latter, there is the supreme godhead, the Infinite Time (Zervan). Mithra, as well as other deities and genii, serves as a link between the godhead and the world. Mithra in particular is the mediator between the primordial divinity and mankind.[2]

The Slavic supreme god is mentioned anonymously in the Russo-Byzantine treaty of 944, where it is said that if the Russians violate the treaty they shall receive no help 'from god or from Perun' (see section 3 below).

Another basic religious and cosmic conception was that of the three worlds. The monk Ebbo, of the twelfth century, describing the sanctuary of God Triglav ('Three-headed') in Stettin says that the god's three heads symbolize the three 'reigns' of which he takes care: Heaven, Earth, and the Netherworld.[3] This corresponds to the shamanic concept of the three cosmic zones.[4]

[1] Helmold, *Cronica Slavorum*, ed. Lappenberg-Schmeidler, 1909, i. 84; C. H. Meyer, *Fontes Historiae Religionis Slavicae*, pp. 45–46; Helmold, *The Chronicle of the Slavs*, Francis Joseph Tschan, translation (New York, 1935), p. 219.

[2] Cf. G. Vernadsky, 'Svantovit, dieu des Slaves Baltiques', *Annuaire*, vii (1939–44), 345–6.

[3] C. H. Meyer, *Fontes Historiae Religionis Slavicae*, pp. 35–36.

[4] See Chapter 1, section 6, above.

In the Russian Chronography several names of deities venerated by the Russian Slavs are mentioned. In Prince Oleg's first
treaty with Byzantium (907) we find the names of Perun and
Volos. Perun is mentioned again in Prince Igor's treaty with
the Byzantines (944). In Sviatoslav's treaty (971) both Perun
and Volos are invoked. A decade later, Sviatoslav's son Vladimir set up on the hills outside his palace in Kiev the statues of
Perun, Khors, Dazhbog, Stribog, Simargl, and Mokosh. In the
Igor Tale (late twelfth century) Veles and Dazhbog are mentioned. In the comments of the Slavic translator of Malalas'
Chronicle on a story about Hephaestus, which was quoted in
the Russian Chronography under A.D. 1114, Dazhbog is called
son of Svarog. Dazhbog is identified by the Slavic commentator
as Helios, and Svarog as Hephaestus.[1] A few names of other
deities occur in old Russian literature, mainly in the admonitions against the survivals of Paganism in Russia. Still other
gods were worshipped by the Baltic Slavs, among them Svantovit and Svarozhich (i.e. 'Svarog's son').

As has been said (see section 1 above), Svarog was apparently
the god of the White Light. He seems to have occupied the
highest place in the Slavic pantheon. Most likely he was the
supreme god of the Slavs mentioned by Helmold, 'the all
powerful one' who 'looks only after heavenly matters'. This
may be the reason why Svarog's name was never openly invoked by the faithful and why there existed no statues of him.
To paraphrase Helmold, other gods, proceeding from Svarog,
discharged the duties assigned to them by him. Among them
were his sons, the Svarozhichi. In Russia, Dazhbog was considered a Svarozhich, and Fire was also called Svarozhich. One
of the most powerful gods of the Baltic Slavs was known by the
name Svarozhich. This was the tribal god of the Ratari who
lived between the lower Oder and the lower Elbe. His sanctuary
was at Radogost (Rethra).

As has been mentioned, the old Russian writers likened
Svarog to Hephaestus. In all probability Svarog was considered
the patron saint of the art of forging weapons. The sword must
have been considered one of his symbols. At the conclusion of
the Russo-Byzantine treaty of 907 the Russians 'swore by their
god Perun, as well as by Volos'. Note that the weapons are

[1] Hypatian Chronicle, *PSRL*, ii, fasc. 1 (3rd edn., Petrograd, 1923), cols. 274–6.

mentioned before Perun and Volos. In the description of the
oath by weapons of the Russians at the confirmation of the
treaty of 944, naked swords are mentioned specifically. It will
be recalled in this connexion[1] that both Scythians and Alans
venerated the naked sword. As has been said 'god' (not named)
was mentioned in the Russo-Byzantine treaty of 944. Presumably it was Svarog. While he was not named—his name must
have been taboo—he was symbolically invoked through his
emblem, the naked sword.

The existence among the Slavs of several names for the Sun-
god does not mean that they had several Sun-gods. There is but
one sun in the heavens. Different names were used to character-
ize its different aspects and functions. The name Khors denoted
the sun in the original sense of the word, that of the luminous
celestial body, and in the moral sense, that of the absolute
Good. The name Dazhbog (Dazhd'bog) has been interpreted
by modern scholars in two different ways. According to some
(including Roman Jakobson) the basic spelling of the name was
Dazhd'bog, and the meaning of the name 'Giver of Wealth'
(from the Old Russian words *dati* 'to give' and *bog* in the sense
of 'wealth'). According to others (including A. Afanasiev), *bog*
here means 'god', and Dazh- is to be derived from the Sanskrit
dah (Avestan *dag*) 'to burn'. The name Dazhbog would then
mean the 'Burning God' or the 'Ardent God'.[2] I believe that
both interpretations are right. Dazhd'bog and Dazhbog must
have been two parallel names, each with its own connotation.[3]
The god was invoked now as the giver of good harvest, and now
as the Ardent God (Iarilo).

Another pair of Sun-god's names is Veles and Volos. The
origin of neither name has been satisfactorily explained so far.
As regards 'Volos' it is identical with the Russian word *volos*
(Old Slavic *vlas*) 'hair'. The identity may be purely accidental.
On the other hand, the hair was considered by many peoples,
including the Slavs, a depository of magic strength (consider
the Biblical Samson). On that ground the name Volos may have
meant the 'hairy god', the hair being the emblem of his power.

---

[1] See Chapter 1, section 6, above.

[2] A. N. Afanasiev, *Poeticheskie vozzreniia Slavian*, i. 65; Roman Jakobson, 'Slavic
Mythology', *Funk and Wagnalls Standard Dictionary of Folklore*, ii (1950), p. 1027.

[3] On the variety of names of Slavic gods see Y. Arbatsky, *Etiudy po istorii russkoi
muzyki*, p. 62.

In popular notions Volos was indeed 'hairy'. In many places of Russia, as late as the nineteenth century, the women reapers following an old tradition used to leave several ears of wheat or rye intact in a corner of the field. One of the women marked these ears beforehand by tying them together, saying, 'this is to Volos for his beard'.[1]

The twin deity Veles-Volos was akin to the Greek Apollo, god of poetry and music as well as of flocks. In the *Igor Tale* the inspired poet Bayan is called 'Veles' grandson'. Veles, then, was Apollo the Kitharaoidos. According to an old tradition, Veles is the Holy Spirit. Volos was the protector of flocks. In the Russo-Byzantine treaties of the tenth century he is called 'the god of cattle'.

Breath (wind in the sense of respiration) was considered an emanation of the spirit. Breath (wind) is also a medium of singing and music (wind instruments). From this point of view there is a connexion between Veles and Stribog. Stribog's element was the atmosphere. In the *Igor Tale* the winds are called 'Stribog's Grandsons'. Stribog's counterpart among the Baltic Slavs was Svantovit. From the description of Svantovit's statue we know that it had four heads. They must have symbolized the four cardinal winds. It should be noted that the cult of the cardinal winds, related to the four seasons, played an important role in Mithraism as well. The Slavic Svantovit is to be compared to the Iranian Wind-god Vat. *Vat* means 'wind' in Avestan. To the Iranian stem *vat* the Slavic *vet* (*vit*) corresponds. In Russian 'wind' is *veter*; in Ukrainian *viter*. The name Svantovit may be interpreted as 'Holy Wind', i.e. 'Holy Spirit'.

In an old Ukrainian song Stribog's breath is likened to Holy Spirit. Yuri Arbatsky has heard in Macedonia an old tale from which it is clear that Stribog produced wind—Holy Spirit— through his nose. When the weather is calm, it means that Stribog is playing his flute, also through his nose. Nose flutes are still used in Macedonia. In Russia they survived in the north, in the Beloozero region.[2] It is still believed in Macedonia that breathing through the nose contains the soul and therefore has a magic power which breathing through the mouth lacks. In the presence of the god of breath, man had to abstain from

[1] A. N. Afanasiev, *Poeticheskie vozzreniia Slavian*, i. 697.
[2] Y. Arbatsky, *Etiudy po istorii russkoi muzyki*, pp. 63–64.

breathing. The high priest of the Svantovit's cult held his breath when he entered the temple's inner sanctuary.

A mighty deity, venerated by many Slavic tribes, was Perun, god of thunder and war. He occupied an important position in the Kievan pantheon as well as in Novgorod. His likeness to the Nordic Thor may have contributed to his popularity at the court of Kievan Rurikids. The oak was considered Perun's sacred tree. Cocks were sacrificed to him. In Russian folk-lore Perun often appears as a beneficent deity. In the spring he comes with thunder and lightnings and fertilizes the earth with rains. He then chases the clouds away to let the sun shine.

The only feminine deity in the Kievan pantheon was Mokosh. It would be tempting to connect this name with the Sanskrit *mokṣa*, which means 'liberation', 'redemption'. The term is used to express the merging with deity, the state of supreme beatitude of the human soul. This is, however, an abstract philosophical notion. *Mokṣa* was never personified in Indian religious literature and art, while the Russian Mokosh appears to have been a concrete deity. Because of this I am inclined to accept Roman Jakobson's interpretation of the name Mokosh as 'most' (in Old Russian *mokosh* means 'moisture').[1] Mokosh may be considered the successor of the Great Goddess of the Scythians—Api-Anahita.[2]

Moisture helps the earth to produce. From this point of view, the old Russian concept of the 'Mother Moist Earth' (*Mati Syra Zemlia*) must be associated with Mokosh. In one of the admonitions against Paganism Mokosh is called Bereginia, 'shore deity' (from the Russian *bereg* 'shore' of a river, or of a lake). According to N. F. Lavrov, Mokosh as a feminine deity was especially venerated by women and was considered the sponsor of spinning and weaving.[3] She was represented as a woman with long hands. It should be noted in this connexion that in Khorezmian art, in the wall paintings of Pianjikent of the seventh and the eighth centuries, and on some Kushan coins, a feminine deity with four hands is represented. This apparently is Api-Anahita, also called Oksho.[4]

[1] R. Jakobson, 'Slavic Mythology', p. 1027.   [2] See Chapter 1, section 6, above.
[3] N. F. Lavrov, 'Religiia i tserkov', *Istoriia Kultury drevnei Rusi*, ed. by B. D. Grekov and M. I. Artamonov (Moscow and Leningrad, 1948–51, 2 vols.), ii. 69.
[4] S. P. Tolstov, *Drevnii Khorezm*, p. 200; *Zhivopis drevnego Piandjikenta* (Moscow, 1954), p. 69.

There is a certain similarity between the names Oksho and Mokosh, which may be entirely accidental. The deity itself seems to be identical with Mokosh.

One more name of the Kievan pantheon remains to be dealt with—Simargl. This deity is to be identified as the Iranian magic bird Simurg (Senmurv) which is also mentioned in Ossetian folk-lore.[1] According to a Middle Persian cosmological treatise, *Bundahišn*, Senmurv abided on 'the Tree of Semen'. When flying, Senmurv spread the semen in water so that the rain could cover the earth with it. The cult of Simurg must have been quite popular in Russia. In a twelfth-century Persian poem by Khaqani the Russians are called Simurgs. In the *Igor Tale* Simurg appears as Div ('Demon'). Simurg means 'radiant bird' (in Avestan *Hšaena Meregha*). As the late A. D. Kalmykow noted, Simurg survived in Russian folk-lore under the name of 'Fire Bird' (*Zhar-Ptitsa*).[2]

A number of names of other deities and spirits may be found in Russian folk-lore, among them that of Lel, spirit of spring and love. Note that in Hungarian *lélek* means 'soul', 'spirit'. The belief in home and wood sprites as well as in nymphs was widespread among the Slavs. Procopius (7. 14. 23) states that they revered 'both river and tree nymphs and some other spirits'. The river and tree nymphs were known as *rusalki* (singular *rusalka*). According to Zelenin, the rusalki were the spirits of those women and maidens whose death was 'unclean', that is a result of violence.[3] In many places of Russia, remnants of the veneration of trees, rivers, and rocks could be observed as late as the nineteenth century.

Not much is known about the priests of the Slavic cults. In Old Slavic they were known as the *volsvy* (in Modern Russian *volkhvy*; singular *volkhv* in both Old and Modern Russian), i.e. magi. The verb *volkhovati* means 'to conjure', 'to practice sorcery'.

From Masudi's report on the Slavs we may conclude that the Slavic priests had a reputation for being experienced sooth-

---

[1] See Chapter 1, section 6, above.

[2] A. D. Kalmykow's daughter, Miss Alexandra Kalmykow, kindly let me read her late father's unpublished study on this matter. See also A. D. Kalmykow, 'Iranians and Slavs in South Russia', *JAOS*, xlv (1925), 68–71.

[3] D. K. Zelenin, *Ocherki russkoi mifologii* (Petrograd, 1916); id., *Russische (Ostslavische) Volkskunde* (Berlin and Leipzig, 1927), p. 392.

sayers, well versed in astronomy. The priest of Svantovit's sanctuary in Arkona was held in high esteem not only by the heathen Slavs but also by some of their Christian neighbours. Several foreign kings, including the king of Denmark, sent their gifts to God Svantovit.

Many a Slavic *volkhv* must have been a skilled physician and surgeon. According to T. Anda,[1] Magyar surgeons of the ninth and tenth centuries were able to perform difficult operations of trepanation of the skull. One skull with marks of such operation was found in Kiev, and several others in Hungary. Anda suggests that these operations were performed by the priests of the Magyar Pagan cult and that they had learned the technique from the Turkish healers of central Asia. The latter, Anda thinks, must have been familiar with the methods of Arabic medicine. In my opinion the Hungarian surgeons might have been smiths (see on the smiths as surgeons and healers in section 4 below). As has been said,[2] the Hungarian surgeons, whether priests or smiths, must have been in close contact with the Slavic *volkhvy* (consider the similarity of Slavic and Hungarian terms for 'miracle' and 'magics'). Therefore we may think that some of the Slavic volkhvy were acquainted with the same methods of healing and surgery. The trepanated skull found in Kiev might have been that of a Hungarian since, as we know,[3] there was a Hungarian settlement in Kiev in the ninth century. But Slavs lived in the neighbourhood and their magi were probably acquainted with the activities of their Hungarian colleagues.

It should be added that, according to Anda, the Hungarian surgeons used some kind of narcotic, presumably an extract from poppy-juice. They also knew certain methods for stopping haemorrhage and understood the necessity of sterilizing the wounds. On one of the trepanated skulls the opening was covered by a silver plate.

Two of the old Russian princes were, in the opinion of their contemporaries, endowed with the supernatural powers of the magi. One was Oleg of Kiev, known in Norse as Helgi Helgi

---

[1] T. Anda, 'Recherches archéologiques sur la pratique médicale des Hongrois à l'époque de la conquête du pays', *AAAH*, i (1951), 251–316.
[2] See Chapter 3, section 4, above.
[3] See Chapter 3 above.

(Helgi the Holy). The other was Vseslav of Polotsk (*regnabat* 1044–1101). His case is especially interesting since he lived in Christian times and, officially, was a member of the Christian Church. In the Chronography it is said about Vseslav that 'his mother bore him by enchantment, for when his mother bore him, there was a caul over his head, and the magi bade his mother bind his caul upon him, that he might carry it with him the rest of his life. Vseslav accordingly bears it to this day, and for this reason he is pitiless in bloodshed'. In the *Igor Tale* Vseslav is represented as an accomplished wizard.

> Vseslav cast lots for the coveted maiden [presumably, a personification of 'city']. Craftily, leaning on his spear he leaped to the city of Kiev, and touched with the spear-shaft the golden Kievan throne.
>
> Wrapped in the pall of a blue mist he leaped like a ferocious beast at midnight out of Belgorod.
>
> Some three times he snatched a streak of good luck, he opened the gates of Novgorod, and smashed the glory of Iaroslav.
>
> Like a wolf he leaped towards the Nemiga. . . .
>
> As prince he ruled the cities, but at night he coursed like a wolf: he would course from Kiev to Tmutorokan before cock-crow, wolf-like crossing the path of the great Khors.
>
> In Polotsk, the bells of St. Sophia's would ring in the morning for him, but he heard these bells in Kiev.[1]

As Roman Jakobson has convincingly shown,[2] Vseslav is also described in a popular bylina under the name of the bogatyr Volkh Vseslavich (Volkh, i.e. Volkhv, son of Vseslav). Like Vseslav, Volkh was familiar with occult sciences and could turn into a wolf or any animal. He could pass through the wall of the enemy's city turning himself and his warriors into ants.

From the legends of Vseslav and of Volkh Vseslavich we may understand what the Russians of the eleventh century considered the characteristic traits and methods of the secret wisdom of their magi. Casting lots was one of these methods. Leaning on a weapon (a spear in this case) or touching a symbol of the magus's objective by the shaft of the weapon had appa-

[1] S. H. Cross's translation (slightly revised in the last verse) in 'La Geste du Prince Igor', ed. by H. Grégoire, R. Jakobson, *et al.*, p. 173.

[2] R. Jakobson, 'The Vseslav Epos', *Russian Epic Studies* (Philadelphia, 1949), pp. 13–86.

rently a magical meaning. It helped to achieve the objective.
The magi were credited with the supernatural capacity of hearing the bells at a great distance. While church bells are mentioned in the legend, they probably are a substitute for the
magic bells of the shamans. The magus could move through
space in a miraculous way with miraculous speed. He could
envelop himself in a cloud of mist. Finally, the magus could
turn himself into a wolf or any animal. It should be noted that
the belief in werewolves was widespread in old Russia as well as
in the Balkan peninsula since time immemorial. Herodotus
(iv. 105) relates of the Neuri (whom some of the scholars consider the ancestors of the Slavs) that 'every Neurian once a year
becomes a wolf for a few days, at the end of which time he is
restored to his proper shape'.

The supernatural powers with which the Slavic magi were
said to be endowed are in some respects akin to those of the
shamans. The ability of the magi to hear and see distant events,
as well as to transport themselves instantly to distant places,
reminds us of the similar powers of the Indian gods and of the
Taoist sages of China.

3. *Community and social order*

One of the basic Russian words in the cycle of notions bearing
on social organization is *mir*. In Modern Russian it means both
'peace' and 'world'. In a specific sense it denotes 'village community'. In Old Russian *mir* meant both 'peace agreement' and
'community agreement'.

In ancient Russia the clan, the zadruga, and, originally, the
verv', were social units based on kinship. For a growing society,
especially in the cities, the framework of these original units
soon proved too narrow. A community based on mutual interests and neighbourhood, not on kinship only, was the next step
in the development of social organization. That companionship
was the mir in the sense of 'community agreement'.

The life of a clan centred around the clan cult. The mir also
had a religious foundation. As Roman Jakobson rightly observed, the Slavic term *mir* 'is connected with the Iranian
Mithra'. It should be noted that the Middle Persian form for
'Mithra' is *Mihr*. In Middle Persian *mihr*, as an abstract notion,

has a connotation of 'friendship', 'association'.[1] *Mir* is the Slavic equivalent of *mihr*.

Mithraism, as it developed in old India and old Iran, had many aspects. One of the important ones was the social. Besides being the god of victory, Mithra was also the god of social order. Some of the Yashts (hymns) of the *Avesta* are addressed to 'Mithra in peace'. In the Yashts Mithra is often called the 'ruler' (*dahyupatis*). Mithra's characteristic epithet is *rtāvan* 'the just' (*urvata* means 'fundamental law').[2]

The concept of Mithra the Ruler was reflected in some of the old Slavic princely names, those ending in -*mir*, like Vladimir and Iaromir.[3] In my opinion 'Vladimir' means 'the Ruling Mithra'; Iaromir, 'the Ardent Mithra'.

As 'the Just', Mithra was the guarantor of justice and laws. There are two Old Slavic words denoting 'law', *pravda* and *zakon*. *Pravda* in Modern Russian means 'truth'. In Old Russian it also had the connotations of 'justice' and 'law'. The old Russian code of laws of the eleventh and twelfth centuries was known as *Pravda Rus'ka*, 'the Russian Law' (Lex Russica).

Zakon in Modern Russian means 'law'. In Old Russian it also meant 'law', but more specifically 'state law' and 'religious law'. As has been mentioned,[4] this word was used by the Khazars and the Magyars. Constantine Porphyrogenitus, describing the ceremonies of the inauguration of the Magyar voevoda Almos as prince under the suzerainty of the Khazar kagan, states that the inauguration followed 'the custom and law' [*zakanon*, i.e. *zakon*], of the Khazars'.[5] Furthermore, from Constantine we know that the Pechenegi also used the term *zakon*.[6] Constantine says that the Pechenegian envoys took their oaths to confirm their loyalty to the emperor, 'according to their laws' (*zakana*, i.e. *zakony*, plural form). At the confirmation of the Russo-Byzantine treaty of 907 the emperors Leo and Alexander 'kissed the cross' and Oleg took the oath (*rota*). 'Oleg's men, according to the Russian law [*zakon*], swear by their weapons

[1] E. Herzfeld, *Zoroaster and His World* (Princeton, 1947, 2 vols.), ii. 483.
[2] Ibid., p. 440.
[3] See note K, p. 319.
[4] See Chapter 3, sections 3–4, above.
[5] Constantine Porphyrogenitus, *De Administrando Imperio*, Greek text edited by Gy. Moravcsik, English translation by R. J. H. Jenkins (Budapest, 1949), p. 172.
[6] Ibid., p. 56.

and by their god Perun and Volos.'[1] Note that for Oleg himself, the rota was considered a strong enough pledge.

Mithra was the avenger of all the violations of social order, and men's obligation was to co-operate with the god. Any infringement of justice, any crime, was a crime against Mithra. The community—be this a clan or a mir—had not only the right, but the sacred duty to avenge the murder of any of its members. The murderer was not only an offender against men; he was one 'who injures Mithra' (*mithradrugš*). Eventually 'mithra', as an abstract notion, assumed the connotation of the moral obligation upon which the society was founded.[2] In ancient times, blood-revenge was the proper method of upholding justice. Later on, blood retaliation was replaced by money-fine (composition). In medieval Russia the murderer had to pay both the amends to the relatives of the murdered man (*golovnichestvo*; in Anglo-Saxon 'bot'), and a fine to the prince (*vira*; in Anglo-Saxon 'bloodwite'). The prince in this case received the share formerly belonging to the god.

Mithra was the god of loyalty to contracts. Impersonally, the word *mithra* had, among its connotations, those of 'contract', 'religious sanction', 'promise', 'vow'. To be religiously valid, every promise is made under oath, and every breach of it means perjury. The Old Russian word for 'oath' is *rota*. The stem of this word is to be connected with the Old Indic *vratam* 'precept', 'law', 'vow', as well as with the Avestan *urvata* 'law', 'dogma'.

According to Mithraic beliefs, breaking the vow would be avenged by Mithra. In the Russo-Byzantine treaty of 944, God's punishment was invoked twice as sanction for any violation of the treaty, both at the beginning of the treaty and at the end. Since among the Russian warriors of Igor's army there were both Christians and heathens, both the Christian God and Pagan gods were invoked. To quote from the sanction formula at the beginning of the treaty.

If any one from the Russian land violates the amity, let those who have been christened be condemned to eternal damnation by God

---

[1] *Povest' Vremennykh Let*, ed. by V. P. Adrianova-Peretts, text prepared for publication by D. S. Likhachev (Moscow and Leningrad, 1950, 2 vols.), i. 20. English translation S. H. Cross and O. P. Sherbowitz-Wetzor, *The Russian Primary Chronicle* (Cambridge, Mass., 1953), p. 65.

[2] E. Herzfeld, *Zoroaster*, ii. 483.

Pantokrator; and let those who have not been christened receive no help from God [Svarog?] or from Perun; let them not be protected by their shields, let them be slain by their own swords, by their arrows, or any of their own weapons, and let them become eternal slaves.[1]

The conclusion of the sanction formula is highly significant: 'Let them be eternal slaves.' Whose slaves? Apparently slaves of the god whose precepts they violated. In Mithraic terms they will become *mithradrug*̌ 'those who injure Mithra'. This means that they lose their personality and are outlawed for ever with no hope of salvation. The position of the 'eternal slave' in this sense is similar to that of the Ossetian *fældyst* 'consecrated'.[2]

The rota played an important role in the old Russian court procedure. The modes of proof at the disposal of the contestants at the court trial in medieval Russia were threefold: witnesses; appeal to God's judgement; and, in civil litigations, deeds, notes, and other documents. The habitual approach to God in the court procedure was to have one of the contestants, or the witnesses, take the oath. This was the rota. In the Christian times, the rota was gradually replaced by kissing the cross. In more complicated cases the rota was supplemented by ordeals. These were of the same kind as in the old Germanic law, by water and iron. Reminiscences of the judicial rota, and of the sanctions for perjury, may be found in a number of Russian oaths, such as 'let my eyes burst' (i.e. in case of perjury), 'let me sink through the earth', 'let God kill me', and so on.

Besides the rota and the ordeals there were many other magic rites in the old Russian law. Some remnants of juridical symbolism survived in Russian customary law down to the modern period. One of such symbolic customs was known as the 'sprinkling' of each transaction such as the sale of property or the signing of a contract: to confirm the act, both parties had to drink liquor—and more often than not they both would get drunk. In the old times both men had to drink wine from the same bowl. This is a rite preserved from the Scythian times.[3] Another similar custom was the symbolic 'clapping of hands' (*rukobitie*). When the agreement was reached, the representative

---

[1] *Povest' Vremennykh Let*, p. 35; Cross and Sherbowitz's translation, p. 74.
[2] See Chapter 1, section 2, above.
[3] See Chapter 1, section 2, above.

of each side had to clap the right hand of that of the other side by his right hand.

When land was bought, the former owner had to hand the new owner a piece of turf from the ground symbolizing the sale of the whole plot of land. Hence the formula 'to buy with turf' (*oderen'*) in the old Russian land deeds. The turf symbol was also used in litigations about land. Ivan Pososhkov, a noted writer of Peter the Great's times, says that the litigant, to prove his rights, would put a piece of turf on his head, take an icon in his hands, and thus proceed along what he considered the lawful boundary. Pososhkov adds that he knew cases in which such litigants had tried to cheat and had died on the spot. As late as 1870, in north Russia, the same mode of proof was used. If all attempts at agreement failed, the litigants decided that the 'Mother Moist Earth' must judge them. Whereupon one of them dug a piece of turf, put it on his head, and proceeded along the boundary.[1] Here, in the notion of 'Mother Moist Earth', we have again a survival of the pre-Christian past, in fact of the Scythian era.

To return to the rota, the oath of loyalty was an important element of the 'sworn brotherhood', an old institution which had existed in the Scythian age,[2] and continued to exist in Russian both before and after her conversion to Christianity. In Christian times the rite of 'sworn brotherhood' (*pobratimstvo*) was blessed by the church. A special kind of military fraternity in old Russia was that of the Norsemen—the *variagi* (Varangians) from the Old Nordic *vaeringr* 'associate under oath'. *Var* in Old Norse means 'fidelity', 'surety', 'vow'.

Of the non-military type were the companies of hunters and trappers, as well as of fishermen, known in old Russia as *vatagi* (singular *vataga*) from the Alanic (Ossetian) *fætæg* 'leader'. The head of the vataga was called *vataman* (in Modern Russian *ataman*) or *vatazhok*. Another term denoting a professional fraternity was *bratchina* (from *brat* 'brother'). The bratchina, as well as the vataga, had the judiciary authority over its members. The term *bratchina* also had the connotation of the 'fraternal

---

[1] P. Matveev, 'Sbornik narodnykh iuridicheskikh obychaev', *Zapiski Russkogo Geograficheskogo Obshestva po otdeleniiu etnografii*, viii (1878), 18; N. P. Pavlov-Silvansky, *Sochineniia*, iii (St. Petersburg, 1910), pp. 427–8; G. Vernadsky, *Zvenia Russkoi Kultury* (Bruxelles, 1938), p. 182.

[2] See Chapter 1, section 2, above.

banquet' as well as 'banquet fraternity'. This was an important
institution in old Russia's community life. In medieval Novgorod and Pskov the banquet fraternities were usually connected
with merchants and artisan guilds.

Of a different type is the 'concealed concord' (*skriveni zalog*)
of conjurers, healers, musicians, and smiths, which survived in
the Balkans until our days. Yury Arbatsky came in contact with
it in the 1930's during his researches there. Its symbolic de-
lineation, 'Rotu', is revealed to the few only. In my opinion,
this symbol derives from the same stem as *rota* 'oath'. The concord has its own esoteric philosophy and language. Among its
basic philosophical concepts is *ruxs* 'light', 'enlightenment'.
This may be compared to the 'White Light' of the Russian
Book of Deep Wisdom (*Glubinnaia Kniga*, cf. section 1 above).

4. *Magic in agriculture, hunting, and crafts*

The productiveness of the soil depends on sun and moisture,
and because of this, as we have seen (section 2 above) Slavic
agriculture was intimately connected with Slavic mythology—
the Sun-worship and the cult of the Mother Moist Earth.
According to Slavic beliefs, the harvest was the gift of the divine
forces. Man's work alone, however hard, was not sufficient to
secure a good harvest. The deities had to be placated by sacrifices and prayers. The success of every stage in the works of the
agricultural cycle was to be secured by magic and symbolic
rites. Remnants of a number of such rites could be observed in
rural districts of Russia as late as the nineteenth century. In
many places in central Russia, before the sowing, the village
priest with all the parishioners proceeded to the field and sang
a *Te Deum*. This, undoubtedly, is a continuation of an ancient
tradition. In pre-Christian times, on such occasions, heathen
deities were invoked instead of the Christian God. In central
Russia, in the Vladimir region, at the time when rye started
earing, the rite of 'leading the ear' was staged. Young men and
maidens stood in pairs facing each other in two parallel lines.
They then joined hands thus forming a kind of bridge. A small
girl decorated with bright ribbons walked along this bridge.
As she walked, the rear pair ran ahead and became the front
pair. The live bridge was thus constantly moving forward.
When it reached the field, the girl jumped from the 'bridge',

picked a few ears, ran back to the village and put the ears in front of the church. This again must have been a survival of a very old rite. In pre-Christian times the ears must have been brought to the sanctuary of a heathen divinity.

The custom of reserving a few ears for Volos at the time of reaping has been already mentioned (see section 2 above). Several other rites preceded and concluded the reaping and harvesting. The first sheaf was brought to the barn to await the threshing. The last sheaf was solemnly brought to the village, or to the lord of the estate. In some places in Russia and Ukraine, on such occasions, the girl reapers cast lots to elect one of them as the principal of the procession. She was clothed in white and crowned with a wreath of field flowers. Other girls put wreaths, or sickles, on their heads. Each of them bowed three times to the East, and then all of them, forming a long line, marched to the village at the head of the procession.

In his description of Scythia, Herodotus (iv. 5) relates that during the rule of the three sons of the first man who lived in Scythia, 'there fell from the sky four implements, all of gold— a plough, a yoke, a battle-axe, and a drinking cup'. Here we have an old tradition of the divine origin of agricultural tools. Belief in the magic nature of the tools and of weapons were widespread among the old Slavs.[1] The representation of Death with a scythe is universal in European art. In Russian folk-lore, Death, besides the scythe, uses, on various occasions, a sickle or a rake. The plough was used in old Russia in magic rites for the prevention of epidemics and epizootics. Some of the Russian peasants, especially womenfolk, believed in the old times that rinderpest was caused by a witch called 'the Cow's Death'. She was represented as an old woman with a rake instead of fingers. To prevent her entering the village, a magic circle was marked around the village by a light plough (*sokha*). The ceremony was performed during the night. All of the participants were women. No man was admitted. One of the women, preferably a widow, pulled the sokha, with another woman at the handle. Others were armed with scythes and sickles which they swayed constantly in order not to let the witch get inside the

[1] On the magic nature of tools see D. K. Zelenin, 'Magicheskaia funktsiia primitivnykh orudii', *Izvestiia Akademii Nauk, Otdelenie Obshchestvennykh Nauk*, 1931, No. 6, pp. 713–54.

village before the magic circle had been completed. Any living being, be it a man or an animal, happening to appear in the vicinity would be immediately killed by the women of the procession. Sometimes the whole ceremony took place in complete silence. In other cases, appropriate songs were sung.[1] Similar rites were performed at the time of epidemics, especially of cholera.

As regards the use of agricultural tools for their direct purpose —agricultural work—it seems that in the ancient times the Russians believed that each such tool was endowed with supernatural energy of its own. The man only had to let them go. According to an old Russian concept, each man had inalienable rights on the plot of land he tilled as long as he continued to till it.[2] In the old formulas of rights on land, the area of the landed estate was often defined in the words: 'As far as the axe, the scythe, and the plough went.' This is an evidence of the belief that the tools, while wielded by man, play a role of their own in the cultivation of land and in establishing rights on land.

Weapons and implements of hunting were likewise believed to have a magic strength of their own. As regards bow and arrow, which was the old Russian hunter's main implement, there is a characteristic story in the bylina of Ivan Godinovich. The bogatyr of that name kidnaps a princess, fiancée of a Tatar khan. The khan pursues Ivan, overtakes him, and with the help of the princess ties him to an oak tree to be executed at leisure. At that moment two doves appear in the air and admonish the khan not to kill Ivan. The infuriated khan seizes Ivan's bow and arrows and aims at the birds. Ivan prays to his bow and arrows not to serve the khan but to kill the khan instead of the birds. And lo! When the arrow is shot, it reverts to the khan and kills him.[3] We have here the motif of sacred birds and magic arrows. The belief that the arrow could be directed by sorcery was apparently widespread among the hunters, not only among the Russians but among the Finns and Turks as well. It is known

---

[1] N. Poznansky, *Zagovory* (Petrograd, 1917), pp. 313–14; D. Zelenin, *Russische (Ostslavische) Volkskunde* (Berlin and Leipzig, 1927), pp. 66–68.
[2] V. B. Eliashevich, *Istoriia prava pozemelnoi sobstvennosti v Rossii*, i (Paris, 1948), 26–33.
[3] A. F. Gilferding (Hilferding), 'Onezhskie Cyliny', *Sbornik Otdeleniia Russkogo Iazyka i Slovesnosti Akademii Nauk*, xc (1896), 684; B. A. Rybakov, *Remeslo drevnei Rusi* (Moscow, 1948), pp. 286–7.

that the Ostiaks used to bring their best bow to god's sanctuary for blessing. A bow with which several animals had been killed was sacrificed to the gods.[1]

The old Russian hunters had special rites and invocations to secure the success of each of their undertakings. Survivals of these rites could be observed in Russia in the late nineteenth century. A. N. Naumov, a landowner and marshal of nobility of the Samara Province, described in his memoirs a bear hunt which took place on 1 January 1895 in which he participated.[2] Scouting took place in the last two days of December. The hunters (there were fourteen of them) spent the night of 1 January in a hut in the forest. They got up at dawn and were instructed by the master of ceremonies (a Chuvashian) to sit quietly for a while. A gallon bottle of vodka (*shtof*) was put on the table. The master of ceremonies rose first and prayed in front of the icon. The others followed him, prayed to God for the success of the hunt, and made the sign of the cross. After that, each was handed a bowl of vodka which he had to drink making the sign of the cross. No food was served. Naumov comments that it was an exacting performance. Incidentally, the hunt was quite successful. In ancient times, heathen deities or spirits must have been invoked at similar ceremonies instead of Christian saints, and the rite itself was probably more elaborated. Generally speaking, the old rites of hunting were better preserved among the Finnish and Turkish tribes of Russia than among the Russians.

Let us now turn to the magic of the crafts, particularly to those of the art of forging metals and producing weapons and tools. This art was connected with magic from time immemorial. Both the smiths and their tools were looked at with awe. It will be recalled that the heavenly smith Kurdalagon occupied a prominent place in Ossetian folk-lore.[3] The Caucasus was one of the oldest centres of metallurgy, and there cannot be any doubt that this art developed in Russia under the influence of the Caucasian masters.

In many places of the Caucasus, the forge was considered a

---

[1] A. P. Smirnov, 'Ocherki drevnei i srednevekovoi istorii narodov Srednego Povolzhia i Prikamia', *MIAS*, xxviii (1952), 251.

[2] A. N. Naumov, *Iz utselevshikh vospominanii* (New York, 1954), pp. 227–33.

[3] See Chapter 1, section 6, above.

kind of sanctuary, and not only the smith but his assistants as well enjoyed a privileged position in the village. Both sledge-hammer and anvil were sacred objects. In Abkhasia the anvil was used as an altar for the annual prayer service. Oaths were taken in front of the anvil. In Kakhetia every Saturday wax candles were lighted on the anvil; each smith apprentice kneeled and kissed the anvil. In Abkhasia, goats, hens, and wax candles were brought to the anvil as sacrifice. In Samurzakan (a region between Abkhasia and Mingrelia) a belief was widespread that the anvil had a magic healing power.[1] The smith himself was regarded as a healer, and actually, many a smith was an experienced surgeon. It will be recalled that in the Ossetian tale of the Nart Batradz, that bogatyr asked the smith Kurdalagon to temper his body in the heavenly forge. Many a smith combined surgery with the use of medicinal herbs.[2]

In old Russia the smith, likewise, had the reputation for being a magician and a healer. In an old Russian *zagovor* (charm, incantation) both the forge and the sledge are invoked for curing the disease. In the last part of this charm the two patron-saints of the smiths, Kuzma and Demian, are implored to beat the disease with their sledges.[3] (After Russia's conversion to Christianity, two Christian saints, Cosmas and Damien—in collo-quial Russian, Kuzma and Demian—replaced heathen deities as patrons of the smiths).

Tools and weapons produced by the smith had magic powers, as well. The key and the lock were invoked in love charms as well as in charms for the safety of the herds. The lock and the axe also played an important role in the magic rites on the spring St. George's Day (23 April) intended to keep the cattle in good condition during the summer.[4] St. George, as well as St. Blaise and SS. Florus and Laurus, were considered protectors of cattle in Christian Russia. In Russian fairy-tales the smith is often represented as a sorcerer, able to produce magic devices. In the tale of the *Seven Simeons*, one of the seven brothers is a smith. He forges an iron column reaching from the earth to heaven, which enables the brothers to achieve all their aims.

[1] B. E. Degen-Kovalevsky, 'K istorii zheleznogo proizvodstva Zakavkazia', *IGAIMK*, cxx (1935), 376.

[2] Ibid., p. 379.

[3] N. Poznansky, *Zagovory* (Petrograd, 1917), pp. 231–2.

[4] Ibid., p. 239.

The magic nature of weapons, in particular of the sword, has been already mentioned (section 3 above). In Russian folk-lore 'the self-swung sword' (*mech-samosek*), as well as 'the hidden sword' (*mech-kladenets*), is often mentioned. In one of the Russian spiritual songs of the late Middle Ages, that on St. George, the 'self-swung sword', by the saint's order, cuts off the head of the Tatar tsar. The 'hidden sword' is not self-swung, the bogatyr has to wield it, but it is endowed with magic force nevertheless, being much more powerful than an ordinary sword. A number of philologists doubt that the Russian epithet of this sword (*kladenets*) derives from *klad* 'hoard',[1] but whatever is the linguistic origin of the term, the fact is that in Russian fairy-tales this sword is usually represented as hidden under a rock, or under a sacred tree, and the bogatyr's first task—and not an easy one —is to find it.

Survivals of ancient magic rites may be observed in other crafts as well. Suffice it to mention here a few customs connected with the art of spinning and weaving. This was a woman's craft, and it was but natural that its supreme sponsor was a goddess, Mokosh. Women made sacrifices to her, and as late as the sixteenth century one of the questions in the list of questions the priest was supposed to ask his women parishioners at confession was: 'Did you not go to Mokosh?' There was a belief that Mokosh, if satisfied with the woman's oblation, could herself do the woman's work. Stories were told about the mysterious hum of the spindle deep at night when Mokosh was supposed to work. After the conversion to Christianity, St. Paraskeva (identified with Friday, *piatnitsa*; hence called Paraskeva-Piatnitsa) took over Mokosh's functions. Women used to bring to St. Paraskeva's icon the first sheaf of flax as well as samples of their work, such as towels, to be blessed by the priest in the name of the saint.[2]

There were several rites connected with spinning and weaving. In some villages of the Smolensk province the rite of the initiation of the girl to the art of spinning was observed. When

---

[1] See Max Vasmer, *Russisches etymologisches Wörterbuch*, i. 565.

[2] N. F. Lavrov, 'Religiia i tserkov', *Istoriia Kultury drevnei Rusi*, ii. 69. On the veneration of St. Paraskeva-Piatnitsa see A. N. Veselovsky, 'Opyty po istorii razvitiia khristianskoi legendy', *ŽMNP*, clxxxiii (1876), 241–87; clxxxv (1876), 326–67; clxxxix (1877), 186–252; N. V. Malitsky, 'Drevnerusskie Kulty selskokhoziaistvennykh sviatykh po pamiatnikam iskusstva', *IGAIMK*, xi (10) (1932), 5–12.

the girl reached the age of five, she was taught to spin. After she had spun her first thread and had wound it up, it was burned, and the young spinner had to eat the ashes and then a piece of bread.[1] The whole process of spinning and weaving was vividly imitated in its successive stages in an old Russian round dance. Girls only participated in it. The dance consisted of four acts. In Act I the circle of the dancers was severed in one spot. The girl at one side of the break remained standing, while all the others continued moving, so that they gradually wound up around the standing girl. In Act II three girls sat in three different bases forming a triangle as it were; others joined their hands and went around the sitting girls so that two of the sitting ones remained inside the circle, and one outside. In Act III one girl stood inside the circle while each of the others joined hands with her two neighbours. They raised their arms, and the centre girl went round them. Act IV was dedicated to the imitation of the final stage of weaving. The girls stood in pairs, face to face, forming two lines, and joined hands. They represented the warp. At each end of the passageway formed by the two lines stood a girl representing a weaver. One of these brought a small child and handed it to the nearest pair of girls in the passageway. The child was then handed from one pair to another down to the passageway and then back again. The child represented the woof. All through the performance appropriate songs were sung.[2]

5. *The word, the song, and the sacred drama*

The notion of 'word' (*slovo*) is one of the key concepts of the old Slavic culture. In Old Slavic *slovo* had a much wider range of connotations than the English *word* or the French *mot*. The Slavic *slovo* may be rather compared to the Avestan *sravah* 'word', 'doctrine', 'saying', as well as to the Greek *logos* 'word', 'saying', 'tale', 'speech'. According to Liddell-Scott's classical definition, logos is 'the outward form by which the inward thought is expressed and made known; also, the inward thought or reason itself'. Logos is 'the power of mind which is manifested in speech'. This definition of logos is applicable to

---

[1] V. Vsevolodsky (Gerngross), *Istoriia Russkogo teatra*, i (Leningrad and Moscow, 1929), p. 125.

[2] Ibid., pp. 123–5; P. V. Shein, *Velikoruss* (St. Petersburg, 1900), pp. 348–9.

the Old Slavic slovo as well. It may be added that according to
the old Slavic beliefs 'the power of mind' was of divine origin.
Hence the sacred nature of slovo. Close to slovo in its meaning
is the Ossetic *uac* (pronounced 'wats') which means 'word' and
also has the connotation of 'holiness'. Thus, Wac-Illa (Saint
Elias). Ilya Gershevitch states that *uac* denotes both 'word' and
'spirit'.[1]

In Russian folk-lore slovo has sometimes the epithet *zheleznoe*
(iron). In the *Igor Tale* a wise slovo is called 'golden'. The
assumption is that the 'word' is 'coined' ('forged', *vykovyvaetsia*)
—obviously, in the Heavenly Forge. Here we have a connexion
between the idea of the divine origin of slovo and the magic
powers of the Heavenly Smith. In Russian and Ukrainian fairy-
tales we also find evidence of the belief that the smith can forge,
for a man or woman who asks for it, a new voice of any pitch
desired, high or low.

The belief in the magic nature of slovo lay at the basis of the
Old Russian *zagovory* (singular *zagovor* 'charm incantation').
Many of these charms are addressed to celestial bodies or forces
of nature—to sun, moon, stars, dawn, wind, fire, thunder, and
rain. After Russia's conversion to Christianity some of the old
'charms' were adjusted to the new beliefs. In some of them,
Christ, the Holy Virgin, and saints are invoked. However, the
basic part of many charms is very old. Some may be compared
to the ancient Babylonian and Greek magic incantations.[2]

The old Russian charms were used for a wide range of purposes, such as keeping in good health; preventing or curing
diseases; sending a disease or any other curse on an enemy;
provoking love; charming one's tools or weapons for their better
efficiency; evoking rain; and so forth and so on. In fact there
were charms for almost any possible occasion. Besides, charms
constituted an essential part of most of the magic rites used in
agriculture, hunting, and crafts, some of which have been
described in the preceding section (section 4 above).

At the basis of the charm lay the belief that with the help of
proper magic man can induce the spirit or god to fulfil man's
needs and desires; also, that the sacred word is man's most

---

[1] See V. I. Abaev, *Osetinskii iazyk i folklor*, i (Moscow and Leningrad, 1949),
85/6; Ilya Gershevitch, 'Word and Spirit in Ossetic', *BSOAS*, xvii/3 (1955), 478–9.
[2] N. Poznansky, *Zagovory* (Petrograd, 1917), pp. 32–34.

appropriate medium for materializing the power of his mind and his will. A favourite charm formula was that of symbolic parallels. 'As the sun dries the dew, so let love desiccate so-and-so' (this is a love charm). 'As the ore in the entrails of the earth is afraid of the sunshine, so let the blood running from my wound hide itself' (a charm to stop bleeding). It should be noted in this connexion that the Slavic word for 'ore' (*ruda*) has also the connotation of 'blood' (*krov'*). In Old Russian the adjective *rudyi* means 'ruddy'; in Ukrainian the word is still used in the sense of 'red-haired'. In Czech *rudý* means 'red'.

Most of the charms have a special descriptive introduction. Here is an example: 'I, servant of God, so-and-so, shall get up early, bless myself, wash my face with dew, dry it with homespun towel, and turn to the East.' Then follows the practical part of the charm, the statement of one's want. The formula ends: 'Let my words be firm and sticky: let no word be added, none omitted; be my saying firmer than stone and iron.' Or: 'I am locking my words, I am throwing the lock's keys under the burning rock Alatyr''. (According to some scholars 'Alatyr' derives from the Greek word *elektron* 'amber', but there is no consensus of opinion on the origin of the name.)

Some of the charms were purely vocal; others were combined with certain symbolic actions. According to an old formula for curing a sty, the person having the sty has to throw into the fire a few barley grains and say: 'As this barley burns, so let this sty disappear from my eye.' It should be noted that this spell is based on a play of words and therefore is untranslatable. In Russian the word for 'sty' is identical with that of 'barley' (*iachmen'*). Another example of a charm combined with action is a formula for having the cow stand still while she is milked. One has to plane off a few shavings from a stable pillar, to throw them into a pail, and let the cow drink from that pail. While she drinks, one has to recite the charm: 'As this pillar stands firm and does not shake, so let thee, my dear beast, stand and not shake.'

The charm of this type is the nucleus of more elaborate magic rites, as well as of the sacred drama. Like the forms of magic rites in general, the texts of such charms must have originated in the milieu of the magi, the volkhvy. These latter must have thus played an important role in the development of the Old

Slavic language. It is they who must have coined ('forged')
many a word and many a spell.

The charms were scanned rhythmically. The songs connected
with agricultural and other magic rites were sung. Here we are
at the sources of Old Russian rhythmic prose, metrics, and
poetry, in fact at the origin of the whole 'oral literature'(*ustnaia
slovesnost'*) of the Russian people.

In his preface to *Russian Fairy Tales*, Roman Jakobson makes
a sharp distinction between the Old Russian 'written literature'
which 'remained almost entirely subject to the [Christian]
church' and the 'oral literature'.

The old Russian laity [he says] possessed a copious, original, manifold, and highly artistic fiction, but the only medium for its diffusion
was oral transmission. The idea of using letters for secular poetry
was thoroughly alien to the Russian tradition, and the expressive
means of this poetry were inseparable from the oral legacy and oral
traditions.[1]

That peculiar dualism developed in the Kievan period after
Russia's conversion to Christianity and continued through the
Muscovite era. Prior to the Conversion, almost no 'written
literature' existed in Russia except for state purposes, like the
Russo-Byzantine treaties of the tenth century. On the contrary,
'oral literature' thrived from time immemorial. However, that
literature of old cannot be dubbed 'secular' (as Jakobson calls
it) without reservations. Its sources likewise were religious and
magical. The oldest Russian songs are the ritual, and these are
obviously of religious origin.

At that juncture we have to face two complex problems. The
first is that of our sources for the study of 'oral literature'. The
second is that of the 'authors' of this literature.

The 'oral literature' naturally left no ancient texts for our
benefit. We have to depend on late versions of the oral traditions as preserved in the 'folk-lore'. Systematic work of writing
down, and later of phonographically recording the songs and
other forms of Russian 'oral literature', started only at the end
of the eighteenth century. Most of the work was done in the
nineteenth century. Only few specimens of oral literature had
been made available in written form in the earlier periods. It

[1] *Russian Fairy Tales* (New York, 1945), pp. 632–3; G. Vernadsky, *Kievan Russia*
(New Haven, 1948), p. 247.

is true that the folk-singers and reciters always tried to keep the old forms intact, but alterations in the course of time were inevitable.

In his 'Studies in Comparative Slavic Metrics' Roman Jakobson says that:

The romantic conception of folk-poetry as a miraculous shrine preserving survivals from a prehistoric age ultimately provoked a violent reaction. Nearly everywhere in Europe the antiquity and originality of the popular tradition were called in question, and folk-lore came to be regarded as a comparatively recent popularization of the creative work of the upper classes—the *gesunkenes Kulturgut* of the German phrase.[1]

Jakobson takes exception to the extremities of this theory. While recognizing the controversial nature of the problem he does not consider the task of reconstructing the old foundations of folk-lore hopeless. He states that 'we are acquiring methods of penetrating into the prehistoric past more deeply than was once believed possible'. In his opinion, the task may be approached both through comparative linguistics and through a study of musical and literary norms and fixed formulas.

Let us now turn to the problem of the 'authors' of the oral literature. It was often assumed that 'folk-literature' was created by 'the people', and that one cannot speak of any individual authors in this field, but only of 'collective creations'. As a contrast, the theory of the 'sunken cultural wealth' (*gesunkenes Kulturgut*) is based on the assumption that individual creations of the literature of the upper classes were absorbed, in a debased form, by the lower classes. As a matter of fact some such diffusion of culture of the upper classes cannot be denied for recent periods. In Russia it undoubtedly took place in the eighteenth and the nineteenth centuries, in regard to both literature and music. However, the process of the diffusion of the culture of the gentry in imperial Russia was of a peculiar kind, since it had to overcome the contrast between two different types of civilization—the Western and the old Russian. The remnants of the latter survived by that time only among the lower classes. Prior to the beginning of the great cultural and religious schism in Russia in the middle of the seventeenth century, Russian

---

[1] Roman Jakobson, 'Studies in Comparative Slavic Metrics', *OSP*, iii (1952), 21.

culture was much more homogeneous, and consequently the elements of the old culture had a better chance for survival. Because of the magnitude of the cultural contrast in the imperial period between the culture of the gentry and that of the lower classes, the new literary forms, which penetrated into the life of the Russian peasants under the influence of the gentry and city intelligentsia, did not merge with the old forms but constituted a separate intermediary group in the poetry and music of the peasants. The old forms were gradually dying but for a number of decades they kept their ground in remote rural areas, especially in northern Russia.

An earlier stage of a gulf between the cultures of the ruling circles and the masses had been that caused by Russia's conversion to Christianity in the late tenth century. However, as has just been said, Christianity affected chiefly the 'written literature' and not the 'oral literature'. It was only gradually that Christian notions penetrated into the realm of oral literature, and under the thin Christian veneer the old contents were preserved almost intact in many cases.

In view of the religious nature of the main body of ancient Russian 'oral literature', it may be supposed that many of its specimens were created by the volkhvy or by their associates and people about them. Such might have been the origin of many charms, as well as of invocations to gods, hymns, and prayers. The smiths likewise might have been authors of many a charm or of a song.

In the clan cult, the clan elders, not the volkhvy, officiated. The veneration of Rod must have been an important source of what we may call 'clan sacred literature'. The most important events in the life of the members of the clan, such as marriage, birth of children, and death, called for appropriate charms and ritual songs. In the funeral rites the women played the leading role: they were the weepers. In clan husbandry, the works of the agricultural cycle, special incantations and songs were required at every stage. Warfare and military exploits were reflected in epic poetry. This latter was an essential element in spiritual and artistic life at the princely courts.

It must be realized that in most cases the 'authors' of ancient 'oral literature', as well as of music, were at the same time its reciters. The reciters followed the established forms but they always improvised within the framework of the general pattern. Improvisation is a basic principle of the process of folk-creation. Because of this, no sharp dividing line between the 'author' and the performer can be established. In that sense only may we speak of 'collective creation' in the realm of 'oral literature'. The oral literature was created by the artistic élite of each community. The process of creation was facilitated by the homogeneity of the whole spiritual background of the people. The religion of Sun, the cult of the genius of procreation, the veneration of the forces of nature—all that constituted the common spiritual patrimony on which both Life and Art were based. The patterns of ancient literature, and of music, were not imposed on the old Slavs from outside. Those patterns grew out of the old traditions, we may say out of the depth of the soul. They were part of the feelings and mentality of the old Slavs, of their world philosophy.

The song is sung, the word in it is merged with music. The musical aspects of the Russian folk-songs will be dealt with in the following section (section 6 below). Here it would not be amiss to say a few words on the texts of the songs. The importance of the word as a basic element of the song is aptly characterized by an old Russian saying: 'No word can be omitted in the song' (*Iz pesni slova ne vykinesh*). One of the best collections of the texts of Russian folk-songs is P. V. Shein's *Velikoruss*.[1] Among the recent publications, Elsa Mahler's *Die russische Totenklage* and *Altrussische Volkslieder* are of great importance.[2]

It is the consensus of scholarly opinion that the ritual songs represent the oldest stratum in the Russian poetical folk-lore. They can be grouped in three classes: (1) funeral laments; (2) wedding songs; and (3) songs of the celebrations of the successive plays of the sun-cycle.

We may be sure that the lament for the dead was one of the oldest forms of oral literature and that it had originated in the milieu of the clan. In the same time, as Elsa Mahler remarks, it is one of the most tenacious forms of oral tradition, presumably still alive in remote communities in Russia. As an outlet for the most natural feelings, the grief at the death of a beloved mem-

---

[1] P. V. Shein, *Velikoruss* (St. Petersburg, 1900).
[2] Elsa Mahler, *Die russische Totenklage* (Leipzig, 1936); id., *Altrussische Volkslieder* (Basel, 1951).

ber of the family, the dirge, while following a basic old pattern, may be adapted to individual cases in the continuous process of creation of this type of 'folk-lore'.

The dirges accompanied all of the successive stages of the funeral rites. In pre-Christian times many of the Slavs cremated the bodies of their dead.[1] In some communities the ashes of the cremated were kept in the 'house of death', a communal depository.[2] It seems, however, that in the eighth, and the ninth and the tenth centuries, the prevailing custom was to bury the ashes or the body of each deceased in a separate grave. Individual princely graves are specifically mentioned in the Chronography. After their conversion to Christianity, the Russians followed the common practices of the Christian Church and buried the bodies. Funeral services were held at the church whenever possible, though in the Kievan period there were almost no churches in rural districts. The memorial service of the Byzantine rite (called *panikhida* in Russian) was based on funeral chants created by St. John Damascene. These chants belong to the heights of religious poetry. They always were, and still are, deeply appreciated by Russian congregations. The old dirges were not abandoned, but they were chanted outside the church.

All women in a clan, or a village community, were considered born weepers and were expected to take part in the mourning. Naturally, some of them proved more skilful than the others. There was usually at least one woman weeper endowed with an exceptionally good memory and high musical abilities, and in a large community there might be quite a number. These were recognized adepts of the craft. As they aged, they trained the ablest girls of the younger generation. In that way the tradition was kept alive in some localities in north Russia down to the twentieth century. Undoubtedly this process had been going on uninterruptedly from time immemorial.

Not only the members of the family, but the whole clan or the whole community participated in the funerals—'the kith and kin, and the good neighbours, and all the people, all good

[1] On the different funeral rites among the Slavs see Iu. V. Gotie, *Zheleznyi Vek v Vostochnoi Evrope* (Moscow, 1930), pp. 239–45; Tadeusz Lewicki, 'Obrzędy pogrzebowe pogańskich Słowian w opisach podróżnikow i pisarzy arabskich', *Archeologia*, v (1952–3; published in 1955), 122–54; French and Russian resumés, 437–8.

[2] See Chapter 3, section 5, above.

men', as an old saying puts it. The wailing rites began at the moment of death. When the body had been washed, covered with a shroud, and put on a bier, the lament took the form of questions addressed to the deceased: 'Where art thou going?' And the weeper answered for the deceased: 'To the ardent sun, to the moon, to the stars innumerable.' Then the widow of the deceased bewailed her fate. 'There is now no ploughman in our fields any more, no mower in our meadows, no fisher in our lake.' She then asked the neighbours to help her and her children. Special laments were chanted at the moment when the coffin was lowered into the grave, at the return from the funeral, and on entering the house. Additional wailing rites were performed at the grave for at least forty days. The grave of the deceased relative remained a sacred place for the Russian and his family. Psychologically, this attitude represented the continuation of the ancient traditions of the ancestral cult. Every year, on Monday or Tuesday of St. Thomas week (i.e. the week following Easter week) the relatives were supposed to visit the grave and to bring Easter eggs for the deceased. The Easter eggs may seem evidence of the influence of Christianity, but the egg is an ancient symbol of revival. The custom of visiting the grave at that time of year and offering food to the deceased is undoubtedly a pre-Christian one. The day was known as *Radunitsa*. According to the noted Ukrainian philologist Potebnia, the word derives from the same stem as *rod*.[1]

There were different forms of dirges depending on the occasion. There were widow's laments for her deceased husband, and vice versa; daughter's or son's laments for her or his deceased father or mother; and parents' laments for children. It should be noted that the weeping for the wife was in most cases performed not by her husband but by a female relative. There were special dirges to be chanted at the grave urging the deceased to awake and to come back to life. Here is an example of such an exhortation to the deceased mother which was recorded by Elsa Mahler in the Pechory district of the Pskov region in 1937:

> Blow, you violent winds,
> Split open, O Mother Earth!
> Split open, O coffin planks!

[1] See M. Vasmer, *Russisches Etymologisches Wörterbuch*, ii. 483.

> Awake and rise up, my dear mother,
> Let us sit at the moist grave,
> Let us talk through the whole dark night.

In some laments, man's death is likened to the sunset, or to the dying of a tree for the winter. Here we have the same set of notions as in the rites of the sun cycle.

When the family and kin returned home after the burial, a memorial banquet was served. It consisted of a kind of wheat pudding (in modern times usually rice pudding with raisins), compote of dried fruits, and wheat pancakes. Seats were reserved at the table for the deceased. The women weepers chanted special dirges, turning in the direction of the cemetery.

In some of the north Russian laments we find examples of the daughter addressing her deceased mother or father (as the occasion might have been), and offering her (or him) a drink.

> O mother, my own,
> Do thou deign accept
> A glass of strong beer,
> A bowl of green wine,
> From me, poor orphan,
> For thee.[1]

The memorial banquet had been an old institution among many peoples.[2] The Old Slavic word for it was *strava*. It will be recalled that the funeral banquet for Attila was so called.[3] In the Kievan period the memorial banquet was known as *trizna*.

In the old times the body of the deceased was conveyed to the grave not in a cart, but in a sledge (even in summer). According to the Chronography, when Prince Vladimir the Saint died in 1015, his attendants placed his body upon a sledge and then brought it to Kiev and 'laid it in the Church of the Virgin that Vladimir himself built'. When, on 20 May 1072, the relics of the prince-martyrs, SS. Boris and Gleb, were transported to the new church erected in their honour in Vyshgorod, near Kiev, 'they took Gleb in a stone coffin and laid it upon a sled, which they pulled along by means of ropes attached to it'. In his

---

[1] E. V. Barsov, *Prichitaniia Severnogo kraia*, i (Moscow, 1862), 79; E. Mahler, *Die russische Totenklage* (Leipzig, 1935), p. 667.

[2] On the Ossetian funeral banquet see Chapter 1, section 2, above.

[3] See Chapter 2, section 4, above.

'Testament' Prince Vladimir Monomakh of Kiev (d. 1125) uses the expression 'to sit upon the sledge' in the sense of 'to be about to die'.

The use of the sledge at the funerals was an old rite, known also in ancient Egypt. 'Sledge' in Russian is *sani*, a plural form. The singular *san'*, is not used in Modern Russian; in Old Russian it meant both the 'runner' of the sledge and 'snake'. Veneration of the snake was widespread from the very earliest times among many peoples, including the Slavs and the Lithuanians. The snake was a symbol of death and of rebirth. In Macedonia a special death and rebirth dance was performed. The leader of the dance held a snake, or more often the effigy of a snake, in his hand.[1] Yury Arbatsky saw live snakes so used. According to him, the name of the dance is *smrtno kolo* ('death round dance'), but this appellation is taboo. Even the substitute name, *bezimeno* ('anonymous'), is only pronounced unwillingly.[2] Reminiscences of the death dance survived in Podolia until the nineteenth century. According to this custom, observed in the village Sokol, when the father or mother died and his or her body was put on the bier, the children, joining hands and singing, danced three times around the house.[3] No snake was mentioned on this occasion.

When a prominent leader—a hero—died, memorial services for him assumed a tribal, or we may say, a national character. In many cases, the lament for a dead hero proved the nucleus for an epic poem or poems about him. In that case the funeral dirge would become the source of an epos.

According to the Chronography, when Prince Oleg of Kiev died in 912, 'All the people mourned for him in great grief. His tomb stands there [on the hill where he was buried] to this day, and it is called the Tomb of Oleg.' It is presumably from the funeral dirges for Oleg that a cycle of epic poems about him was created. Later, excerpts from these poems were inserted into the Chronography. When Prince Igor of Kiev was killed by the rebellious Drevliane (945), his widow Olga went to the place where he was buried and there 'wept for her husband'. The

[1] J. Kunst, 'Cultural Relations between the Balkans and Indonesia', *Royal Tropical Institute, Mededeling CVII, Afdeling Culturele en Physische Anthropologie*, No. 47 (Amsterdam, 1954), p. 11, fig. 56.

[2] Ibid., p. 11.

[3] E. Mahler, *Die russische Totenklage*, p. 118.

chronicler describes in detail the stratagems she used for defeating the Drevliane and avenging Igor's death. In this case, again, the chronicler must have used the epic tales which grew out of Olga's lament for her husband and of the memories of her revenge. We may be sure that both the dirges for the dead hero and epic poems in his memory had been composed by the Slavs in ancient times as well. A lament for Attila is known in Latin translation. Franz Altheim believes that the original dirge was in Turkic.[1] In view of the fact that the funeral banquet for Attila is mentioned in a Latin text under the Slavic term for such occasions, I am inclined to think that there also existed a Slavic lament for Attila.

Of course, not all of the epic literature grew out of the funeral dirge. This was only one of its sources. In the Russian literature of the Kievan period we find evidence of epic poems composed during the hero's life. Thus we know that there was a poem on Prince Mstislav of Tmutorokan, the son of Vladimir the Saint, and on his duel with the 'Kosogian Prince Rededya', who was actually the Alanic bogatyr Iry Dada, 'Father of the Iron', i.e. the Ossetians (1022). Boyan's poem of the duel between Mstislav and 'Rededya' is mentioned in the *Igor Tale*. There is also a description of the duel in the Chronography. Recently, Dzambulat Dzanty has made available the text of an Ossetian tale on the same theme, *Iry Dada* which he wrote down as he heard it from the old Ossetian reciter, Khulyx, in 1910.[2] Thus, it is now possible to study the interrelations between the Russian and the Alanic epos.

Another example of an epic poem on a living hero is the famous *Igor Tale* itself, in which Prince Igor's unsuccessful raid on the Polovtsy in 1185 is described. Here again we have the story of the events recorded in the chronicles, in this case the Kievan Chronicle.

There cannot be any doubt that poems on living heroes were also popular among the Slavs in ancient times. Not all of them were composed by professional reciters. As was the case in the Alanic society, the notion of 'valour' (Alanic *æxsar*, Greek *arete*) played an important role among the Slavic chieftains of old

---

[1] Franz Altheim, *Attila und die Hunnen* (Baden-Baden, 1951), pp. 146–52.
[2] G. Vernadsky and D. Dzanty, 'The Ossetian Tale of Iry Dada and Mstislav', *Journal of American Folklore*, lxix (1956), 216–35.

(Menander's 'archons' of the Antes). The Old Slavic word for 'valour' is *doblest'*. In the Old Russian epos, the word *buest'* ('daring') was used in approximately the same sense. As we know, the old code of valour also included the duty of revenge for the murder of or offence against any member of the clan or family (cf. Princess Olga's revenge). Each outstanding deed of an 'archon', or of any member of the clan, served to strengthen the morale of the whole clan. It was not, or at least not only, the desire to boast that induced the hero to tell his comrades about his exploits. In a sense, it was his duty to do so. It was this competition in valour which enabled the clan to keep up its glorious traditions. On that basis, we may suppose that many an epic poem of old was composed and recited by the hero himself.

Poems on historical characters were the foundation for popular epic fiction—the *stariny* (conventionally called 'byliny') in which the valiant knights (*bogatyri*) were glorified. As has been mentioned (see section 2 above), an actual historical character, the prince-sorcerer Vseslav of Polotsk, served as the prototype for the epic bogatyr Volkh Vseslavich. In certain cases, traits of two or more historical characters were combined in an image of a bylina hero. Presumably the roots of epic fiction of this kind go deep into the past. In pre-Christian times, mythological themes have been mixed with tales of human heroes, as they are in the Ossetian legends of the Narts. Traces of such themes may be discerned in some of the Russian byliny of the Kievan period.

Let us now turn to what may be called the theatrical element in old Russian culture. Through the traditional folk-rites, the main events in the course of the life-cycle of works of any person, as well as of a clan, were permeated with histrionics. Consider the ritual of the funerals, for example. From the moment of death, an elaborate course of rites and of songs was followed, down to the interment, or in ancient times to the cremation. Each funeral was a drama, but performed in actual life, not on the stage.

Likewise, the cycle of the old Russian wedding ceremonies, even as late as the nineteenth century, amounted to a play in which not only the bridegroom and the fiancée but the kith and kin and the 'good neighbours' participated, each man and woman having to perform a part of his or her own. Characteristically, Russian peasants, even in recent years, when referring to a wedding used to say 'to play a wedding' (*igrat' svad'bu*). The cycle consisted of several acts, beginning with the coming of the kinsmen of the bridegroom to the house of the father of the fiancée, usually at night, as the old ritual required. The performance lasted for several days in the homes of the relatives of each side in turn. A variety of songs was an essential feature of the ceremonies, special songs being considered proper for each day and each stage of the occasion. At the early stages, the fiancée was expected to lament the loss of her girlhood freedom, as well as the parting with her parents. At the betrothal, the women of her family lamented over her, bewailing her impending departure to 'the land of strangers'. When they had finished, the fiancée herself would begin to sing sadly:

> No leisure have I to be sitting here,
> To be talking and chattering.
> The season for works has come,
> The mowing time and the haymaking.

[Ralston's translation here and in the following verses.]

A dramatic moment was the unplaiting of the fiancée's braid. The fiancée laments:

> O my plait, my plaiting,
> My dear plait,
> Ruddy and golden!

The assisting girls replied:

> Early is it to unplait thee,
> And for the long journey,
> The long one to prepare thee.

When the fiancée's tresses had been combed out, she sang.

> Not for gold do I mourn,
> Nor mourn I for bright silver.
> For one thing only do I mourn,
> For the maiden beauty
> Of my ruddy braid.

If the fiancée was an orphan, she expressed her grief at the thought that she had no parent to bid her God-speed on her

new path of life, but she asked the departed parents to bestow
a blessing on her in any case:

> Split open, O Mother Moist Earth,
> Fly asunder ye coffin-planks!
> Unroll, O brocade of gold!
> And do thou rise up, O father!
> Say farewell, and give me thy blessing.

It will be noticed that the theme of this exhortation is very similar to that of some of the funeral dirges.

There were also many theatrical elements in the rites connected with agriculture and crafts (see section 4 above). Some
of these rites, as, for example, that of the 'leading the ear' and
the imitation of the process of spinning and weaving, amounted
each to a short play. In the festivities of the sun-cycle (see section 2 above) remnants of magic performances and in some
cases of the sacred drama are even more obvious.

Performances of fragments of the sacred dramas of old could
be observed in remote rural districts of Russia as late as the
early twentieth century. By that time the exact meaning of the
ceremonies was not any more understood either by the actors
or by the audience. It was believed, nevertheless, that the rites
were needed to secure the fertility of the soil and to obtain a
good harvest.

The horse and the goat played an important part in these
rites. Both of them are sun-animals (see section 2 above). The
late N. N. Evreinov was present at performances of plays of both
types. In a village of the Spassk district of Tambov Province,
Evreinov saw a play in which the horse was the central figure.
The time was late spring, soon after Radunitsa (no exact date
is given by Evreinov in this case). The play was apparently
part of the 'Rusalia' cycle; it was called 'Parting with the
rusalka' (*Provody rusalki*) but no rusalka appeared. The performance took place at sunset on the fringes of a forest. The
spectators stood in a semicircle facing the forest. The horse was
represented by two young men placed one behind the other
and covered by burlap. The one at the front held a pole on the
top of which an effigy of the horse's head was fixed. Mane and
tail were made of hemp. The 'horse' emerged from the forest,
being led by an old man whose face was blackened with soot.

He was called the 'Gipsy'. When the 'horse' had entered the
semicircle of the spectators, a small boy was put on its 'back'.
A musician played gay tunes on an accordion, and the 'horse'
began to dance but soon fell on the ground. The 'Gipsy' succeeded in 'reviving' it, and it 'galloped' back to the forest. Then
the girls among the audience sang a song in which they expressed their hope that spring will come back again.[1]

It should be noted that this performance took place at the
time of Radunitsa, and that Radunitsa was the day for the
commemoration of the dead. In view of this we may think that
the play Evreinov saw was a fragment of the sacred drama of a
phase of the sun-cycle representing death and future rebirth.
In the art of the Alanic-Tokharian sphere, to which the old
Slavic art belonged, we find especially on embroideries a
symbolic representation of the ride of the souls of the departed
on horseback (or on a deer). The souls are represented either as
birds or as human figures.[2]

In December 1915 Evreinov attended, in the village of
Babino, near Bobruisk, Belorussia, the goat play. This was part
of the winter solstice festivities, of the Koliada cycle. In the
centre of the procession walked an old man (*ded* 'grandfather')
with a staff in his hand. He led a 'goat'. The latter was imperso-
nated by a boy clad in a goat-skin. He wore a mask made of
birch and pine bark, representing a goat's head. The horns were
made of straw and the beard of flax. The other characters were
two 'gipsies' represented by girls in men's clothes. Their faces
were blackened with soot. Singers and musicians followed suit.

The essence of the drama, as in that with the horse, was the
sudden death of the goat and its revival. When the 'goat' fell
'dead' on the ground, the actors feigned dismay. Then the
chorus advised the 'grandfather' to press the goat's 'vein'. By
that the organ of copulation was meant. The 'grandfather' did
as he had been told, and the 'goat' rose up and began to dance.
The audience rejoiced.[3]

While the performance of this type was a rare occasion in
modern Russia, the 'goat' was a common character in the
Yuletide masquarades in many a Russian home. In these

[1] N. N. Evreinov, *Istoriia Russkogo teatra* (New York, 1955), pp. 35–36.
[2] J. Kunst, 'Cultural Relations', figs. 35, 39, 51, 63.
[3] N. N. Evreinov, *Istoriia Russkogo teatra*, pp. 29–32.

mostly the youth and children participated. In some villages special songs were sung on such occasions in which the goat appeared as a symbol of the fertility of the soil. The Russian word for 'goat-song' is *kozloglasie*. This corresponds exactly to the Greek *tragoidia*.

Evreinov compares the fragment of the sacred drama he saw in Belorussia in 1915 with the rustic Dionysia of Ancient Greece as described briefly by Plutarch in his essay 'Of the Love of Wealth'. Evreinov likens the 'grandfather' of the Russian play to the priest of the Greek Dionysia, and the 'gipsies' to the phallophori. The latter's faces were blackened too.

Dionysiac elements in the old Slavic sacred drama could have originated independently of the Greek Dionysia. However, a possibility of some influence of the Bacchanalia on the old Slavs is not excluded. It will be recalled that in the Scythian era, there were a number of Greek cities on the north Pontic shore. Besides, there existed a Greek settlement deep in Scythia itself. In his description of Scythia, Herodotus mentions, among other non-Scythian tribes, the Budini. These might have been Slavs.[1] According to Herodotus (iv. 108), there is a city in the land of the Budini

called Gelonus, which is surrounded with a lofty wall, thirty furlongs each way, built entirely of wood. All the houses of the place and all the temples are of the same material. Here are temples built in honour of the Grecian gods, and adorned after the Greek fashion with images, altars, and shrines, all in wood. There is even a festival, held every third year in honour of Dionysus, at which the people fall into the Bacchic fury. For the fact is that the Geloni were anciently Greeks, who, being driven out of the factories along the coast, fled to the Budini and took up their abodes with them. They still speak a language half Greek, half Scythian.

6. *Music*

The music of the old Slavs was a branch of an ancient musical culture which originated in the 'pre-historic' era and thrived in a vast area stretching from Scotland to Indonesia. Musical instruments almost identical with those of the Slavs were used (and in some cases are still used) by a number of Lithuanian, Finnish, and Turkish peoples, as well as in Indonesia in the east,

[1] See Chapter 2, section 2, above.

and in Scandinavia, southern Holland, Scotland, the Alps, and the Pyrenees, in the west. Most of the old instruments found, or represented on wall paintings and art objects, among the Greco-Scythian antiquities of the north Pontic area, belong to the cultures of the Middle East and Egypt of the third and second millenniums B.C. Old melodies of Russian folk-songs, especially of the funeral laments, are related to the same musical systems as those preserved in the Balkans. The musical system of the Montenegrian folk-singer T. Vucić, studied by Gerhard Gesemann and Gustav Becking, seems to be a product of pre-Homeric epoch.[1] It may be added that elements of Hebrew music were discovered by Yury Arbatsky in Albania in the 1930's, among the remnants of three small Balkan nomadic tribes—Birko, Bejdbejta, and Djoj (now almost extinct). The religious practices of these tribesmen seem to have been related to Judaism.[2] It should also be noted that in some of the Russian byliny, 'Jerusalem melodies' are mentioned.

According to Arbatsky, the Balkan nomadic tribes, whose music he studied, believed in the divine origin of music, as well as in that of singing and dancing. This belief must have been part of the philosophy of all the ancient Slavs, in fact of all the peoples whose spiritual and musical background was similar to that of the old Slavs. This aspect of the old Slavic world-philosophy may be best defined as the worship of the Holy Spirit ('Holy Wind'), closely connected with Sun-worship (see section 2 above). It follows that the sources of the old Slavic music were religious and magical. Music was an important element in charm incantations, conjurations, and magic rites. Through ecstasy, music was a basic element in prophetic inspiration.

In the same way as we have seen in their attitude towards weapons and tools (section 4 above), the Slavs believed in the magic nature of musical instruments. For the Slavs, the musical

---

[1] Gerhard Gesemann, 'Ueber jugoslavische Volksmusik oder zur Wahrung des kulturellen Ansehens von der Welt', *Slawische Rundschau*, iii (1931); Gustav Becking, 'Der musikalische Bau der montenegrinischen Volkslor', *Archives Néerlandaise de Phonétique expérimentale* (Amsterdam, 1933); Y. Arbatsky, *Etiudy po istorii Russkoi muzyki*, p. 142.

[2] Y. Arbatsky, *The Roga, a Balkan Bagpipe, and its Medico-Magical Conjurations* (read at the Annual Meeting of the American Musicological Society, 1953, mimeographed).

instrument was alive and could work by itself. The musician's task in playing the instrument was only that of letting the instrument go and of revealing the divine music. Of course, the musician himself must be initiated into the mysteries of the craft. In the *Igor Tale*, it is said that the poet Boyan 'laid his own magic fingers upon the living strings [of the zither] and they would of themselves sound forth the glory of the princes'. We have here two notions intimately connected: the magic fingers of the musician and the living strings of the instrument, i.e. Divinity and Matter.

As regards the sacred nature of musical instruments, the spiritual head (Ava) of the above-mentioned Balkan nomadic tribes used the *roga* (a kind of bagpipe) for medico-magical conjurations. On the chanter of his roga, the *girana* (a symbol whose meaning was taboo) was branded. The upper part of it represented the snake symbol (*naga*). The snake symbol was used in the Balkans for, among other things, warding off vampires.[1] The roga might not be called by name during the full moon. Instead, an old Slavic phrase *sosud slovesa neizrečena* ('container of the inexpressible word') was used.[2]

In medieval Russia there existed companies of musicians and actors known as *skomorokhi*.[3] They must have preserved many an old tradition, but they also introduced some new elements from Byzantium, the Near East, and western Europe. In earlier times, sacred musical traditions were kept alive among the Slavs by the élite of the initiated. In view of the magic meaning of music, it is but natural that the musicians were associated with the conjurers, the healers, and the smiths. Of such type is the 'concealed concord' Arbatsky came in contact with in Albania.[4] The fraternity centred around the monastery of St. Ion Vladimir, near Elbasan in Albania.[5] Presumably such secret fraternities existed in ancient Russia as well. It is through them that the *Books of Deep Wisdom* (*Glubinnye Knigi*) might have found its way to Russia.

---

[1] There is a drawing of the girana symbol in Arbatsky, *Roga*, p. 5, and a picture of the Naga symbol in Kunst, 'Cultural Relations', p. 12.

[2] See Y. Arbatsky, *The Roga*, p. 3.

[3] On the *skomorokhi* see N. Findeizen (Findeisen), *Ocherki po istorii muzyki v Rossii*, i (Moscow and Leningrad, 1928), 145–70.

[4] See section 3 above; also J. Kunst, 'Cultural Relations', p. 11.

[5] Y. Arbatsky, *The Roga*, p. 3.

Of musical instruments used in Scythia we know from both written sources and archaeological evidence. Plutarch (*Concerning Music*, 14) relates that 'the sacred presents of the Hyperboreans were sent of old to Delos, attended with the auli, the syringes, and the kitharae'. (The aulos is the double oboe; syrinx, in this case, Pan-pipe; kithara, a kind of lyre.) In his 'Glossary' (*Onomasticon*, iv. 60 and 76) Julius Polydeuces, who lived in the second century of our era, ascribes to the Scythians the invention of the pentachord. He also says that the Scythians, as well as the Androphagoi, the Melanchlaeni, and the Arimaspi, sound the hollow bones of eagles and kites using them as flutes. Martinus Capella, who wrote in the fifth century an encyclopaedia of the Seven Arts under the title 'Of the Nuptials of Philolology and Mercury' (ix. 925), states that the Amazons exercised in military art to the tunes of the reed-pipe (*calamus*).

As regards archaeological data, a fragment of an aulos made of beech tree was found near Kerch in 1830. In the barrow at Sakhnovka, Kiev region, a golden plaque was excavated on which a Scythian playing the lyre is represented. Among other musical instruments in the north Pontic area of which we know from archaeological evidence, are the horns, shell-trumpets, trigonons (harps), Pan-pipes, lutes, and zithers.

Musical instruments of all these types were known to the Slavs and used by them. The bone-flute (tibia) is still used among the Balkan peoples. The Albanian mountaineers of the Shala tribe sound the bone-flute at the burials as well as at the phallic dances. While the flute is a symbol of the male element, the shell-trumpet is that of the female. Among the Greeks of the southernmost Peloponnese (the promontory between the gulf of Messena and the gulf of Laconia) the flute and the shell-trumpet are sounded simultaneously during the weddings. On such occasions, the free end of the flute is to be inserted into the mouth of the shell. The shell-trumpet is also used ritually in the case of women who have conceived for the first time. Such a woman has to perform a special dance to the tune of the shell-trumpet.[1]

The horn made of tree-bark, like the shell-trumpet, originated during the stone age. Its various derivations were used in Russia—medieval and modern—by herders and shepherds.

[1] Id., *Etiudy po istorii russkoi muzyki*, p. 37.

The size of these horns varies from 30 centimetres to 1 metre. Aurochs horns were used for religious ceremonies in Slavic temples, and also in war. Such horns often were silver-mounted with incrustations and elaborate ornamentation. A horn of this type of the Scythian period was found near Simferopol in the Crimea. Two horns of a later period (the tenth century) were excavated near Chernigov.[1] As has been said (see sections 1 and 2 above), horns were also used as ritual vessels.

Like the Hebrew *shofar*, the Slavic horn was supposed to have magic power. It was believed that its mighty sound could affect the forces of nature (consider the story of the capture of Jericho in the Bible). In the Russian bylina of the bogatyr Vasili Okulevich, it is said that when Vasili sounded his horn for the first time, high mountains were shaken. When he sounded it for the second time, dark forests fell down. When he sounded it for the third time, a tempest started over the sea.

Another musical instrument is the *zhaleika*, a kind of clarinet made either of reed or of tree-bark. It also occurs in the form of a double clarinet. Curt Sachs found a representation of a similar double-clarinet on an Egyptian bas-relief dated 2700 B.C.[2] Like the flute, the zhaleika was originally an instrument of musical magic, never merely of entertainment.

In musicological literature the zhaleika is often confused with the *brelka*. The latter is widespread in Russia. Brelka also belongs to the clarinet type but is made of tree-bark, and the bell, according to an old tradition, has to be made of horn.[3]

Several string instruments, such as the lyre, zither, lute, and trigonon, were used by the Slavs. In old Russia the generic name for most of these instruments was *gusli*. It should be mentioned in this connexion that the terminology of the old Russian instruments was not stable, and the same name was used in various periods and by various authors for different types of instruments. The name *svirel*, for example, was applied to the double oboe (aulos), as well as to the flutes and to clarinets of various kinds.[4] We really do not know what kind of string instrument Boyan played (a kind of zither?) except that it

---

[1] See Count I. I. Tolstoy and N. P. Kondakov, *Russkie drevnosti* (St. Petersburg, 1889–99, 6 vols.), v, figs. 10–15.

[2] See Y. Arbatsky, *Etiudy po istorii russkoi muzyki*, p. 40.

[3] Ibid., pp. 39–40 and 44.

[4] Ibid., pp. 46–47, 125–128.

had ten strings. The Ossetian zither of old (*fændyr*) had twelve strings.

The early type of fiddle (in old Russian *gudok*) was brought to western Europe from central Asia around the ninth century. Presumably it appeared in Russia about the same time. In any case, it is much younger than the instruments mentioned before. The tambourine (in Russian, *bubny*) and the kettledrum (*nakra*) seem to have penetrated into Russia from the Near East at about the same time as the gudok.

As Arbatsky aptly remarks, one of the primary characteristics of the musical culture, to which the old Slavic music belongs, is

variability within a pattern; and the very vitality of the music is a result of the principle of improvisation. A folk-artist will never repeat the same song in the same manner: on the contrary, he will strive for variety. It is easy, however, to recognize that a certain fundamental form is repeated and that the musician follows a scheme of his mind which he elaborates quite consciously. It must be remembered that folk music is organically living and that it rises out of more or less fixed musical schemes which must be newly shaped and composed while performed.[1]

The archaic musical systems, to which the most ancient Russian songs belong, are based on microtone, that is one step shorter than semitone. Remnants of Slavic microtonic songs are very rare. However, some of the dirges of the Chernigov region and of north Russia are based on microtone. Besides, microtonic elements are used in some Russian songs for a kind of 'chromatic' treatment of the pentatonic formations.[2]

The Russian folk-song was studied, in its musical aspects, by a number of ethnographers and musicologists. Outstanding among them were Paul Iakushkin (1820–72), whose musical notes unfortunately perished in a fire; Julius Melgunov (1846–93); Eugenia Lineva (1854–1919),[3] and Alexander Kastalsky (1856–1926).[4] Of great importance is Yury Arbatsky's work, 'Studies in the History of Russian Music' (*Etiudy*) (1956).

The Russian song is polyphonic. Russian folk-polyphony

[1] Id., *Beating the Tupan in the Central Balkans* (Chicago, 1953), p. 5.
[2] Id., *Etiudy po istorii russkoi muzyki*, pp. 77–78.
[3] E. Lineva, *Velikorusskie pesni v narodnoi garmonizatsii* (St. Petersburg, 1904–9, 2 vols.); id., *Ukrainskie pesni v narodnoi garmonizatsii* (Moscow, 1902).
[4] A. Kastalsky, *Osobennosti narodno-russkoi muzykalnoi systemy* (Moscow and Petrograd, 1923).

represents a musical system of great vitality with its own peculiar methods and devices. The song is begun by the chanter,
who carries on the main theme. Around that main theme other
singers improvise a system of *podgoloski* (singular *podgolosok*,
'co-ordinate voice', i.e. 'subordinated melody'). Each podgolosok is a variant of the main melody; the variant is, however,
so close to the main melody that, were it performed separately,
it would give a clear idea of the song. Thus, the system of
podgoloski presents a simultaneous collective elaboration of a
given melodic model. In the course of the performance, some
of the 'co-ordinate voices' would drop their particular part
and join another part; other voices would add a new variant.
Thus, a varied number of podgoloski (from two to five) co-
operate spontaneously with the main 'voice'.

The technique of the performance of Russian songs has been
accurately and vividly described by Lineva on the basis of her
intense studies and her personal contacts with folk-singers. Bio-
graphical sketches of some of the outstanding Russian folk-
singers may be found in Lineva's works, as well as in the works
of other ethnographers and musicologists. Most of these singers
were uneducated, from the contemporary point of view, and
some of them illiterate. One of the famous 'weepers' of north
Russia, Irene Fedosova, told the noted student of Russian folk-
lore E. V. Barsov in the 1860's: 'I am not literate through letters, but instead I have the power of mind' (*Ia gramotoi ne gra-
motna, zato pamiatiu ia pamiatna*).[1] It should be noted that in
Russian folk-speech 'memory' (*pamiat'*) is synonymous with
'mind' and 'knowledge'. In western Macedonia they used to
speak of a man with a keen intellect and memory as of one 'who
remembers knowledge' (*pamecu pamjatan*).[2]

Like Fedosova, most of the outstanding Russian folk-singers
were endowed with exceptional memory, and, of course, with
high musical abilities. They were, undoubtedly, great artists.
But each folk-singer capable of improvising the podgoloski was
obviously an artist in his or her own right. They all belonged

[1] E. V. Barsov, *Prichitaniia severnogo kraia*, i (Moscow, 1862), 315.
[2] Y. Arbatsky's communication to me. See also Y. Arbatsky, *Etiudy po istorii
russkoi muzyki*, p. 106. It would not be amiss to compare the interrelation of Slavic
notions of 'memory' (*pamiat'*) and 'mind' (*um*) with that in English. The first
definition of 'mind' in Webster is 'memory' (or 'power of remembering or recognizing').

to the same milieu and were permeated with the same traditions. Theirs was teamwork in the best sense of the word.

By its nature, Russian folk-polyphony may be compared in
many respects with the polyphonic system of medieval Europe.
It belongs to the so-called 'horizontal' tone structure as opposed
to the 'vertical' (harmonic) chord-structure of modern Western
music. Paul Bekker[1] compares the horizontal tone-structure to
the republic and the vertical to the monarchy, since in the former all parts (in Russian folk-songs, the podgoloski) are independently active; and in the latter, most of the voices are
subordinated to the leading voice.

7. Fine arts

Sixty years ago the great Russian archaeologist N. P. Kondakov, discussing the problem of the origins of the early Russian
art, stated that 'Until recently we knew nothing of the
Russian antiquities hoarded in the burrows. . . . Now the Russian
museums are being filled with ample collections of antiquities
coming in from every part of Russia. These antiquities await
the attention of investigators who will have to reveal the picture
of varied cultural life of the early tribes of Russia'.[2] Kondakov
meant, in this statement, the antiquities of the Russian tribes
as well as those of the Finnish and Turkish tribes closely connected with the Russians in contrast to the classical and
Scythian antiquities which had attracted the interest of the
archaeologists much earlier.

After 1890 the work of excavating and collecting Russian
antiquities, as well as that of studying them, progressed rapidly.
Kondakov himself took an active part in these studies. Among
other outstanding workers in this field V. A. Gorodtsov, A. A.
Spitsyn, and V. V. Khvoiko may be mentioned here. The latter
was an amateur but nevertheless succeeded in making important discoveries. During the period of the First World War and
the civil war in Russia (1914–22) systematic archaeological
work became impossible. After that, however, it was not only
resumed, but even better co-ordinated. The technique of excavations was improved, and a number of modern methods of
study and analysis of antiquities were introduced. On the

[1] Quoted by Y. Arbatsky, *Etiudy po istorii russkoi muzyki*, pp. 100–1.
[2] Count I. I. Tolstoy and N. P. Kondakov, *Russkie Drevnosti*, v (1897), 1–2.

negative side, the political terror of the 1930's resulted in deci-
mating the ranks of Russian archaeologists, many of whom were
imprisoned or exiled.[1] In the 1940's archaeological researches
were greatly expanded. Among the prominent Russian archaeologists of this period, M. I. Artamonov, A. V. Artsikhovsky,
B. A. Rybakov, S. P. Tolstov, and P. N. Tretiakov may be
named here. Tolstov directed the archaeological excavations in
Khorezm which achieved results of great significance. The
other four concentrated their attention on Russian antiquities
proper.

Owing to the intensive archaeological research of the last
sixty years, and especially that of the last decade, a new picture
of early Russian art and life has emerged. What could have
been only surmised thirty years ago, is now being revealed. Of
course, there are still many gaps in our knowledge of old Russia,
and the validity of the interpretation of the meaning of many a
find given by the authors, or editors, of recent Russian works,
may be questioned in some cases, but this does not undermine
the primary importance of the finds themselves.

One of the significant results of recent archaeological research in Russia is that the gulf between the art of the Scytho-
Alanic era and that of early Russia is gradually being filled.
Many a problem in the history of Slavic art and its relation to
the development of oriental and western art can now be approached from a new angle and in a new way.

As a result of a series of migrations, both the animal style and
the geometric style of the Alanic-Tokharian sphere[2] spread
westward and were reflected in the early medieval antiquities of
Hungary, the Balkans, Italy, Germany, France, and Spain, as
well as those of the British Isles and Scandinavia. Fantastic
figures of entwined animals and the use of the plait motif are
among the characteristic traits of the Scandinavian art. Similar
traits occur in the early Slavic art. Can it be said on that ground
that Slavic art originated in Scandinavia? Kondakov doubted
it. 'The Scandinavians', he said, 'themselves borrowed much
from the south, through the intermediary of the Slavs, if not
solely from them.'[3] The noted Austrian art historian Josef

---

[1] See M. A. Miller, *Arkheologiia v SSSR* (München, 1954).
[2] See Chapter 1, section 7, above.
[3] *Russkie Drevnosti*, v. 17–18.

Srzygowski, in his book *Die altslavische Kunst* (1929), likewise came to the conclusion that the roots of the north European art are to be found in Asia and that the peoples of eastern Europe played an important role in the process of spreading the north and middle Asiatic patterns westward.[1] From this point of view he emphasized the importance of the place occupied by the old Slavic art in the general development of European art. The dependence of the north European art on the art of the Eurasian nomads and of China has also been documented by W. Anderson in 1937 in his article 'Nordische Bildkunst der ersten Jahrtausends'.[2]

After these preliminary remarks let us now survey briefly some of the aspects of the old Slavic art. The task is not easy, especially in regard to monumental art, since so little of it survived. Most of the old Slavic temples were made of wood, and none of them has been preserved. We have to rely on the descriptions of buildings in literary sources, and on archaeological data which have revealed only the foundations of temples, not the temples themselves.

The temple of God Svantovit in Arkona, island of Rügen, was described by Saxo Grammaticus in the late twelfth century. It was situated on a promontory facing the sea. Archaeological excavations by Carl Schuchhardt and Robert Koldewey (1921), which revealed a considerable part of the temple's foundations (part was washed off by the sea) confirmed the accuracy of the main lines of Saxo's description.[3] According to Saxo, the temple was wooden and of exquisite craftsmanship (*opere elegantissimum*). It was covered with a red roof. The inner sanctum was separated by partitions from the outer temple; it was accessible through the roof only. Both the temple as a whole and the sanctum were of square shape.[4] Strzygowski comments that the Iranian fire-altars were of the same shape. Herbord, an author of the twelfth century, mentions the so-called *continae* in Stettin, buildings

[1] Josef Strzygowski, *Die Altslavische Kunst* (Augsburg, 1929), p. 263.
[2] W. Anderson, 'Nordische Bildkunst der ersten Jahrtausends', *Annales de l'Institut Kondakov*, ix (1937), 23–38. See also D. Carter, *The Symbol of the Beast: the Animal Style Art of Eurasia* (New York, 1957), p. 151; T. T. Rice, *The Scythians* (New York, 1957), pp. 29, 169, 185–8, 192.
[3] Carl Schuchhardt, *Arkona, Retra, Vineta* (Berlin, 1926).
[4] Saxo Grammaticus, *Gesta Danorum*, xiv, reprinted in C. H. Meyer, *Fontes Historiae Religionis Slavicae* (Berlin, 1931), p. 49.

which served as Slavic community centres of religious character. He says that the main contina was built 'with remarkable care and artistry' (*mirabili cultu et artificio*).[1]

There is no description of old Russian temples in literary sources. In Kiev a stone foundation of what was first considered a whole temple, was excavated by Khvoiko in 1908. It is of oval shape. Recent investigations show that the foundation discovered by Khvoiko is that of the inner sanctum of the temple. The temple as a whole must have been an enormous edifice.[2]

No other foundations of large temples have been, so far, discovered in Russia. The sanctuary of God Perun, excavated in 1948–52 by the Novgorod Archaeological Expedition (directed by A. V. Artsikhovsky), had no temple in the proper sense of the word. The sanctuary was situated on a promontory formed by the bank of the Volkhov River, close to Lake Ilmen. It consisted of a round platform (21 metres in diameter) enclosed in a circular moat with eight semicircular bulges on its outer side; the radius of each semicircle is 7 metres.[3] We have here a pattern of two concentric circular lines (the edge of the platform and the outer rampart of the moat). This may be compared to the plan of Koy-Krylgan Kala in Khorezm.[4] The design of the plan of the sanctuary resembles an eight-petal flower. It is supposed that the design was intended to symbolize one of the flowers dedicated to Perun, for several flowers are called 'Perun's flowers' in Slavic folk-lore.

In the centre of the sanctuary the lower part of a wooden pillar was revealed. It is supposed that the pillar served as the foundation for Perun's statue. In the circular moat, at the base of each bulge, piles of charred wood were found. These apparently were accumulations from ritual fires kindled there at the Perun festivals, or perhaps they were fires kept permanently burning. No traces of any building were found. Apparently it was an open-air sanctuary.

It should be noted that all the above three sanctuaries—Svantovit's, the Kievan one, and Perun's—were situated on

---

[1] Herbordus, ii. 30–32, in C. H. Meyer, *Fontes Historiae Religionis Slavicae*, pp. 25–26.

[2] See Igor Grabor, *Istoriia Russkogo Iskusstva*, i (2nd edn., Moscow, 1953), 88–89.

[3] V. V. Sedov, 'Drevnerusskoe iazycheskoe sviatilishche v Peryni', *KS*, l (1953), 100, fig. 44.

[4] See Chapter 1, sections 1 and 5, above.

promontories directed towards East and facing water (sea at Arkona, rivers in Russia). This obviously must be connected with Sun-worship and veneration of water among the old Slavs.

While there were, apparently, few large temples in pre-Christian Russia, it may be supposed that there existed there buildings similar to the Stettin continae, serving as community centres of religious character. These might have been managed by the elder volkhvy. Such buildings, assuming that they existed, must have been made of wood, especially so in northern Russia. The art of carpentry flourished in Russia, and particularly in Novgorod, in the Kievan period. It was undoubtedly based on very old traditions. Both large houses and fortresses were built. The tower was an important element of the fortress walls.[1]

After the conversion of the Slavs to Christianity, old religious temples and sanctuaries were destroyed and Christian churches built instead. These followed the new patterns, Western among those Slavs who accepted Christianity from Rome, and Byzantine among the eastern Slavs and most of the southern Slavs. In a number of cases, foreign architects were engaged to build the new churches. In many cases, however, native workers were also employed, as a result of which certain traditional pre-Christian architectural traits and devices seem to have affected the architecture of the new churches to a certain extent at least.

Approaching the old Slavic architecture from this point of view, Josef Strzygowski finds it possible to state that the architecture of some of the early Christian churches in Croatia and Dalmatia reflects old pre-Christian Croatian traditions. Strzygowski considers the plan of the cupola superimposed over a square foundation with the use of funnel-shaped niches, one of the basic old Croatian architectural forms.[2] This form Strzygowski derives from Iran and Armenia. Strzygowski also thinks that many of the old wooden Christian churches in Galicia, Germany (in the area of the early Slavic settlements), Norway, and north Russia contain very old architectural elements.

As regards the early Christian churches in Russia, N. N. Voronin and M. K. Karger emphasize the impact of the tradi-

---

[1] N. N. Voronin and M. K. Karger, 'Arkhitektura', *Istoriia Kultury drevnei Rusi*, ii. 246–9.
[2] J. Strzygowski, *Die altslavische Kunst*, pp. 66, 76–82.

tional wooden architecture of old Russia on the architecture of Christian churches. As Voronin and Karger say, 'The same carpenters [who had built the pre-Christian temples and continae] built the first Christian churches which hardly differed much from the buildings of the heathen times'.[1] The experience the old Russian architects had acquired in the building of community centres and fortresses may be felt in the architecture of the first large Christian churches of Russia. The first (wooden) Sancta Sophia of Novgorod presented a complex of thirteen towers. It may be supposed that the tops of these towers were of pyramidal shape. According to Voronin and Karger, a characteristic trait of the old Russian wooden architecture was the predilection for high tower-like edifices in the architecture of both houses and temples.

Statues of gods were amply used in Slavic cults. The statue of Svantovit at Arkona was described by Saxo Grammaticus in the following words:

> In the temple there stood an immense idol, much larger than human size. It had four necks and four heads; two heads seemed to face forward, and two backward. Approached from the front or from the back, one head seemed to look to the right, and the other to the left. The beard was shaven, the hair clipped in the manner of the Rugii. The idol held in its right hand a horn made of various metals. . . . The left hand held a bow, the arm resting along the side of the body. A tunic covered the body down to the skin. The tunic was made of diverse kinds of wood and was so skilfully attached to the knees that the point of contact could be discerned only after a close examination. The feet rested on the ground but it could not be seen on what foundation were they fixed.[2]

While stating that the tunic on Svantovit's statue was made of wood, Saxo does not say of what material the statue itself was made. Presumably it was hewn of stone.

A number of other Slavic gods were polycephalic. Triglav, as the name itself shows, had three heads; Porevit, five heads; and Rugevit, a head with five faces.

In 1848, owing to a prolonged drought, the river Zbrucz became shallow and a statue became noticeable on a shoal, not far from Husiatin in Galicia. The statue was later brought to

---

[1] *Istoriia Kultury drevnei Rusi*, ii. 248.
[2] C. H. Meyer, *Fontes Historiae Religionis Slavicae*, p. 49.

the Kraków Museum. It is a quadrangular pillar of hard lime-
stone 2·59 metres high. On each side the figure of a divinity in
human shape (perhaps one of four emanations of the same
divinity) is represented, as well as a series of other figures.
Taken as a whole, the idol has four heads, or rather four faces
oriented to four quarters. The napes merge together, and all
four heads are covered by the same headgear.[1] The headgear
resembles that of the Russian princes of the Kievan period. The
representation of the divinity occupies the upper part of each
side of the pillar. In the lower part of each side various figures
are arranged in two tiers. On one side, the lower tier is blank.

According to some scholars, including B. A. Rybakov, of the
four divinities represented on the pillar, two are male and two
female. Not having seen the monument I cannot judge, since
reproductions available to me are not clear enough. One
allegedly female divinity holds an aurochs horn in its right
hand. Another, obviously male, is provided with a sheathed
sword or sabre; at the god's feet, a horse is represented. According to Rybakov,[2] the third supposedly female divinity holds a
bracelet in its right hand, though another scholar thinks it is a
cup and not a bracelet. The fourth divinity (male) has no
attributes. In the upper tier below the divinity, on each side
there is a human figure, which according to Rybakov is the
figure of a man on two opposite sides of the pillar, and that of a
woman on the other two sides. In the lower tier there is a figure
of a kneeling man on each of the three sides: the fourth, as has
been mentioned, is blank.

Zakharov refers the idol to the ninth or the tenth century.[3]
Rybakov dated it in the tenth century; Zakharov considers it
Pecheneg or Magyar; Rybakov believes it to be Slavic. In my
opinion there cannot be any doubt that the idol is Slavic. It
may be compared to the Arkona idol in many respects. In the
first place, the idol's four heads facing the four quarters correspond to the four heads of Svantovit's idol at Arkona, even if
from Saxo's description we may think that the heads of the
Arkona's idol were oriented in a slightly different way. Besides,
the sword or sabre of one of the emanations of the divinity

[1] See figure in I. Grabar, *Istoriia Russkogo iskusstva*, i (1953), 76.
[2] B. A. Rybakov, 'Iskusstvo drevnikh Slavian', in I. Grabar, op. cit., pp. 76–77.
[3] A. A. Zakharov, 'The Statue of Zbrucz', *ESA*, ix (1943), 346.

represented on the Zbrucz idol finds its parallel in the sword
which lay in front of the Arkona statue. As regards the motif of
the divinity with the horn, we know that the Arkona idol held
a horn in its right hand. The horse reminds us of the sacred
horse at Svantovit's sanctuary in Arkona. Furthermore, as
Rybakov points out, a statue made of grey granite, apparently
of a woman with the representation of a horn on her chest, was
found at Rosenberg, West Prussia.[1] It may be added that a
statue of a man, with beard and moustache, holding a horn in
his right hand, was also found in Rosenberg.[2]

As regards the statues of the gods of the Kievan pantheon,
only one is briefly described in the Russian Chronography,
namely, that of Perun. It was 'made of wood with a head of
silver and a moustache of gold'.

When Prince Vladimir accepted Christianity he ordered
'that the idols should be overthrown, and that some should be
cut to pieces and others burned'.[3] The statues to be 'cut to
pieces' were apparently made of stone.

Besides its independent role as in statues, sculpture was also
used by the old Slavs as an element of architecture. According
to Thietmar of Merseburg, in the sanctuary of God Svarozhich
at Retra the outside walls of the temple were adorned with the
effigies of gods and goddesses 'admirably sculptured' (*mirifice
insculptae*).[4] In the main contina at Stettin there were sculptures
on the walls, both outside and inside. The figures, in high
relief, of men, birds, and animals were of such vivid expression
'that one could think they were alive and breathed'.[5] The outside images were painted; the paint was so durable that neither
rain nor snow could either darken or wash it off.

Both the temple at Retra and the continae of Stettin were
apparently made of wood. The sculptures, therefore, must have
been carved in wood also. There cannot be any doubt that the
Slavic wood-carvers achieved the highest level of artistry.
Wood-carving was widespread in Russia, one of its main centres
being Novgorod. While no specimen of the earliest Novgorodian
wooden sculpture has been preserved, we may suppose that

[1] L. Léger, *La Mythologie Slave* (Paris, 1901), p. 223, fig. 6.
[2] Ibid., fig. 7.
[3] *Povest' Vremennykh Let*, i. 80; Cross and Sherbowitz's English translation, p. 116.
[4] C. H. Meyer, *Fontes Historiae Religionis Slavicae*, p. 10.
[5] Ibid., p. 26.

some creations of the later period (eleventh and twelfth centuries) which are known to us represent the continuation of the old traditions of craftsmanship (see, for example, the human head, carved in wood, of the twelfth century).[1]

As we have seen, the idol of Zbrucz is of stone. So presumably was Svantovit's idol in the Arkona temple. Besides, several stone figures were found in the area of the Baltic Slavs. These are rather crude. It seems that stone sculpture was more developed among the Slavs of the Kievan area as well as among the southern Slavs. Unfortunately, we can judge of it mostly on the basis of its traditions as preserved in the monuments of later periods.

The only example of major sculpture in the south Slavic area known to us is the so-called 'Madara horseman', the huge rock relief in Bulgaria, and this, as we know, closely followed central Asian and Iranian patterns.[2] Of what origin were the sculptors we do not know.

Sculpture as an element of architecture flourished in old Croatian art. Strzygowski believes that the ornamental technique of Croatian monuments of the early Christian period is based on pre-Christian traditions. One of the characteristic forms of the old Croatian sculptural ornamentation is that of multi-striped plait, of two or more entwined strands. Strzygowski derives this technique from Iran. He also points out that this type of ornamentation grew out of wood-carving technique. On some of the Croatian ornamented stone-tables and capitals, figures of animals and birds occur.[3] It may be mentioned in this connexion that on an ancient tomb at Ubosco, Bosnia, the souls of the dead, represented as birds, ride on deer (one of them on a goat). On another Bosnian tomb human figures appear— dead warriors riding on horses to the Country of Souls.[4] On an old Bulgarian stone-plate and on fragments of a frieze of the seventh and the eighth centuries from Stara Zagora and Drenovo we find figures in bas-relief of a lion, of a gryphon, of a double-headed eagle.[5] On a capital from Stara Zagora of the same period a gryphon attacking an herbivorous animal which

[1] *Po Sledam drevnikh kultur: Drevniaia Rus'* (Moscow, 1953), plate facing p. 240.
[2] See Chapter 1, section 7, above.
[3] See J. Strzygowski, *Die altslavische Kunst*, figs. 151 and 153.
[4] J. Kunst, 'Cultural Relations', fig. 52.
[5] B. D. Filov, *Starobŭlgarskoto izkustvo* (Sofia, 1924), Plate II.

B. Filov defines as an elephant is represented.[1] All these motifs
and themes belong to the art and mythology of the Alanic-
Tokharian sphere.

As regards the old Russian stone sculpture, a number of
specimens of it dated in the eleventh and twelfth centuries have
been preserved, and, as in the case of Croatian art, it may be
presumed that in some of them elements of older traditions
survived. From this point of view, the fragment of carved white
stone, found during the excavations at the site of the Cathedral
of Annunciation in Chernigov (built in 1186), deserves attention. The stone presumably belonged to the altar ciborium.[2]
The nature of the sculptural ornamentation of this stone,
especially the elements of multi-striped plait, may be likened
to that in the old Croatian art. The plait-like strands in some
parts of the figures in relief of St. Theodore Stratilates and a
Russian prince (possibly, Mstislav, son of Vladimir Monomakh)
likewise seem to correspond to the Croatian technique.[3] Consider the representation of the lower part of the tunics, as well
as that of the horses' manes and tails, which can be compared
with the plait-like feathers of the bird of the St. Donatus's
capital at Rab. It may be surmised that certain features of both
the old Croatian and the old Russian sculpture are based on
common traditions.

In some of the old Russian metal works we find elements
reminding us of the Scandinavian type of ornamentation. Consider, for example, the entangled design on a mould for casting
bracelets found in Kiev;[4] also, that on the silver bracelets of the
same period (twelfth or thirteenth century).[5] The ornamentation of the silver mounting of the aurochs horn found near
Chernigov (see section 6 above) likewise resembles, in parts,
the Scandinavian style.

Can we say that these art objects belong to the Scandinavian
art or represent an influence of Scandinavian art on the old
Russian art? The problem is very complex. The bracelet mould
found in Kiev shows that such bracelets were produced in Kiev.
Of course, it is possible that the artist who made the mould was

[1] B. D. Filov, *Starobŭlgarskoto izkustvo*, p. 11, fig. 5.
[2] B. A. Rybakov, 'Prikladnoe iskusstvo i skulptura', *Istoriia kultury drevnei Rusi*, ii.
454, fig. 230, 1.
[3] Ibid., p. 443, fig. 221, 2.   [4] Ibid., fig. 213, 1.
[5] Ibid., p. 431, fig. 214.

a Varangian settled in Kiev, but there is no direct evidence of it. As regards the Chernigov horn, it probably was made in Chernigov. The two human figures (archers) represented on it are not Norsemen. They seem to be Turks or Magyars (there was a Turko-Magyar tribe—the Koui—in the vicinity of Chernigov at that time.[1] Besides, there are also elements of Middle-Eastern ('Sassanian') art patterns in the ornamentation of the horn.[2] As has been mentioned, Kondakov and Strzygowski think that the sources of Scandinavian art are to be sought in Middle-Eastern art or in the Scytho-Alanic art; according to my terminology, in the Alanic-Tokharian sphere. From this point of view, the old Croatian, the old Bulgarian, the old Russian, and the Scandinavian art all derive from the same cultural milieu.

As regards old Russian minor sculpture, ornaments, and jewellery, there is an abundance of specimens revealed by archaeological excavations, with much variety in form, style, and technique. In some cases it is not easy to determine whether the artifact in question belongs to the Slavic art or to the art of one of the other peoples who lived in the territory of Russia together with the Slavs. In any case, however, we may speak of the artistic patterns which had originated in the Scytho-Alanic era and continued to develop in the same geographic area. The Slavs, certainly, played an important role in this process.

A general survey of the applied arts of old Russia, on the basis of recent research, has been given by B. A. Rybakov in his *Remeslo Drevnei Rusi* (1948), chs. i–iii (see also Rybakov's chapter on 'Applied Art and Sculpture' in vol. ii of *Istoriia Kultury Drevnei Rusi* (1951), as well as his surveys of the 'Art of the Old Slavs' and of the 'Applied Art of Kievan Rus'' in vol. i of the second edition of Grabar's *Istoriia Russkogo Iskusstva* (1953)).

Ornaments of various kind, both men's and women's, have been found on the territory of Russia in great quantities. Among them are torques, fibulas, bracelets, diadems, ear-rings, pendants, and amulets. Among the pendants, those of the Radimichi and the Viatichi are of considerable interest from the sociological point of view. These pendants are seven-petalled.

---

[1] See Chapter 3, section 4, above.
[2] Id., *Remeslo drevnei Rusi* (Moscow, 1948), pp. 284–6.

Each petal of the Viatichian pendant is shaped like an oblong shield, while the Radimichian has a triangular shape. In my opinion this pendant may be considered the tribe emblem, the number of petals indicating the number of clans which had constituted the tribe.[1]

Many sites of foundries were found, with remnants of equipment, such as moulds and special tools. This indicates that most of the objects were manufactured in Russia. Kiev was an important centre of such industries.

Among the antiquities of the eleventh and the twelfth centuries a number of enamelled ornaments was found. Apparently the technique of *cloisonné* enamel was highly developed in this period. As regards the earlier times, Rybakov states that the middle Dnieper River region was an important centre of *champlevé* enamel works in the fourth and the fifth centuries, and probably in the following three centuries as well.[2]

Clay figures of various kind were found at the excavations of old sites of settlements as well as in those of the Kievan period. Among their themes are the horseman; the woman with a child; the horse; the cow; the bird. These must have been originally lekans or amulets. Later on the same themes were reproduced in children's toys.[3]

Ornamental textiles and embroideries represented an important branch of applied arts in old Russia. Fragments of woollen fabrics with traces of stamped geometric ornamentation in dark colour were found in the barrows of the Severi. In the upper Dnieper region (the land of the Krivichi) fragments of woollen fabrics of the eleventh and twelfth centuries were excavated. They have a complex woven ornament based on the form of rhomb. From the old times Slavic women were expert embroiderers. Embroidery was always popular in Russia. The old traditions survived in Russian peasant art. The themes of many folk-embroideries reflect pre-Christian religious beliefs. More often than not the figure of the Great Goddess of the Scythian age (Mother Moist Earth, Moksha in Russian mythology) occupies the centre of the composition. Sometimes the goddess

---

[1] See Chapter 3, section 2, above.

[2] B. A. Rybakov, *Remeslo drevnei Rusi*, p. 53.

[3] See L. A. Dintses, 'Drevnie cherty v Russkom narodnom iskusstve', *Istoriia kultury drevnei Rusi*, ii. 465–91.

holds in each of her hands a blossoming bush or a bird. Two horses or other animals (deer, leopards) usually stand on two sides of the divinity. Often riders are represented on horses (the theme of the riding souls of the departed). On many embroideries the Tree of Life replaces the human figure of the goddess in the centre.

It is obvious that the ornamentation of the old Russian embroideries was permeated with ancient mythological notions. Even after Russia's conversion to Christianity the image of the Great Goddess must have been for many centuries secretly revered, especially by women, as that of the Mother Moist Earth.

5

THE RUSSIAN KAGANATE

1. *The Norsemen and the Rus*

IN the eighth and the ninth centuries a new dynamic element came to the fore in Russia—the Norsemen. They were known in Russia under the general name of Varangians. A group of Norsemen merged with the Alano-Slavic tribe of Rus and assumed their name.

The nature of the connexion between the Norsemen and the Rus is one of the most controversial problems of the early Russian history. A variety of hypotheses was offered by both philologists and historians; the literature of the subject is vast and constantly growing. A comprehensive survey of that literature, down to 1930, was given by V. A. Mošin in two studies (both in Russian) published in 1931.[1] The reader can find a brief outline of the problem in my book *Ancient Russia* (1943), ch. vii (especially in section 4 of that chapter). Among the recent publications, Ad. Stender-Petersen, *Varangica* (1953), must be mentioned here.

There are two aspects in the 'Varango-Russian' problem which have not been, so far, sufficiently disentangled: the question of the Norse element in the ethnic background of the Rus and that of the origin of the Rus themselves. The third relevant question is that of the origin of the name 'Rus'.

The confusion concerning these questions started as early as the beginning of the twelfth century, at the time when the Russian Chronography took its final shape. In the Hypatian version of the Chronography the Russes are mentioned among the tribes who negotiated an agreement with the Varangians, A.D. 862: 'The Rus, the Chud, the Slovene, the Krivichi, and the Ves, said [to the Varangians]. . . .'[2] In the Laurentian ver-

---

[1] V. A. Mošin, 'Nachalo Rusi', *Byzantinoslavica*, iii (1931), 38–58, 285–307; id., 'Variago-Russkii Vopros', *Slavia*, x (1931), 109–36, 343–79, 501–87.

[2] *PSRL*, ii, fasc. 1 (3rd edn., Petrograd, 1923), col. 15; see also *Povest' Vremennykh Let*, p. 18.

sion it is the Rus whom the other tribes call to rule over them:
'The Chud, the Slovene, the Krivichi, and the Ves said to the
Rus. . . .'[1] Then the chronicler adds: 'These particular Varangians were known as Russes, just as some are called Swedes,
and others Norwegians, Angles, and Gothlanders, for they were
thus named.' In another passage of the Chronography (A.D.
898) it is said that 'the Slavs and the Russes are one people, for
it is because of the Varangians that the latter became known as
Rus though originally they were Slavs'.[2]

In order to understand the meaning of this statement of the
editor of the Chronography we have to go back to the first
dated entry in the Chronography—A.M. 6360 (A.D. 852). We
read here: 'In the year 6360, the 15th of the indiction, at the
accession of the Emperor Michael, the land of Rus was first
named. We have determined this date from the fact that in the
reign of this Emperor Russes attacked Tsargrad [Constanti-
nople], *as is written in the* Greek Chronicle' (italics are mine).[3]

It is obvious that the occasion on which, from the point of
view of the editor of the Chronography, the Russes had been
'first named', was their first attack on Constantinople, A.D. 860
(on this attack see section 5 below). The Russian scholar of the
twelfth century found this information in the Greek sources as
he plainly said. It was Patriarch Photius who described this
attack, and the subsequent conversion of part of the Russes
to Christianity. It was Photius who emphasized the fact that this
was the first appearance of the Rus before the Imperial City
(see section 5 below).

From the classical sources the Byzantine scholars, including
Photius, knew of the existence of the ancient tribe of the Roxo-
lani, but they did not connect the old name (or rather, the first
part of it—Ros) with the Russes (Ros) of 860. Among these new
Russes, Norsemen played a prominent role, and so the name
Ros was now connected with the Norsemen. It is in this sense

---

[1] *PSRL*, i, fasc. 1 (2nd edn., Leningrad, 1926), col. 19. In the Troitsa Codex
which, in its earlier part is close to the Laurentian Codex, the reading is 'The Rus',
as in the Hypatian Chronicle (not 'to the Rus'), M. D. Priselkov, *Troitskaia Letopis'*
(Moscow and Leningrad, 1950), p. 58. See also the variants in *Povest' Vremennykh
Let*, ii. 184, note 51. In Cross and Sherbowitz's translation, p. 59, 'to the people of
Rus'.

[2] *Povest' Vremennykh Let*, i. 23; Cross and Sherbowitz's translation, p. 63.

[3] *Povest' Vremennykh Let*, i. 17; Cross and Sherbowitz's translation, p. 58.

that we may best understand the Russian chronicler's remark that the 'land of Rus' was 'first named', in the reign of Emperor Michael, 'because of the Varangians'.

On the basis of the above considerations we may assert that, in the opinion of the Russian chroniclers of the eleventh and the early twelfth centuries (that was the period during which the Russian Chronography was compiled), the name Rus was given to the people Rus by the Greeks.

This theory is an example of the profound influence of the Byzantine traditions on Russian scholarship of the eleventh and the twelfth centuries. The theory can hardly satisfy us since it contradicts what we know of the deeper historical background of the peoples of the Pontic area. As we know, both the people Rus and the name Rus existed for centuries before the first Russian attack on Constantinople. The new element in the situation was the Norsemen. From the historical point of view, the main problem in this case is that of when and how the intimate connexion between the Norsemen and the Rus was established.

The era of the Vikings, a period of the turbulent expansion of Scandinavian peoples, began in the middle of the eighth century.[1] Long before that, however, the Norsemen had explored the southern and eastern shores of the Baltic Sea. In the sixth century a group of them settled at the mouth of the western Dvina. In the seventh century the kings of southern Sweden had overseas possessions in Kurland. By the beginning of the eighth century Livonia and Estonia were considered part of the realm of Ivar, king of southern Sweden and Denmark. Having consolidated their control over the Livonian littoral, the Norsemen began to penetrate deeper into the country. The course of the western Dvina offered a natural road inland, and it became the first path to facilitate the Norse advance into Russia. The native population along the banks of the western Dvina consisted of small tribes of Balts and Finns and was both scarce and lacking in unity, so that the Norsemen met no trouble and no serious opposition in both trading with the natives and subduing them.

Reaching the upper parts of the river the Norsemen penetrated into the area of Slavic colonization. It appears that in

[1] See note L, p. 320.

their further drive inland the Norsemen at first by-passed the strong Slavic centre of Novgorod. Due to the mutual proximity of the sources of the western Dvina, Dnieper, and Volga, once the Norsemen reached the upper parts of the western Dvina they were in position to explore the upper parts of both the Dnieper and the Volga. As regards the Dnieper, the Norsemen could hardly go down it very far since the Lithuanian and Slavic tribes in the upper Dnieper region must have been strong and well organized. Their most important centre in that area was at the site of Gnezdovo, near Smolensk.

On the other hand, the Norsemen met with no organized resistance in the upper Volga basin down to the area of the future towns of Rostov and Iaroslavl. The Rostov region was inhabited by the Finnish tribe of Meria. In the Iaroslavl region, a site of an old settlement of the Slavic type of the period from the third to the fifth centuries has been recently excavated near the village of Berezniaki.[1] From the Iaroslavl–Rostov area, using portages between the tributaries of the upper Volga and the lower Oka, the Norsemen might easily have penetrated to the Oka basin, probably around A.D. 700. The Rostov region also attracted new Slavic settlers from among the Slovene of Novgorod and the Krivichi of the Smolensk area. The Norse colonization thus merged here with the Slavic. Archaeological research revealed ample antiquities of both Norse and Slavic types in this area, as well as those of the Finnish tribe of Meria. Most of the objects found are referred to the eighth and the ninth centuries.

The above data concerning the early Norse colonization in north Russia are generally accepted and seem to stand firm. Less certain is the possibility of the Norse expansion further east. In the introductory part of the Russian Chronography we find a list of tribes of north and east Russia belonging to 'the share of Japheth'.[2] In that list besides the Rus, the Poles (Liakhs) and a number of Finnish and Lithuanian tribes are mentioned. According to the chronicler, the Liakhs, the Prussians, and the Chud (a Finnish tribe) 'border on the Varangian Sea' (i.e. the Baltic Sea). Then the chronicler adds: 'The Varangians dwell on the shores of that same sea, and extend to the eastward as far

---

[1] See Chapter 3, section 5, above.
[2] *Povest' Vremennykh Let*, i. 9–10; Cross and Sherbowitz's translation, pp. 51–52.

as the portion of Shem.' The Chronography states that 'to the lot of Shem fell the Orient'. Among the countries belonging to the portion of Shem according to the Chronography, Bactria is the nearest to Russia. In the statement of the Chronography about the eastern extension of the Varangians we may thus see an indication of the existence of the early Norse settlements in central Asia. The editors of the Chronography might have based their statement on an old tradition.

Traces of the same tradition may be found in the writings of Khorezmian and Persian scholars of the Middle Ages. The noted cosmographer Biruni, who lived in the late tenth and the early eleventh centuries, mentions together the Asii and the Varangians (*Asiu-o-Varang*).[1] Nizami, who wrote in the twelfth century, in his poem on Alexander the Great (*Iskandernamah*), describes an attack on the town of Derbend by the Russes and their allies, the Alano-Varangians (*Alan-Varag*).[2] In both these cases the Varangians are connected with the As-Alans. This is an indication of the existence, in the medieval Khorezmian and Persian literature, of the belief that the Varangians belonged to the same historical and geographical background as the Alans, that is, to the northern Caucasus and central Asia.

Further evidence pointing in the same direction may be obtained by a systematic comparative study of tribal and clan names. Consider, for example, the name of one of the Turkmen tribes, Yom.[3] It is known that many of the central Asian Turkish tribes represent, historically, a mixture of Alans, Tokhars, and Turks.[4] Since the name *yom* does not seem to be Turkic, we may refer it to the pre-Turkish population of central Asia. According to Vambery *yom* is an old word meaning 'people'. Now, the name yom is identical with that of a militant Varangian fraternity which, in the late tenth and the first half of the eleventh centuries, centred around the island of Jom in the estuary of the Oder River in the Baltic Sea (known as the Joms-Vikings). It may be added that the island of Jom (pronounced Yom) was known in Slavic as Volyn, and it will be recalled that the name Volyn seems to be a Slavic form of the name 'Khorezm'.[5]

---

[1] Analysed by N. A. Rast, *Les Alains dans la littérature, la poésie et la langue Persanes* (not yet published).   [2] Ibid.   [3] See note M, p. 320.
[4] See Chapter 3, section 3, above.   [5] See Chapter 3, section 5, above.

It will be recalled in this connexion that there are striking parallels in the Alanic and Nordic folk-lore which seem to point out that the two peoples had been intimately connected one with the other in remote antiquity.[1] Consider, for example, the Ossetian tale of Odin of which a French paraphrase has been published by Dzambulat Dzanty.[2] In this tale, the miraculous birth of Odin (in Ossetian *uyd-dæn* 'I am the soul'); his discovery of smelting the bronze; his exploits in the Caucasus; his journey to Scandinavia and final return to the Caucasus are described. Furthermore, according to Georges Dumézil, an important character of the Ossetian legends, the crafty and mischievous Syrdon closely resembles the Nordic god Loki.

Even more significant is the generic name of the Nordic gods —Æsir. This name is similar to that of the people Asii (in Old Russian As or Ias) who, as we know, had merged with the Alans in deep antiquity. The feminine form of the Nordic As (singular for Æsir) is *asynja*. This is identical with the Old Russian word *asynia* (variant *iasynia*), feminine of As ('an As [Ossetian] woman').[3]

As a matter of fact, the Nordic sagas themselves connect the Æsir with the country of the Asii (Alans). We read in the Ynglinga Saga: 'The land in Asia to the east of the Tanakvisl [Tanais, i.e. Don River] was called Asaland or Asaheim and the chief town in the land was called Asagard [As-Grad, i.e. City of the As].'[4]

To all this it should be added that the sources of Nordic art are to be found in the Alanic-Tokharian sphere.[5]

The question before us now is how to co-ordinate and to reconcile the evidence of the early ties between the Norsemen and the peoples of the Alanic-Tokharian sphere, on the one hand, and that of the Norse expansion from Scandinavia in the era of the Vikings, on the other. In my opinion the answer is basically the same as in the case of the Slavs and the Goths. Both the Slavic and Teutonic tribes migrated from central Asia

---

[1] See Chapter 2, section 1, above.
[2] D. Dzanty, 'Odin', *Oss-Alanes*, ii (1953), 11–13.
[3] G. Vernadsky, *Ancient Russia*, p. 274 and n. 38.
[4] C. C. Rafn, *Antiquités Russes d'après les monuments historiques des Islandais* (Copenhague, 1850, 2 vols.), i. 246; E. Monsen, ed., *Heimskringla, by Snorre Sturlason* (New York, 1932), p. 2.
[5] See Chapter 4, section 7, above.

to Europe not all at once but through several stages of migration. As regards the Norsemen we may suppose that a considerable number of them had reached Scandinavia and settled there in remote antiquity. Other groups of them might have remained in the east much longer and moved westward in the later periods.

We now may attack the crux of our problem of the connexion between the Norsemen and the Rus. Since, as I believe, both the Rus and the Norsemen originally belonged to the same background—that of the Alanic-Tokharian sphere—it is theoretically possible that part of the Norsemen might have merged with the Rus long before the era of the Vikings. However, there are a number of considerations on the basis of which we may think that the mergence of the two elements—the tribe of Rus and a group of Norsemen—took place only as late as the second half of the eighth century. It is at that time that the Rus emerged as an aggressive and expansive factor in the turbulent political history of the Pontic area and the Caucasus. The Rus had shown, indeed, a similarly dynamic character much earlier when they were associated with the Alans and were known as the Roxolani. Subsequently, however, in the period from about the fourth to the middle of the eighth centuries, the Russes, while keeping their ground in south Russia, undertook no distant campaigns of their own, or at least there is no record of any such campaigns.

In the late eighth century the situation changed. Around 790 the Russes attacked the town of Surozh (old Sugdaea, present-day Sudak) in the Crimea. In the 830's the Russes apparently presented a menace to the Khazars since the latter engaged Byzantine engineers to build a fortress on the lower Don River as a protection against the inroads of an enemy—in all probability of the Russes. About 840 the Russes attacked Amastris, a town on the southern shore of the Black Sea, and finally, in 860, they appeared before Constantinople. The increasing aggressiveness of the Rus is clear evidence of their rapidly growing military strength, and it is most likely that this was the result of the assistance given the Rus by the Norsemen.

In my opinion, it is the Russes themselves who might have asked the Norsemen for assistance. When the Khazar kaganate had come to existence, the Russes, together with the Slavs, the

Alans, and the Magyars, had recognized the kagan as their suzerain. As long as the Khazar kaganate was strong, it offered sufficient protection for its subjects and allies. But in 737 the Arabs broke the line of Khazar defences and raided the Don area capturing 20,000 Slavs who were then moved to Transcaucasia.[1] This event must have produced a painful impression on the Slavs and Russes alike. It is possible that part of the Slavs taken prisoner by the Arabs were Russes. In any case the Slavs and the Russes were now left to their own resources and had to think of strengthening their armies or to look for allies and protectors outside the Khazar kaganate. It seems that the Russes solved this problem by engaging the assistance of a group of Norsemen. These Norsemen may have come from the Oka region. However, it is theoretically possible that the first contingent of Norsemen came to south Russia not from the north but from the east, from among the 'Aso-Varangians' and 'Alano-Varangians'. Later on, groups of Norsemen from Scandinavia must have joined them. From the Bertinian annals we know that there were Swedes among the Russes in 839.

The first aggressive undertaking of the Russes was their attack on Surozh in the late eighth century. The story of that attack is found in an appendix to the Life of St. Stephen of Surozh.[2] St. Stephen died in 786. The attack took place 'a few years' later, that is around 790. The Life of St. Stephen of Surozh is available in two versions of which the short is in Greek and the expanded one in Russian. Both are known in later manuscript copies, the earliest known manuscript of the Russian version being referred by V. G. Vasilievsky to the sixteenth century. Both versions, according to Vasilievsky, have preserved the tradition of their early original. The Slavic version must have circulated in Russia at least as early as the fifteenth century since on its basis the story of the Russian attack on Surozh was mentioned in the life of a Russian saint of the fourteenth century, St. Dimitri Prilutsky (d. 1391).[3] The Russian life of St. Stephen contains four appendixes in which various miracles wrought by the saint both in life and after his death are described. It is in the third appendix that the story of the attack is told. According to the

---

[1] See Chapter 3, section 3, above (p. 96).   [2] See note N, p. 320.
[3] V. O. Kliuchevsky, *Drevnerusskie zhitiia sviatykh kak istoricheskii istochnik* (Moscow, 1871), pp. 188–9; V. G. Vasilievsky, *Trudy*, iii, pp. cclx–cclxii.

story, the Russian prince was stricken by palsy at the moment when he burst into the church of St. Sophia and reached St. Stephen's tomb. He then expressed the desire of being christened. After baptism he was miraculously healed.

The appendix containing the story of this miracle is entitled 'On the coming to Surozh of Prince Bravlin with his army from Novgorod the Great'. In the text we read: 'A few years after the death of the saint [St. Stephen] there came a large Russ army from Novgorod—Prince Bravlin, very strong.' Note that in the text, 'Novgorod' and not 'Novgorod the Great' is mentioned. Apparently 'the Great' has been added by a late editor. It is most likely that under 'Novgorod' the old Scythian town of Neapolis, near present-day Simferopol, is meant.[1] It seems hardly possible that the inhabitants of Novgorod the Great— far in the north—would have been able to organize a campaign to the Crimea as early as the eighth century. Most likely the Russian army came from the Don–Donets area, not from north Russia. Neapolis (Simferopol) is strategically located on the way from northern Tauria to the southern shore of the Crimea and no invader coming through the Perekop Isthmus could by-pass it.

The name of the Russian prince, Bravlin, seems dubious. No such name occurs in any source of this and the following periods. In some of the manuscripts we find the reading *branliv* ('belli-cose') instead of Bravlin. It may be assumed that this is the correct reading. Apparently no name of the prince was men-tioned in the original and the prince was only characterized by the epithet 'bellicose'. The opening sentence of the story may be tentatively emended as follows: 'A few years after the death of the saint there came a large Russ army [under the command of] a bellicose and very strong prince.'

The Russian attack on Surozh constituted the climax of their Crimean campaign. Before coming to Surozh they had raided the whole southern littoral of the Crimea, from Korsun (Cher-son) to Kerch (Bosporus), plundering many churches. The Russes had besieged Surozh for ten days before they succeeded in storming the city. After the conversion of their prince the loot was returned to the churches.

There is no evidence concerning the motives of the Russes

[1] See Chapter 2, section 2, above.

which caused them to attack the Crimea around 790. It seems probable that their campaign was provoked by Byzantine diplomacy. As has been mentioned,[1] Byzantine interests conflicted with the Khazar in the Crimea. The region of the Crimean Goths, whose main stronghold was the city of Doras (Dor-As, 'The Rock of the As', now known as Eski-Kermen) in the mountainous region of south-western Crimea, constituted a Byzantine protectorate. Around 787, as we know from the Life of St. John of Gothia, the Khazars seized Doras, and a Khazar governor was appointed there. Before long the Goths revolted against the Khazars, but the uprising was crushed by the latter.[2] It is presumably at that juncture that the Byzantine diplomats decided to use the Russians against the Khazars and that the Russians responded to the call. At that time both Surozh and Kerch were apparently controlled by the Khazars. It appears from the story of the miracle that the Russians, not contented with attacking Kerch and Surozh, also plundered Korsun (Cherson) which was under Byzantine protection. However, as has been already said, they later made the necessary amends. On the whole, the Russian campaign brought the desired results from the Byzantine point of view. In the 790's Doras was again under the rule of a Gothic official (*toparch*) responsible to Byzantium.

It seems likely that part of the Russes who participated in the Surozh campaign were converted to Christianity, following the example of their leader. It also appears that a number of Russes settled in the Crimea for good. From the Russo-Byzantine treaty of 944 (of which more will be said later),[3] we know that the prince of the Russes controlled certain Crimean cities at that time. Presumably there were Russes among the inhabitants of these cities. Many of them must have become Christians. In 962, when the Khazars again attempted to subdue the Crimean Goths, the Goths asked 'their adherents' in Crimea to help them. These 'adherents' advised the Goths to seek protection of 'the ruler north of the Danube . . . from whose people they [the adherents] did not differ in customs and manners'. That ruler was Prince Sviatoslav of Kiev. According to the late

---

[1] See Chapter 3, section 3, above.
[2] See V. G. Vasilievsky, *Trudy*, ii (St. Petersburg, 1912), 397–8, 416–20.
[3] See Chapter 6, section 3, below.

A. A. Vasiliev, the Crimean 'adherents' of the Goths must have been Russes.

2. *The kaganate*

I

At the time of the Surozh expedition the commander of the Russes had the title of 'prince' (*kniaz'*). By 838 the Russ ruler assumed a much more ambitious title—that of 'kagan'. It will be recalled that the title 'kagan' was borne by the mighty rulers of the Steppe empires of world importance. It corresponded, more or less, to the Western title of 'emperor'. Among the western extensions of the steppe empires, the title 'kagan' was used by the rulers of the Avars and the Khazars. The Russes, as we know, had been for some time subjects of the Khazar kagan. The assumption of the title 'kagan' by the head of the Russes amounted to the declaration of his independence from the Khazars. More than that, it was a declaration of the claims of the Russes to the universal character of their own newly born empire, an attempt to take over the political legacy of the Khazars and to replace the Khazar empire by their own.

It appears that around 825 the Arabs renewed their offensive against the Khazars. The historian Muqaddasi, who wrote in A.H. 375 (A.D. 985/6), says the following: 'I have heard that Mamun attacked the Khazars from Gurjania [Khorezm] and compelled their king to accept Islam.' According to Josef Marquart, this is a reference to the Abbasid Caliph Mamun (813–33).[1] W. Barthold suggested that another Mamun, who became the ruler of Khorezm after 995, is meant here.[2] However, Muqaddasi wrote his book ten years before the other Mamun became Khorezm Shah. There can hardly be any doubt that Muqaddasi was speaking about the Caliph Mamun.[3] Because of this, Marquart's identification of Mamun is to be preferred to Barthold's. If we accept that the Khazar power was temporarily shattered by the Arabs around 825, that would seem an appropriate moment for the Russes to assert their formal independence from the Khazars, and for the prince of the Russes to assume the title of kagan.

[1] J. Marquart, *Osteuropäische und ostasiatische Streifzüge* (Leipzig, 1903), p. 3.
[2] W. Barthold, 'Khazar', *EI*, ii. 936.
[3] D. M. Dunlop, *The History of the Jewish Khazars* (Princeton, 1954), p. 247, n. 57.

Because of their defeat by the Arabs, the Khazars must have tried to resume friendship with Byzantium. To achieve this they had to abandon their claims on the Gothic city of Doras. The agreement between the Byzantines and the Khazars was directed not only against the Arabs, but against the Russes as well. The Byzantines, who formerly had used the Russes against the Khazars, now proved ready to help the Khazars to contain the Russian menace.

Around 833 the Khazar kagan dispatched envoys to Emperor Theophilus asking him to send competent engineers to build a fortress on the river Don, because of a danger from enemies. Neither the author of the continuation of Theophanes' chronicle nor Constantine Porphyrogenitus, both of whom recorded that episode, cared to explain what enemies were meant. Some modern historians attempted to identify these 'enemies' as the Pechenegi (Patzinaks); others were ready to see Magyars in them. However, the Pecheneg inroads reached their climax much later, and the Magyars were still at that time the Khazar kagan's vassals. Therefore we must agree with J. B. Bury and A. A. Vasiliev who identify the Khazars' enemies as the Russes.[1] The fortress was needed by the Khazars to prevent the Russes from penetrating to the lower Volga region.

Emperor Theophilus agreed to assist the Khazars and sent them an impressive expedition headed by an important Byzantine official, Petronas Kamateros. Petronas's flotilla set forth for Cherson (Korsun) where it was joined by another squadron sent from Paphlagonia. In Korsun the materials were reloaded into smaller boats, in which the troops and the engineers were then shipped through Kerch Strait and across the sea of Azov to the mouth of the Don, and up the Don to the site selected for the fortress, at the mouth of Tsymla River near the modern town of Tsymlianskaia. The fortress was built on the left bank of the Don. The central castle was of white stone, while the outer wall was of brick with boulders used as foundation. Brick had been made on the spot in kilns built by Byzantine technicians. The fortress became known as Sarkel, which means in

[1] Constantine Porphyrogenitus, *De Administrando Imperio*, ch. xlii, Moravcsik's edition and Jenkins's translation, pp. 182–9; Theophanes Continuatus, ed. Bekker (Bonn, 1838), pp. 122–4; J. B. Bury, *A History of the Eastern Roman Empire* (London, 1912), p. 418; A. A. Vasiliev, *The Goths in the Crimea*, p. 111; G. Vernadsky, *Ancient Russia*, pp. 304–5.

Ugric 'White House'. The Russian chroniclers call it the 'White Tower' (*Belaia Vezha*).[1] It is probable that smaller forts were built along the Don both above and below.

Having executed his mission, Petronas presented to his government a general report in which he stressed the desirability of strengthening the imperial power in the Crimea by appointing a military governor (*strategos*). The project was approved by Emperor Theophilus, and Petronas himself was appointed to the post with the title of 'Military Governor of the Climata', as the mountain districts of the Crimea inhabited by the Goths were known. The city of Cherson, which had been autonomous since about 705, was now subject to the new governor.

We may suppose that before long the Russes must have felt painfully the new pressure imposed on them by both the building of Sarkel and the consolidation of Byzantine military power in the Crimea, and probably because of this they decided to send envoys to Constantinople for negotiations. The Russian embassy arrived in the Imperial City some time in 838. Nothing is known of the course of the negotiations, but it is obvious that they ended in an impasse. The Russ envoys were not allowed to return home directly but instead were obliged to join the Byzantine embassy which was at that juncture being sent to Emperor Louis I at Ingelheim. The arrival of this embassy was recorded in the Bertinian Annals under the date of 17 January 839, and a resumé of the contents of the letter sent by Theophilus to Louis was likewise inserted which, so far as it concerns the Russ envoys, reads as follows:

He [Theophilus] also sent with them [the Byzantine envoys] certain men who stated that their tribe is known as Rus and that their ruler is known as the kagan [Chacanus]; he [Theophilus] asked that the emperor [Louis] allow them to return home across his possessions since the roads by which they had come to Constantinople were cut by wild and cruel tribes, and he did not want them to face danger in case of returning by the same route.[2]

According to the German chronicler, these men (the Russ

[1] See M. I. Artamonov, 'Sarkel', *Sovetskaia Arkheologiia*, vi (1940), 130–65.

[2] 'Annales Bertiniani', s.a. 839, see Prudentius, 'Annales', ed. Pertz, *MGH, Scriptores*, i (1826), 429–54; F. Kruse, *Chronicon Nortmannorum* (Hamburg and Gotha, 1851), pp. 132–3; G. Vernadsky, *Ancient Russia*, pp. 306–7; A. A. Vasiliev, *The Russian Attack on Constantinople in 860* (Cambridge, Mass., 1946), pp. 6–13.

envoys) proved to be Swedes by birth (*gentis esse Sueonum*). Considering them suspicious the Frankish emperor ordered their arrest for more complete investigation. We may suppose that this move was the result of secret advice from Constantinople. Characteristically enough, in his official letter to Louis, Emperor Theophilus did not say that the Russ envoys had refused to return home from Constantinople the same way they had come. He said that *he* did not want them to face danger by returning by the same route. Most likely, he did not want them to get back at all, or in any case wanted to delay their return home.

We do not know whether the Russ envoys finally succeeded in getting back to Russia from Ingelheim or not. In any case the detention of their envoys must have irritated the Russes, and their relations with Byzantium must have become even more strained than before the embassy of 838. A drastic move of the Russes against Byzantium would be natural under such circumstances, and indeed in the Life of St. George of Amastris we find a story of the Russian attack on that city (Amastris). According to Vasilievsky, the Life was written not later than 842. We may tentatively date the attack to 840.

The attack is described in the following words:

There occurred the invasion of the barbarians, of the Ros, a people which is, as every one knows, utterly wild and rough, devoid of any traces of humaneness. Similar to wild beasts, inhuman in their deeds, they evidenced their bloodthirstiness by their very appearance; they found no pleasure in anything but blood-shedding. They —this people terrible by both their deeds and their name—began their devastations from the Propontis and after having visited other parts of the littoral finally reached the birth place of the saint [i.e. Amastris]. They mercilessly slew [people of] both sexes and every age, not pitying the old, not neglecting the infants, but raising their deadly hand against every one without discrimination, hastening to mete out wholesale ruin as much as they could. They demolish churches, they profane sanctuaries: on the spots where the altars had stood they perform their lawless libations and sacrifices—that old Tauric slaughter of aliens which still flourishes among them. They kill maidens, men, and women; and there was no one to help the victims, to oppose [the barbarians]. They reverence fields, springs, and trees. The Divine Providence allows this, perhaps in order that lawlessness spread around—which, as we know from the Scriptures, Israel had had to suffer many times.

The text of the Life of St. George of Amastris was published by Vasilievsky in 1893.[1] Vasilievsky himself believed in the authenticity of the story, and his point of view was at first generally accepted. Later on, voices of doubt were raised. In her study 'Y eut-il des invasions russes dans l'Empire Byzantin avant 860?' Mme G. da Costa-Louillet vehemently denied the validity of the Life of St. George of Amastris as an historical source.[2] A. A. Vasiliev, who at first had accepted Vasilievsky's conclusions, later on changed his opinion, and in his book *The Russian Attack on Constantinople of 860* (1946) seconded da Costa-Louillet's point of view.

In my opinion, Vasilievsky's conclusions still stand firm in spite of the recent criticism of his argumentation. One of the main points the critics held against him is the assertion, in the story of the Russ invasion, that the Russes came to Amastris from the Propontis. The Greek word *propontis* in its generic sense means 'fore-sea', but it also has a specific meaning, denoting the sea of Marmora. According to Vasilievsky, the word, in the Life of St. George, was used in its generic sense and thus could have denoted the Bosporus. The critics rejected this interpretation and insisted that 'Propontis' could mean only the sea of Marmora and nothing else. And they argued that it would be utterly impossible for the Russes to penetrate into the sea of Marmora in 840.

In this controversy Vasilievsky is right and not his opponents. The decisive evidence is presented by a Byzantine historian of the eleventh century, Michael Attaliates. In his description of the Byzantine-Russian war of 1043 he says that the Russians had reached the Propontis.[3] Now, from Attaliates's own account of that war, as well as from other sources, both Byzantine and Russian, it is perfectly clear that in 1043 the Russians did not penetrate deep into the Bosporus, not to mention the sea of Marmora. The naval battle which ended in Russian disaster took place at the entrance to the Bosporus. It is obvious that

[1] Reprinted in V. G. Vasilievsky, *Trudy*, iii (Petrograd, 1915), 1–71 (Greek text and Vasilievsky's Russian translation).

[2] *Byzantion*, xv (1940–1), 231–48. Mme Da Costa-Louillet also tried to reject the authenticity of the Life of St. Stephen of Surozh, see note N, p. 320.

[3] Michael Attaliates, *Historia*, W. Brunet de Presle, ed. (Bonn, 1853), pp. 20–21; G. Vernadsky, 'The Byzantine-Russian War of 1043', *Südost-Forschungen*, xii (1953), 57–58.

Attaliates used the word 'Propontis' in the same sense as Vasilievsky tried to interpret it.

Returning to the story of the Russian invasion in the Life of St. George of Amastris, it appears that the Russes at that time first came to the entrance of the Bosporus, but for some reason did not dare to enter it and instead cruised along the southern shore of the Black Sea eastward to Amastris.

Among the comments of the author of the 'Life' on the Russes, his statement that the Russes (Ros) are terrible not only by their deeds but also by their name deserves attention. Presumably this is a reference to the Biblical Ros (Rosh). It should be noted that at the time of the Hunnic invasion of 433, Patriarch Proclus had recalled Ezekiel's prophecy (Ezek. xxxviii. 2) concerning the Prince of Rosh.[1] The author of the Life of St. George apparently followed the same tradition. In this case the Biblical reference sounded even more convincing since the name of the invaders was actually identical with the Biblical name.[2] Another interesting comment in the story of the Russian attack on Amastris is the comparison of the human sacrifices of the Russes to those of the ancient Tauri. Apparently the author of the Life connected the Russes with Tauris (Crimea). It may be mentioned, in this connexion, that in Byzantine chronicles the Russes are often called 'Tauroscythae'. Leo Diaconus calls them simply 'Tauri'. Of considerable importance is the remark of the author of the Life that the Russes 'reverence fields, springs, and trees'. This remark shows that he —or his informer—was a keen observer well acquainted with the religious notions of the Russes. On that basis we may think that the story of the Russian attack on Amastris was based on reliable and authentic sources.

II

The use of the title 'kagan' by the ruler of the Russes is confirmed by oriental writers. Ibn-Rusta, describing the Russes, says: 'They have a king who is called Khaqan Rus' (*khaqan* is

---

[1] See G. Vernadsky, *Ancient Russia*, pp. 138–9.

[2] The Biblical name 'Rosh' was in Greek pronounced 'Ros', identically with the name of the Russes (Ross). It would not be amiss to mention that the Biblical 'Rosh' may be compared to 'Rusa', a royal name in the kingdom of Urartu.

the Arabic transcription of kagan). Gardizi has 'Khaqan of Rus'; *Hudud al-Alam* 'Rus-Khagan'.[1]

Both Ibn-Rusta and Gardizi state that the main head-quarters of the Russes were on an island. According to Gardizi:

Rus is an island, which is placed in a sea [Ibn-Rusta says: 'a lake'] and this island is three days' journey in length and breadth and it is all trees and thickets, and its ground is very moist, so much that if you put your foot on the moisture, the ground quakes from its dampness. . . . In this island there are men to the number of 100,000, and these men constantly go out to raid the Slavs in boats, and they seize the Slavs and take them prisoner and they go to the Khazars and the Bulgars and sell them there.[2]

They have no landed property nor villages nor cultivated land; their only occupation is trading in sables and grey squirrel and other furs, and in these they trade and they take as the price gold and silver and secure it in their belts. . . . The Russes have many cities and they expend much money on themselves. (Ibn-Rusta.)[3]

Their king seizes a tithe from the merchants. Constantly 100 or 200 of them come to the Slavs and by force seize from them maintenance while they are there. From the Slavs many men go and serve the Russes in order that through their service they may be safe. (Gardizi.)[4]

Most of the oriental writers laud the military prowess of the Russes:

These people are vigorous and courageous and when they descend on open ground, none can escape from them without being destroyed and their women taken possession of, and themselves taken into slavery. The Russes are strong and observant, and their raids are not made riding, but their raids and fights are only in ships. . . . They have Sulaymani swords, and when there is any call to war, they go out all together, and do not scatter, but are as one hand against their foes until they have conquered them. (Ibn-Rusta.)[5]

They are a mighty nation with vast frames and great courage. They know not defeat, nor does any of them turn his back till he slay or be slain. It is the practice of the individual among them to carry his armour, while bearing suspended upon his person an artisan's outfit, axe, saw, hammer, and the like. He fights with spear and shield; he wears a sword and has hung upon him a lance

---

[1] V. F. Minorsky, *Hudud al Alam*, p. 159.
[2] C. A. Macartney, *The Magyars in the Ninth Century*, p. 213.
[3] Ibid.   [4] Ibid., p. 215.
[5] Ibid., pp. 214–15.

and an instrument resembling a poniard. They fight on foot. (Ibn-Miskawaih, D. S. Margoliouth's translation.)[1]

The children of the Russes were imbued with martial spirit from an early age:

When a child is born to any man among them, he takes a drawn sword to the new-born child and places it between his hands and says to him: I shall bequeath thee no wealth and thou wilt have naught except what thou dost gain for thyself by this sword of thine. (Ibn-Rusta.)[2]

The Russes honour their guests and are kind to strangers who seek shelter with them, and everyone who is in misfortune among them. They do not allow anyone among them to tyrannize over them, and whoever among them does wrong or is oppressive, they find out such a one and expel him from among them. (Ibn-Rusta.)[3]

As we know, in the Khazar kaganate a system of 'dual kingship' prevailed, the kagan being the spiritual ruler and the beg the military commander. Traces of duality of the supreme power are noticeable in the Russ kaganate as well. There, however, the kagan seems to have held full military authority. Judicial authority, on the other hand, belonged to the college of 'doctors' (*volkhvy*).

They have doctors who act as judges, whose judgement is esteemed above that of the king, who are like gods to them. These men order them to come forward with what they desire to their Creator, of women and men and horses, and when the doctors have decreed a thing there is no escape from fulfilling their behest, and the doctor takes the man and the beast from them and casts a rope about his neck, and hangs him from a beam, until his soul has departed, and the doctor says this is an offering to God. (Ibn-Rusta.)[4]

The picture of the Russ kaganate, as drawn by oriental writers, is that of a mighty military and trading state in which, under the authority of the kagan and the volkhvy, all Russes are equal ('they do not allow anyone among them to tyrannize over them'). Trade was the economic foundation of the Russ state. Large landed estates, which were to grow rapidly in the Kievan period, played no role of any importance at the early

---

[1] N. K. Chadwick, *The Beginnings of Russian History* (Cambridge, 1946), p. 138.
[2] C. A. Macartney, op. cit., p. 213.   [3] Ibid., p. 214.
[4] Ibid. Cf. V. F. Minorsky, *Hudud al-Alam*, p. 159.

stage of the history of the Russian kaganate. Grain and other food products were supplied by the Slavic tribes subjected to the Russes. From Gardizi's book it is obvious that the Russes used periodically to collect tribute. That tribute came partly in money, but mostly in kind—slaves, food products, and furs. Besides, the tributary Slavs had to supply maintenance to the personnel of the Russ detachments while the Russes were collecting tribute.

Similar administrative methods were used by the Kievan princes in the tenth century as we know from both Constantine Porphyrogenitus and the Russian *Chronography*. Usually in November the prince of Kiev and the members of his retinue (*druzhina*) would start their tour of the Slavic tribes subject to tribute in order to collect it. This was known as *poludie* ('touring the people'). By that time, a definite quota of tribute was established. The subject tribes paid it without resistance as long as the quota was not raised. However, when Prince Igor, in 945, attempted to collect additional tribute from the tribe of the Drevliane, he was killed by the latter.

The staples of the Russ trade, according to most oriental writers, were furs and slaves. Besides, honey, wax, and walrus tusks, as well as woollen cloth and linen, were exported to the oriental countries by Russ merchants. With Byzantium the Russes, in the tenth century, traded in furs, honey, wax, and slaves. In the ninth century the Russes presumably traded in those goods with the Greek cities in the Crimea but, until 866, had no regular commercial relations with Constantinople. However, since war for the Russes was an opening stage for trade, we may suppose that when the Russes undertook their raid on Amastris they may have had in mind the advantages of a new market for their goods in the future.

The Russ merchants not only visited their immediate eastern neighbours, the Volga Bulgars and the Khazars, but appeared in Baghdad as well. According to a notice inserted into the book of Ibn-Khurdadhbih, who wrote around 847, the Russian merchants went first to 'Tanais, the Slavic River' (Don), and then, by a portage, to the bend in the lower Volga near the present city of Stalingrad.[1] From there they sailed down the Volga and through the Caspian Sea to Iran and Iraq.

[1] See note O, p. 320.

We have now to tackle two moot problems concerning the Russ kaganate, that of the location of the kaganate and that of the ethnic composition of the people Rus.

There is no consensus of scholarly opinion on the situation of the Russ kaganate. Some scholars, including A. A. Shakhmatov, would locate it in north Russia, around Novgorod;[1] P. P. Smirnov places it around Rostov in the upper Volga region;[2] A. A. Vasiliev, in Kiev;[3] E. E. Golubinsky and V. A. Mošin, in Tmutorokan.[4] In my opinion, the latter hypothesis is to be preferred.

Let us examine the above four hypotheses one by one, starting with Novgorod.

(1) *Novgorod.* At first glance there would appear to be enough reasons for considering Novgorod-the-Great the centre of the Russ kaganate. Of the large cities of old Russia Novgorod was the closest to Scandinavia and easily accessible to the Norsemen via the Baltic Sea and the Neva–Lake Ladoga–Volkhov River route. It is known that after the middle of the ninth century there was a large Varangian colony in Novgorod. Besides, Ibn-Rusta's statement that 'Russia' was an island 'around which is a lake' would fit the location of Novgorod on the banks of the river Volkhov close to Lake Ilmen.

There are, however, a number of considerations which make the Novgorod hypothesis unacceptable. In the first place, it will be recalled that in their earlier drive through the upper parts of the Dvina River to the upper Volga and lower Oka region the Norsemen seem to have by-passed Novgorod. It was only in the middle of the ninth century, with the coming of Rurik, that Novgorod assumed a leading role in north Russia. It would be hard to imagine that the Russian raid on the Crimea in about 790 could have been directed from Novgorod. Nor does it seem possible that the centre of the Russ kaganate was in Novgorod in 838, at the time the envoys of the Russian kagan appeared in Constantinople. Besides, the very title 'kagan'

---

[1] A. A. Shakhmatov, *Drevneishie sudby Russkogo plemeni* (Petrograd, 1919), p. 56. See also S. F. Platonov, 'Rusa', *Dela i Dni*, i (1920), 1–5.

[2] P. P. Smirnov, *Volzkyi shliakh i starodavni Rusy* (Kiev, 1938).

[3] A. A. Vasiliev, *The Russian Attack on Constantinople in 860* (Cambridge, Mass., 1946), pp. 66–69, 173–5, 177–82.

[4] E. E. Golubinsky, *Istoriia Russkoi tserkvi*, i, Part i (Moscow, 1901), 41–45; V. A. Mošin, 'Nachalo Rusi', *Byzantinoslavica*, iii (1931), 293–6.

could hardly be assumed by any ruler of Novgorod. The title belongs to the milieu of the Eurasian steppes, not to the Scandinavian background. Furthermore, had the centre of the Russian kaganate been in Novgorod, it would be natural to expect that the oriental writers would mention the rigidity of the north Russian climate. Even of Galicia Ibn-Rusta says that 'in this country the cold is very severe, and it reaches such severity that a man there digs himself in like a wild animal under the earth'. The only oriental author who says that the country of the Russes 'is an exceedingly cold country' is Ibn-Miskawaih in his description of the Russian raid on Berdaa in Transcaucasia. But Ibn-Miskawaih also states that the country of the Russes is close to the Caspian Sea. For the inhabitants of Transcaucasia everything north of the Caucasian range seems a 'cold country'.

(2) *The Rostov area.* P. P. Smirnov's hypothesis is based on the assumption that the Volga was the main way of communication which the Russes used both in their oriental trade and their military undertakings. Actually, however, the Russes were able to use, at the time of the flourishing of their kaganate, only the upper part of the course of the Volga as far as the city of Bulgar, and the lower course which they reached—as Ibn-Khurdadhbih states—from the Don area. The middle course of the Volga was controlled by the Volga Bulgars. Besides, the same consideration about the absence of any indication of the severity of Russia's climate in the basic oriental works on the Russes, which points against centring the Russian kaganate around Novgorod, speaks against the Rostov theory of P. P. Smirnov. In addition, there is no suitable 'island' in the Rostov region to fit the description of 'Russia' by Ibn-Rusta and Gardizi.

(3) *Kiev.* After its seizure by Oleg, around 878, Kiev became the capital of the Russian state.[1] It would seem possible that Kiev had been an important Russ centre long before Oleg. However, we know that in the 840's and 850's Kiev was controlled by the Magyars (see section 4 below). This excludes the possibility of its being the centre of the Russ kaganate at the early stage of the latter's development. Furthermore, Kiev is not situated on an island.

(4) *Tmutorokan.* Tmutorokan is located at the mouth of the Kuban River on the Taman peninsula which is washed by the

[1] See Chapter 6, section 2, below.

Black Sea in the south, the Kerch strait in the west, and the sea of Azov in the north. The Taman 'peninsula' is actually an island, since it is separated from the mainland by the channels of the Kuban delta. The swamps and thickets mentioned by both Ibn-Rusta and Gardizi actually abound along the lower stretches of the Kuban River. It will be recalled in this connexion that in the seventh century Tmutorokan was known as 'the Bog of the Ros' (Mal-Ros).[1] Furthermore, as has been mentioned, Ibn-Miskawaih says that the country of the Russes is close to the Caspian Sea. Of all the four proposed locations for the centre of the Russian kaganate this statement fits only Tmutorokan. Tmutorokan is even closer to the Crimea (across the Kerch strait). On many occasions and in many periods Tmutorokan (ancient Phanagoria) and Kerch (ancient Panticapaeum) were politically united, being part of the same state. Such was the situation at the time of the kingdom of Bosporus, as well as in the later periods. Geopolitically, Tmutorokan belonged to the Crimea. And as we know, many a Byzantine writer connected the Ros with the Crimea. Some of them called the Russes 'Tauroscythae' or 'Tauri'. This is understandable if we place the Russes in Tmutorokan but would contradict any other of the four proposed locations of the Russ kaganate.

Tmutorokan is situated close to the heart of the Khazar empire. From this point of view it seems natural that when the Russ ruler decided to assert his independence from the Khazars, he assumed the title of the Khazar ruler, that of 'kagan'. It should be noted that in the Kievan period, when Tmutorokan was the capital of an autonomous Russian principality, only those Russian rulers who were connected with Tmutorokan were known as kagans. The following Russian princes are so called in Russian sources of the eleventh and the twelfth centuries: Vladimir the Saint, who controlled Tmutorokan after 989; Iaroslav the Wise, who became master of Tmutorokan after the death of his brother Mstislav, prince of Tmutorokan and Chernigov, in 1036; and Prince Oleg of Chernigov (contemporary of Vladimir Monomach), who had ruled Tmutorokan before his accession to the throne of Chernigov. Presumably, two other Russian princes of the Kievan period, the above-mentioned Mstislav and his grandfather Sviatoslav, also

[1] See Chapter 2, section 3, above.

had this title. In the Ossetian tale of *Iry Dada* Mstislav is called *padishah* (emperor) and not simply *ældar* (prince). As regards Sviatoslav, who attempted to build up a huge empire,[1] and who conquered the Khazar kaganate, we may safely suppose that he had the title of 'kagan'.

Both Ibn-Rusta and Gardizi say that the Russes raided the Slavic tribes in boats. This also fits the location of Tmutorokan. Sailing across the sea of Azov the Russes could easily reach its northern shores, and from there to go up the Don and Donets rivers into the lands of the Slavic tribes of the Severi and the Viatichi. Besides, via some smaller rivers discharging into the sea of Azov, like Berda and Kalmius, and then using the portages to the eastern tributaries of the Dnieper, like the Konskaia and the Volchya and the Samara, they could easily penetrate into the Dnieper basin. Furthermore, it seems likely that part of the Russes lived in the Don–Donets area as well as in some sections of the Crimea. The close connexion between Tmutorokan and Chernigov (in the land of the Severi) in the eleventh century was possible precisely because of the existence of a convenient system of riverways in northern Tauria and the Azov region.

One more consideration in favour of centring the Russ kaganate in Tmutorokan is the latter's proximity to the Caucasus. In the late ninth, the tenth, and the early eleventh centuries, the Russes undertook several expeditions in the Caucasus and Transcaucasia. Undoubtedly, Tmutorokan served as the main base for these campaigns.

While Tmutorokan seems to have been the headquarters of the Russ kagan, we should not think that all of the Russes lived there. The figure of the Russ population—100,000 men—as given by Gardizi might refer to the whole Russ tribe, not to Tmutorokan alone. Presumably only part of the Russes stayed in Tmutorokan. Other groups of them, as has just been mentioned, might have lived in the Crimea, and in the Don–Donets area (where they are located by Zacharias Rhetor); still others in the Kievan region (on the banks of the Ros River). A Russ colony also was established in north Russia, around the town of Rusa, south of Lake Ilmen (see section 3 below).

Tmutorokan apparently served as the political, religious,

---

[1] See Chapter 6, section 3, below.

and military centre of all the Russes. In the *Igor Tale* the 'Tmutorokan Idol' (*bolvan*) is mentioned. This, presumably, was the statue of a divinity worshipped by the Russes. We may think that the college of the Russ 'doctors' (*volkhvy*) resided in Tmutorokan. Military supplies of various kinds must have been stored in Tmutorokan as they were, centuries later, stored in the Zaporozhie *sech*, the stronghold of the Ukrainian Cossacks below the Dnieper cataracts, in the sixteenth, seventeenth, and eighteenth centuries.

Commercially, Tmutorokan seems to have been the main base of the Russes for their oriental and Caucasian trade. It is from Tmutorokan that furs and other goods collected by the Russes from the Slavs and other tributary tribes were shipped, across the sea of Azov, to the Don, and then to the Volga River and the Caspian Sea (consider Ibn-Khurdadhbih's evidence). It should be mentioned that the French translator of Ibn-Khurdadhbih's work in the *Bibliotheca Arabicorum* makes the Russian merchants 'descend the Don' (*descendent le Don*). Such a translation is apparently based upon the preconceived idea that they must have arrived directly from Novgorod. Now, in the Arabic original it is simply said that the Russian merchants 'go' (*sārū*)[1] the way of the Don, and it is almost certain that they used to come from the sea of Azov up the stream and not downstream from the north. In Ibn-al-Faqih's revision of Ibn-Khurdadhbih's work (903) the town of Samakars is mentioned as one of the stations used by the Russian merchants. The name 'Samakars' (or 'Samkush', as M. J. de Goje would have it) may refer to either Kerch (Sam-Kerch) or to Tmutorokan (in case we consider it a corruption of 'Tamatarcha', the Byzantine name of Tmutorokan).

In the *Book of Lands* by al-Istakhri (written in 951) we find a somewhat puzzling statement that

the Rus are divided into three tribes. According to Istakhri, one Russ tribe lives near the Bulgars; their king lives in the city of Kuthaba, which is greater than Bulgar. The second tribe is called Saqlab, the third Utanie, and their king lives in Artha. Merchants only come to Kuthaba; to Artha none goes, because the inhabitants

---

[1] I offered this interpretation of *sārū* in my book *Ancient Russia* (1943), p. 283. Recently Tadeusz Lewicki has accepted my version, see his *Źródła arabskie*, i (1956), 133.

kill every stranger and throw him into the water. Therefore no one reports of their affairs, and they have no connection with anyone. From Artha black fox furs and lead are exported.[1]

Kuthaba (or Kuyaba) may be identified as Kiev; Saqlab (the Arabic name of the Slavs), with the land of the Slovene, i.e. Novgorod. The two names of the third Russ tribe, Artha and Utanie are not self-evident. Therefore the location of that Russ tribe remains a moot problem. V. A. Mošin places it in Tmutorokan, with which I agree. The very name 'Utanie' (or 'Artha-Utanie') seems to be a corruption (or, rather, an imitation) of 'Tmutorokan'.

As Tmutorokan was a military base of the Russes, it is natural to suppose that unknown foreigners would not be allowed to enter it without permission, and those who entered might have been killed. The statement concerning the export from 'Utanie' of furs and metals should not be interpreted in the sense that furs and metals were native products of the country 'Utanie'. As has been mentioned, Tmutorokan served as the main base for the Russ trade with the Orient. Various goods, obtained from different quarters, must have been stored there, ready for export. Furs must have been brought from north Russia and metals from the Caucasus.

In my opinion, al-Istakhri's statement must be referred to the first half of the tenth century, that is to the period of the reigns of Oleg and Igor. At that time Kiev, Novgorod, and Tmutorokan were united under the same authority—the suzerainty of the Grand Prince of Kiev.

III

As regards the ethnic composition of the Russ people in the ninth and tenth centuries, while the extreme 'Normanists' consider the Russes pure Norsemen, the extreme 'Antinormanists' consider them pure Slavs. Both sides neglect the early Alanic background of the Russes. The extreme 'Normanists' even disregard or deny the existence of the name Rus (Ros) in south

---

[1] C. A. Macartney, *The Magyars in the Ninth Century*, p. 221. See also V. F. Minorsky, *Hudud al-Alam*, pp. 159, 434–8. On al-Istakhri and his information on the Slavs and Russes see T. Lewicki, 'Świat Słowiański w oczach pisarzy arabskich', *Slavia Antiqua*, ii (1949/50), 360–3; T. Lewicki, 'Ze studiów nad źródłami arabskimi', I, *Slavia Antiqua*, iii (1952), 162–3.

Russia centuries before the coming of the Varangians. In the opinion of some of them, the Russes received their name from the Finnish *Ruotsi*, the Finnish name of the Swedes, in the middle of the ninth century.[1] From the linguistic point of view the derivation of *Rus'* from *Ruotsi* is theoretically possible. From the historical point of view, however, the hypothesis is untenable. The name 'Rus' ('Ros') is an old name as is well certified by our sources. More likely than not it derives from the Alanic 'Ruxs'. Personally I have no doubt about it.

The Normanists are on much firmer ground when they assert the presence of the Norse ethnic element in the Russ people of the ninth and the tenth centuries. In the first place, we have the evidence of the Bertinian Annals (839) that the Russ envoys who came to Ingelheim proved to be Swedes. The second important piece of evidence is that of the Russo-Byzantine treaties of 911 and 944. Most of the names of the Russ envoys listed there are obviously Norse. Thirdly, we have the names of the Dnieper cataracts both in 'Russian' and in Slavic as recorded by Constantine Porphyrogenitus, who wrote between the years 948 and 952.[2] Most of the 'Russian' names may be easily derived from the Norse. On the other hand, there is evidence to the contrary showing the importance of the Slavic element among the Russes. In the report on the Russ merchants in Ibn-Khurdadhbih's book the Russes are called 'a kind of Slavs' (or 'a tribe of Slavs'). Furthermore, in the Russian Chronography it is stated that 'the Slavs and the Russes are one people'. In the tenth and eleventh centuries 'Slav' (Slovenin) was used to denote a Novgorodian (one of the Slovene of Novgorod), and 'Rus' (Rusin), a Kievan.

The best way to reconcile the contradictions in the evidence available to us concerning the ethnic composition of the Russes of the ninth and tenth centuries is to admit the presence of both the Norse and the Slavic elements in the people of Rus at that time, in other words to consider them a symbiosis of Slavs and Norsemen. From this point of view it may be seen that in the

---

[1] For a succinct review of various explanations of the origin of the name 'Rus' see Max Vasmer, *Russisches etymologisches Wörterbuch*, ii. 551–2. It should be noted that the existence of the name Ros (also in the form Rus) in antiquity and the early Middle Ages is not even mentioned by Vasmer.

[2] Constantine Porphyrogenitus, *De Administrando Imperio*, ch. ix. See Gy. Moravcsik's edition (and R. J. H. Jenkins's translation), pp. 58–61.

ninth and the first half of the tenth centuries the Russ envoys were usually chosen from among the Russes of Norse extraction. Also, that the names given the Dnieper cataracts by the Norsemen, presumably in the ninth century, were still used in the tenth century. All this indicates that the Norsemen played an important role at the top of Russ society and the Russ state; it does not prove by any means that all the Russes were Norsemen in this period.

As has been said, the mergence of a group of Norsemen with the Russes must have taken place in the second half of the eighth century. Most likely the Russes themselves had engaged a company of Norse warriors to strengthen their own army. The commander of the Norse contingent naturally must have occupied an influential position in the Russ army. Eventually, he might have seized the power, proclaiming himself prince (and later kagan) of the Russes. While this is possible, it is not absolutely certain, since there is no information on the nationality of the first Russ kagans. They may have been Norsemen, as the Rurikids in Kiev later were; but they may have been Slavs or Alans. Many Slavic tribes, originally controlled by the Alans, seem to have been ruled by a dynasty of Alanic origin.

The ruler of the Russes used the old *tamga* (clan emblem) of the original royal Russ clan. Owing to the researches of S. P. Tolstov, P. N. Tretiakov, and B. A. Rybakov, we know that the design of the tamga of this type, the trident (variant, two-pronged spearhead), is found on objects of the Alanic-Bulgar antiquities of the fourth to the sixth centuries; in the sites of western settlements of the Khazars (seventh to ninth centuries); and in the antiquities of the Kievan region as well as in those of the land of the Viatichi in the upper Oka region (sixth and seventh centuries). The design is strikingly similar to that used by the rulers of the Bosporan kingdom of the second and third centuries as well as to that of the Khorezmian tamgas. Of the same design are the emblems of the Russian princes of the Kievan period.[1]

Even though the first Russ kagans might have been Norsemen, they used the old Russ tamga. This could have been done by a Norseman who had married a Russ princess. It is said in the Ossetian tale of *Iry Dada* that when Mstislav of

[1] See note P, p. 321.

Tmutorokan married an Alanic princess, Nado of the Bur-galty clan, he put the Alanic tamga on his standard. Dzambulat Dzanty informed me (by letter) that, around 1910, he saw the tamga of the Burgalty clan in the home of a descendant of the clan in the village Senkhay, about nine miles from the town of Mozdok in the northern Caucasus. The tamga is of bronze and had a two-pronged form: ༙. According to Rybakov, a tamga used as the top of a standard (found in the Nalchik district in the northern Caucasus) resembles the trident. A bow-case with a design of Mstislav's tamga was found in Tmutorokan. It is similar to the emblem (trident) of his father, Vladimir the Saint.

Presumably, the Norsemen constituted only a minority among the Russes. The bulk of the people must have been Slavs, or Slavisized Alans. This explains the fact that by the time of the compilation of the Russian Chronography in the late eleventh and early twelfth centuries, Slavic was considered the language of the Rus. Comparatively few Norse words entered the Russian language. Most of them are terms of princely administration, as, for example, *grid'* (bodyguard), *tiun* (steward), and *iabetnik* (agent). Besides, the Russian word *vitiaz'* ('valiant warrior'), which entered all Slavic languages, derives from 'viking'; and, incidentally, 'knout' (in Russian *knut*) is also of Norse origin (*knutr*). It is noteworthy that there are, in the Russian vocabulary, no words of Norse origin bearing on religion and magic, in fact almost none related to spiritual and intellectual life. This enables us to conclude that while the Russ kagans may have been Norsemen, the Russ 'doctors' (*volkhvy*) were Slavs.

While at the time of the coming of the Norsemen the Russes were a separate tribe, eventually they merged with some of the other east Slavic (Antian) tribes, especially with the Poliane and the Severiane. The process of this mergence must have been facilitated by the readiness of many Slavs to serve in the Russ army and administration, for which we have Gardizi's evidence.

3. *The Russes in north Russia and the 'Calling of the Varangians'*

The most precious furs in which the Russes traded with the oriental countries came from north Russia. In this respect north Russia was indispensable to the Russes as a source of their prosperity. North Russia was also important for them from the military point of view as an area through which they could obtain fresh contingents of Norse warriors from Scandinavia every time their own army suffered serious losses from war casualties or diseases.

Furs could be obtained from the hunters and trappers of north Russia either by purchase or by coercion in the form of tribute. Also by a combination of both methods. For purchase, a network of commercial agents was needed. For coercion, military forces were indispensable. Because of this, the Russes had to keep part of their men on duty in north Russia. These could always be reinforced by new-comers from Scandinavia. Of the latter, some were Varangian bands in search of adventure who were eager to enter the Russ service for a specified term. These would not lose their ethnic identity. The trouble with them was that they were inclined, whenever circumstances allowed, to seize power and to collect tribute for themselves instead of for their employers.

Other Norsemen proved willing to join the Russes for good and eventually merged with them. The upshot of all this was that gradually a sizeable group of the Russes, which consisted of both the Russes from the south and the new-comers from Scandinavia, established itself in north Russia. It must have centred around the town of Rusa, south of Lake Ilmen, as the town's name itself indicates. (The town later became known as Staraia Rusa, i.e. 'Old Rusa'). This Russ group may be called the northern branch, or northern extension, of the Russian kaganate.

The connexion between south Russia and the northern branch of the kaganate could have been maintained through the land of the Severi and Smolensk via a network of riverways and portages. The upper stretches of the Donets and the Oskol rivers come close to the upper Seim River. Continuing down the Seim and then up the Desna River one could easily reach the land of Smolensk. It was also possible to travel from the land of the Severi to that of Smolensk via the tributaries of the Oskol and the Don, and then those of the Oka, a stretch of the Oka itself, and the Ugra River. Some of the small rivers in that system of riverways are quite shallow at present but they were navigable in the earlier times.

The Russes in north Russia were not strong enough to establish their own administration over the local Slavic and Finnish tribes. Instead, they had to come to terms with them. Together all of them formed a kind of federation. As we may conclude from the story of 'Calling the Varangians' in the Russian Chronography, the following tribes were members of this federation: the Russes, centring around Rusa; the Chud, a Finnish tribe in Estonia; the Slovene, centring around Novgorod; the Krivichi, centring around Smolensk; and the Ves, a Finnish tribe west of Beloozero. Presumably each of these tribes had to contribute its quota of furs and each had its share of profits in the commercial undertakings of the Russes. In this way the economic systems of north and south Russia were closely inter-related. The prosperity of the Russian kaganate as a whole depended on the prosperity of the northern area, and vice versa.

From what has been just said, it is clear that the land of the Severi was the most important link in the network of communications between the lower Don region and Smolensk, that is —in regard to the two terminal points—between Tmutorokan and Rusa.

When the Khazars had begun their policy of containing the Russes in the 830's, they were well aware of the importance for them of severing the connexion between south Russia and north Russia. The fortress of Sarkel was intended to bar to the Russes the way to the upper Don as well as to the lower Volga. The Donets riverway was still open to the Russians, but the Khazars were now in position, using Sarkel as their base, to patrol the course of the lower Donets in order to prevent the Russ commercial caravans from using this route. Not satisfied with this, the Khazars undertook a series of campaigns to the north and north-west with the aim of extending their control over the Slavic tribes in the wooded steppe zone. As we know from the entry in the Russian Chronography under A.D. 859 (the date to be adjusted to around 850), the Khazars imposed tribute 'upon the Poliane, the Severi, and the Viatichi, and collected a silver coin and a *veveritsa* from each hearth'.[1]

---

[1] The silver coins which circulated in Russia at this time were mainly Arabic dirhems. According to B. A. Romanov, the *veveritsa* (presumably, 'squirrel') was reckoned as one-fourth of the dirhem, see *Istoriia Kultury Drevnei Rusi*, i. 285; T. Lewicki, 'Z dziejów peniadza arabskiego w Europie Wschodniej', *Archeologia*, iii (1949), 228–9. According to V. L. Ianin, one dirhem corresponded to one Russian *kuna* 'martin' (25 of which corresponded to 1 Russian grivna); 1 kuna was

The establishment of the Khazar control over the Severi was a serious blow to the Russes. The Khazars, of course, were not numerous enough to patrol the whole land of the Severi, and small detachments of Russes probably could go through, but large commercial caravans would be easily detected by Khazar scouts and thus exposed to the danger of the Khazar attack.

The clogging of the commercial ways between south and north Russia must have resulted in a serious economic crisis in north Russia. To add to the troubles of the tribes of the northern federation, the Varangians got out of control and began raiding the country. In the same entry of the Russian Chronography where the establishment of the Khazar control over the southern tribes is mentioned we read that 'the Varangians from beyond the sea imposed tribute upon the Chud, the Slovene, the Meria, the Ves, and the Krivichi'. In this list we find the name of the Finnish tribe Meria (in the Rostov region) which does not occur in the list of the tribes who, later on, 'called the Varangians'. On the other hand, the Russes are not mentioned in the former list. Presumably, the Russes refused to pay tribute to the Varangians but were not able to protect the other tribes of the north Russian federation from the Varangian oppression.

Part of the Varangian invaders must have been Danes. According to the Life of St. Anscarius a number of Danes sailed in 852 across the Baltic Sea and seized a city in the land of the Slavs. This city may be identified as Novgorod. Receiving a large ransom, the Danes went home.[1] It is possible that the same episode has also been recorded in the Russian Chronography under A.D. 862. It should be noted in this connexion that the dates in the early parts of the Chronography are not reliable and have to be adjusted with the help of other sources available. The date 862 seems to correspond to 852. The chronicler applied that latter date to the accession to the throne of Emperor Michael III, which actually occurred in 842. The entry in question reads as follows: 'And they [the Slovene] chased the Varangians away and did not give them [permanent] tribute, and set out to govern themselves.'

---

equal to 6 veveritsas, see V. L. Ianin, *Denezhnovesovye sistemy Russkogo Srednevekovia* (Moscow, 1956), pp. 40, 100, 160.

[1] Rimbert, *Vita Anskarii*, ed. G. Waitz (Hanover, 1884), p. 43; G. Vernadsky, *Ancient Russia*, p. 335.

While the Danes were repulsed, the situation in the Novgorod area did not improve, especially since the road south was not cleared. Therefore the crisis continued 'and there was no justice in the administration, and clan rose against clan, and a civil war started'. It was at that juncture that the tribes of the north Russian federation decided to 'seek a prince who may rule over us, and judge us according to the law'. As a result of this decision, as the chronicler informs us, they sent envoys overseas to 'call the Varangians'.

Let us now examine that famous story as recorded in the Hypathian version of the Chronography (A.D. 862).[1]

The Rus, the Chud, the Slovene, the Krivichi, and the Ves, said [to the Varangians]: our land is great and abundant but there is no order in it. Come to rule and reign over us. And three brothers chose to come with their clan. . . . The oldest, Rurik, located himself in Novgorod; the second, Sineus, in Beloozero; and the third, Truvor, in Izborsk [a town near Pskov]. After two years, Sineus and his brother, Truvor, died, and Rurik assumed the sole authority. He assigned cities to his followers, Polotsk to one, Rostov to another, and to another Beloozero. In these cities there are thus Varangian colonists, but the first settlers were, in Novgorod, Slovene; in Polotsk, Krivichi; at Beloozero, Ves; in Rostov, the Meria; and in Murom, the Muroma [a Finnish tribe].

In order better to understand the background of the story we have to take into consideration the time when it was edited. There cannot be any doubt that the wording of the story was adapted by the editor of the Chronography to the circumstances of his own time. The chronicler, as well as his readers, tried to find, in the old historical events, answers to their own vexing problems, and at times involuntarily interpreted the past in the light of the present.

The project of compiling a History of Russia (*Povest' vremennykh let*, i.e. 'Chronography'), on the basis of previous records, was started by the monks of the Crypt Monastery (*Pechersky monastyr'*) around 1110, in the reign of Prince Sviatopolk II of Kiev. Presumably one of these monks was Nestor who was, for a long time, considered the author of the whole work. Sviatopolk died in 1113. The first redaction of the Chronography was finished after his death (1114). It did not, however, satisfy the

---

[1] *Povest' Vremennykh Let*, i. 18; Cross and Sherbowitz's translation, p. 59.

advisers of Sviatopolk's successor Vladimir Monomach. By the order of the new government the copy of the work was taken from the Crypt Monastery and sent to another one more favoured by Vladimir—the St. Michael Monastery at Vydubichi. There the manuscript was revised by Abbot Sylvester (1116). In 1118 a new edition was prepared by an anonymous writer.[1]

While the first redaction was favourable to Sviatopolk in describing the events of his reign, the redaction of 1116 is rather critical of him and favourable to Vladimir Monomach. It should be borne in mind in this connexion that during the reign of Sviatopolk a serious economic crisis developed in Russia. There was a sharp contrast between the rich at the top of society and the poor at the bottom. The latter complained of the exorbitant rates of interest collected by Kievan capitalists on loans. The plight of the identured labourers (*zakupy*) was hard. The salt monopoly introduced by Sviatopolk, which resulted in high prices on salt, added to the general discontent. Sviatopolk's death on 16 April 1113 released the forces of opposition. Riots started in Kiev. The populace plundered the houses of the high officials and the rich. A social revolution seemed imminent. To avoid it, the Kievan *veche* (city assembly), disregarding the order of seniority of the Russian princes (descendants of Rurik), called to the throne not the senior but the most popular among them, the prince of Pereiaslav, Vladimir Monomach, known for his righteousness. Immediately after his accession to the throne of Kiev, Vladimir initiated a far-reaching programme of social reforms. Peace was restored and public confidence in the princely power reaffirmed.[2]

It is in the light of these events that we may best approach the interpretation, by the editor of the second redaction of the Chronography, of the meaning of the 'Calling of the Varangians'. According to him, riots had preceded the decision of the federated tribes to 'seek a prince who may rule over us, and judge us according to the law'. The main reason of the 'calling the Varangians' in the ninth century, as interpreted around 1116, was that of restoring order in the country. That was done

---

[1] See G. Vernadsky, *Kievan Russia* (New Haven, 1948), pp. 285–6; D. S. Likhachev, *Russkie Letopisi* (Moscow and Leningrad, 1947), pp. 145–72.

[2] G. Vernadsky, *Kievan Russia*, pp. 93–94.

by Vladimir Monomach in the early twelfth century, and that, precisely, was expected from Rurik, according to the chronicler who was a contemporary of Vladimir.

When coming to Novgorod, Rurik assumed the leadership over the Russes in north Russia, and his clan merged with the Russes. Because of this, in the Laurentian version of the Chronography his clan is called 'Rus'. It is noteworthy that in the list of the Varangian tribes, inserted into the Chronography on the occasion of the 'Calling of the Varangians', we find no Danes but instead (in the Laurentian version) the Rus. Rurik must have been a Dane.

Rurik may be identified with Roric of Jutland of Western annals. Such identification was first suggested by Friedrich Kruse in 1836, but not then accepted. In 1929 the late N. T. Belaiew approached the problem once more and with the use of some new materials and certain new arguments fully confirmed Kruse's theory. In my opinion the identification is valid.[1]

We are thus in a position to make a brief sketch of Rurik's life. His father, of the clan of Skjoldung, had been ousted from Jutland and had pledged allegiance to Charlemagne, from whom around 782 he received Friesland as his fief. Rurik was born about the year 800. His childhood was passed in turbulent surroundings since his father and, after the latter's death, his elder brother were constantly at war with the usurping rulers of Jutland. In 826, or thereabouts, Rurik's elder brother Harald, who had succeeded in seizing part of Jutland but was later expelled from it, placed himself under the protection of Emperor Louis the Pious and was baptized at Ingelheim, near Mainz. As Harald came thither with all his family we may surmise that Rurik was baptized as well. If so, he can hardly have taken his conversion seriously, for he later returned to paganism.

After Harald's conversion the emperor granted him as his fief the district of Rustringen in Friesland. Rurik received his share in it and after his brother's death became lord of the whole fief. Even before Harald's death the two brothers had to

---

[1] F. Kruze (Kruse), 'O proiskhozhdenii Riurika', *ŽMNP*, ix (1836), 47–73; N. T. Belaiew (Beliaev), 'Rorik Iutlandskii i Riurik nachalnoi letopisi', *Seminarium Kondakovianum*, iii (1929), 215–70; G. Vernadsky, *Ancient Russia*, pp. 337–9. Recently, Baron Michael de Taube took exception to Kruse and Belaiew's views, see M. de Taube, 'Nouvelles Recherches sur l'histoire politique et religieuse de l'Europe Orientale', *Istina*, 1957, No. 1, pp. 27–32.

fight stubbornly to protect their lands from attack on the part of the king of Denmark, and after the death of Emperor Louis Rurik's position became quite precarious. According to the Treaty of Verdun (843) Friesland was included in Lothaire's portion of the empire and it appears that Rurik lost his fief. During the next few years Rurik led the life of an adventurer, taking part in several raids both on the Continent and on England. In the annals of those years he became known as *fel Christianitatis*, 'the gall of Christendom'. In 845 his boats sailed up the river Elbe, and in the same year he raided northern France. In 850 Rurik launched a fleet of 350 boats with which he looted the coastal district of England. In the next years he turned his attention to the mouth of the Rhine and to Friesland. Lothaire was compelled to compromise and returned Friesland to Rurik on condition that he would defend the shores of the empire from the attacks of other vikings. Since Rurik was now prevented from looting the shores of the North Sea he must have thenceforth shifted his attention to the Baltic, being probably well informed of the Danes' raid on Novgorod of 852.

Rurik's interest in the Baltic area must have received a new impetus when he was forced by Lothaire to give up Friesland once more and was granted in its place another fief in Jutland (854). Becoming master of southern Jutland, Rurik acquired direct access to the Baltic Sea and was thus in an even better position than before to take active part in Baltic affairs.

Presumably Rurik set forth for Russia in 855 or in 856. The chronicler states that Rurik came to Russia with two brothers, Sineus and Truvor. No such names are recorded in Western annals. According to N. T. Belaiew, Sineus and Truvor must be interpreted not as personal names but as epithets for Rurik himself. In Norse 'Signjotr' means 'victorius' and 'Thruwar' 'trustworthy'. In medieval story-telling the legend of three brothers founding a city or a state was a popular motif.

To complete the story of Rurik, he seems to have stayed in the Novgorod area for about thirteen years, putting in order his new possessions. He continued, however, to watch the development of events in the west, and in 867 made a vain attempt to regain Friesland with the help of the Danes. The death in 869 of Lothaire, king of Lotharingia, who had in 854 received Friesland as a fief from his father the emperor Lothaire, called for a general redivision of all the holdings in the Frankish empire, and Rurik decided that the moment was propitious for presenting his claims as well. He went, accordingly, to Nimwegen for an interview with Charles the Bald, a brother of the Emperor Lothaire, and promised to support him in return for his backing. In 873 Rurik received Friesland back, and thereafter his name receives no further mention in the Frankish annals. Presumably he died not long after regaining his old fief.

4. *The Russes in Kiev*

As has been said (see section 3 above), the Kievan chronicler of the early twelfth century considered the internal disorders in north Russia in the middle of the ninth century, amounting to a civil war, the cause of the 'Calling of the Varangians' by the peoples of north Russia. It cannot be denied that north Russia was at that time in the grip of a serious political and economic crisis. But the causes of this crisis were not local. Besides the invasions of the Varangian bands from overseas, the main cause of the crisis was the severing of the roads between north and south Russia by the Khazars and the Magyars, as we shall presently see. The clogging of the lines of communications between Tmutorokan and Rusa resulted in the disintegration of the whole mechanism of the oriental trade of the Russ kaganate.

In view of this, restoration of order in administration would not, in itself, be sufficient for restoring prosperity in north Russia. It was only part of the task for which Rurik was called to Novgorod. The other part, which was more difficult, was to clear the roads to the south and to re-establish the communications between north and south Russia. For this the forces of the northern tribes alone had proved to be insufficient, and this may have been one of the main reasons for their 'Calling the Varangians'. They needed more troops for an expedition to the south.

Under the leadership of Rurik and with the assistance of his Danish retinue, the Russes of north Russia were apparently able to extend their control over north Russia, including the Rostov area, within a few years. Even before that task had been completed, Rurik encouraged a group of his followers to go south. According to the chronicler, Rurik 'had two men [Askold and Dir], not of his own kin, but boyars, and they asked his permission to go to Constantinople with their kin, and they went, accordingly, down the Dnieper River'. This story is inserted in the Chronography under the same date as the 'Calling of the Varangians' (862). We may tentatively refer Askold's departure to 856.

The chronicler's statement that the aim of Askold's campaign was Constantinople deserves special attention. Apparently the Russes contemplated at this time not merely clearing the road to Tmutorokan, but opening a new road—to Byzantium.

Constantinople, the Imperial City (in Norse 'Miklagard'; in Slavic 'Tsargrad'), lured by its wealth and splendour many would-be invaders, including the Huns, the Avars, the Bulgars, and the Arabs. While the Russes, at the time of their raid on Amastris, did not dare to enter the Bosporus and to attack Constantinople, their Amastris expedition showed the feasibility of reaching the heart of the Byzantine empire. Since Tmutorokan was a Russian stronghold, and since a number of Russes settled in the Crimea in the late eighth and the early ninth centuries, the Russes were in a position to obtain, through the Crimean Greeks, reliable information on Byzantine affairs. They must have watched closely the course of events in Byzantium and the intricate moves of Byzantine diplomacy. Through the Russes the the Varangians could easily get information about Constantinople. With Rurik's coming to Novgorod and with his assuming leadership over the northern group of the Russes, relations between the Russes and the Varangians, in other words between the eastern and the western Norsemen, became even closer. Rurik himself had been a leading figure in the western expansion of the Norsemen, and now when he had associated himself with the Russes he was in the pivotal position of a middleman between the east and the west. The eastern and the western Norsemen could now think of co-ordinating their efforts for reaching Constantinople. In view of this we may think that Rurik attributed great importance to Askold and Dir's expedition even though he was not able to give them more troops. I cannot accept Baron Michael de Taube's theory, proposed by him in 1947, according to which Askold acted entirely on his own and independently of Rurik.[1]

[1] Baron Michael de Taube, *Rome et la Russie avant l'invasion des Tatars, I. Le Prince Askold, l'origine de l'Etat de Kiev et la première conversion des Russes* (Paris, 1947).

In 844 the western Norsemen, sailing through the strait of Gibraltar, entered the Mediterranean and attacked Sevilla in Spain. Fifteen years later they appeared at the delta of the Rhone in southern France, and in 860 sailed to the bay of Spezia, in Liguria, and captured and pillaged Pisa, Luna, and some other Italian cities. Simultaneously they began exploring the eastern part of the Mediterranean and finally succeeded in reaching the sea of Marmora. Thus, while the Russes made preparations for an attack on Constantinople from the north, through the Black Sea, the western Norsemen approached it through the Mediterranean, as if trying to close the ring.

The compiler of the Russian Chronography was well aware of the existence of this ring of maritime and river ways. He says:

A trade route connected the Varangians with the Greeks. Starting from the Greeks, this route proceeds along the Dnieper, above which a portage leads to the Lovat. By following the Lovat, the great Lake Ilmen is reached. The river Volkhov flows out of this lake and enters the great lake Nevo [Lake Ladoga]. The mouth of this lake [i.e. the Neva River] opens into the Varangian Sea. Over this sea goes the route to Rome, and on from Rome overseas to Tsargrad [Constanti-nople].[1]

Several years had passed before Askold and his associates were able to reach Constantinople, for they had stopped in Kiev on their way. To continue the chronicler's record of their voyage:

they went down the Dnieper River and saw a town on the hill and asked: 'Whose town is it?' And they [the townspeople] said: 'There were three brothers, Kiy, Shchok, and Khoriv, who founded this town and perished, and we belong to their clan and live in it and pay tribute to the Khazars. Askold and Dir stayed in the town and assembled many Varangians and began ruling over the land of the Poliane [which centred around Kiev].[2]

While much is uncertain in the narrative about Askold and Dir, the story must have preserved sound historical features. A number of historians expressed their doubts about certain points in the story. Some suggested that 'Askold' and 'Dir' were two names of the same person, not two persons. However, there

---

[1] *Povest' Vremennykh Let*, i. 11–12; Cross and Sherbowitz's translation, p. 53.
[2] *Povest' Vremennykh Let*, i. 18–19; Cross and Sherbowitz's translation, p. 60.

is nothing unusual in the dual leadership if we suppose that the expedition was organized by two clans who joined their forces for the purpose. Both names are Norse. As A. A. Vasiliev rightly points out, in a later entry of the Chronicle (under A.D. 882) the exact location of the tomb of Askold and that of Dir is mentioned, which shows that there was in Kiev a firm local tradition about the two of them.[1]

As regards the reasons which compelled Askold and Dir to stop in Kiev, one of them is implied in the chronicler's statement that they 'assembled many Varangians'. Their own forces must have been small and they needed reinforcements before proceeding farther. The Poliane of Kiev seem to have been at that time a peaceful people preferring to pay tribute to an invader rather than fight him, and they hardly would be eager to supply troops for a distant campaign. Judging from the name of the Ros River south of Kiev we may think that a group of Russes lived on its banks and these may have been induced to co-operate with Askold and Dir, but they probably were not numerous. Much more assistance could be obtained from the Tmutorokan Russes. We may think that Askold and Dir sent messengers to Tmutorokan soon after their arrival in Kiev in order to establish joint plans for a campaign against Constantinople. It will be recalled in this connexion that the northern shore of the sea of Azov could be easily reached from Kiev via the eastern tributaries of the Dnieper. The Tmutorokan group of the Russes must have been at that time much stronger than the Kievan. Besides, a number of Varangians, possibly those belonging to the Jom fraternity, could also come to Kiev in response to Askold and Dir's calls for assistance. All this, however, required much time, and meanwhile the Kievan leaders had to strengthen their position in Kiev and to negotiate with the Magyars. The latter controlled the lower part of the Dnieper region as well as the steppes of northern Tauria and thus were in a position to bar Askold's further drive to the Black Sea.

According to the Russian chronicler, the people of Kiev told Askold and Dir that before their arrival they had been tributaries of the Khazars. In an earlier entry of the Russian Chronography (under A.D. 859) it is likewise said that the Khazars had imposed tribute upon the Poliane, and on two other east Slavic

---

[1] A. A. Vasiliev, *The First Russian Attack on Constantinople*, pp. 178–81.

tribes. On the basis of the evidence of other sources we may think, however, that the tribute from the Poliane was collected not directly by the Khazars but through the latter's vassals—the Magyars. Presumably, the tribute was authorized by the Khazar kagan and thus the statement of the Russian chronicles is technically correct. Actually, however, Askold and Dir had to deal with the Magyars, and not with the Khazars.

It will be recalled that there existed a Magyar settlement in Kiev in the ninth century and that a Magyar chieftain, the voevoda Almos (called Olma in Russian chronicles), had been in control of Kiev as well as of the lower Dnieper region from about 850.[1] It is with Almos, then, that Askold and Dir had either to fight or to come to an agreement. Apparently they chose the latter alternative and agreed to serve as Almos's lieutenants in the land of the Poliane. The Almos palace (*Olmin dvor*) in Kiev became their headquarters. Presumably, Almos was entitled to receive part of the tribute collected by Askold and Dir from the Poliane.

Be this as it may, we may be sure that some kind of agreement between the Norse leaders and Almos must have been reached. Otherwise, Askold and Dir's expedition to Constantinople would not have been feasible, and we know that that expedition actually took place in 860. While the advantages of the agreement for the Russes were obvious, it is not clear what the Magyars could have gained by it. Most likely they were promised part of the prospective war booty.

5. *The Russian attack on Constantinople*, A.D. *860–1*

The study of the Russo-Byzantine war which began in 860 and lasted for almost a year has been greatly facilitated by the late A. A. Vasiliev's admirable monograph on the subject.[2] Vasiliev's work contains a critical survey of the sources and literature of the Russian invasion as well as a careful analysis of its dramatic events. While I would rather take exception to Vasiliev's interpretation in certain cases, I have been guided mainly by his work in the following outline of the course of the war.

[1] See Chapter 3, section 4, above.
[2] A. A. Vasiliev, *The Russian Attack on Constantinople in 860* (Cambridge, Mass., 1946).

Of the Russian sources of the war the two most important accounts are found in the Chronography, which was completed, as we know, in the early twelfth century, and in the Nikon Chronicle. The latter was compiled in the middle of the sixteenth century but in many cases was based on earlier records which are otherwise unavailable to us. The account of the campaign in both chronicles depends on the Greek sources but contains also some information which apparently represents an old Russian tradition.

Let us first quote in full the account of the Chronography, inserted there under A.D. 866.[1]

Askold and Dir went against the Greeks and came [to Constantinople] in the fourteenth year of the reign of the Emperor Michael. At that time the emperor had set forth against the Agariane [i.e. Arabs]. When he had reached the Black River [in Asia Minor], the eparch [prefect of Constantinople], sent him word that the Russes were approaching Tsargrad [Constantinople], and the emperor turned back. Meanwhile the Russes entered the Bosporus, made a great massacre of the Christians, and besieged Tsargrad in two hundred boats. The emperor succeeded but with difficulty in entering the city. The people prayed all night with the Patriarch Photius at the church of the Holy Virgin in Blachernae. With hymns they carried the sacred garment of the Virgin and dipped it in the sea. The weather was still and the sea was calm, but lo! a gale came up, and great waves rose straightway, smashing the boats of the godless Russes. It threw them upon the shore and broke them up, so that few escaped such disaster and returned to their native land.

The Nikon Chronicle contains a similar account as well as some additional information taken from later Byzantine sources not used by the compiler of the Chronography. The Nikon Chronicle also adds two statements apparently based on Russian tradition. Speaking of the Arab invasion of Byzantine possessions in Asia Minor which had preceded the Russian attack, the Russian chronicler says: 'Hearing this, the Kievan princes Askold and Dir went on Tsargrad and did much evil.' The story of the war in the Nikon Chronicle is concluded by the following remark: 'Askold and Dir returned from Tsargrad with a small retinue [*druzhina*], and there was great weeping in Kiev.'[2]

---

[1] *Povest' Vremennykh Let*, p. 19; Cross and Sherbowitz's translation, p. 60.
[2] *PSRL*, ix. 7.

The first question which faces us is that of the causes of the war. After having discussed this problem, Vasiliev says:

> No particular cause for the attack of 860 is known. We must explain it, for the time being, by the same causes which stimulated the Normans to make their raids over Western Europe, rapacity, and desire for devastating, and for acquiring booty and wealth. . . . Rumour of the fabulous wealth of Constantinople was widespread, and this was the chief reason for the Russian attack of 860.[1]

As regards the basic psychological attitude of the Norsemen towards war, Vasiliev's statement is certainly adequate. However, Vasiliev does not take into consideration the specific background of Russo-Byzantine relations. Since Byzantium had supported the Khazar policy of containing the Russes, the latter must have considered not only the Khazars, but the Byzantines as well, their enemies.

The Russian raid on Amastris in about 840, which followed in the wake of the failure of the Russ embassy to Constantinople in 838, achieved no decisive results. It was, however, an important landmark in the development of the Russo-Byzantine relations. While Vasiliev, in his earlier works had believed in the authenticity of the Amastris story, in his monograph on the Russian attack of 860 he abandoned his former point of view and refused to bring the Amastris episode into the picture. By this, in my opinion, he made the proper understanding of the causes of the war of 860–1 more difficult for the subsequent students of Russo-Byzantine relations. If we accept the authenticity of the Amastris story, as I do, the whole background of the Russ attack of 860 becomes clear. We may assume that the Amastris raid was followed by a period of 'cold war'. The Byzantines might have dismissed the possibility of a further Russian invasion in the near future, but the Russes must have begun thinking of such a move soon after their return from Amastris.

The Khazar drive on the Slavic tribes of the wooded steppe zone, which had resulted in the establishment of the Khazar and Magyar control over the Viatichi, the Severi, and the Poliane, and had severed the communications between the north Russes and Tmutorokan, weakened the Russes and pre-

---

[1] Vasiliev, op. cit., p. 186.

vented them from undertaking at once another campaign against Byzantium. The Tmutorokan Russes had to wait for reinforcements from the north. Meanwhile, however, they closely watched the development of events in Byzantium in order to strike at the most appropriate moment when—and if—they themselves were ready to do so.

With the arrival of Askold and Dir at Kiev, about 856, and with the coming of the Varangians (Jomsvikings?) summoned by Askold and Dir, the military position of the Russes in south Russia was greatly strengthened. Combining their forces, these three groups—Askold and Dir's retinue, the Varangians summoned by them, and the Tmutorokan Russes—were now strong enough to launch a campaign against Byzantium. And precisely at that time the attention of the Byzantines shifted from the affairs in the north to those in the south, from the Russes to the Arabs and the western Norsemen.

A continuous struggle was going on with the Arabs in Sicily and south Italy, and with the Cretan Arab pirates, who across the Aegean managed to enter the sea of Marmora, and there were frequent Norman raids in the eastern Mediterranean, which extended also as far as the Aegean and the sea of Marmora. Accordingly, the Byzantine fleet was removed from Constantinople into the southern waters and was exceedingly occupied there with generally unsuccessful operations. . . . So in 860 Constantinople was practically devoid of any naval forces and was almost defenceless against any sea assault from the north.[1]

On land the situation was not much better. An intermittent war was going on between the Byzantines and the Arabs in Asia Minor. In 859 the Byzantines waged a rather successful campaign there. In the summer of 860 the young Emperor Michael III and his powerful uncle, the caesar Bardas[2] set forth again, and a stubborn new fight was raging in Asia Minor. 'The capital lacked any substantial land defence.'[3] The situation, thus, was extremely favourable to the Russes.

From the Nikon Chronicle it is clear that the Russes knew of

[1] Vasiliev, op. cit., p. 150.

[2] The title 'Caesar' (in Greek 'Kaisar', in Slavic 'Kesar'') signified the highest rank in Byzantine administration next to the emperor (in Greek *basileus*, in Slavic 'tsar').

[3] Vasiliev, op. cit., p. 150.

the absence of the Byzantine army. Undoubtedly, they were also aware of the absence of the fleet.

Both the early Russian Chronography and the Nikon Chronicle consider Askold and Dir the sole leaders of the Russian expedition of 860 and Kiev its only base. There is no mention of any role the Tmutorokan Russes could have played in the campaign. This may be explained by the general tendency of the Chronography (on which, for the early Kievan period of Russian history all of the later chronicles were based) to consider Kiev, the 'Mother of Russian Cities', and the House of Rurik the only rightful dynasty of Russia. While Askold and Dir did not belong to Rurik's clan, it was Rurik who, according to the chronicler, had authorized them to attack Constantinople.

It is an interesting fact that nowhere in the Chronography is the title 'kagan' applied to Russian rulers. The reason apparently is that that title had been originally associated with a different dynasty and different place. That Vladimir the Saint and Iaroslav the Wise had the title 'kagan' we know from the sermons of the Metropolitan Hilarion, not from the chronicler. In view of this, it seems quite understandable that the Kievan chronicler should have given full credit for the organization of the campaign of 860 to the Kievan rulers—emissaries of Rurik —not even mentioning either the Russ kagan of Tmutorokan or the Tmutorokan Russes at large.

There is no consensus of scholarly opinion on the question of from where the Russes attacked Constantinople in 860. While some historians, including Golubinsky, think that the Russes came from Tmutorokan (or from the Crimea), others, including Vasiliev, insist on Kiev as the starting-point of the expedition.

Vasiliev says: 'Only a well organized state could have thought out and executed such a daring attempt, and Kiev was at that time such a state.'[1] The validity of this statement may be questioned. From the Chronography we know that at the time of the arrival of Askold and Dir at Kiev, the Poliane were tributaries of the Khazars (through the Magyars, as has been explained). There was apparently no local prince in Kiev, or at least none is mentioned in the story of Askold and Dir. The latter met no opposition on the part of the Kievans. All this contradicts Vasiliev's hypothesis of the existence, at that time,

[1] Vasiliev, op. cit., p. 175.

of a 'well organized state' centring in Kiev. Askold and Dir had to 'assemble the Varangians' for their further advance, which shows that there was no sufficiently strong Kievan army at their disposal. To be sure, during their four years' stay in Kiev prior to the Tsargrad expedition they must have succeeded in gathering a number of warriors and, undoubtedly, in building a number of boats needed for the raid, but all these measures were of an emergency nature.

In view of the above consideration it does not seem likely that Kiev was the only base of the expedition. The main base of the Russes must have been located elsewhere. In my opinion it could only have been at Tmutorokan.

Vasiliev argues that it would not have been possible for the Russes to organize the expedition in the Crimean region because both the Byzantine authorities in Cherson and the Byzantine allies—the Khazars—would have prevented it. But Tmutorokan was out of reach of either the Khazars or the Byzantines. Besides, there were many elements in the Crimea friendly to the Russes, and, as we may suppose, there were a number of Russes themselves settled in the Crimea after 790.

As regards the Khazars, they could be expected to try to contain the Russes not only in the Crimea, but in Kiev as well if they had enough strength to do so. After all, Kiev was under the suzerainty of the Khazar kagan (through the Magyars), and it seems that the Khazars would have been able to prevent the Russes from organizing an expedition there even more so than in the Crimea. In my opinion the Khazar intervention in Kiev was forestalled by Askold and Dir's agreement with the Khazar vassal, the Magyar voevoda Almos. It so happened that the Khazars were not in a position to help the Byzantines either in the Crimea or in Kiev.

As to the Byzantine commander (*strategos*) of the Chersonian district (*theme*), he had, apparently, no sufficient forces at his disposal at that time. It will be recalled that, as Vasiliev himself made clear, the whole Byzantine fleet was occupied in the southern waters. The Cherson strategos might have been left a few patrol vessels, but these would not have been in a position to interfere with the movements of the flotilla of the Tmutorokan Russes.

It should be mentioned that the Byzantines themselves considered the Crimean region the main base of the Russian operations in the war of 860, as they had done at the time of the Amastris raid. In his account of the war of 860 the Byzantine chronicler John Zonaras, who wrote in the twelfth century but used earlier records, calls the Russians 'a Scythian race who live around Taurus'.[1] The same information is given in the chronicle of Skylitzes—Cedrenus.[2] Vasiliev himself has to admit that 'certain groups of Normans reached the south of present-day Russia including the Tauric Peninsula before 860'.[3] Besides, we know that the Russes were well aware of the absence of the Byzantine army and fleet from Constantinople, and we may think that they had obtained this information in the Crimea. The Tmutorokan Russes were certainly closer to the Crimea than the Kievan Russes. It seems, therefore, that it is the Tmutorokan Russes who were in charge of the intelligence work in the Crimea. The most important news was, of course, conveyed by them to Kiev.

According to our sources, the Russian armada which reached Constantinople consisted of 200 vessels. This is a smaller figure than those given for some of the later Russian raids on Constantinople. Oleg's armada of 907 is said to have consisted of 2,000 boats.[4] During the Russian campaign of 1043, 400 Russian vessels took part in the naval battle at the entrance to the Bosporus according to Michael Attaliates.

Masudi, speaking of Russian vessels, says that each was manned with 100 men. Oleg's boats carried 40 men each. As regards the campaign of 860, we may assume that the Russian boats, based on Tmutorokan, were larger than those built in Kiev. While Kievan boats had to sail down a river (the Dnieper) to reach the sea, Tmutorokan was located right on the sea. If we suppose that half of the Russian armada of 860 consisted of larger ships (100 men per boat), and half of smaller (50 men per boat), we may estimate the number of the Russ warriors engaged in the expedition at around 15,000.

Since, as I have supposed, the Russian expeditionary force must have consisted of three separate groups, each must have been represented in the council of war. We may thus think that in that council the Russ kagan, Askold and Dir, and the leader

---

[1] Vasiliev, op. cit., p. 111.   [2] Ibid., p. 103.   [3] Ibid., p. 174.
[4] See Chapter 6, section 2, below.

of the Varangians were the top members. Presumably, the two flotillas—the Tmutorokan and the Kievan—met in the Dnieper estuary in May 860. After the final preparations had been completed the combined Russ armada sailed to the Bosporus and appeared before the walls of Constantinople on 18 June.

Constantinople was at that time a large city. Her population is estimated at around 500,000. She was protected by formidable fortifications—a twelve-mile circuit of strong walls. The city, prior to the age of fire-arms, was practically impregnable as long as the Byzantine government was strong and there were no internal dissensions among the people. It was only because of internal discord in the Byzantine empire that the knights of the Fourth Crusade were able to capture Constantinople. At the time of the conquest of Constantinople by the Ottoman Turks in 1453, she was almost a ghost city, its population having shrunk to some 40,000. The last Byzantine emperor had only about 6,000 soldiers at his disposal. The people did not support the government because of the religious discord between the Orthodox and the Uniates. The besieging Turkish army is estimated at about 80,000, and, besides, the Turks had strong artillery. Even so, the siege lasted almost seven weeks.

All this shows that the Russes had little chance, if any, to capture the city in 860, especially since the Byzantine government at the time of their attack was strong and efficient, and the people spiritually united around the church under the inspired leadership of Patriarch Photius.

The defence of the capital was entrusted to the prefect of the city, Nicetas Ooryphas, who seems to have displayed appropriate energy and vigour. Later on he was appointed commander of the Byzantine fleet. Patriarch Photius took upon himself the task of fortifying the faith of the people and guiding them spiritually.

Photius preached in the church of Sancta Sophia and organized religious processions which fired the participants with religious fervour. The text of two major sermons (homilies) of his was discovered by a Russian scholar, the Archimandrite (later Archbishop) Porphyrius Uspensky in 1858, during one of his voyages to Mount Athos. The first of these sermons was delivered by Photius soon after the beginning of the Russian attack; the second, some time after the Russian retreat. Photius's basic tendency, as expressed in these sermons, is to imply that calamity has befallen the Greek people on account of their sins and transgressions. He called for a religious revival which would bring salvation and urged the people to pray to the Holy Virgin for protection. Both sermons are composed in a rhetorical style and contain many references to the books of the Old Testament. The ferocity of the Russes and the devastations wrought by them are described in a declamatory and dramatic manner, and the picture given is probably not devoid of exaggeration. Photius's account of the Russian attack is not that of an historian; and yet it is a highly valuable historical document.[1]

In his second sermon Photius calls the Russes an *ethnos agnoston*, which is usually translated as 'unknown people'. However, the basic meaning of the Greek adjective *agnostos* is not 'unknown' but 'not recognized', hence 'forgotten'. In my opinion Photius's phrase is an allusion to the Biblical Rosh (spelled in Greek 'Rhos' and thus identical with the name of the Russes). In his first sermon Photius quotes from the book of Jeremiah (vi. 22–24): 'Behold, a people cometh forth from the north country . . . they shall lay hold on bow and spear; they are cruel, and have no mercy; their voice roareth like the sea.' If Photius had meant the word *agnoston* in the sense of 'unknown', he would have used it in the first sermon rather than in the second. By the time he had delivered his second homily, the Russes were only too well known to the Byzantines—and in a painful way at that.

In his first sermon Photius speaks of the Russians in the following words:

I see that a cloud of barbarians floods with blood our city which is withered because of our sins. . . . Alas for me that I see how the savage and cruel people surround the city and plunder the suburbs, destroy everything, fields, houses, cattle, beasts of burden, women, children, old men, youth; they strike all with the sword, feeling pity for no one, sparing no one. Destruction for all of us! Like locust on corn-field, like mildew on vineyards, or rather like a hurricane or typhoon or flood or I cannot say what, they have attacked our country and eliminated the whole generations of inhabitants. [English translation by Vasiliev here and hereafter.]

[1] For the text of Photius's two 'Homiliae' see Augustus Nauck, ed., *Lexicon Vindobonense* (St. Petersburg, 1867), Appendix, pp. 201–32; C. Müller, *Fragmenta Historicorum Graecorum*, v, Part I (Paris, 1870), 162–73.

In the second sermon Photius emphasizes 'the mercilessness of the barbarous race and the harshness of their temper and the savagery of their habits'. They 'despoiled the surroundings and plundered the suburbs, cruelly massacred captives and safely established themselves around all this [city], showing in their greed for our wealth such conceit and arrogance that the inhabitants did not even dare to look on them with level and undaunted eyes'.

The deliverance of the city from the Russian terror Photius ascribed not to the efforts of the Byzantine government and army but to the protection of the Holy Virgin.

Since we were deprived of any help and were in great want of power of men, we rested our expectations upon the Mother of our Lord and God, and were comforted; we implored her to appeal to her Son to break down the audacious rashness of the barbarians, to pull down their insolence, to defend the people in despair, to fight for her own flock. . . . Thus through the marvellous benevolence of the free petition of the Mother, God has inclined towards us, wrath has been averted, and the Lord has shown mercy upon His flock.

There is no detailed chronological outline of the course of the war in the sources available to us. It seems that the Russes at first attempted to seize Constantinople by surprise. When this attempt failed, they turned their attentions to plundering the suburbs as well as the churches and palaces along the shores of the Bosporus. They also entered the northern section of the sea of Marmora and devastated the Prinkipo Islands. They undoubtedly amassed a large booty and found the expedition profitable enough to continue it as long as they could. Meanwhile they kept the Byzantine authorities and the people of Constantinople in a state of suspense. Since the Russes controlled the Bosporus, the Byzantines were not in a position to bring in any large reinforcements from Asia Minor. It was only the return of the Byzantine fleet that could have changed the situation, but the fleet was still engaged in the Aegean. In view of all this it seems that the Russes were prepared to stay for a long time. They had nothing to lose and much to gain in case of the success of another attempt to break the defences of Constantinople or the spirit of the Greeks. Besides, the Russes might have counted on the eventual arrival of the Norse fleet from the west.

From a sermon of Photius's chancellor, George of Nicomedia, preached on 21 November 860, we may conclude that at that time the Russes were still continuing their raiding operations around Constantinople. By March 861 the situation became more favourable to the Byzantines, and the danger, for the city itself in any case, was almost over. Otherwise, as Vasiliev points out,[1] it would have been impossible for an important church council attended by the Papal legates (the so-called 'First and Second Council') to hold its sessions in the Church of the Apostles in Constantinople in March and April 861.

It is presumably in March 861 that the procession with the garment of the Virgin Mary, mentioned in the Russian chronicles, took place. Photius speaks of it in his second sermon.

The entire city bore with me Her garment for the repulse of the besiegers and the protection of the besieged; we offered prayers and made a litany. . . . It went around the walls, and the enemy inexplicably turned their backs. It protected the city, and the stronghold of the enemy collapsed as if by a sign. . . . As soon as the Virgin's garment had been borne round the wall, the barbarians raised the siege and withdrew, and we were released from impending captivity and received unexpected salvation. Unexpectedly befell the aggression of the enemies; beyond all hopes has proved their withdrawal.

According to another tradition (reflected in the Russian chronicles) the relic was not only borne in procession round the walls but was dipped in the sea, which at that time was dead calm; suddenly a violent storm arose and dispersed the ships of the godless Russes, so that only a few of them escaped danger and in complete defeat returned to their own country. Vasiliev comments:

The miraculous storm of wind needs no miracle for explanation. A sudden storm is a phenomenon which occurs often and suddenly in the Black Sea. We may very reasonably assume that such a storm arose and dispersed the Russian ships. The weather in the Black Sea in January, February, and March is often very stormy.[2]

According to Vasiliev[3] the end of the siege of Constantinople was officially celebrated on 22 March by singing a newly composed hymn (the so-called *Akathistos*) in honour of the Holy Virgin, 'the Victorious Leader' (*Strategos Hypermachos*). It

---

[1] Vasiliev, op. cit., pp. 215–17.
[2] Ibid., p. 221.
[3] Ibid., pp. 97–98 and 216–17.

should be noted that the hymn is still being sung in both Greek and Russian Orthodox churches. (The initial words in Church Slavonic are *Vzbrannei voevode pobeditelnaia*, which corresponds to *strategos hypermachos*.) It is a song of religious exaltation and triumph.

Even after 22 March 861, small groups of Russian invaders continued to operate in the upper part of the Bosporus and some adjoining regions. But the capital considered itself now safe and free. The final withdrawal of the Russes from the Bosporus seems to have taken place around 5 June 861. This is the commemorative date which was later fixed by the Byzantine Church.

At the very time that the Russ invasion collapsed, probably late in March or in April 861, the Norse flotilla from the west, sailing through the Aegean and the Hellespont, entered the sea of Marmora. According to the 'Venetian Chronicle' (*Chronicon Venetum*), compiled by Johannes Diaconus around A.D. 1008, it consisted of 360 ships. These Norsemen did not even try to attack Constantinople but rewarded themselves with plundering the shores and islands of the sea of Marmora. How long they stayed there is not known, but according to Johannes Diaconus they returned in triumph—that is, as we may think, unmolested and carrying rich booty.[1]

As a contrast, from the Russian chronicles we know that Askold and Dir came back to Kiev in a pitiful condition. The losses of the Tmutorokan Russes were probably as great as those of the Kievan. The Russ expedition as a whole proved a failure. Yet it was an event of great historical importance, and it opened a new page in the history of Byzantine-Russian relations.

From the Byzantine chronicle known as the 'Continuation of Theophanes' Chronicle' (Theophanes Continuatus) we know that shortly after the withdrawal of the Russes, a Russ embassy came to Constantinople beseeching to be converted to Christianity, and that this conversion indeed took place.[2] In his circular letter to the oriental patriarchs (867), Patriarch Photius states that the Russes 'have changed their Hellenic and godless

---

[1] Johannes Diaconus's *Chronicon Venetum* was published in Pertz, *MGH, Scriptores*, vii (1846), 4–38 (see especially p. 18); reprinted in Migne, *Patrologia Latina*, cxxxix, cols. 875–940 (see col. 905); new edition by Giovanni Monticolo, *Cronache Veneziae antichissime*, i (Rome, 1890), 59–171 (see pp. 116–17).

[2] Theophanes Continuatus, ed. Bekker (Bonn, 1838), p. 196.

religion for the pure and unadulterated faith of the Christians, and have placed themselves under the protection of the Empire, becoming good friends instead of continuing their recent robbery and daring adventures'.[1] Photius mentions the Russes just after saying that the Bulgars had adopted Christianity. The baptism of the Bulgarian king Boris took place in 864. Presumably, the conversion of the Russes Photius mentions occurred in 866. It seems possible that the date under which the Russian campaign of 860 is recorded in the Russian chronicles (866) actually refers to the date of the treaty which officially terminated the war. We do not have to think, however, that the whole people of Russes were christened at that time. Most of them were still pagans in the tenth century. Presumably only part of them were converted in Photius's time. The new Christian community of the Russes was put under the guidance of a bishop appointed by Photius. Unfortunately we do not know where the see of that bishop was located. It could have been established either in Kiev or in Tmutorokan. Many scholars are inclined to place it in Kiev. However, there is no indication of the existence of a bishopric in Kiev even in the tenth century. On the other hand, the see of Tmutorokan is mentioned in the list of bishoprics of the Eparchy of Gothia which was compiled either in the late eighth century, as many scholars think, or in the 860's. Because of this and other considerations I am convinced that the see of the first bishopric was in Tmutorokan.

After the Byzantine palace revolution of 867 in which the Emperor Michael III was assassinated and Basil I, the founder of the so-called Macedonian dynasty, succeeded to the throne, the Russes sent another embassy to Constantinople, and a new treaty was negotiated (presumably in 868). As regards religious affairs, the patriarch Ignatius (Photius was deposed by Basil I) agreed to grant the Russ bishop the title of archbishop. This change made the position of the young Christian community of the Russes much more stable.

Undoubtedly the treaties of 866 and 868 dealt not only with church affairs but with state matters as well, including trade. From the treaties of the first half of the tenth century we know that by that time trade occupied an important place on the agenda of the Russo-Byzantine negotiations, and that trade

[1] Migne, *Patrologia Graeca*, cii, cols. 736–7. Cf. Vasiliev, op. cit., pp. 229–30.

between the Russes and the Greeks was lively and was well organized. The foundations of this organization must have been laid in 866 and 868. In the treaty of 907 it was stipulated that the Russian merchants who arrive in Constantinople 'shall dwell in the St. Mamas quarter'.[1] As Vasiliev says:

It is almost certain that this suburb of St. Mamas where the Russian traders and envoys were lodged, and which was located on the European shore of the Bosporus, at the modern Beshik-tash, had been designated for this particular purpose not in 907 or 911 but much earlier according to the agreement made with the Russians after their campaign of 860–1.[2]

In the treaty of 911 it was also stipulated that whenever the Byzantine emperor conducted a campaign and needed additional troops, those Russes who 'are desirous to honour' the emperor may come at any time to Byzantium; if they wish to remain in the emperor's service, they are allowed to do so. Vasiliev is 'inclined to believe' that the right of the Russians to serve the emperor as mercenaries goes back to the treaties of the 860's. Vasiliev's surmise is quite plausible. The Byzantines must have been duly impressed by the fighting qualities displayed by the Russes in 860–1 and, because of this, eager to employ their former enemies for strengthening their own army and navy. It thus seems that one of the results of the war of 860–1 was the creation of a corps of Varango-Russian guards (in Russian *druzhina*, in Greek *hetaireia*) in Byzantine service.

[1] See Chapter 6, section 2, below.
[2] Vasiliev, op. cit., p. 233.

6

THE FOUNDATIONS OF THE
KIEVAN STATE

1. *Patriarch Photius and the Apostles of the Slavs*

PHOTIUS was one of the outstanding characters in the history of the Christian Church and one of the great spiritual leaders of the Byzantine world. He held the office of the Patriarch of Constantinople twice: from 858 to 867 and again from 878 to 886.[1]

In spite of the important role Photius played in the events of his time, little is known about the chronology of his life. Presumably he was born around 800 and died around 897, almost a centenarian. In his youth he served in the imperial guards and later in the imperial chancellery. He also taught philosophy in the school of highest learning established in Constantinople by the caesar Bardas, which Vasiliev calls 'Bardas's University'. Photius was a man of universal knowledge based on the study of classical writers. He was well versed not only in theology but also in grammar, philosophy, natural science, law, and medicine. He collected a rich library which was open to his friends. A select circle of these assembled regularly in his house to read aloud and to discuss literature of all kinds, secular and religious, Pagan and Christian. From layman Photius became patriarch in 858, being ordained and elevated through all clerical degrees within a few days. He ascended the patriarchal throne with full awareness of the duties of spiritual leadership expected of him, yet at the same time he could not but remain philosopher and statesman.

In the ninth century Christianity was still united. While there developed differences between the Roman and the Greek churches as regards the ritual and even the dogmas (the addition

---

[1] On Photius see J. Hergenröther, *Photius* (Ratisbonn, 1869, 3 vols.); A. A. Vasiliev, *The First Russian Attack on Constantinople*, pp. 90–94, 165; F. Dvornik, *The Photian Schism. History and Legend* (Cambridge, 1948).

of *filioque* in the Creed by the Roman church), these differences were not serious enough to stop the intercourse between Western and Eastern Christianity. A temporary break between Rome and Constantinople which occurred during Photius's first patriarchate was soon healed, and the unity of the Church restored.

Photius's basic idea concerning the interrelations between Church and State was that of the 'symphony' of the two. This idea was concisely formulated in the Byzantine law manual edited during Photius's second patriarchate, the so-called 'Epanagoge'. According to it, Christian society is guided by two heads—the patriarch (who is 'the living image of Christ') and the emperor. For Photius, especially in view of his background, this was not an abstract theory. As patriarch he took an active part in the shaping of the Byzantine policies. Christian society, as Photius understood it, was universal in nature. Eventually it was to embrace the whole *oecumene* (inhabited world). Hence the importance of the Christian mission in Photius's policies. Photius's enlightened object was to sponsor the advancement of philosophy as the foundation of the Church, and also to spread Byzantine civilization beyond the borders of the empire. Therefore the period of his first tenure of the patriarchal office witnessed a great revival of the missionary activities of the Byzantine church. The conversion of the Russes was only one of several such moves of Photius's policy.

While only part of the Russes had been converted during Photius's time, and while the attempt to convert the Arabs was a failure and that to convert the Khazars only a partial success, the missions to the Bulgars and to the Moravian Slavs brought lasting results and proved events of paramount importance in the religious and cultural development of the Slavs at large, and especially of the eastern Slavs. The final conversion of the Russes in about 990 was but an outgrowth of the Christian missions of Photius's time.

It should be added that Photius's concept of 'symphony' of church and state in the Christian society, and of the patriarch and the emperor as the two heads of that society, was destined to play a significant role in the spiritual life of Muscovite Russia of the sixteenth and seventeenth centuries. This is especially clear in the teachings and policies of the Russian patriarch Nikon (1652–8). Nikon's doctrine of the dual leadership of the patriarch and the tsar over Russia was based on the 'Epanagoge.[1]

The success of the Byzantine missions among the Slavs was facilitated by Photius's approval of the use of Slavic language for the church services in Moravia, as well as by his wise choice of the two heads of the Moravian mission—two brothers—Constantine (whose highest monastic name given him before his death was Cyril) and Methodius, known as 'the Apostles of the Slavs' (SS. Cyril and Methodius).[2] Constantine was Photius's former student in Bardas's University.

The two brothers were born in Salonika, Macedonia, where their father occupied a position of some importance in the army administration. Methodius was the eldest child in the family of seven children and Constantine the youngest (born around 827). Salonika (in Slavic, Solun) was within the area of Slavic colonization, and many Salonican families were bilingual, Slavic being spoken together with the Greek. Such was the case of Methodius's and Constantine's family too. Their familiarity with Slavic proved a great asset in their missionary activities as well as in their work as translators of the Gospel from Greek to the Slavic. Both brothers were deeply religious; both received good education. Constantine was enrolled in the Salonika school and then, because of his fine scholarly record, was accepted as a student in Bardas's University. Among his teachers was the future patriarch Photius. Constantine studied classical literature, philosophy, mathematics, astronomy, and music. After the completion of his studies he was appointed professor of philosophy at the university. Because of this, he later became known as Constantine the Philosopher. While both brothers were outstanding missionaries and inspired church leaders, Constantine was in many respects superior. He was endowed with rare philosophical insight and exceptional philological abilities. Bilingual from childhood, he later easily learned Hebrew and Arabic as well as elements of Turkic (Khazar).

Of the Slavic peoples outside the boundaries of the Byzantine empire, the Bulgarians were closest to Constantinople and

---

[1] G. Vernadsky, 'Die kirchlich-politische Lehre der Epanagoge und ihr Einfluß auf das rußische Leben im XVII Jahrhundert', *Byzantinisch-Neugriechische Jahrbücher*, vi (1928), 119–42.

[2] See note Q, p. 321.

thus more exposed to Byzantine cultural influence than other Slavs. While in the first half of the ninth century the majority of both the proto-Bulgar aristocracy and the Slavs subordinated to them were still Pagan, Christianity made considerable progress in Bulgaria, especially among the Slavs, primarily through the Byzantine captives taken by the Bulgarians during their wars with the empire, and also through Greek merchants. The Bulgar khans, at first, persecuted the 'perverted' and the 'perverters', but the process of gradual Christianization went on steadily, nevertheless.

At the time when Photius became patriarch (858), the ground seemed well prepared in Bulgaria for Christian missions. However, the process of Christianization of Bulgaria was complicated by ecclesiastical disputes between Rome and Constantinople as well as by the foreign policies of Khan Bogoris (Boris) who ascended the Bulgarian throne in 852 and, at one time, wavered between a Byzantine and a German alliance.

Khan Boris had the same dilemma before him as later on Prince Vladimir of Kiev was to face: whether to try to stop the rising tide of Christianity or to ride on it. A conversion to Christianity offered many advantages, such as enhancing the ruler's prestige, both nationally and internationally, and placing a staff of educated men at his service. On the other hand, Boris could not fail to recognize certain political dangers in receiving Christianity from Byzantium. Recognition of the authority of the Patriarch of Constantinople over the would-be Bulgarian Church might lead to the necessity of recognizing the suzerainty of the Byzantine emperor over the Bulgarian state. It seems that Boris would therefore prefer to receive Christianity not from Byzantium but from Rome. In fact he tried to bargain with both sides in order to obtain a certain autonomy for the future Bulgarian Church, or at least in order to have it organized as a separate diocese. Neither Constantinople nor Rome were, at first, ready to grant independence to the Bulgarian Church. In view of the existence in Bulgaria of a number of Christians belonging to the Byzantine Church, whose support he needed, Khan Boris had to agree to receive the Byzantine mission. In 864 he was baptized and received the Christian name of Michael (it was that of the Byzantine emperor). Soon after most of his subjects—both the proto-Bulgar aristocracy and the Slavs—adopted Christianity.

One of the results of the conversion was the mergence of the Turkic and the Slavic groups in Bulgaria.

Greek priests were sent to Bulgaria; Greek was, at first, used there for church service. There is no evidence of any participation of Constantine and Methodius in the conversion of the Bulgarians. Later on, however, the impact of their Moravian mission proved of great significance to Bulgaria. In the late ninth century Slavic became the language of the Bulgarian Church. In 928 the Bulgarian Church became autocephalous. Its first primate had the title of patriarch; his successors that of archbishop.

Prior to their Moravian mission, which proved the main work of their life, Constantine and Methodius had been sent by Photius to Khazaria to preach Christianity there. The chronology of their Khazarian mission is uncertain, but in any case it must have taken place during the Russo-Byzantine war of 860-1. According to the Life of Constantine[1] the Khazar kagan sent his envoys to the Byzantine emperor with the request that preachers be sent to his people. In his message the kagan said that 'We have known God the Lord of everything from time immemorial . . . and now the Jews are urging us to accept their religion and customs, and the Arabs, on their part, draw us to their faith, promising us peace and many gifts'. We may think that besides the religious affairs, political problems were likewise dealt with in the Khazar-Byzantine negotiations of 860. Being attacked by the Russes, the Byzantines must have asked the Khazars for assistance. The Byzantine Christian mission to Khazaria must have had important political implications as well.

Constantine and Methodius went to Khazaria via Cherson (Korsun) in the Crimea. It will be recalled[2] that Constantinople was besieged by the Russes from the sea from June 860 to March 861. Land communications with the capital were not, however, completely severed. It would have been possible for the two brothers and their attendants to reach a port on the western Bulgarian coast of the Black Sea which could hardly have been patrolled by Russian boats, and from there to sail to Cherson.

---

[1] For the Life of Constantine (St. Cyril) and that of Methodius see P. A. Lavrov, 'Materialy po istorii vozniknoveniia drevneishei Slavianskoi pismennosti', *Trudy Slavianskoi Komissii* (Akademiia Nauk), i (Leningrad, 1930), 1-78; for French translation, F. Dvornik, *Les Légendes de Constantin et de Méthode*, pp. 349-93.

[2] See Chapter 5, section 5, above.

The voyage was dangerous, indeed, but the brother missionaries were ready to face dangers. There is no indication in our sources about the exact time of Constantine's sailing to Cherson. In any case, he must have started not later than March 861, probably earlier.

It is obvious that the brothers spent a considerable time in Cherson before continuing their voyage to Khazaria. During his stay in Cherson Constantine recovered the relics of St. Clement (Pope of Rome, A.D. 92) in a crypt long immersed under the sea. He prepared himself for the Khazarian mission by study-ing the Hebrew language and conversing with Jews, residents of Cherson (Arabic Constantine had learned several years before). So eager was his thirst for languages that, meeting a Samaritan, he found time to master the Samaritan dialect. But from our point of view the most important philological discovery made by Constantine in Cherson was that of a manuscript of the Gospel and the Psalms written 'in Russ characters' (*ros'sky pismeny*; variant *rous'ky*).[1]

To quote from the Life of Constantine:

And he found there a copy of the Gospel and the Psalms written in Russian characters and he found a man speaking that language and spoke to him and understood the meaning of what he said, and, adjusting it to his own dialect, he analysed the characters, both for the vowels and the consonants, and praying to God, started quickly to read and speak [Russian].

This passage of the Life of Constantine proved a stumbling block for generations of scholars, and still is for some. In view of the preconceived ideas that the name 'Rus' appeared in south Russia only with the Varangians, that the early Russes were pure Norsemen, and in a wider sense that the ancient Slavs had been a barbaric people prior to their conversion to Christianity, it seemed incredible that a 'Russian' alphabet could have existed in 861. Therefore, a number of hypotheses were suggested to prove that the 'Russian characters', found by Constantine, were not Russian. Some of the philologists attempted to inter-pret 'Russian characters' as Gothic. Others, like A. Vaillant and R. Jakobson, think that the original reading had been 'Syriac' (*soursky*) and not 'Russian' (*rous'sky*), and that the reading

---

[1] *Pismeny* is instrumental case, plural; nominative case, plural, is *pismena*.

'Russian' is a copyist's mistake.[1] However, in no manuscript of the Life of Constantine do we find the reading *Soursky*. Besides, in many manuscripts we find 'Russian' spelled as *Ros'sky* (not *Rous'sky*), and that would have made *Sorsky*, not *Soursky* (Syriac).

In my opinion we have here the case (not unique in the annals of scholarship) of a conflict between a reliable historical source and a firmly established set of opinions of the historians. In such cases, before denying the possibility of a phenomenon which contradicts the picture of historical development created by the scholars, one has, in the first place, carefully to study the wording of the text itself, and secondly to re-examine the traditional interpretation of the historical background of the phenomenon in question.

The first task was accomplished by N. K. Nikolsky in his study on the 'Russian characters' discovered by Constantine.[2] Nikolsky has convincingly shown that the language in which the Gospel found by Constantine in 861 was written could not have been any other than a Slavic dialect. Indeed, from the contents of the story it is plain that the difficulty for Constantine was in familiarizing himself with the characters of the manuscript, and not in understanding the language, which he mastered easily, comparing it with his own speech (*svoei besede prilagaia*)—that is, obviously comparing the Russian with the Macedonian Slavic dialect. Presumably, the language of the Crimean Russes—basically Slavic—contained at that time a number of terms borrowed from the Alanic, Norse, and Gothic.

As regards the historical background, the existence of the Russ settlements in the Crimea in the middle of the ninth century evokes no doubt. Even Vasiliev admits it, as has been mentioned.[3] Some of those settlements might have been established in the ancient period when the Russes were closely associated with the Alans. It will be recalled that the Roxolani penetrated into the Crimea in the late second century B.C.[4] Irrespective of that early background, a number of Russes must have settled in the Crimea in the late eighth century of the

---

[1] A. Vaillant, 'Les Lettres russes de la Vie de Constantin', *RES*, xv (1935), 75–77. R. Jakobson informed me in 1942 that he was in favour of Vaillant's opinion.

[2] N. K. Nikolsky, 'K voprosu o Russkich Pismenakh', *Isvestiia po Russkomy Iazyku i Slovesnosti, Akademiia Nauk*, i (1928), 1–37.

[3] See Chapter 5, section 5, above.

[4] See Chapter 2, section 2, above.

Christian era following the Russian raid on Surozh.[1] From the Life of St. Stephen of Surozh it is known that the Russian prince who had led the attack on Surozh was subsequently converted to Christianity. A number of other Russes presumably followed his example. Those who settled in the Crimea could not but have fallen under the influence of their Christian neighbours—Greeks and Goths. The service in the churches the Russes attended must have been in Greek or in Gothic, depending on the locality. Eventually, however, the Russes might have attempted to establish churches of their own with the use of their own language in the services. In his debates with the German clergy in Moravia, Constantine, defending the right of the Slavs to have their own church language, mentioned a number of peoples using their own language in church services, among them the Sugdaeans, i.e. the inhabitants of Surozh (Sugdaea was the old name of Surozh). These must have been either Alans or Russes. Possibly both these groups were meant by Constantine under the name of Sugdaeans; each could have used their own language.

Irrespective of the question whether the Crimean Russes held church services in their own language or not, we may think that these Russes wanted in any case to have the Gospel translated into their language. This could have been done by those among them who received ecclesiastical education, possibly by priests of Russ origin ordained by Greek or Gothic bishops. The Russ, with whom Constantine conversed in Cherson, was apparently an educated man.

Next comes the problem of the Russ alphabet itself. From time immemorial the Crimea was a meeting place of peoples of diverse ethnic origin and of various religions and cultures. In the ninth century, besides the descendants of the old Tauri (as well as those of the Scythians), Greeks, Goths, Alans, Russes, and Jews lived there. Khazar, Armenian, and Georgian merchants visited the country. Several religions were practised, several languages spoken in the Crimea, and several alphabets were in use by the educated élites of various ethnic or religious groups. In this sense, the Crimea was a convenient place for creating a new alphabet by an ethnic group which found themselves in need of one—the Russes in our case. Such an alphabet could

[1] See Chapter 5, section 1, above.

have been established either by adjusting the characters of some particular existing alphabet to the Slavic, or by combining elements of one or more old alphabets to the requirements of the Slavic and adding new characters if necessary, in other words by inventing a new alphabet. This was, apparently, the method by which the 'Russ' characters found by Constantine in the Crimea were created. It was a full-fledged alphabet containing letters for both consonants and vowels.

The author of the Life of Constantine does not say what shape the 'Russ' characters had. This enigma will be dealt with later on in this section. Now we have to discuss another aspect of the problem, namely, the exact meaning of the term 'Russ' as applied to the 'Russ characters'. At first glance it seems that the term is used in its direct ethnic sense: the characters of the Russes, of the Russ language. This is quite probable. Yet it is also possible that *rus* was used in this case in the original meaning of the word *ruxs*, that is 'light' (to be pronounced 'rookhs'). It will be recalled that in the esoteric language of the Rotu concord *ruxs* means 'light', 'enlightenment'.[1] In Rotu, the ancient Albanian characters are known as the 'Ruxs characters' (*Ruxski pismena*), that is the 'enlightened alphabet', or the 'divinely inspired alphabet'.[2] That might have been also the meaning of the 'Russ characters' discovered by Constantine in 861.

To return now to the course of Constantine's Khazarian mission, the length of his sojourn in Cherson was caused not only by his desire to be better prepared for his task but also, and perhaps even mainly, by political circumstances. The regular way from Cherson to Khazaria was by boat along the southern shore of the Crimea to the strait of Kerch, then across the sea of Azov to the mouth of the Don and up the Don River to the Volga portage. The initial section of this way, however, could not have been used by Constantine since the strait of Kerch was controlled by the Tmutorokan Russes. Presumably Constantine was advised to wait in Cherson until the end of the Byzantine-Russian war. But even when the flotilla of the Tmutorokan Russes returned home in June 861 the Russes still continued to be in hostile relations with Byzantium for some time.

When it became clear to Constantine that there was no sense

[1] See Chapter 4, section 3, above.
[2] I am thankful to Yury Arbatsky for this information.

in waiting in Cherson any longer, he had to set forth to Khazaria by a roundabout way, overland across the Crimea to
northern Tauria. There his party was attacked by the Magyars
who 'howled like wolves' and wanted to kill the Byzantine
travellers. At the time of the attack Constantine had been conducting a litany for his group. The confused Magyars did not
molest them. As we know,[1] the Magyars had had an agreement
with Askold and thus could be expected to be hostile to Byzantium. They had, then, a motive for attacking a Byzantine embassy. When, however, they understood that Constantine's was
a religious mission, they let him and his party continue their
journey. Reaching a port on the north-eastern shore of the sea
of Azov, the missionaries sailed to the mouth of the Don, now
using the regular 'Khazarian way', and finally reached the headquarters of the kagan who, at that time, sojourned near 'the
Caspian Gates of the Caucasian Mountains' (the Daryal Gorge).
There Constantine had to confront his opponents, the Hebrew
and the Moslem scholars, presumably in July or August 861.

According to the Life, Constantine defeated all the arguments
of the Jewish scholars. Any other report of the debates can
hardly be expected in such a literary document as the life of a
saint. However, even from the Life it is clear that the kagan was
not entirely convinced by Constantine's argument. Nevertheless
he allowed his courtiers and his people to be baptized if they
chose. Around 200 of them were actually baptized. It should be
mentioned that by the time of Constantine's mission there had
existed already several Christian communities in Khazaria.[2]
These must have been morally strengthened by Constantine's
appearance there. Politically, Constantine's mission reaffirmed
friendship between the Khazars and the Byzantines. The kagan
wrote a polite letter to the emperor which read in part as
follows:

You have sent us, Sir, a worthy man who by his words and deeds
showed us that the Christian faith is holy; and we have understood
that it is the true faith and we let those who like it be baptized and
hope that we ourselves will be ready to do the same [in due time].
And we are friends and associates of your majesty and are ready to
serve you when you require our service.

---

[1] See Chapter 5, section 4, above.
[2] See Chapter 3, section 3, above.

In seeing Constantine off, the kagan offered him rich presents, but Constantine declined to accept them, asking the kagan instead to do him the favour of freeing the Byzantine captives without ransom, which the kagan agreed to do. Since there had been no war between the Byzantines and the Khazars prior to Constantine's mission, the question naturally arises as to what Byzantine captives were in Khazaria at that time and how they got there. The only possible explanation is that these were Greeks taken prisoner by the Russes during their raid on Constantinople, then brought to Tmutorokan and sold to the Khazars.

For his return Constantine chose the overland route from the Daryal Gorge to the eastern shore of the sea of Azov across arid steppes where both he and his companions suffered much from thirst and exhaustion. There existed a more convenient route down the Kuban River, but this led to Tmutorokan and was thus barred by the Russes. Constantine could not use it, especially since he had with him the freed Byzantine captives.

After crossing the sea of Azov Constantine came back to the Crimea and converted the people of Phullae (most likely Alans) to Christianity. The city of Phullae was situated in the northeastern part of Crimea, near the modern town of Karasubazar. The Phullaeans worshiped a sacred oak which Constantine cut down. From there Constantine proceeded to Cherson. He returned to Constantinople probably late in 861. He had been a man of weak constitution from his childhood. The exhausting journey to Khazaria impaired his health and he needed rest. But he was not to enjoy it for long.

In 862 Prince Rostislav of Moravia dispatched an embassy to the Byzantine emperor, Michael III, and requested the emperor to send to Moravia missionaries capable of preaching and conducting church services in Slavic. By this time part of the Moravian people, including Prince Rostislav himself, were already converted to Christianity, chiefly through German missionaries. The latter, however, were not familiar with the Slavic tongue, which was a serious handicap to their preaching. Moreover, the church books they brought with them and the church services they conducted were in Latin, and so incomprehensible to the natives.

In order to grasp fully the significance of Rostislav's decision to apply to Constantinople for missionaries, we must consider

the involved political and ecclesiastical background of the area
of the middle Danube, known as Pannonia in the wider sense of
the name. Ecclesiastically the area was within the jurisdiction
of Rome, but more specifically the bishop of Salzburg claimed
authority over the region. With regard to international politics,
in the first quarter of the ninth century the area of the middle
Danube was the object of dispute between the Franks and
the Bulgars. Moravia remained within the Frankish sphere of
influence and in 840 King Louis the German installed Prince
Rostislav there as his vassal. Rostislav was at first loyal to Louis,
but later attempted to emancipate himself and his country from
the German domination. Although he had had himself baptized, Rostislav resented the haughty ways of the German
bishops. In 855 Louis sent troops to Moravia, but these were defeated by the Moravian prince. Later, Louis offered to Khan
Boris of Bulgaria, at that time still a pagan, an alliance against
Moravia. It was to forestall the danger of being attacked by
Bulgars in addition to the Germans that Rostislav decided to
ask the Byzantine emperor for assistance, both diplomatic and
ecclesiastical.

The importance of both the political and ecclesiastical implications of Rostislav's move was fully grasped by the Byzantine
authorities. According to the Life of Constantine, Emperor
Michael immediately gathered a special conference of high
state officials and church prelates to consider the matter. While
the name of Photius is not mentioned in the Life in this connexion, there cannot be any doubt that he also took part in the
conference. The conference decided to send a mission to Moravia in accordance with Rostislav's wishes. Thus a momentous
decision was taken—to recognize the Slavic language as one of
the languages of the Church.

In view of Constantine's knowledge of Slavic and his experience as a missionary, it was but natural that the emperor
turned to him and asked him to take over the direction of the
Moravian mission, in spite of his poor health. Constantine
answered that ill and weak as he was, he would gladly assume
the important task. He pointed out, however, that for organizing
a Slavic church it was indispensable to have Slavic books.
Consequently, he was authorized by the emperor (and undoubtedly, by the patriarch, too) to compose a Slavic alphabet

and to translate the Gospel and service books from the Greek into Slavic.

Fully realizing the magnitude of the work, Constantine asked his brother Methodius to help him and gathered a group of other assistants. Constantine prayed with them, and 'Soon he had a revelation, and composed the characters, and began writing the Gospel [in Slavic]: In the beginning was the Word, and the Word was with God, and the Word was God' (Johni. 1).

The question of what the alphabet invented by Constantine in 862 was like is one of the moot problems in Slavic philology. Two old Slavic alphabets are known: the Glagolitic and the Cyrillic. The Cyrillic alphabet is based on Greek uncials with the use of some additional characters to denote sounds not covered by the Greek letters. As to the Glagolitic alphabet, various origins of its characters were suggested. Some scholars derived it from the Greek cursive, others from the Armenian, Georgian, Hebrew, Samaritan, or a number of other oriental alphabets. The earliest specimen of both Glagolitic and Cyrillic script so far known are referred to the reign of Tsar Simeon of Bulgaria (892–927).

The very name of the Cyrillic alphabet is evidence of a tradition which ascribed its invention to St. Cyril (Constantine). However, many scholars think that Constantine invented the Glagolitic alphabet, and not the Cyrillic. They refer the invention of the Cyrillic script to a Bulgarian pupil of Constantine's brother Methodius, at the end of the ninth century. There is no conclusive evidence for this, however.

While recognizing the controversial nature of the problem, I am inclined to disagree with the hypothesis of the invention of the Cyrillic script in Bulgaria. In the first place, if we admit that hypothesis, we would have to admit the existence of not two but three old Slavic alphabets (the 'Russ characters' found by Constantine in the Crimea, the Glagolitic, and the Cyrillic); and yet all old Slavic manuscripts known to us are either in Glagolitic or in Cyrillic. In my opinion the riddle was solved by Nikolsky in 1928. He showed that the Glagolitic alphabet is identical with the 'Russ characters'. An important piece of evidence for this is a note in the so-called Rheims Gospel of the thirteenth century. That manuscript is Slavic; part of it is written in Cyrillic and part in Glagolitic. In the note, written in the fourteenth century, the Glagolitic part is called 'Russian'. By that time only the Cyrillic script was in use in Russia. Consequently the name 'Russian' in the note cannot refer to the Russian script of the fourteenth century. It obviously refers to the 'Russ characters'.

If the Glagolitic alphabet is to be identified as the 'Russ' (or 'Ruxs') characters, then the alphabet Constantine invented in 862 must have been the Cyrillic, which is in accordance with its name. We may think that Constantine at first experimented with the Russ characters he had found in the Crimea, the Glagolitic, but was not entirely satisfied with them and therefore decided to compile a new alphabet, the Cyrillic. The Glagolitic alphabet was not, however, discarded by the group of Slavic scholars assisting Constantine. It might have been used for confidential messages as a kind of cryptic script in which only the most trustworthy of Constantine's disciples were initiated. Cases of the use of the Glagolitic as a cryptic script in some passages of Cyrillic manuscripts are known. Later, after Constantine's death, secrecy might have been lifted and the Glagolitic was then used together with the Cyrillic or, in some regions like Dalmatia, even preferred to it. In Bulgaria and Russia the Cyrillic alphabet eventually prevailed.

In the year 863 Constantine and Methodius appeared in Moravia at the court of Prince Rostislav. The history of their activities there is outside the scope of our present work and we must limit ourselves here to some general remarks only.[1] The specific difficulty of the missionary brothers' position was that they had to be on good terms with Byzantium and Rome simultaneously. As a matter of fact there was as yet no schism between the Western and the Eastern Church. The delicacy of Constantine's and Methodius's position resulted from the fact that they were sent as missionaries by the Patriarch of Constantinople into an area which traditionally belonged to the jurisdiction of the Pope of Rome. Had the brothers coming to Moravia insisted on its ecclesiastical submission to Constantinople, as Photius may have instructed them, they would have committed a breach of canonic discipline. But they did nothing of the sort, being imbued by a truly Christian spirit and not by con-

[1] See G. Vernadsky, *Ancient Russia*, pp. 357–9; F. Dvornik, *The Slavs: Their Early History and Civilization*, pp. 87–101.

siderations of church politics. Their object was to organize a
Slavic Church in Moravia and not to extend the boundaries of
the Byzantine patriarchate. The opposition they met at the onset
was not from Rome but from the German clergy. Since these
latter were canonically subordinated to the Pope, it was to the
Pope that Constantine and Methodius addressed themselves for
a confirmation of their authority in Pannonia. Theoretically,
the Pope had the power to organize a new eparchy in Pannonia
despite any protest of the Bishop of Salzburg. Actually the
Germans put as many obstacles in the brothers' way as they
could. Both the German and the Italian clergy opposed vigor-
ously the use of the Slavic language in church services.

In 868 Constantine and Methodius went to Rome in order to
defend the rights of the Slavic language, a mission in which they
completely succeeded, and Pope Hadrian II solemnly deposited
copies of Slavic liturgical books on the altars of several churches
in Rome. By this time Constantine's health was completely
shattered by his intense labours and he died in Rome after
receiving the highest monastic rank *skhima* under the name
of Cyril (869). Methodius was ready to go on with the work
alone, and in 870 Pope Hadrian II ordained him Bishop of
Pannonia, to have his see at Sirmium (Mitrovica). It seemed
that the cause of the Slavic Church was now secured, but just
at this moment a palace revolution occurred in Moravia. The
Germans skilfully took advantage of disagreement between
Prince Rostislav and his nephew Sviatopolk. With the help of
the Germans Sviatopolk arrested his uncle and seized the Moravian throne for himself. Before long the Germans betrayed him
and invaded Moravia. It was only in 874 that Sviatopolk succeeded in ousting them and restoring his authority.

While opposing the Germans politically, Sviatopolk proved
ready to compromise with them in church matters. He recognized Methodius as archbishop but at the same time sought
the advice of a German priest, Wiching. Wiching opposed the
Slavic liturgy and in various ways intrigued against Methodius,
reporting the latter to the Pope. Methodius went to Rome
once more, but although he succeeded in exculpating himself,
the Pope, in order not to irritate the German prelates, gradually
began to curtail the use of Slavic in the Moravian Church.
Following Methodius's death (885) the use of the Slavic for the

liturgy was barred in Moravia. Methodius's disciples were expelled from the country and had to take refuge in Bulgaria.

While the main results of the Moravian mission were thus
forfeited, the historic work of Constantine and Methodius was
not in vain, for they laid a solid foundation for building up
Slavic letters and Christian Slavic civilization at large, for which
they certainly deserve their name of Apostles of the Slavs. In the
midst of their hard administrative and missionary work, and in
spite of all obstacles, they found time for literary activities of
which the Slavic translation of the Gospels, the Psalms, and some
church service books were the most important fruits. The Slavic
language of Constantine's and Methodius's works, which had
as its linguistic base the Macedonian dialect, became the language
of all Slavic churches—that is, of the Orthodox Slavs—and is
therefore known now as Church Slavonic. It was the language of
most of the Slavic literati during the Middle Ages and early
modern period, and it was also to become the foundation from
which the Russian literary language developed. Thus, while the
blossoming of Slavic letters in Moravia was of short duration,
it lasted long enough to carry the torch first to Bulgaria and
Serbia, and then to Russia.

2. *Oleg and his campaign against Constantinople*

As we know, after the failure of the Russ attack on Constantinople in 860–1 Askold and Dir returned to Kiev 'with a small
retinue'. Their Varangian allies must have deserted them in
search of a more fortunate employer.

The Russo-Byzantine treaty of 866 opened the door for lively
commercial relations between Kiev and Constantinople. Kiev
also traded with Smolensk in the north and Galicia in the west.
Her prosperity must have been steadily increasing. Another important result of the treaty of 866 was the spread of Christianity
among the Russes, both in Tmutorokan and Kiev. Crimean
priests of Russ origin, or Russian-speaking Greek priests from
the Crimea, probably appeared in Kiev. Besides, some of the
disciples of St. Cyril and St. Methodius might have come to Kiev
via Galicia. It is to this period that Nikolsky refers the rise of the
idea of the brotherhood of three Slavic tribes—the Czechs, the

Poles, and the Russes.[1] According to a legend there had lived once upon a time three brothers, Czech, Lekh (Pole), and Rus, who became the progenitors of the three respective tribes. The legend originated in Moravia. It is evidence of the existence of cultural intercourse between the Czechs, the Poles, and the Russes in this period. With the rise of the Slavic Church in Moravia, Christian notions began to spead from Moravia to both Poland and Russia. A number of scholars think that Askold and Dir themselves were converted to Christianity, but there is no definite evidence for such an assumption.

The rise of Christianity in Kiev was soon stopped by the arrival from the north of a heathen Varangian army led by Prince Oleg (according to the Russian Chronography from Novgorod in A.D. 882; but it is usually supposed to have happened in 878).[2] According to the Chronography, Oleg was a relative of Rurik, who died about 873. The chronicler says that before his death Rurik had invested Oleg with princely authority and also appointed him the guardian of his infant son, Igor. Fosterage is an ancient and widespread institution. It existed among the Alans, the Bulgars, the Slavs, the Norsemen, and many other peoples. The usual Norse word for an older man who fulfils the function of foster-parent for the son of an equal is *fostri*.[3] The Old Russian term for it is *kormilets*.

The objective of Oleg's expedition to the south was apparently twofold. In the first place Oleg wanted to unite the resources of north and south Russia: secondly, he was attracted by the prospects of a lucrative Byzantine trade and by the wealth of Constantinople. The Norsemen did not accept the failure of the attack of 860–1 as final. They were eager to have another try.

According to the chronicler, Oleg set forth, taking with him many warriors—the Varangians, the Chud, the Slovene, the Meria, the Ves, and the Krivichi. He thus arrived with his Krivichi before Smolensk, took the city, and set up a garrison there. Thence he went to Lubech, where he also established a garrison. He then came to the hills of Kiev, and was informed that Askold and Dir reigned there. Oleg seized them by ruse

[1] N. K. Nikolsky, 'K voprosu o Russkikh Pismenakh', *Izvestiia po Russkomu Iazyku i Slovesnosti*, i. 16–18. Cf. G. Vernadsky, 'The Origin of the Name Rus', *Südost-Forschungen*, xv (1956), 177–8.

[2] See note R, p. 321.

[3] N. K. Chadwick, *The Beginnings of Russian History* (Cambridge, 1946), p. 25.

and had them killed. 'And Oleg set himself up as prince of Kiev, and declared that it shall be the mother of Russian cities. And he had with him Varangians and Slovene, and others who were now called Russes.'[1] By the 'others', besides the original Russes themselves, the chronicler obviously means the Poliane, the Severi, and certain other Slavic tribes affiliated with them. It should be noted that prior to Oleg's time each of these tribes was known only under its own name. The Russes as yet had constituted a separate tribe. Now the Russes began merging with the Poliane and the Severi. Eventually the name Rus was applied to the whole federation of the east Slavic tribes headed by the princes of Kiev. Only the Novgorod men continued to speak of themselves as 'Novgorodians' and not 'Russians', even in international treaties. That process of unification of the Russian people and of the Russian land was given great impetus by Oleg's policies.

We see, therefore, that in his statement the chronicler aptly summarized the historical significance of Oleg's reign. He not only recorded the important fact that Kiev now became the capital of Russia, but he also noticed the rising consciousness of the unity of the Russian people. The concept of Russian unity was later poetically expressed in the *Igor Tale* of the twelfth century. There the Russian people are called Rusichi, that is, 'sons of Rus', and, besides, 'grandsons of Dazhbog', the Sun-god (see section 5 below). It follows that Rus, the mythical progenitor of the Russes, was considered son of the Sun-god.

It is in Oleg's period that Rus, the progenitor of the Russes, was first mentioned in the sources available to us. Commenting on the Russian attack on Constantinople, usually referred to 907, the compiler of the Byzantine chronicle of the tenth century known as 'Pseudo-Symeon' says that the people of Rhos are so called after a certain Rhos, a mighty man of valour. This information must have been received by Pseudo-Symeon's informer from the Russians themselves.[2]

---

[1] *Povest' Vremennykh Let*, i. 20; Cross and Sherbowitz's translation, pp. 60–61.

[2] A. Soloviev, 'Rusiči and Rus', *Zametki k Slovu o Polku Igoreve*, ii (Kondakov Institute, Belgrade, 1941), 27; R. J. H. Jenkins, 'The supposed Russian Attack on Constantinople in 907', *Speculum*, xxiv (1949), 404–5; A. A. Vasiliev, *The Second Russian Attack on Constantinople*, Dumbarton Oaks Papers, vi (Cambridge, Mass., 1951), pp. 187–95; G. Vernadsky, 'The Origin of the Name Rus', *Südost-Forschungen*, xv (1956), 177–8.

Oleg's administrative activities at the beginning of his reign are tersely described by the chronicler in the following words: 'Oleg began to build stockaded towns and fixed the amount of tribute to be paid by the Slovene, the Krivichi, and the Meria; and he ordered that Novgorod should pay tribute to the Varangians, to the amount of 300 *grivna* a year, according to his agreement with them. This tribute was paid to the Varangians until the death of Iaroslav (1054).'[1]

The statement of the chronicler concerning the tribute to be paid to the Varangians is of great importance for the proper understanding of the position of the Varangians in the Kievan state from Oleg's times down to Iaroslav's. It should be noted that the Russes of Norse origin were not called Varangians in this period. By 'Varangians' military fraternities of Norsemen used by the Russ princes as auxiliary troops were meant. They represented a separate force, an autonomous army within the Russ state. The Varangians were also employed in the same capacity in this period by the Byzantine emperors and used as shock troops or imperial guards. It may be added that Russes also served in the Byzantine army and navy on the same basis as Varangians.

The Varangian troops were indispensable for both Russia and Byzantium because of their high fighting qualities, as well as because of their skill in navigation. But they also caused much trouble to both the Kievan princes and the Byzantine emperors by their greediness and their interference in the politics and the administration of the county they served.

The Varangians were organized in powerful corporations, of which one of the most active was that of the Jomsvikings. The fraternity of the Jomsvikings was not connected with any particular state. It is known that in the tenth and early eleventh centuries the main stronghold of the Jomsvikings was located on the Jom (Volyn) Island in the Oder estuary. We may suppose that the fraternity of the Jomsvikings had been formed much earlier and that the Jomsvikings controlled the Volyn Island and some other islands in that part of the Baltic Sea already in

---

[1] *Povest' Vremennykh Let*, i. 20; Cross and Sherbowitz's translation, p. 61. The Old Russian *grivna* was an ingot of silver weighing 68·22 grammes. In north Russia, by around 950, a smaller grivna came into existence which weighed 51·19 grammes, see V. L. Ianin, *Denezhnovesovye sistemy Russkogo Srednevekovia* (Moscow, 1956), pp. 36–56 and 204.

the late eighth and throughout the ninth centuries. From their stronghold they were ready to seek employment both in the east and the west, in Russia as well as in the British Isles, and if there was no employment, they undertook raids on their own. In Ireland they became known as 'the Black Vikings'. Norsemen of a different corporation were called 'White Vikings' in Ireland. The distinction between the 'Blacks' and the 'Whites' must have been based on the colour of the dress and armour (especially shields) of the two respective groups.[1] It is possible that the medieval names of 'Black Russia' in the upper Nieman River basin and 'White Russia' in the basin of the western Dvina and of the upper Dnieper River reflect the same difference between the Black and the White Vikings. Presumably, the upper Nieman basin had been for some time controlled by the Jomsvikings (the 'Black Vikings'), and the upper Dvina and upper Dnieper basin by the 'White Vikings'.

The international status of the Jomsvikings is somewhat similar to another corporation which was to arise in the thirteenth century in the lower Nieman and the lower Visla region—the Teutonic order. The Jomsvikings were also, in a sense, a religious order, but heathen, not Christian. As the late Grace F. Ward has pointed out, the Jomsvikings represented a revival of militant Norse heathenism which may have been originally associated with the famous heathen fane at Uppsala, a centre of traditional devotion to Odin. In Grace F. Ward's words:

> Odin himself by tradition has reached Sweden, and therefore Uppsala, from some region of the far south-east, the land of the Æsir, with twelve companions, the greatest men of the land, according to Snorri's account, second only to their princely leader. These 'Odin's men' were, like their prince, priests (*godar*) who served the great sacrifices and feasts; and they were also at the same time lawmen to maintain the law, which Odin had given, and warriors to lead the folk. Odin has promised that when these 'Odin's men' despaired victory in battle, and called upon him, he would answer.

This tradition was preserved by the Swedish kings of the Yngling line. There is a story that King Eric appealed to Odin during the battle of Fyris River in about 980. Odin's voice

---

[1] See T. D. Kendrick, *A History of the Vikings* (London, 1930), p. 275; G. Vernadsky, *The Mongols and Russia*, pp. 236-7. For the picture of a viking with the white shield see Bjorn Hougen, 'Osebergfunnets billedev', *Viking*, iv (1940), 104.

declared on that occasion that the Jomsvikings were all 'men of Odin'.[1]

It should be noted that the college of Odin's twelve men is similar to the college of 'doctors' in the early Russ kaganate as described by Ibn-Rusta.[2] The Odin's man was both a 'priest' and a 'lawman'. The 'doctor' in the Russ kaganate was a 'god', and also a 'judge'. However, the Russ 'doctors' were not military leaders.

The Jomsvikings, as well as other Varangian fraternities, constituted a strong link between Russia and Scandinavia, and Russia and England. Hence there were many similarities in the institutions of Russia, Scandinavia, and England of this period, such as the Royal Hirth (*grid'*, *druzhina*), the system of the judiciary (double protection for the king's men), and that of the financial administration. Many medieval administrative terms of the three countries are indentical, and it is not always possible to determine where the Russians borrowed a term from the Norse and where the Norsemen used a Russian word. Grace F. Ward has shown that the English 'Danegeld' is not 'money paid to the Danes', as the term is usually explained, but simply the Russian *dan'* ('tribute').[3] To the Russian *stol* ('princely throne') the identical Norse term corresponds. The Norse *skat* ('money') has its equivalent in the Russian *skot* (in Modern Russian 'cattle', in Old Russian 'money'). Besides, as N. T. Belaiew has shown, there are many similarities between the old Russian and the old English measures and weights.[4]

Remunerating the Varangian troops for their service proved one of the most exacting problems for the Kievan princes. The Varangians demanded a permanent fixed income in cash for their services in peace-time. In the case of a distant campaign, such as an expedition against Constantinople, they expected additional bonuses in the form of reserving for themselves a large

[1] The late Grace Faulkner Ward's study on the Jomsvikings has not been published in full so far (Miss Ward had been kind enough to let me read a carbon copy of part of the typescript of her work). A fragment of her study appeared posthumously under the title 'Jomsburg Brethren in England', *Scandinavian Studies*, xxviii (1956), 135–41.   [2] See Chapter 5, section 2, above.

[3] Grace F. Ward, 'The English Danegeld and the Russian Dan", *ASEER*, xiii (1954), 299–318.

[4] N. T. Belaiew (Beliaev), 'O Drevnikh i nyneshnikh Russkikh merakh protiazheniia i vesa', *Seminarium Kondakovianum*, i (1927), 246–88, see especially pp. 250, 251, 260, 263, 264, 267, 271, 281.

share in the prospective war booty. In such cases, thousands of fresh Varangian troops from overseas would answer the call of the Prince of Kiev, or even would come unsolicited.

The amount of the annual tribute from Novgorod was far from sufficient to satisfy all the Varangian troops serving the Prince of Kiev even in peace-time. For 300 grivny (this is the plural of *grivna*) only a small company of Varangians could be maintained, not over fifty men. And yet, even in peace-time, the Varangian troops in Russia numbered many more than that—at least several hundred, probably more. Thus, more funds were needed to satisfy them. The problem was partly solved by the system which was known in Old Russian as *kormlenie* ('feeding'). A number of Varangian chieftains were appointed town and district governors in various places of Russia, so that they and their retinue could 'feed themselves' off the land. They were entitled to keep for themselves a considerable proportion of the local taxes and court fees.

Besides, in certain cases, the commander of the main body of the Varangian troops was authorized by the prince to collect tribute from some of the tribes who were subject to tribute. In this way the Varangian auxiliary army became a permanent factor in the administration of Russia in the tenth century. During the reigns of Igor and Sviatoslav (see section 3 below) the commander of the Varangian troops, Sveneld (Sveinald), received the title of voevoda and became, practically, a co-ruler of the prince of Kiev. From the story of Igor's death (see section 3 below) it is obvious that Sveneld and his men were entitled to a larger share of the tribute from the land of the Drevliane than Igor and his retinue.

Oleg enjoyed a greater prestige among the Varangian troops than his successor, Igor. We may think that Oleg was an 'Odin's man' himself. He was considered by his contemporaries a volkhv, which is the meaning of his Russian epithet *veshchii*. In Norse he was known as Helgi Helgi (Oleg the Holy). The Russian chronicler represents him as a man of supernatural wisdom. Even during his life Oleg became an epic character in both Russian and Norse epos. The saga of Oleg became a source for the account of his reign in the Russian Chronography. The story of his death as described by the Russian chronicler is closely similar to that of the Norse hero Orvar-Oddr.

Oleg's seizure of Kiev and the murder of Askold and Dir, who were Almos's lieutenants, could not but result in a conflict between Oleg and the Magyars. There is no mention of a war between Oleg and Almos in Russian chronicles, but under A.D. 886 the chronicler records a war between Oleg, on the one hand, and the Ulichi and the Tivertsy, on the other. These two Antian tribes lived in the basins of the lower Bug and the lower Dniester and undoubtedly were at that time controlled by the Magyars. Apparently the war was indecisive. The Magyars were unable to recover Kiev, but kept the lower Dnieper and lower Bug region, barring the road to the Black Sea.

Meanwhile Oleg occupied himself by extending his authority over the Slavic tribes both west and east of Kiev. He defeated the Drevliane and imposed upon them tribute of one black marten skin per hearth. Next he conquered the Severi and forbade them to pay any more tribute to the Khazars. To encourage them, he required from them for himself only a light tribute. The Radimichi were likewise ordered by Oleg to cease paying tribute to the Khazars and instead had now to pay him the same amount, one shilling per hearth. By establishing his rule over these three tribes (in addition to his control of the Poliane), Oleg greatly expanded his original Kievan base and also gained access to the sea of Azov which must have facilitated his contact with the Tmutorokan Russes. Of the northern Slavic and Finnish tribes Oleg controlled the Slovene, the Krivichi, and the Meria. He thus succeeded in building a large kingdom for himself.

We should not think, however, that Oleg was the only ruler of all these tribes. From the preamble to the Russo-Byzantine treaty of 911 we know that Oleg had the title of the 'Russian Great Prince' (*veliki Kniaz' Ruski*), but that, under his suzerainty there were other 'serene and great princes'. The treaty was concluded, on the Russian side, in the name of all these princes, as well as in that of Oleg's 'great boyars'. These latter were apparently the Russ grandees. As to the 'serene and great princes', the Russ kagan of Tmutorokan and the regional rulers of other parts of Russia must have been meant. Some of them were probably Norsemen of royal descent; others, tribal chieftains of Alanic and Slavic origin.

Towards the end of the ninth century an event occurred which cleared the way to the Black Sea for Oleg and thus made it possible for him to prepare a campaign against Constantinople. Under the combined pressure of the Danubian Bulgars and the Pechenegi, the Magyars were compelled to move westward, left south Russia, and established themselves in the Slavic area of the Middle Danube region which subsequently became known as Hungary (897–9). The immediate result of the Magyar drive was the downfall of the Slavic kingdom of Moravia. Most of it was occupied by the Magyars. White Khorvatia—that is Galicia—pledged allegiance to Oleg. For the latter the most important result of the Magyar migration was that the whole Dnieper river-way from Kiev down to the Black Sea was now at his disposal. The tribe of the Tivertsy, in Bessarabia, formerly subordinated to the Magyars, recognized Oleg's authority.

The Pechenegi were as yet not dangerous to the Russes. The Pechenegi (in Turkic 'Badcnak', in Byzantine Greek 'Patzinakai') were a Turkish people, partly of Iranian origin. In the late ninth century they succeeded in piercing the Khazar defences along the lower Volga and the lower Don, and several groups of them entered the Pontic steppes. They were at that time not strong enough to control south Russia by themselves, but were ready to offer their services to any prospective employer. Tsar Simeon of Bulgaria was the first to take advantage of the situation and used them against the Magyars.

Oleg must have realized the importance of having the Pechenegi on his side too. Besides, as we may think, he attempted to co-ordinate his policies with those of Tsar Simeon of Bulgaria. According to Baron Michael de Taube in A.D. 899 Oleg sent a detachment of auxiliary troops to Simeon.[1] The latter, following his victory over the Magyars, turned his attention to the Byzantine empire. The empire, at that time, was already in trouble because of the Arabic naval raids in the Ægean. In 904 the Arabs sacked the city of Salonika. The Bulgarian offensive was quite successful, and Emperor Leo the Wise had to sue for peace. By the terms of the Bulgar-Byzantine treaty of 904 Tsar Simeon obtained all the Slavic lands of southern Macedonia, except the city of Salonika, and southern Albania which until this time had

[1] On Baron de Taube's study see note R, p. 321. In my opinion Baron de Taube's statement on Oleg's assistance to Simeon in 899 fits well to the background of Oleg's relations with both Bulgaria and Byzantium.

belonged to the Byzantine empire. As a result of all this, the empire was greatly weakened and the situation became extremely favourable for Oleg's plans.

There are many aspects of Oleg's expedition against Constantinople which need clarification. A detailed account of Oleg's campaign has been preserved in Russian chronicles only, and has been coloured by stories derived from epic tradition. Because of this, a number of historians, especially in recent times (among them G. Laehr, H. Grégoire, G. da Costa-Louillet, and R. H. Dolley), denied the authenticity of the account of Oleg's campaign in Russian chronicles and came to the conclusion that no such campaign ever took place.[1] However, quite a number of scholars (among them George Ostrogorsky) voiced their belief in the historicity of Oleg's expedition.[2] I concur with their opinion. In the first place, the story of Oleg's expedition in the Russian chronicles must have been based not only on the Oleg epos, but on the usually reliable old records as well. Secondly, epos is not, or not always, myth. On many occasions epos preserves actual facts in a more vivid manner than the chronicles. Thirdly, besides the account of Oleg's expedition, the Russian Chronography contains a resumé of Oleg's trade convention with the Byzantines of 907 as well as the full text of the Russo-Byzantine treaty of 911 which the chronicler must have copied from the authentic documents in the princely archives of Kiev. In his careful study of the Russo-Byzantine treaties of 911, 944, and 971, S. Mikucki has recently (1953) come to the conclusion that the analysis of these treaties from the point of view of diplomatics fails to reveal any traits which could be used as an argument against the authenticity of the treaties ('Un resultat paraît certain, notamment que l'analyse diplomatique ne révéle pas d'argument contre l'authenticité de ces traités').[3]

Furthermore, while there is no systematic outline of Oleg's

---

[1] G. Laehr, *Die Anfänge des Russischen Reiches* (Berlin, 1930, pp. 34–35, 95–99, 130–1; H. Grégoire, 'La légende d'Oleg et l'expédition d'Igor', *Bulletin de la classe des Lettres et des Sciences Morales et Politiques de l'Académie royale de Belgique*, xxiii (1937), 79–80; G. da Costa-Louillet, 'Y eut-il des invasions russes dans l'Empire byzantin avant 860?', *Byzantion*, xv (1940–1), 231–48; R. H. Dolley, 'Oleg's Mythical Campaign against Constantinople', *Bulletin . . . de l'Académie royale de Belgique*, xxxv (1949), 106–30.

[2] G. Ostrogorsky, 'L'Expédition du Prince Oleg contre Constantinople en 907', *Annales de l'Institut Kondakov*, xi (1939), 47–62.

[3] S. Mikucki, *Études sur la diplomatique russe la plus ancienne* (Kraków, 1953).

expedition either in Byzantine or oriental sources, there are definite references in both to the Russ campaign, some of them very precious. All these references have been recently examined by A. A. Vasiliev in his valuable monograph *The Second Russian Attack on Constantinople* (1951). Of the Byzantine authors the most important in this case are Leo the Wise, Constantine Porphyrogenitus, and Pseudo-Symeon. Of the oriental writers, the works of Masudi and Marvazi contain some information on the Russian attack.

Masudi, in his *Golden Meadows*, refers the readers for details to two other works of his, *The Historical Annals* and *Middle History*. Unfortunately, these works have not yet been discovered. In the *Golden Meadows* we find a few lines on a king of the Slavs whose name Masudi spells as Alawang. Vasiliev sees in this name an Arabic adaptation of the name Oleg.[1] Masudi says that King Alawang 'possessed vast cultivated lands, numerous troops, and many military resources. He fought the Greeks, the Franks, the Nokabard, and other peoples. And the war between them had various chances.' The importance of this statement for our purpose consists, first, in the very mention of the name Oleg—so far the only known mention of Oleg's name in a non-Russian literary source. Secondly, Masudi confirms our notion of Oleg as a mighty ruler commanding vast economic and military resources. Thirdly, it is a corroboration of the fact of a war between Oleg and the Greeks—it would be out of place here to discuss the question of how the Franks and the 'Nokabard' got into the picture.

Turning now to the Byzantine sources, Pseudo-Symeon's information on the Rhos, progenitor of the people Rhos, has been already quoted. Another important evidence presented in Pseudo-Symeon's work is a list of names of various places situated not far from Constantinople. This list, according to R. J. H. Jenkins, is related to Oleg's expedition. The 'Tactica' of Leo the Wise, written at the outset of the tenth century, contains an interesting comparison between the Arabic and the Russian fleets. 'The barbarians [i.e. Saracens] use larger and slower vessels [*koumbaria*] and the Scythians [i.e. Russians] smaller, lighter, and faster boats [*akatia*], because in order to get into the Black Sea through the rivers they cannot use bigger ships.'[2]

---

[1] A. A. Vasiliev, *The Second Russian attack on Constantinople*, p. 178.
[2] Quoted by A. A. Vasiliev, op. cit., p. 183.

According to R. H. Dolley this paragraph in Leo's 'Tactica' was written in 905, that is a year after the Arab raid on Salonika.

In his work *De Administrando Imperio*, Constantine Porphyrogenitus says that the Russians cannot 'come to this imperial city of the Romans [i.e. Constantinople], either for war or for trade, unless they are at peace with the Pechenegi'.[1] 'So long as the emperor of the Romans is at peace with the Pechenegi, neither Russians nor Turks [i.e. Magyars] can come upon the Roman dominions by force of arms, nor can they exact from the Romans [i.e. Byzantines] large and inflated sums in money and goods as the price of peace.'[2] The last sentence is an adequate characterization of Oleg's demands, as we shall see presently.

In addition to the Byzantine sources surveyed by Vasiliev, a Bulgarian inscription in Greek of 904 deserves attention. This inscription is on a marble stela found in the village Naruš, north of Salonika. The stela was a landmark of the new Byzantine–Bulgarian boundary established in 904. It was studied by Theodore (Fedor) Uspensky in 1898 and published by him in the *Izvestiia* of the Russian Archaeological Institute at Constantinople the same year.[3] The inscription reads as follows: 'In the year A.M. 6412 [A.D. 904]. [This is] the boundary between the Romaei [i.e. Greeks] and the Bulgars. In the time of Simeon, the installed-by-God prince of the Bulgars. In the presence of [*epi*; the following three words are in the genitive case] Theodorou Olgou trakanou; [and] in the presence of the prefect [*komit*] Dristr.'[4] *Trakanos* (metathesis for *tarkanos*) is the Greek transliteration of the well-known Bulgar and Alanic title *tarkhan* (*tarxan*) 'commander', 'prefect', 'official'. As to Olgos (supposed nominative case of Olgou), Uspensky understood it as the Slavic name 'Oleg'. He believed that this tarkhan had two names, one Old Slavic (Oleg) and the other Christian (Theodore). Henri Grégoire took exception to this opinion and interpreted *olgou* not as a personal name but as the Turkic adjective *ulug* 'great', and on that basis suggested that Theodore's

[1] Constantine Porphyrogenitus, *De Administrando Imperio*, ch. ii, Moravcsik's ed. and Jenkins's translation, pp. 50–51.

[2] *De Administrando Imperio*, ch. iv (pp. 50–51).

[3] Fedor I. Uspensky, 'Dve istoricheskie nadpisi', *Izvestiia Russkogo Archeologicheskogo Instituta v Konstantinopole*, iii (1898), 184–94.

[4] B. Beševliev, 'Prvobulgarski nadpisi', *GSU*, xxxi (1935), 1–162, Inscription No. 48.

title was 'great tarkhan' (*ulug tarxan*).[1] Karl H. Menges, while considering Grégoire's interpretation possible, submitted a different one, proposing to read *oglu* instead of *olgou*. *Ogul* means 'son' in Turkic.[2]

It should be noted that in no proto-Bulgar inscription do we find either the supposed title *ulug tarxan* or that of *oglu tarxan*. 'Olgou' occurs only once—in our stela of 904. Therefore I believe that Uspensky was right in understanding 'Olgou' as 'Oleg'. Contrary to him, however, I think that this Oleg was not a Bulgarian but a Russ, in fact the great prince of Kiev himself. I interpret *Theodorou Olgou trakanou* as 'Theodore, Oleg's tarkhan', that is, 'Theodore, an official of Oleg'. The implication is that a representative of Oleg guaranteed the new Bulgaro–Byzantine boundary. Presumably, there existed at that time a formal alliance between Oleg and Simeon of Bulgaria.

Let us now quote in full the story of Oleg's campaign as recorded in the Russian Chronography.[3]

A.M. 6415 [A.D. 907]. Oleg set forth against the Greeks, leaving Igor in Kiev. He took with him a multitude of Varangians, Slovene, Chud, Krivichi, Meria, Drevliane, Radimichi, Poliane, Severi, Viatichi, Khorvaty, Duleby, and Tivertsy who are Tolkoviny;[4] all these tribes are called Great Scythia by the Greeks. And with this entire force, Oleg sallied forth by horse and by ship, and the number of vessels was 2,000. And he came to Tsargrad [Constantinople], and the Greeks locked [the entrance to] the Golden Horn with chains, and closed the city. And Oleg disembarked, and began waging war, and slaughtered many Greeks around the city, destroyed many palaces, and burned the churches. Of the prisoners the Russes captured, some they slew, some they tortured, others they shot with arrows, and still others they cast into the sea. And the Russes inflicted many other woes upon the Greeks, as is usual with the soldiers.

And Oleg commanded his warriors to make wheels and to put boats on wheels. And the wind was favourable, they spread the sails and the boats moved toward the city across the fields. When the Greeks saw it, they were terrified, and sending messengers to Oleg,

---

[1] H. Grégoire, 'La Légende d'Oleg et l'expédition d'Igor', *Bulletin . . . de l'Académie royale de Belgique*, xxiii (1937), 85.

[2] Karl H. Menges, 'Altaic Elements in the Proto-Bulgar Inscriptions', *Byzantion*, xxi (1951), p. 99.

[3] *Povest' Vremennykh Let*, i. 23–24; Cross and Sherbowitz's translation, p. 64.

[4] 'Tolkoviny' has been interpreted by various scholars in different ways, as 'Translators', 'Turks', and 'Allies'.

they implored him not to destroy the city and offered to submit to
such tribute as he should desire. And Oleg halted his troops. And
the Greeks brought out to him food and wine, and he did not accept
it; it proved mixed with poison. The Greeks were overawed and exclaimed: 'This is not Oleg but St. Demetrius whom God sent upon us.'
And Oleg demanded that the Greeks pay tribute for his 2,000 ships at
the rate of 12 grivny per man, with forty men reckoned to a ship.

Most of the historians who dealt with Oleg's expedition assumed, on the basis of the date in the Russian Chronography, that
the campaign took place in 907. I believe that this is a wrong
assumption and that the date, 907, refers to the trade convention
concluded after the campaign and not to the expedition itself.
Under 903 we find, in the Chronography, the entry concerning
Igor's marriage with Olga. From the story of the expedition
(under 907) we know that Oleg, when starting for the campaign,
left Igor in Kiev. Presumably, preparing himself for the expedition and having in mind to appoint Igor his lieutenant in
Kiev for the duration of the campaign, Oleg arranged for Igor's
marriage in order to have him well settled as his future successor.
Then there follow in the Chronography three dates—904, 905,
and 906—with no entries at all, and then, under 907, both the
story of Oleg's campaign and the resumé of the trade convention
concluded after the campaign. It is most likely that the expedition started in 904 and continued through 905, and perhaps
through part of 906 as well. We know that the Russo–Byzantine war of 860–1 lasted for almost a year. The Russes, at
that time, had had to lift the siege only because of the shattering
of their fleet by a severe tempest. No such disaster occurred during
Oleg's expedition. From its description in Russian chronicles
we know that Oleg's expedition was better prepared and on a
larger scale that that of 860–1. Askold's resources were tiny in
comparison with those at Oleg's disposal. Therefore, there is
nothing against the supposition that Oleg's expedition lasted
longer than Askold's.

Besides, the general political situation was more favourable
for a Russian campaign against Constantinople in 904 than in
907. In 904 the Arabs raided Salonika and the Bulgars were making rapid progress towards Constantinople. In 907 there was no
war between Byzantium and the Bulgars, and no assistance could
have been expected from the latter by the Russians. Therefore

it is likely that Oleg began the expedition in 904. As has been mentioned, a representative of his seems to have guaranteed the new Bulgaro-Byzantine boundary of 904. In any case, the mere prospect of the coming of the Russes would be in favour of the Bulgars since the news of the impending Russian attack must have made the emperor more amenable in his negotiations with Simeon. That the Greeks knew in advance of the approach of the Russian fleet is clear from the fact that they had had time enough to lock the entrance to the Golden Horn (from the Bosporus). Here the evidence of the Russian chronicles is corroborated by an oriental writer of the early twelfth century, Marvazi. After mentioning Russian raids in the Caspian Sea, Marvazi says: 'They [the Russes] sail to Constantinople in the sea of Pontus, in spite of the chains in the Gulf.'[1] It should be noted in this connexion that among the sources used by Marvazi was the work of Jayhani, a contemporary of Oleg's expedition. Jayhani's work was written in Bukhara between 892 and 907. The date of the termination of his work (907) is another argument in favour of dating Oleg's expedition slightly earlier than in 907. It would seem probable that at least several months should have elapsed before a detailed report of the Russian attack could have reached Bukhara.

Furthermore, we have to take into consideration that Leo the Wise's comparative characterization of the Arabian and Russian fleets was written in 905. Leo must have written it under the fresh impressions of both the Arab raid on Salonika (904) and the appearance of the Russian fleet in the Bosporus (904 or 905). As we have seen, the Russian chronicler mentions the belief expressed by Greeks that Oleg was St. Demetrius 'whom God has sent upon us'. The idea that Russian invasions were allowed by God for the punishment of the Greeks for their sins had been expressed by Greek religious writers on earlier occasions—after the Russian raid on Amastris about 840 and after their attack on Constantinople in 860. Apparently, Oleg's invasion was interpreted in the same spirit. But why St. Demetrius? Presumably because he was the patron saint of the city of Thessalonika (Salonika), and because the Russian attack followed in the wake of the Arab raids on Salonika in 904. In Salonika St. Demetrius fulfilled God's will negatively by not helping the citizens to de-

---

[1] V. F. Minorsky, *Marvazi on China, the Turks, and India* (London, 1942), p. 36.

fend themselves against the Arabs. In Constantinople, as some of the Greeks apparently felt, St. Demetrius took an active part in the punishment of the city through the person of Oleg. We may think that the legend originated among the Greek or Slavic refugees who came from Salonika to Constantinople in 904. The Salonikans must have blamed the Constantinople authorities for not protecting Salonika against the Arabs. Now the people of Constantinople had to suffer in their turn.

Oleg undoubtedly was the leader of the Russian expedition of 904–5, but it is most likely that the Russ kagan of Tmutorokan also took part in the campaign. The main part of the Russ army and navy, however, was mustered by Oleg.

According to the chronicler, Oleg set forth 'by horse and by ship'. This is the first mention in our sources of the use of cavalry by the Russes. We can hardly think by that time the Russes had built up a large cavalry force. Most likely, the bulk of Oleg's cavalry consisted of hired squadrons of Pechenegi. If we suppose that Oleg had begun his campaign in 904, before the end of the Bulgaro-Byzantine war, we may then think that the Bulgars agreed to let the Pechenegi, their former allies, ride through their territory to Byzantine Thrace.

Oleg's fleet, the chronicler says, numbered 2,000 vessels. Vasiliev calls it a 'normal exaggeration'. The figure 2,000 is that which Oleg used in his negotiations with the Greeks after the close of the campaign as the basis for calculating the amount of contribution he demanded. We should not think that all of these boats sailed at once to Constantinople at the very beginning of the campaign. If, as I believe, the expedition lasted for more than one year, the Russian expeditionary force must have received reinforcements and supplies from home from time to time. In his demands presented to the emperor in 905 or 906, Oleg must have counted all of the boats the Russes had used in the expedition at one time or another. In a sense it was a bill of damages. The boats of Oleg's flotilla were small, each carrying only forty men. This indicates that the strength of Oleg's expeditionary army (not including cavalry) was about 80,000. This figure, again, refers to the total number of men employed during the whole campaign.

While Oleg's warriors hailed from a number of various tribes, the boats were navigated by those among them who had had enough experience in sailing; i.e. the Varangians, the Russes,

and the Slovene of Novgorod. The chronicler relates an anecdote which reflects the rivalry between the Russ and the Slovene
sailors. Before leaving for home after the conclusion of the peace
agreement, 'Oleg gave orders that silken sails of brocade be
made for the Russes and linen ones for the Slovene. . . . The
Russes unfurled their brocade sails and the Slovene their linen
sails; and the wind tore them [the sails of the Russes]. And the
Slovene said: let us keep our simple sails, we have no use for
brocade sails.'[1] The anecdote must have originated among the
Slovene sailors. The Slovene had been apparently offended that
the Russes received a larger share of costly fabrics than themselves and now tried to make fun of the Russes.

Oleg's armada was assembled and finally equipped at the
Dnieper estuary where it was probably joined by the Tmutorokan flotilla. Pseudo-Symeon calls the Russians 'Dromitae'.
Vasiliev, very ingeniously, derives this term from 'Achilles'
Dromos' ('race course').[2] By this name a long narrow stretch of
shore at the mouth of the Dnieper River had been known from
ancient times. Apparently, Oleg used the Dromos as his headquarters during the final preparations for his campaign.

On the basis of Pseudo-Symeon's list of place names which,
according to Jenkins,[3] is related to the Russian invasion, we may
conclude that the Russians first reached Mesembria and Midia
on the south-western shore of the Black Sea. There part of them
disembarked and marched across Thrace to the sea of Marmora,
reaching it at Selybria. The Russ flotilla, or part of it, continued
down the coast and turned into the Bosporus, stopping at
Hieron. The Russes also gained a footing on the Bithynian
coast at Mount Trikephalos. In this way the Russes established for
themselves a large base for their operations against Constantinople. By controlling Mesembria and Midia they secured their
connexions with Bulgaria and Russia. Their dash to the sea of
Marmora cut the land route from Macedonia to Constantinople.

---

[1] *Povest' Vremennykh Let*, i. 25; Cross and Sherbowitz's translation, p. 25. There is
some confusion in the English translation since the sails of the Slovene are there
called 'silken'. See D. S. Likhachev and B. A. Romanov's translation into Modern
Russian, *Povest'*, i. 221–2.

[2] A. A. Vasiliev, *The Second Russian Attack on Constantinople*, pp. 193–5.

[3] Symeon Magister (Pseudo-Symeon), ed. I. Bekker (Bonn, 1838), p. 707;
R. J. H. Jenkins, 'The Supposed Russian Attack on Constantinople in 907',
Speculum, xxiv (1949), 403–6.

The Russes did not hasten to storm the walls of Constantinople but were in a position to harass and plunder the outskirts of the city at their will. They apparently were taking their time, being sure that sooner or later the Byzantine government would offer them a huge ransom for lifting the siege.

And indeed, probably in 905, or early in 906, the Byzantines gave in and sued for peace. Oleg first demanded an enormous contribution of 12 grivny per man. The Greeks agreed to begin formal negotiations. Oleg retired a short distance from the city and sent his envoys to the emperor. A compromise was reached. The rate of the contribution was changed from 12 grivny per man to 12 grivny per rowlock. This meant cutting the contribution to one-half of the original demand, since each rowlock was manned by two men rowing in turns. On the other hand, the Byzantines agreed to pay special stipends to the cities of Kiev, Chernigov, Pereiaslav, Polotsk, Rostov, Lubech, 'and others'. The chronicler comments: 'In these cities there were established great princes subject to Oleg'.[1]

Having agreed to pay the contribution ('tribute' as the Russian chronicler calls it), the emperors Leo and Alexander made peace with Oleg, confirmed by oath. Before departing Oleg hung his shield upon the gate of Constantinople. This was the traditional Norse symbol of peace (the Russian chronicler calls it a symbol of victory). Oleg then went home with the main part of his army. He came to Kiev 'bearing gold, silken fabrics, fruit, and wine, along with every sort of adornment'.

It seems likely that some of the Russes and Varangians, instead of returning to Russia or Scandinavia, entered the Byzantine service. Some of these may have participated in the naval battle between the Byzantine and Arab fleets in the Ægean in 906. The Byzantines won that battle. Of the next major engagement between the Byzantine and Arab fleets, that of 910, we know positively that 700 Russes took part in it. In that second battle the Byzantine fleet was defeated.

When departing for Kiev, Oleg left his plenipotentiaries in Constantinople to negotiate a trade convention. It was concluded in 907. The resumé of its provisions in the Chronography reads as follows:[2]

---

[1] *Povest'*, i. 24; translation, p. 64.
[2] *Povest'*, i. 24–25; translation, pp. 64–65.

When the Russ diplomatic agents come [to Constantinople] they are to receive [from the Greeks] maintenance according to their wishes. And when the Russ merchants come, they shall receive a monthly allowance for six months, including bread, wine, meat, fish, and fruit. And baths shall be prepared for them according to their wishes. When the Russes return homewards they shall receive from your emperor, for their voyage, food, anchors, cordage, and sails, as many supplies as they need. And the Greeks agreed to it, but the emperors and the members of the council stipulated that only those Russes who are bona fide merchants are entitled to the monthly allowance. The Russian prince shall lay injunction upon such Russes as journey hither that they shall do no violence in the towns of our country. And when the Russes come, they shall dwell in the St. Mamas quarter, and our government will send officials to record their names, and they shall then receive their monthly allowance, first the men from Kiev, and then from Chernigov and Pereiaslav, and from other cities. They shall enter the city through one gate, unarmed, fifty men at a time, and may trade as much as they want, not paying any customs duties.

The provisions of the convention of 907 must have been partly based on the experience of the previous Russo-Byzantine trade relations. Now a great expansion of this trade was expected, and more definite rules were established. The trade was apparently of great value to the Byzantines as well as to the Russes, which explains the readiness of the Byzantine government to provide for the maintenance of the Russian merchants during a six-month period each year.

The actual rise of the Russo-Byzantine commerce following the convention of 907 proved much greater than anticipated, and it soon became clear that a new more comprehensive treaty was needed to protect the interests of both the Byzantines and the Russians. In 911 a Russ embassy appeared in Constantinople to discuss the provisions of a new treaty. The treaty was formerly concluded on 2 September 911. The full text of the Russian version of this treaty was kept in the Kievan princely archives and later inserted into the Russian Chronography.[1]

The provisions of the convention of 907 were not repeated in the 911 document although they undoubtedly were still valid. By the new treaty, the procedure of settlement of mutual offences, murders, thefts, and other crimes perpetrated by the

[1] *Povest'*, i. 25–29; translation, pp. 65–69.

nationals of one state against those of the other was regulated, with special attention to the case of fugitive slaves. All provisions were made in the spirit of the complete equality of the two nations. A remarkable feature of the treaty is the promise on each side to help the shipwrecked merchants of the other. This was contrary to the so-called 'strand law' practised in most European countries at the time, by which in a case of shipwreck the local rulers were entitled to confiscate all stranded goods of the shipwrecked merchant and to enslave him and his crew. The law was abolished in Italy in the twelfth century, and in England and Flanders in the thirteenth century, though at first only with respect to the Hanseatic merchants. General abandonment of the practices of strand law in Europe took place even later.

After the conclusion of the treaty of 911

Emperor Leo honoured the Russian envoys with gifts of gold and costly silken fabrics, and assigned to them his officials as guides to show them the beauty of the churches, the Golden Palaces, and the riches contained therein—much gold, silken fabrics, precious stones, and the relics of our Lord's Passion: the crown, the nails, and the purple robe, as well as the relics of saints. And the Greeks instructed the Russes in their faith, and expounded to them the true belief. And thus the emperor dismissed them to their native land with great honour.

3. *Russia in the tenth century*

I. *Preliminary remarks*

Oleg's treaties with Byzantium inaugurated a new era in Russian history. The rapidly expanding Byzantine trade greatly stimulated the prosperity in Russia. Oriental trade likewise continued to occupy an important place in Russia's economy. Russian commercial flotillas sailed not only down the Dnieper River to Byzantium, but also down the upper Volga River to Bulgar. The coming of one such Russ flotilla to Bulgar was described by Ibn-Fadhlan who visited the city of Bulgar in 921. The Tmutorokan Russes continued to trade with the Orient through the Khazar way. Khazar merchants also used to come to Kiev. Their settlement in Kiev is mentioned in the chronicles under A.D. 944.

As we look back through the ages on the events of the tenth century we cannot fail to note the dynamic character of both the Russian economic development and of Russian politics in this period. We observe the working in Russia of powerful biological and social forces, a protracted conflict between a reckless military group looking for further expansion and adventures and the conservative elements of the society desiring to consolidate the gains already achieved. The military group had its day under Igor's son Sviatoslav, but his attempt to build up a huge Russ empire failed dismally. While Sviatoslav's campaigns wasted much of Russian military strength, they did not shatter the foundations of the Kievan state nor did they prevent further consolidation of the Russ federation. That federation centred around Kiev. At first it consisted of the ruling group of cities and tribes controlled by the Russes, the lands of the Poliane and of the Severi. 'Outer tribes' had at first to pay tribute to the Russes. By the middle of the eleventh century, however, most of them acquired an equal status with the Poliane and the Severi, and all of them became known as Russians.

Closer contacts with the Greeks resulted in the gradual spread of Byzantine culture in Russia. The rise of Christianity in Kiev, checked for a while by 'Odin's men', now resumed its upward trend. It seems that some of the Russ envoys to Constantinople whom were shown the churches and sacred relics of the Imperial City by Emperor Leo in 911 were deeply impressed by what they saw. Some of them might have been converted to Christianity. In any case it is obvious that Christianity made rapid progress among the Russes during the first decades after 911. All of Oleg's envoys in 911 were heathen. Among those of Igor, who negotiated the treaty of 944, part were heathens, but part Christians. We know from this treaty that by that time there existed a Christian church in Kiev—St. Elias's. After Igor's death his widow Olga was converted to Christian faith (about 956). Their son Sviatoslav was a fervent observer of the ancient faith and refused to be baptized. His son Vladimir, at first passionately opposed Christianity but later not only was converted himself (988 or 989), but made Christianity the state religion of Russia, which it continued to be until 1917.

While the Christian faith was in the ascendancy in tenth-century Russia, we should not think that it was a mass movement. It spread at first only in the cities, and prevalently among Russes. Other tribes were in that period but slowly affected by Christian notions. Some of the foreign merchants residing in Kiev, like the Khazar for example, were Christians. But on the whole Christian communities constituted but a thin layer in Russian society of the tenth century, although those who accepted the new faith were deeply inspired by it. We cannot properly explain the appearance in Russia in the first half of the eleventh century of Christian leaders of such inspiration and culture as the Metropolitan Hilarion unless we suppose that the process of the formation of a well-educated Christian élite had been steadily going on in Russia for several decades before the official acceptance of Christianity.

11. *The reign of Igor*

Oleg died around 912.[1] According to the chronicler, a sorcerer (*kudesnik*) had warned him that his death would come through his steed. Impressed by the prophecy, Oleg took care not to ride it. Later, being shown the horse's carcass, he stepped upon it, abusing the sorcerer; at that moment a snake crept out of the carcass and bit him, causing his death.[2] As we know, Oleg himself was *veshchii*, that is endowed with the supernatural power of a volkhv. The legend of his death is obviously didactic, its object to prove that even the wisest man is helpless before Fate. The same idea was later poetically expressed in the *Igor Tale* in regard to another prince-sorcerer, Vseslav of Polotsk: 'Neither a shrewd and experienced man, nor a prudent bird can escape the God's judgement.'

Igor was Oleg's ward and must have been trained by Oleg as his prospective successor. Apparently the Russ boyars recognized Igor as the new ruler without any objections. Outer tribes subject to the Russes submitted to the decision except for the Drevliane who revolted immediately. Igor crushed the rebellion and as punishment imposed a heavier tribute on the Drevliane than they had paid to Oleg.

The success of Oleg's expedition against Constantinople encouraged the Russes to undertake another distant campaign, this time in the Caspian region. Tmutorokan undoubtedly served as the main base for this campaign. Preparations for it must

---

[1] Baron M. de Taube (see note R, p. 321) refers the death of Oleg to A.D. 925.

[2] *Povest' Vremennykh Let*, i. 29–30; Cross and Sherbowitz's translation, p. 69. See also A. I. Liashchenko, 'Letopisnye skazaniia o smerti Olega Veshchego', *Izvestiia Otdeleniia Russkogo Iazyka i Slovesnosti Akademii Nauk*, xxix (1924), 254–88.

have started soon after the conclusion of the Russo-Byzantine treaty of 911 which secured firm peace with Byzantium.

Around 913 the Russes went up the river Don to the Volga portage and down the Volga to the Caspian Sea. They received the permit of the Khazar kagan to go through his possessions for a promise of a share in the booty. The Russes plundered the south-western shores of the Caspian Sea using the Apsheron peninsula (the Baku region) as their base for supplies and the storage of booty. They maintained the base for several months, after which, their ships heavily loaded with plundered goods, they set forth homeward. In spite of the fact that they had sent the kagan his agreed share, as soon as they entered the Volga estuary they were treacherously attacked by his troops and completely defeated. According to Masudi, about 30,000 Russes perished in the massacre (914).[1]

The disastrous results of the Caspian expedition impaired Russian military strength for a number of years. Meanwhile the Pechenegi grew stronger in the Pontic steppes and thus presented a new potential menace. In 920 Igor waged a war against them which apparently ended in a stalemate.

A new eruption of Russ aggressiveness took place in 941–4. It was directed against both Byzantium and the Caspian area. The Russian and Greek sources describe only the Byzantine campaign; Arabic sources speak of the Russian invasion of Transcaucasia, while a Hebrew document throws some light on the connexion between the two.

The reason, or the pretext, for Igor's break with Byzantium is not known. According to 'The letter of an Unknown Khazar Jew of the Tenth Century', the Russian attack on Byzantium was instigated by the Khazars.[2] The number of Russian boats, according to both Byzantine and Russian sources, amounted to 10,000, which is an obvious exaggeration. In any case, the Russian expeditionary force must have been quite large since the Byzantines had to muster several armies before they succeeded in repelling the invaders. The main blow of the Russian attack fell this time not on Constantinople but on the southern (Anatolian) shore of the Black Sea. The Russes first sailed to the

[1] See B. A. Dorn, 'Kaspii', *Zapiski Akademii Nauk*, xxvi (1875), pp. vi–viii, 15, 16, 28; J. Marquart, *Osteuropäische und Ostasiatische Streifzüge* (Leipzig, 1903), pp. 333–5.

[2] P. K. Kokovtsov, *Evreisko-Khazarskaia perepiska v X veke* (Leningrad, 1932), p. 120.

Bithynian coast and then some went westward to Heraclia and some eastward to the Bosporus. Entering the Bosporus they sailed along its Asiatic shore to Chrysopolis (now Scutari), facing Constantinople. As was the case during their previous invasions, the Russes tortured prisoners, burned churches, palaces, and villages, and amassed enormous booty.

When stopped by the Byzantine troops, the Russes took to their ships, but their flotilla was attacked by the Byzantine fleet containing 'siphonophore' vessels able to project an explosive compound known as the 'liquid fire' (or the 'Greek fire'). Thrust out by special tubes or siphons this compound burst into flames when it struck the vessel of the enemy. A number of the Russian boats were thus destroyed. The Russes were terrified and turned home in haste. The Russian prisoners captured by the Greeks were put to death.[1]

While the Russes were defeated, their losses were apparently not catastrophic, since Igor immediately began preparations for another campaign, this time aiming at Constantinople. He started mobilizing the military forces of Russia and sent messengers to the Varangians urging them to attack the Greeks. In 943 Igor set forth from Kiev by ship and horse. Besides the Varangians and the Russes, he had in his army contingents of the Slovene, the Krivichi, and the Tivertsy. He also hired a horde of Pechenegi. According to the Russian chronicles, 'the Chersonians, upon hearing of this expedition, reported to [Emperor] Romanus that the Russes were advancing with innumerable ships and covered the sea with their vessels. Likewise the Bulgarians sent tidings to the effect that the Russes were on their way and that they had won the Pechenegi for their allies.' The Byzantines were worried by this threat of another Russian invasion, and the emperor sent his highest officials to Igor to negotiate a peace, promising to pay the Russes the same contribution as to Oleg and even more. Simultaneously the emperor sent presents to the Pechenegi—'silken fabrics and much gold'.

By that time Igor's army and navy reached the lower Danube. Igor convoked the Russ boyars for a council. The boyars

[1] Igor's first campaign against Byzantium took place in 941. See *Povest' Vremennykh Let*, i. 33; Cross and Sherbowitz's translation, pp. 71–72; K. Bártova, 'Igorova výprava na Cařihrad r. 941', *Byzantinoslavica*, viii (1946), 87–108; G. Vernadsky, *Kievan Russia* (New Haven, 1948), p. 34; A. A. Vasiliev, *History of the Byzantine Empire* (Madison, Wis., 1952), pp. 321–2.

advised acceptance of the Byzantine offer. 'If the emperor speaks thus, what do we desire beyond receiving gold, silver, and silken fabrics without having to fight for them? Who knows who will be victorious, we or he? Who has the sea for his ally? For we are not marching by land, but through the depths of the sea. Death spares no one.' Igor heeded their advice and agreed to call off the expedition. However, he bade the Pechenegi ravage Bulgaria. 'He himself, after receiving from the Greeks gold and silken fabrics for his whole army, led it back and returned to Kiev in his native land.' From the Byzantine sources it is known that the Pechenegi succeeded in reaching the Byzantine Thrace and that the emperor concluded a five-year armistice with them (943).[1]

The emperor then sent his envoys to Kiev to negotiate a permanent peace with the Russes. A preliminary agreement was reached and Igor dispatched his envoys to Constantinople to conclude a formal treaty (944).

In the Russo-Byzantine treaty of 944 both the provisions of the trade convention of 907 and many of the clauses of the treaty of 911 were included in a slightly different form.[2] By the commercial clauses of the treaty of 944 the Russ merchants were limited in their purchase of costly silken fabrics. Each Russ merchant was allowed to buy silk only up to the value of fifty gold coins. The provision of 907 concerning the exemption from customs duties was not repeated in the treaty of 944.

The main difference between the treaty of 911 and that of 944 is that the former was a treaty of friendship and the latter a treaty of both friendship and alliance. In 911 it was stipulated that the Russes desiring to enter the Byzantine service might do so. In the treaty of 944 instead of this clause we find the following provision: 'And if our empire needs military assistance from you against our adversaries, we shall write to your Great Prince, and he shall send us as many troops as we require. And so other nations shall learn what amity the Greeks and the Russes entertain toward each other.'

[1] *Povest' Vremennykh Let*, i. 33–34; Cross and Sherbowitz's translation, pp. 71–73.
[2] For the text of the Russo-Byzantine treaty of 944 see *Povest' Vremennykh Let*, i. 34–39; Cross and Sherbowitz's translation, pp. 65–68. In my opinion, both the English translation and the translation into modern Russian by Likhachev and Romanov (*Povest' Vremennykh Let*, i. 231–6) are to be treated with caution since both misinterpreted the original on some occasions.

Besides this general clause stipulating military assistance of the Russes to the Byzantine empire, two special clauses were inserted into the treaty according to which the 'Russian prince' undertook not to let the Black Bulgars[1] attack the Crimea; also he was authorized to wage war against those Crimean cities which refused to submit to him and, in such cases, he was promised military assistance by the Byzantines.

The meaning of this latter clause was misunderstood by quite a number of scholars, and the problem thus needs our special attention. Somehow it was supposed that the clause was meant to *prevent* the Russian prince from attacking the Crimea. In the text of the treaty (in the Chronography) we have a phrase which reads as follows: 'Let him [the Russian prince] wage war in those localities' (*da voiuet*). This phrase was understood as part of the same sentence as the preceding one, and together they were interpreted as follows: 'The Prince of Rus shall not have the right to harass these localities' (S. H. Cross's translation). In the new edition of the Chronography by V. P. Adrianova-Peretts (1950), and in the translation into Modern Russian by D. S. Likhachev and B. A. Romanov, the phrase is understood in the same sense: 'Let the Russian prince not have the right to wage war in those regions.'[2]

Such an interpretation contradicts the conclusion of the clause, according to which the Russian prince is entitled to Byzantine military assistance in case he needs it.

Here is the English translation of the full text of the clause as I understand it:

On the Crimea. Wherever there are cities in that part of the country which is not under the authority of the Russian prince, let him wage war in those localities, and [if] a locality does not submit to him, then, if the Russian prince asks us for troops [to help him] to wage war, let me give him as many [troops] as he needs.

Obviously, this clause contains no injunction forbidding the Russian prince to wage war in the Crimea. On the contrary, it is an agreement of co-operation between the Russes and the Byzantines of a joint Russo-Byzantine action in the Crimea.

---

[1] Under the 'Black Bulgars' either that branch of the Bulgars which remained in the northern Caucasus after the dispersion of the Bulgars, or that of the Volga Bulgars, is meant.

[2] *Povest' Vremennykh Let*, i. 234.

Action against whom? The only possible adversaries threaten-
ing both the Byzantine and Russian interests in the Crimea at
that time were the Khazars. The political situation in the Crimea
was quite complex. In the south-western part of the peninsula the
city of Cherson and the region of the Crimean Goths were under
the authority of the Byzantine emperor. In the easternmost part
of the Crimea the city of Kerch (Bosporus) was controlled by the
Tmutorokan Russes. Some of the other cities of the Crimea were
subject to the Khazars; in any case the Khazars apparently
claimed them. Now the Byzantine emperor and the 'Russian
prince' announced their alliance against the Khazars.

Who was that Russian prince? Not Igor, since the latter had
the title of 'great prince'. Most likely, the 'Russian prince'
of this clause was the leader of the Tmutorokan Russes, that is
the Russ kagan. In Chapter X of his *De Administrando Imperio*,
Constantine Porphyrogenitus says that the 'ruler of Alania'
can attack the Khazars. He explains that: 'Nine regions of
Chazaria are adjacent to Alania, and the Alan can, if he be so
minded, plunder these and so cause great damage and dearth
among the Chazars: for from these nine regions come all the
livelihood and plenty of Chazaria.'[1] As early as 1874 the Russian
historian N. P. Lambin came to the conclusion that under the
title 'Ruler of Alania' Constantine Porphyrogenitus meant here
the ruler of the Tmutorokan Russes.[2] Lambin's assertion passed
almost unnoticed, and yet it is quite plausible. Both geographi-
cally and historically Tmutorokan may be considered part of the
Alanic world. Constantine's notes on the attacks of the 'ruler of
Alania' on the Khazars may relate to the war the 'Russian prince'
was encouraged by Byzantium to wage against the Khazars. In
the first half of the eleventh century the Alans were allies of
the Russian prince of Tmutorokan, Mstislav, and it is possible
that the situation was identical in the tenth century.

At the time Igor was negotiating with the Byzantine emperor,
the Tmutorokan Russes and the Varangians launched another
major campaign in the Caspian and Transcaucasia. When the
armistice between the Byzantines and the Russians had been

---

[1] *De Administrando Imperio*, Moravcsik's ed., and Jenkins's translation, pp. 62–65.
[2] N. P. Lambin, 'Tmutorokanskaia Rus', *ŽMNP*, clxxi (1872), 67–69. Cf. G.
Vernadsky, 'The Rus in the Crimea and the Russo-Byzantine Treaty of 945',
Byzantina-Metabyzantina, i (1946), 253–4 (note 22 to p. 253).

concluded in 943, the Varangians must have received their share of the Byzantine contribution. However, most of them, as we may think, did not return home but preferred to go east.

This time the rich city of Berdaa in Azerbaijan was chosen by the Tmutorokan Russes for their invasion. As in their preceding oriental campaign, they went through Khazaria, via the lower Don and the lower Volga, and sailed south along the western shore of the Caspian Sea to the mouth of the Kura River. The Arabic writer Ibn-Miskawaih, who described the Russ campaign in detail, dates it in A.H. 332 (A.D. 943–4).[1] As they approached Berdaa the Russes issued the following proclamation: 'There is no dispute between us on the matter of religion; we only desire sovereignty; it is our duty to treat you well and yours to be loyal to us.' The city refused to capitulate. The Russians then stormed it and ordered all the population to evacuate it within three days. Those who remained after that term were either slain or obliged to pay huge ransoms.

Using Berdaa as their base the Russians plundered the country around it and amassed immense booty. They spent several months there but, as Ibn-Miskawaih says, 'they indulged excessively in the fruit of which there are numerous sorts there. This produced an epidemic among them . . . and their numbers began thereby to be reduced.' Encouraged by the waning of the Russian strength, the Moslems approached Berdaa and attempted to lure the Russes into an ambush. The Russes made a sally, their commander riding on an ass. The Moslems did not succeed in encircling them, but the Russes lost 700 warriors, including their commander, after which they retreated to the Berdaa fortress. Gathering more troops, the Moslems

continued to attack and besiege the Russes till the latter grew weary. The epidemic [among the Russes] became severe in addition. . . . When their numbers were reduced, they left by night the fortress in which they had established their quarters, carrying on their backs all they could of their treasure, gems, and fine raiment, boys and girls as they wanted, and made for the Kura River, where the ships in which they had issued from their home were in readiness with their crews, and 300 Russes whom they had been supporting with portions of their booty. They embarked and departed, and God saved the Moslems from them.

[Ibn-Miskawaih, Margoliouth's translation.]

[1] See note S, p. 321

The events of the years 941–4 are also briefly described, in a somewhat confused way, in the above-mentioned Hebrew letter of the tenth century. In that letter, the Byzantine and the Transcaucasian campaigns of the Russes are presented as closely interrelated. It is said there that after the failure of his Byzantine campaign the king of the Russes, Halgu, 'went to Persia by ship' and perished there.[1] 'Halgu' is obviously the same name as Oleg (Helgi in Norse). Apparently this was the name of the Russ kagan of Tmutorokan. He might have been a relative of Igor. We may think that it was he who led the sortie from Berdaa, riding on an ass, and was subsequently killed, according to Ibn-Miskawaih.

One year after the conclusion of the Russo-Byzantine treaty of 944 Igor was killed by the Drevliane. The circumstances which led to his death are of considerable interest for understanding the mechanism of the Russian administration of this period. It will be recalled that the Drevliane revolted against Igor at the beginning of his reign and were punished by a heavier tribute imposed on them. The name 'Drevliane' means 'Forest People'. They were a proud although somewhat backward tribe ruled by their own prince who had to recognize the suzerainty of the Great Prince of Kiev. To compel them to pay a heavy tribute, military pressure was necessary.

According to information preserved in the Nikon Chronicle, Igor authorized Sveneld to collect tribute from the Drevliane.[2] Besides holding the office of the general of the army (*voevoda*) in the Kievan state, Sveneld was the captain of the company of Varangian guards. Sveneld's appointment to the position of the commissioner in charge of the land of the Drevliane probably took place in 940, at the time Igor was preparing for his Anatolian campaign. Upon his return from his second, unfinished, Byzantine campaign in 943, Igor did not dare to deprive Sveneld of the latter's Drevlianian commission. And yet both Igor and the members of his retinue resented the loss of an important source of their income. 'Igor's retinue said to him: Sveneld's huscarls (*otroki*) are adorned with weapons and fine raiment and we are naked. Go forth with us, O Prince, after tribute, that both you and we may get it.'

[1] P. K. Kokovtsov, *Evreisko-Khazarskaia perepiska*, p. 120.
[2] *PSRL*, ix. 26–27.

Igor heeded their advice and decided to impose extra tribute on the Drevliane in addition to the regular tribute collected by Sveneld. Thereupon Igor led his druzhina to the land of the Drevliane and in spite of the latter's protests collected the extra tribute. Apparently most of it went to the boyars and Igor returned once more to the Drevliane accompanied by but a few retainers to round his personal share in the tribute. This time the Drevliane were not prepared to stand the extortion. Their prince Mal said to the people: 'If a wolf comes among the sheep, he will take the whole flock one by one, unless he is killed.' The Drevliane then attacked Igor and his men and slew them all.[1]

III. *The regency of Olga*

To avenge Igor's death his widow Olga inflicted a cruel punishment on the Drevliane. Her crafty stratagems are described in detail in the chronicles, obviously on the basis of the epic tradition. The Kievan army led by Olga and the voevoda, Sveneld, stormed the capital of the Drevliane, Iskorosten, and burned it. The Drevlianian elders were arrested; many of the prominent citizens were massacred; others given as slaves to the members of Olga's retinue. Most of the commoners were not molested, but a heavy tribute imposed on them.[2]

Olga ruled that two-thirds of the Drevlianian tribute be sent to Kiev, that is, into the princely treasury; and one-third to her own apanage town, Vyshgorod, that is, to her own treasury. Olga then marched through the Drevlianian land earmarking for herself hunting-preserves, establishing encampments, and appointing definite quotas for taxes and liabilities of the Drevliane. The next year Olga went north to the land of the Slovene and made similar arrangements there. All this amounted to an important administrative reform. Annual expeditions for collecting tribute (*poludie*) were replaced by a network of permanent local agencies.[3]

Olga was born in Pskov. The date of her birth is not known. According to the chronicler she was given in marriage to Igor in 903. Her son Sviatoslav, probably not her first child, was born around 940. She could hardly have been over fifty when

[1] *Povest' Vremennykh Let*, i. 39–40; Cross and Sherbowitz's translation, p. 78.
[2] *Povest'*, i. 40–43; translation, pp. 78–81.
[3] *Povest'*, i. 43; translation, pp. 81–82; G. Vernadsky, *Kievan Russia*, pp. 39–40.

she gave birth to him. Consequently we may think that she was born about 890. This would mean that she became Igor's bride at the age of thirteen. Early marriages were rather common among the Russian princes. Olga's name is Norse, Helga (feminine form of Helgi, Oleg). She probably was a Norse princess. N. K. Chadwick thinks that Olga was Oleg's daughter.[1] Be this as it may, it appears that Olga's prestige was high among both the Russes and Varangians. She ruled not in her own name but in the name of the boy Sviatoslav, whom she took along both to the Drevlianian campaign and on her journey to the land of the Slovene. However, until Sviatoslav's coming of age, she was the actual ruler of Russia.

From the point of view of intellectual history the most important event in Olga's life was her conversion to Christianity. According to the Chronography Olga was baptized in Constantinople in 955. This information is contradicted by the official record of Olga's reception at the imperial palace in Constantinople in Constantine Porphyrogenitus's book *De Ceremoniis Aulae Byzantinae*. This document gives the year 957 as the date of Olga's visit to Constantinople; it also makes plain that at the time of her visit Olga was already Christian.[2] Most likely, Olga was baptized in Kiev, around 956, and went to Constantinople afterwards. She accepted the Christian name of Helen, which was that of the Emperor Constantine's wife.

While Olga's conversion must have strengthened the Christian party among the Russes, it was not followed by the conversion of the whole nation. The Pagan party was still strong, centring as it did around Sviatoslav, a lad in his teens at the time of his mother's baptism. In vain Olga tried to instruct him in the Christian faith. 'He did not heed her exhortation, answering: "How shall I alone accept another faith? My druzhina will laugh at that."' Obviously he was under the influence of Odin's men.

As was the case with Boris of Bulgaria, and as later it was to be the case with Olga's grandson Vladimir, Olga wanted to secure some kind of autonomy for the Christian Church in Russia before attempting to convert the whole nation of the Russes. Therefore she turned to Emperor Otto of the Holy Roman Empire

---

[1] N. K. Chadwick, *The Beginnings of Russian History* (Cambridge, 1946), p. 21.
[2] Constantine Porphyrogenitus, *De Cerimoniis Aulae Byzantinae*, ii, ch. xv, in *Patrologia Graeca*, cxii. 1108–12.

asking him that a bishop and priests be sent to Kiev from Germany. The monk Adalbert of Trier came to Kiev but was not accepted by Olga (962). M. D. Priselkov believes that his failure must have been the result of a misunderstanding between Olga and Otto. The latter, apparently, wanted the Russian Church to be subordinated to the German ecclesiastical authorities.[1]

iv. *Sviatoslav—the would-be empire builder*

Olga's failure to secure a national organization for the Russian Church resulted in the ascendancy of the Pagan party. Its leader, Sviatoslav, now assumed full power in Kiev (962). The name 'Sviatoslav' is Slavic meaning 'of Holy Glory'. Apparently by the middle of the tenth century the Slavic language prevailed in the princely family. Sviatoslav's 'fosterer' was, however, a Norseman, judging from his name Asmund.

The Russian chronicler likens Sviatoslav to a leopard for the swiftness of his movements. Little did he care for the amenities of life. 'Upon his expeditions he carried with him neither wagons nor kettles, and boiled no meat, but cut off small strips of horse-flesh, game, or beef, and ate it roasting it on the coals. Nor did he have a tent, but he spread out a piece of saddle cloth under him, and set his saddle under his head.'[2] A characteristic story is told by the chronicler about the gifts the Byzantine envoys once brought to Sviatoslav. They first laid before the Russ prince gold and silk. Sviatoslav, without paying any attention to the presents, bade his servants keep them. Then the envoys displayed a sword and other weapons. These Sviatoslav accepted personally, praised and admired them, and returned his greetings to the emperor.

Sviatoslav observed strict rules of warfare. He never attacked the prospective enemy without a formal declaration of war. An envoy would deliver his message, which was always brief: 'I am setting forth against you.'

Sviatoslav's first war was fought against the Khazars.[3] In 962 the Khazars attempted to subdue the Crimean Goths. The Goths asked the Crimean Russes to help them. At the joint conference

[1] M. D. Priselkov, *Ocherki po istorii tserkovno-politicheskoi istorii Kievskoi Rusi* (St· Petersburg, 1913), pp. 12–13.

[2] *Povest' Vremennykh Let*, i. 46; Cross and Sherbowitz's translation, p. 84.

[3] On Sviatoslav and his policies see G. Vernadsky, *Kievan Russia* (New Haven, 1948), pp. 42–47.

of the Goths and the Russes it was decided to ask Sviatoslav for protection. An embassy was then sent to Kiev and a treaty concluded according to which the Crimean Goths and Russes recognized Sviatoslav as their suzerain and he in turn promised to defend them against the Khazars. On their return trip the members of the embassy observed an interesting astronomic phenomenon: 'Saturn was at the beginning of its passage across Aquarius, while the sun was passing through the winter signs.' According to the astronomical calculations, Saturn held such a position among the stars at the outset of January 963. It was then in 963, not in 965 (the date given in the Chronography), that Sviatoslav attacked the Khazars.[1]

Sviatoslav's main blow was directed at the Khazar fortress of Sarkel on the lower Don river. Having stormed Sarkel, Sviatoslav turned south, marched along the eastern shore of the sea of Azov to the northern Caucasus and conquered the Alans (Ossetes) and the Kasogi (Circassians). Undoubtedly, Sviatoslav's first campaign was concluded by his entrance into Tmutorokan. On the grounds of the previous treaty between Sviatoslav and the Crimean Russes we may think that he was acclaimed in Tmutorokan as the Russ kagan.

The immediate Khazar danger for the Crimea and the Azov region was now eliminated, but the new Russian kagan was not satisfied; his intention was to conquer the whole Khazar empire. For this he needed to control the entire course of the Volga, which in its middle section was held by the Volga Bulgars, and in its lower section by the Khazars. Access to the realm of the Volga Bulgars was barred by the Viatichi, who at this time still paid tribute to the Khazar kagan. Consequently, Sviatoslav's next blow was directed against this tribe, which he defeated around 964 (966 according to the Chronography).[2] After that Sviatoslav was in a position to attack the Volga Bulgars. Their capital, Bulgar, was stormed and plundered by the Russes about 965.

It was only then that Sviatoslav could start preparations for a final campaign against the Khazars. However, at this juncture his attention was attracted to the Balkans, since the Byzantines asked Sviatoslav's help against the Danubian Bulgars. According to the treaty of 944 the Great Prince of Kiev had to

[1] A. A. Vasiliev, *The Goths in the Crimea* (Cambridge, Mass., 1936), p. 121.
[2] *Povest' Vremennykh Let*, i. 47; Cross and Sherbowitz's translation, p. 84.

send auxiliary troops against Byzantium's foes if so asked by the emperor. Accordingly the representative of the emperor, the chief magistrate of Cherson, Kalokyras, conferred with Sviatoslav, and the latter agreed to attack the Danubian Bulgars.[1]

In 967 Sviatoslav invaded Bulgaria, with Kalokyras at the head of the Greek troops brought from the Crimea. By autumn the whole of northern Bulgaria was overrun by the Russians, and Sviatoslav established his winter quarters at Pereiaslavets (Little Preslav), the fortress which commanded the Danubian delta. In despair the Bulgarian tsar turned to the Pechenegi for assistance. The latter made straight for Kiev and besieged the city. The Kievans received some help from the Severi, and the Pechenegi failed to storm Kiev, but even the combined forces of the Kievans and the Severi were not strong enough to defeat the enemy. Sviatoslav's mother Olga, who with his sons resided in Kiev, sent a messenger to Pereiaslavets, imploring Sviatoslav to rescue her and the city.

Leaving a garrison to hold Pereiaslavets, Sviatoslav with his druzhina hastened by horse to Kiev and drove the Pechenegi back to the steppes. He did not intend to stay in Kiev, however, 'I do not care to remain in Kiev', he announced to his mother and the boyars, 'but should prefer to live in Pereiaslavets on the Danube, since that is the centre of my realm, where all riches come to: gold, silks, wine, and various fruits from Greece, silver and horses from Hungary and Czechia, and from Russia furs, wax, honey, and slaves.'[2] Olga, who was old and in precarious health, begged him to bury her and then to go wheresoever he would. 'Three days later Olga died. Her son wept for her with great mourning as did likewise her grandsons and all the people. They carried her out and buried her in her tomb. Olga had commanded them not to hold a funeral feast for her, for she had a priest who performed the last rites over the sainted princess.'

During his sojourn in Kiev Sviatoslav made preparations for another campaign against the Khazars. There is no mention of

---

[1] Leo Diaconus, *Historiae Libri decem*, ed. B. Hase (Bonn, 1828), p. 77; Skylitzes, in G. Kedrenus, *Historiarum Compendium*, ed. J. Bekker (Bonn, 1838–9, 2 vols.), ii. 372; N. D. Znoiko, 'O posolstve Kalokira v Kiev', *ŽMNP*, viii (1897), 253–64; V. Zlatarski, *Istoriia na Bŭlgarskata Država*, i, Part 2 (Sophia, 1927), 576–7. See also D. Anastasijević, 'Godina saveza Fokina s Bugarima protiv Rusa', *Bulletin de la Société Scientifique de Skoplje*, xi (1932), 51–60.

[2] *Povest' Vremennykh Let*, i. 48; Cross and Sherbowitz's translation, p. 86.

it in Russian chronicles, but the Arab writer Ibn-Hauqal states that in the year A.H. 358 (A.D. 968–9) the Russians, descending from Bulgar, attacked and plundered the main cities of Khazaria, Itil, and Semender.[1] There is no indication that Sviatoslav personally participated in the expedition, the conduct of which was probably entrusted to some of his generals. He himself set off back to Bulgaria soon after Olga's funeral.

Since Sviatoslav intended to stay in Bulgaria for good, before his departure he installed his three sons as local princes in Russia, to rule under his suzerainty. His eldest son Iaropolk he appointed prince of Kiev, and the second, Oleg, prince of the Land of the Drevliane. The Novgorodians likewise asked for a prince for themselves and received Sviatoslav's youngest son Vladimir as their ruler. It is noteworthy that two of these three princes bore Slavic names. Since that time Slavic names prevailed in the house of Rurik.

Had Sviatoslav's plans materialized, he would have created a huge east Slavic empire in which both Russia and Bulgaria would be included, and which also would have superseded the Khazar kaganate on the lower Volga. However, Sviatoslav's forces proved unequal to the task. In the first place, the shattering of the Khazar empire opened the gate from central Asia to the new hordes of the Pechenegi and other Turkish peoples. Secondly, the situation in the Balkans soon became unfavourable to the Russes. The Bulgarians settled their differences with the emperor, and the Russes had now to face a joint front of Bulgarians and Greeks. Sviatoslav counted on a palace revolution in Constantinople which his Crimean friend Kalokyras tried to engineer. It was, however, not Kalokyras but another adventurer, the noted general John Tzimiskes, who succeeded in seizing the throne. The fortunes of war turned against Sviatoslav. Defeated in several battles, the Russes finally sought refuge in the fortress of Dorostol (Silistria), where they were besieged. Their casualties running high and food running short, they sued for peace. The meeting between Emperor John Tzimiskes and Sviastoslav at the Danube River has been vividly described by the Byzantine historian Leo Diaconus.

The emperor arrived at the bank of the Danube on horseback,

[1] V. V. Grigoriev, *Rossiia i Aziia* (St. Petersburg, 1872), pp. 6–12; W. Barthold *La Découverte de l'Asie*, French translation by B. Nikitine (Paris, 1947), pp. 194–6.

wearing golden armour, accompanied by a large retinue of horsemen in brilliant attire. Sviatoslav crossed the river in a kind of
Scythian boat; he handled the oar in the same way as his men. His
appearance was as follows: he was of medium height—neither too
tall, nor too short. He had bushy brows, blue eyes, and was snub-
nosed; he shaved his beard but wore a long and bushy moustache.
His head was shaven except for a lock of hair on one side as a sign of
the nobility of his clan. His neck was thick, his shoulders broad, and
his whole stature pretty fine. He seemed gloomy and savage. On one
of his ears hung a golden ear-ring adorned with two pearls and a
ruby set between them. His white garments were not distinguishable
from those of his men except for cleanness.[1]

The treaty of peace was concluded in July 971.[2] Sviatoslav had
to promise never to attack any Byzantine possessions, nor Bulgaria, nor the Crimea. On that condition, friendship and alliance between Byzantium and Russia was resumed.

His imperial plans shattered, Sviatoslav set forth back to Kiev.
Meanwhile the Bulgarians sent word to the Pechenegi to inform
them that the Russes were returning with rich booty but few
troops. The Pechenegi immediately concentrated their forces
in the region of the Dnieper cataracts. In view of this Sveneld
advised Sviatoslav to return by horse, not by ship. This would
have meant abandoning most of the booty, and Sviatoslav decided to go by ship. The Russes spent the winter in the Dnieper
estuary and set forth homewards the next spring. As might be
expected, they were attacked by the Pechenegi in the region of
the cataracts. Sveneld went through to Kiev with his cavalry
squadron but Sviatoslav was killed in the battle. Kuria, prince of
the Pechenegi, ordered a cup to be made of his skull, overlaid
with gold, and drank from it on solemn occasions. Such was
the end of Sviatoslav.

v. *Russian state and society in the tenth century*

The early Russ state was, in its essence, a dictatorship of a
strong military group, representing the Russ tribe, superimposed on a number of other tribes—Slavic and Finnish—subject

---

[1] Leo Diaconus, *Historiae Libri decem*, ed. Hase, pp. 156–7.

[2] For the text of the treaty see *Povest' Vremmenykh Let*, i. 52; Cross and Sherbowitz's translation, pp. 89–90. For the chronology of Sviatoslav's war with Tzimiskes
and of the treaty see D. Anastasijević, 'Lev Diakon o gode otvoievaniia Tsimis-
khiem Bolgarii ot Russkikh', *Seminarium Kondakovianum*, iii (1929), 1–4; G. Ostrogorsky, *Geschichte des Byzantinischen Staates* (München, 1940), pp. 208–9.

to tribute. The pattern of this government was similar to that of other military realms of eastern Europe and western Eurasia, including the Huns, the Avars, and the Khazars. The Russ system of tribute (*dan'*) was similar to that established in the Khazar state. As the Russes emancipated themselves from the authority of the Khazar kagan and as they extended their control over the tribes formerly subject to the Khazars, they kept the Khazar system of tribute and in most cases did not change the amount of the tribute. The Russes applied the same system to the other tribes they conquered which had not been previously under the Khazar authority, as for example the Drevliane.

The core of the Kievan state in the tenth century was the middle Dnieper region, the lands of the Poliane and the Severi. This was the Russ land (*Rus'*) in the proper sense of the word. It was called *Rosia* by Constantine Porphyrogenitus. The areas of the peripheral tribes were called 'Outer Russia' (*Exo Rosia*) by Constantine. With the rise of the authority of the great prince of Kiev and with the economic growth of the country as a whole, the 'Outer' tribes gradually acquired more rights, and 'Outer Russia' eventually merged with the core of Russia. Thus, the Russ federation arose under the supreme authority of the prince of Kiev. This process was more or less completed by the middle of the eleventh century. By that time the tribute was transformed into a regular tax, collected per 'hearth' or per 'plough', even though the old term *dan'* was still kept. Larger cities were exempt from any direct taxes. Of the rural populations, only a special category of peasants, the *smerdy*, had now to pay the *dan'*.

The process of transformation of the tributary state into a free federation of cities and 'lands' may be illustrated by the example of the city of Novgorod and the land of the Slovene. As we know, Oleg imposed the tribute on the Slovene, and subjected Novgorod to a yearly contribution of 300 grivny for the upkeep of the Varangian guards. Presumably, Novgorod was for some time controlled by the captain of the Varangian guards. In 968 the Novgorodians asked Sviatoslav to appoint one of his sons prince of Novgorod. Sviatoslav's third son, Vladimir, was appointed, with the consent of the Novgorodians. Vladimir's uncle Dobrynia accompanied him as adviser and became the first *posadnik* (lieutenant) of Novgorod. The status of Novgorod in the Kievan state was thus considerably raised, but the Novgorodians had to pay a high price for it. The tribute they used to pay to the Varangians was increased tenfold, from 300 grivny to 3,000 grivny.[1] Of this amount, the Novgorod prince had to send two-thirds to the great prince of Kiev, keeping one-third for the wages of his soldiers in Novgorod.

This regulation was valid until the times of Vladimir's son Iaroslav. After Vladimir's death there was a struggle between his sons for power. Iaroslav finally won the throne of Kiev with the assistance of the Novgorodians. As a reward to them, he granted them a special charter by which he equalized their rights with those of the Kievan Russes. After that, Novgorod ceased to be a tributary city, and the Slovene a tributary tribe.

As regards the organization of the government and administration of the Kievan state in the tenth century, at the head of it stood the great prince (*velikii kniaz'*). The gradual consolidation of his power may be illustrated from the data of the Russo-Byzantine treaties of this period. From the preamble to the treaty of 911 we know that under the suzerainty of Oleg there were other 'serene and great princes' in Russia. Under Igor (944) the subaltern rulers were called just 'princes'. In the treaty of 971 only the voevoda, Sveneld, is mentioned after the Great Prince Sviatoslav, and no princes at all. Of Sviatoslav's son Iaropolk the chronicler says that he was 'the sole ruler' of Russia (977). Iaropolk's younger brother, Vladimir the Saint, was called 'monocrator' (*edinoderzhets*) by the Metropolitan Hilarion.

The 'great princes' and 'princes' under Oleg and Igor belonged to different clans and were of various national descent (Norse, Alanic, Slavic). After Sviatoslav, only princes of the House of Rurik were entitled to rule Russia. Each great prince used to give apanages to his sons. Because of this, the principle of 'monocracy' could not be upheld for long, but until about 1200 the prince of Kiev was considered the senior ruler in Russia.

While the authority of the great prince of Kiev ascended, that of the Russ kagan of Tmutorokan gradually declined. Under Oleg, the Russ kagan must have been one of the 'serene and great princes'; under Igor, he became 'the Russian prince'. As has

---

[1] It will be recalled, however, that by that time the weight of the north Russian grivna decreased from 68·22 grammes to 51·19 grammes (see n. 1, p. 245, above).

been mentioned, Sviatoslav seems to have assumed the title of 'kagan' himself, in addition to that of 'great prince'. Of Sviatoslav's son Vladimir the Saint we know definitely that he had the title of 'kagan'. The kaganate thus merged with the Kievan state.

Vladimir's clan emblem (*tamga*) had the form of the trident. As has been said,[1] it was a variant of the old Alanic tamga used in Khorezm, in the Bosporan kingdom, and among the old Russes (Ros) from ancient times. If, as I believe, Vladimir's father Sviatoslav was the first of the Kievan rulers to assume the title of kagan, he must have been also the first of them to use the old Russ tamga. After Vladimir all of the latter's descendants used this clan emblem, and only the Suzdalian princes in the late twelfth century replaced the trident by the leopard.

Each prince in Kievan Russia was entrusted to a 'fosterer' (*kormilets*) from his childhood. The kormilets guided the prince in his youth, and more often than not remained his close adviser throughout his life. Sometimes the kormilets also held the office of voevoda. The voevoda was the prince's main assistant in the army administration. After the reign of Sviatoslav a position of considerable importance was that of the great prince's lieutenant (*posadnik*) in Novgorod. Later on, when Novgorod emancipated itself from the princely rule, the office of posadnik became elective, and the posadnik became the mayor of the city. The first posadnik of Novgorod was Vladimir the Saint's maternal uncle Dobrynia. Dobrynia's son Constantine filled the office after him, and after Constantine, the latter's son Ostromir. Ostromir's son Vyshata was voevoda of Kiev. Later, Vyshata's son Ian held the same office. Ian died a nonagenarian in 1106.[2] Many of his stories of the bygone years were written down by the compilers of the Chronography. Ian certainly knew intimately the affairs of the Kievan state of his time, and also, through his father, the events of the latter's time. Ian's information must be considered one of the most reliable sources of the Chronography.

From Ian's family background, as well as from other sources, we know that the highest offices of administration in the Kievan

---

[1] See Chapter 5, section 2, above.

[2] See D. S. Likhachev's 'Commentaries' to the Russian Chronography, *Povest' Vremennykh Let*, ii. 469.

state became almost hereditary. It is obvious that most of them, if not all, were filled by men belonging to a small circle of prominent clans centring around the great prince of Kiev. This was very important for the stability and continuity of princely policies. It is also this group of clans which nurtured and kept alive the national traditions of the Russ state.

It seems certain that the great prince of Kiev, already in the tenth century, had a well organized chancellery. When Olga came to Constantinople she was accompanied by several officials —the *apokrisiarii* (secretaries), *pragmateutae* (clerks), and *hermeneutai* (translators). It is owing to the efficiency of the princely chancellery that the Russes were able to draft the provisions of the treaties of 907, 911, and 944, as well as to translate the Greek texts of the imperial charters. Some of the princely clerks must have been Bulgarians, others Russians.

The state treasury was distinguished from the private treasury of each prince. As we know, Olga ruled that two-thirds of the Drevlianian tribute be sent to the princely treasury and one-third to her own treasury. Of the Novgorod tribute, two-thirds went to the princely treasury at Kiev, and one-third was spent by the great prince's lieutenant in Novgorod.

The consolidation of the power of the great prince of Kiev was facilitated by the dynamics of three socio-political forces: the army, the boyars, and the cities.

The army of the Kievan state consisted of three separate groups: the Varangians; the princely retinue; and the contingents of the tribal troops. The Varangians fought under the command of their own captains. As has been mentioned, Sveneld appears to have combined the state office of the voevoda with the captainship of the Varangian guards, which gave him a great influence on state and army affairs. The princely retinue (*druzhina*) consisted of heterogeneous elements bound by oath of personal loyalty to the prince. There were both Varangian and Russes among the princely retainers, as well as warriors of other national origin, such as Alans, Kasogi (Circassians), Turks, and Magyars. The princely retinue was a highly mobile and well trained force.

The tribal army was counted as a 'thousand' (*tysiacha*), even though it actually was sometimes smaller or larger. It was headed by a chiliarch (*tysiatsky*). In some cases that official was also known as voevoda. Thus, the head of the Severian troops which helped the Kievans to hold their city against the Pechenegi in 968 until the return of Sviatoslav is called *voevoda* in the Chronography. Eventually, the office of the voevoda in the old sense merged with that of the chiliarch. Thus Ian (son of Vyshata) was appointed voevoda of the Kievan 'thousand' (1089). With the growth of the cities the tribal army was replaced by city militia which were now called the 'thousand'. The term chiliarch was then used in the sense of the commander of the city militia. In the land of Pereiaslav the militia was organized in units of one hundred (*sotnia*), each under the command of a centurion (*sotnik*).

From ancient times most of the Slavs fought on foot. However, both the Slovene and the Antes had also cavalry squadrons, some of which were used by Belisarius against the Goths. Of the Russes, we may conclude, on the basis of Zacharias Rhetor, that at that time (sixth century) they had no cavalry. In the early period of the Russ kaganate (eighth to the first half of ninth centuries), the Russes, as we know from Ibn-Rusta, made their raids by ship, not by horse.

The first mention in the chronicles of the cavalry in the Russ army is on the occasion of Oleg's campaign against Constantinople. However, as has been said (see section 2 above), most of that cavalry must have been supplied by the Pechenegi. With the expansion of the Kievan state, cavalry force became indispensable for the Kievan rulers. According to Constantine Porphyrogenitus, expeditions for collecting tribute began usually in November. At that time, rivers in north and central Russia were frozen, or about to be frozen, and riverways could not be used. The expeditionary squads undoubtedly went by horse. Furthermore the Russians needed cavalry to defend their southern boundaries against the steppe peoples—the Pechenegi, and later the Polovtsy.

It seems certain that in the course of the tenth century the Kievan rulers paid much attention to the horse. By the time of Sviatoslav the princely retinue became a cavalry squadron. Great efforts were taken to improve the breed of horses. In the periods when the Russians were at peace with the Pechenegi the Russians bought horses (as well as horned cattle and sheep) from the Pechenegi. The Russian princes established huge stud farms. According to the 'Russian Law' (*Pravda Russkaia*) of the eleventh century, any damage to the horse from a princely stud involved a heavy fine. When a prince died, his favourite horse was buried with him. This practice continued for some time even after the conversion of the Russes to Christianity.

In the course of the incessant fight with the steppe nomads the Russ druzhinnik (member of the druzhina) became an accomplished horseman. His spirit is well characterized in the *Igor Tale*:

And said the dashing aurochs, Vsevolod [prince of Kursk] to his brother Igor [prince of Novgorod-in-Severia]: saddle, o brother, your swift horses, and mine are ready, saddled in Kursk beforehand. And my men of Kursk are horsemen of renown: Swaddled under trumpets, fostered under helmets, nurtured with the spear's point. The paths [in the steppes] are known to them, the ravines familiar. Their bows are drawn, their quivers opened, their sabres sharpened. They race like the grey wolves in the fields, seeking honour for themselves and glory for their prince.[1]

The horse-lore was also reflected in many a bylina and folktale. The horse is described as the bogatyr's faithful companion and close friend.

While the druzhina was an efficient fighting force, it was not large. Because of this the Kievan princes had to use Turkish horsemen as auxiliaries. When Vladimir the Saint set forth against the Volga Bulgars (985), he went by boat down the Oka River, and his allies the Torks rode overland along the banks of the Oka. Later on, a number of Turkish tribes—Torks, Black Caps (Karakalpaks), and others, as well as the Koui (remnants of the Lebed Magyars), were settled along the northern fringe of the steppes in the vicinity of Kiev and Chernigov. Besides, beginning with Vladimir, the Russian princes built a line of forts and ramparts to protect the southern Russian lands from the attacks of the Pechenegi and the Polovtsy.

The upper stratum of the Russian society of the tenth century was the boyars. The term is of Bulgar origin.[2] In the later periods, large landed estates constituted the economic foundation of the

---

[1] H. Grégoire, R. Jakobson, *et al.*, 'La Geste du Prince Igor', *Annuaire*, viii (1948), 42 (Old Russian text), 153 and 155 (S. H. Cross's English translation). My translation here is slightly differently worded than that of S. H. Cross.

[2] See Chapter 3, section 2, above.

boyar class. In the tenth century the boyars derived much of their income from the Byzantine and oriental trade and were thus closely connected with the top layer of the merchants. However, we may think that more and more of them acquired landed estates through the division of clan lands, or by princely grant or else by purchase. By around A.D. 1000 land must have become the main source of the income of the boyars—in addition, of course, to their share of war booty at the time of major campaigns. An important item of this booty was war prisoners held for ransom. If not able to pay the ransom they had to work for the amount of the ransom on the princely and boyar estates. In addition there were hereditary slaves owned by both the princes and the boyars. Slavery was an important source of labour on the boyar estates. As has been said,[1] slaves must have been originally owned by the clan but later, with the division of the clans into families, the ownership was transferred to individual families of heads of the family.

The boyars filled the higher offices of princely administration and constituted the senior group of the princely druzhina. Their service to the prince was, however, entirely voluntary. They were under no obligation to serve in the druzhina, and they could withdraw from the service if they were not satisfied with it. Their landed estates were their own. Even if a boyar withdrew from the druzhina, his rights on land were not forfeited.

The council of the boyars assisted the prince in all matters of state. No important decision was taken by the prince without the advice of the boyars. International treaties, like the Russo-Byzantine treaties of the tenth century, were concluded in the name of both the princes and the boyars. Igor accepted the Byzantine offer of contribution and peace in 943 only after the boyars' approval of it. Vladimir convoked the boyars and the city elders before taking his momentous decision to accept Christianity.

Let us now turn to the growth of the cities as another important factor in the consolidation of the Kievan state. As we know, trading cities existed in south Russia from the Scythian era, rising and falling in the vicissitudes of great migrations and wars. In the Khazar period trading centres flourished in the Volga

[1] See Chapter 3, section 5, above.

region as well as in the Crimea. Of the Russ and Slavic towns of this period information is scanty. Tmutorokan, as we know, was a military stronghold and a storage place for goods. Presumably Kerch (Bosporus) thrived on Tmutorokan trade. In the north, Rusa might have been a trading town of considerable importance, though later to be superseded by Novgorod. Kiev, we may think, traded with Smolensk, Moravia, and Bulgaria.

Numerous finds in Russia of Byzantine, Western, and oriental coins dated in the ninth and the subsequent centuries, as well as of jewellery, are an indication of the growth of commercial relations between the people of these regions and Byzantium, the Orient, and the West.[1] It is significant that the Khazars collected the tribute from the Poliane, the Severi, and the Viatichi not only in furs, but in silver coins as well (entry in the Chronography under A.D. 859). In 885 the Radimichi paid the Khazars one shilling from each hearth, and Oleg ordered them to pay him the same amount.

The rise of trade and, in a sense, of money economy, could not but serve as a background for the rise of the cities. By the time of Oleg's campaign against Constantinople three cities emerged in the middle Dnieper region as important bases for the Byzantine trade: Kiev in the land of Poliane, and Chernigov and Pereiaslav in the land of the Severi. A share of the contribution the Byzantines had had to pay Oleg was reserved to each of these cities (and some others) by the agreement of 906. In the trade convention of 907 merchants of Kiev, Chernigov, and Pereiaslav were specifically mentioned among the Russ traders entitled to receive maintenance from the Byzantine government during their six-month sojourn in Constantinople each year. It is obvious that powerful corporations of merchants existed in these three cities at that time. They must have co-operated with the great prince and the druzhina in forming and equipping the yearly commercial flotilla plying from Kiev to Constantinople. This was, indeed, a huge undertaking. The assemblage and the sailing of these Russ commercial flotillas was described in detail by Constantine Porphyrogenitus in Chapter IX of his *De Administrando Imperio*.[2]

---

[1] See note T, p. 321.
[2] Constantine Porphyrogenitus, *De Administrando Imperio*, Moravcsik's ed. and Jenkins's translation, pp. 56–63. A volume of Commentaries to *De Administrando*

Preparations for the yearly caravan were made in the preceding winter. The great prince with his druzhina made their tour of the tributary tribes collecting tribute in kind, such as furs, wax, and honey. In addition, the Russ merchants also bought these products. An important staple of the Russian trade with Byzantium was slaves. Towards the spring, huge quantities of various goods for export were ready.

Meanwhile, Slavs living in the upper reaches of the Dnieper would be engaged in making bottoms of boats by hollowing out the trunks of trees, and early in the spring these were floated down to Kiev and there sold to the Russes. Boats of this kind were called *monoxyla* ('single-strakers') by Constantine Porphyrogenitus. In Kiev the boats would be finished, equipped with rowlocks, and loaded. Each year in April and May Kiev must have looked like a great shipyard bursting with human activity. In June, when everything was ready, the flotilla moved downstream. In the region of the Dnieper cataracts, the Russes, before each major barrage, disembarked most of the men, leaving only a few on each boat to convey it through the rapids, punting with poles. At the fourth barrage, the big one, the Russes partly dragged their boats, partly carried them on their shoulders. At this barrage, the Russes took all the goods from the boats and ported them overland; they also conducted the slaves in their chains along the bank. The remaining three cataracts were easier to pass. Throughout all this procedure the Russes had to keep vigilant watch for the Pechenegi.

Reaching the island of St. Gregory (Khortitsa), the Russes sacrificed live cocks before a gigantic oak-tree. The next stop was at the island of St. Aetherius (Berezan) in the Dnieper estuary. There the Russes rested for two or three days and equipped their boats with rudders, masts, and sails. From there they proceeded along the shore of the Black Sea to the Dniester estuary, then to the mouth of the Danube, and sailed farther south down to Mesembria which was the terminal point of the journey. On their return trip (not described by Constantine) the Russians

---

Imperio has been prepared for publication by Professor Jenkins. Commentaries on Chapter IX were written by Dimitri Obolensky. Concerning the problem of the names of the Dnieper cataracts see George Y. Shevelov (Yury Šerech), 'On the Slavic Names for the Falls of the Dnepr in the De Administrando Imperio of Constantine Porphyrogenitus', *Slavic Word*, xi, No. 4 (Dec. 1955), 503–30.

carried goods of more delicate kind—silk fabrics, spices, wines, and fruits.

The major Russian cities of this period were not only trading bases, however. They were simultaneously centres of various crafts. Recent excavations in Novgorod, conducted by A. V. Artsikhovsky, revealed numerous remnants of workshops of smiths, tanners, shoemakers, carvers on bone, jewellers, toy makers, and so on.[1] Some of them may be referred to the tenth and the eleventh centuries. Similar crafts must have flourished in other large cities as well.

With the growth of the cities, the urban people became conscious of their strength. Thus, under the superstructure of the princely and boyar administration, the city assembly (*veche*) gained momentum and eventually became an important element of power. The prince had to reckon with it, especially in cases of emergency. When Kiev was besieged by the Pechenegi in Sviatoslav's absence (968), the people of Kiev took matters into their own hands and decided to send a messenger to the Severi across the Dnieper to ask for their assistance. This is the first record in the chronicles of the activities of the Kievan veche. The same year the Novgorodian envoys came to Sviatoslav asking him to send one of his sons as their prince. They threatened to find an independent ruler for themselves if he refused. As has been mentioned, Sviatoslav sent Vladimir to them as their prince and his uncle Dobrynia as posadnik. The readiness of the Novgorodians to pay a tenfold tribute for their new status is an indication of the rapid growth of Novgorod's population and wealth in the tenth century. All these matters were undoubtedly discussed and approved by the Novgorod veche.

The general social structure of Russia in the tenth century underwent many far-reaching changes. The old clans were breaking, being partly superseded by the 'greater family' communes of the zadruga type. The number of individual families was growing both in the cities and among the landowners in the rural districts. The old rural commune based on kinship (*verv'*) was in process of transformation into a neighbourhood community. A peculiar form of association was that of co-operative ownership

---

[1] A. V. Artsikhovsky, 'Novye otkrytiia v Novgorode', *Desiatyi Mezdunarodnyi Kongress Istorikov v Rime, 1955, Doklady Sovetskoi delegatsii* (Moscow, 1956), pp. 171–88.

of a landed estate by several co-owners (*siabry*). *Siaber* is an archaic Slavic word (akin to the German *Sippe*). Presumably, the siabry association developed from the family commune.

The Russian society of the tenth century was that of free men. There were no impenetrable barriers between various groups of freemen, no hereditary castes or classes, and it was easy to pass from one group of occupation to another. It is only with reservations that one can speak of the existence of social classes in Russia in this period. The boyars together with the richest merchants may be called Russia's upper class of that age. The middle class in the cities must have consisted of the merchants of average means and of master artisans; in the rural districts, of the owners of smaller estates and members of neighbourhood communities and co-operative associations. The lower classes were represented by the poorer artisans and unskilled labour in the cities as well as by the peasants settled on state land, the so-called *smerdy*. The latter were under the special jurisdiction of the prince, and their legal status was somewhat restricted, although they were free men, not serfs. In my opinion, the term *smerd* (this is the singular form) derives from the Iranian *mard* 'man'. I believe that the smerdy were the descendants of the 'serf tribes' of old which had been subjected to foreign conquerors, such as the Alans, the Goths, and the Magyars. Now they found themselves under the authority of the Russ princes.

Outside the pale of the free society were the slaves—a leftover of the Ancient World. The class of slaves seems to have been quite numerous in the beginning of the tenth century. In the eleventh and twelfth centuries the number of slaves decreased considerably. It is one of the peculiarities of Russian social history that the institution of slavery continued in Russia throughout the Middle Ages and the early modern period down to the age of Peter the Great, at which time the slaves were merged with the serfs. Incidentally, it would not be amiss to mention that serfdom developed in Russia much later than in western and central Europe. In fact, down to the late sixteenth century the Russian peasants were free men.

4. *Vladimir: Russia's conversion to Christianity*

After Sviatoslav's death his eldest son Iaropolk became prince of Kiev with the assistance of Sveneld. For some time Sviatoslav's second son Oleg remained prince of the land of the Drevliane and the youngest son Vladimir prince of Novgorod. Peace among the three brothers did not last for long, however. Sveneld claimed the land of Drevliane, or at least part of it, for himself. Sveneld's son Lut went there for hunting and was killed by Oleg as a poacher. Sveneld then 'egged Iaropolk on to attack Oleg and seize his property, because he wished to avenge his son'. In the ensuing war between Iaropolk and Oleg, the latter was defeated and fled to the fortified town of Vruchi [Ovruch]. As his soldiers stampeded on the bridge across the moat, Oleg was pushed into the ditch. 'Many men fell in, and the horses crushed the soldiers.' After Oleg's body was found, 'Iaropolk came and wept over him, and remarked to Sveneld: See the fulfilment of your wish.'[1] After this, there is no more mention of Sveneld in the Chronography. In all probability he was dismissed by Iaropolk. A new voevoda was appointed, namely Blud.

When Vladimir heard that Iaropolk had killed Oleg, 'he was afraid, and fled abroad. Then Iaropolk sent his lieutenants to Novgorod, and became thus the sole ruler of Russia' (977). Vladimir did not intend, however, meekly to accept Iaropolk's rule. He hired a strong force of Varangians (possibly Jomsvikings) and with them returned to Novgorod. He ordered Iaropolk's lieutenants to go back to their prince and to give him the following message: 'Vladimir is setting forth against thee: be prepared to fight.'

The war between Vladimir and Iaropolk ended in the victory of the former. Iaropolk was betrayed by the voevoda Blud and murdered by Vladimir's Varangian guards. Vladimir must have been supported in his campaign by the militant heathen groups of both Varangians and Russes. Iaropolk's wife, a former Greek nun captured by Sviatoslav in Bulgaria, was a Christian and Iaropolk himself seems to have been favourably inclined towards Christianity. In a sense, Vladimir's campaign against Iaropolk was a new crusade of Odin's men.

Iaropolk and Vladimir were Sviatoslav's sons by different mothers. Vladimir's mother was princess Olga's stewardess (*kliuchnitsa*) Malusha, sister of Dobrynia. According to the Chronography, Malusha's and Dobrynia's father was a certain Malok of Lubech (Lubech is a town on the Dnieper north of

---

[1] *Povest' Vremennykh Let*, i. 53; Cross and Sherbowitz's translation, pp. 90–91.

U

Kiev.) Princely and boyar stewards and stewardessess in old Russia were usually slaves. And, indeed, when Vladimir asked the prince of Polotsk to give him in marriage his daughter Rogned, the latter answered that she did not want to marry the son of a slave.

Under A.D. 1000 the chronicler noted: 'Malfred died.' It has been suggested by a number of scholars that the entry must be referred to Vladimir's mother Malusha, and that consequently the latter's real name was Malfred. This is just a surmise. The Malfred who died in 1000 might have been Sviatoslav's sister or daughter, or some other princess of the house of Rurik. N. de Baumgarten considers her one of Vladimir's wives.[1] Another hypothesis supported by some scholars is that Malusha and Dobrynia were children of Sveneld's son Lut and consequently Sveneld's grandchildren.[2] Again there is no sufficient evidence for this. Malusha and Dobrynia might have been of Norse extraction in spite of their Slavic names. But they might have been Slavs. This latter alternative seems even more likely in view of the fact that Malusha was Olga's slave.

Vladimir was a man of great abilities and of a dynamic personality. Metropolitan Hilarion characterized him in the following words:

> This celebrated [ruler], born of celebrated [ancestors], a noble born of nobles,[3] our Kagan Vladimir, grew strong from childhood, and was filled with energy and strength; he excelled in valour and intelligence and became sole ruler of his land, having subdued peripheral countries, some by peaceful negotiations, others by sword. And, as he thus lived and shepherded his land with justice [*pravda*], valour, and good sense, then there came God's visitation upon him [and Vladimir decided to accept Christianity].[4]

It should be noted that Hilarion does not ascribe Vladimir's good qualities to his conversion to Christianity only. According

---

[1] N. de Baumgarten, 'Généalogies et mariages occidentaux des Rurikides russes du Xᵉ au XIIIᵉ siècle', *Orientalia Christiana*, xxxv (1937), 7.

[2] D. S. Likhachev's Commentaries to the Chronography, *Povest' Vremennykh Let*, ii. 295, 353–4, 469.

[3] Hilarion apparently had in mind Vladimir's father and grandparents, not his mother. Vladimir identified himself in his 'Church Statute' as 'son of Sviatoslav, grandson of Igor and of the blessed Princess Olga'.

[4] Hilarion, 'Eulogy of Kagan Vladimir', *Pamiatniki drevnerusskoi tserkovno-uchitelnoi literatury*, i (St. Petersburg, 1894), 69–76.

to Hilarion, Vladimir was endowed with many spiritual gifts from his childhood; he was a great ruler even long before his conversion. The conversion came as a result of God's visitation, as the sanctioning of Vladimir's natural abilities, of his innate reason, and sense of justice.

Vladimir's name means 'the Ruling Mithra'.[1] In Russian folk-lore Vladimir is called 'the Ardent Sun' (*Krasnoe Solntse*), which is a Mithraic epithet. Even before his conversion to Christianity Vladimir must have been a deeply religious man, conscious of his duties as a ruler. Mithra was the god of war, but also the god of justice and of the 'wide pastures'. Vladimir shepherded his land 'with justice, valour, and good sense'.

Vladimir was, however, not only a man of reason, but of violent passions as well. A characteristic trait of his nature was his insatiable sexual desire. He had several wives and many concubines. He could be quite brutal to a woman if she refused to accept his wooing. According to the Chronography, when Rogned of Polotsk refused to marry him, Vladimir attacked Polotsk, killed Rogned's father and two brothers, and married her against her will. In a later chronicle we find a story that Vladimir violated Rogned in the presence of her parents and then had the latter killed. It is added that Vladimir was instructed to do so by his uncle Dobrynia. Here we have a different motive—Dobrynia's revenge for Rogned's calling his sister, Vladimir's mother, a slave.

Vladimir was a skilful diplomat. Whenever possible he tried to achieve his aims by diplomacy rather than by war. He reckoned with realities and avoided any adventures. The objectives he posed for himself were always attainable. He had no dreams of creating a world empire like his father Sviatoslav. His aim was more realistic—to round off and consolidate his own realm —Russia. And in this he fully succeeded.

While Vladimir observed his father's rule of never beginning a war without a formal declaration of it, once the war started he used all possible means to win it, including cunning and deceit. In his war with Iaropolk, instead of storming the latter's stronghold, Kiev, Vladimir sent a secret message to the Kievan voevoda Blud urging him to betray Iaropolk and to arrange for the

[1] See Chapter 4, section 3, above.

surrender of the city. Thus, no blood was shed at the final stage of the war except for Iaropolk's.

Vladimir's 'fosterer' was his maternal uncle Dobrynia. He guided Vladimir in his youth and he remained Vladimir's closest adviser during most of his reign. After his conversion to Christianity, Vladimir often consulted Christian clergymen, especially the priest Anastasius of Cherson.

From the military point of view Vladimir owed his victory over Iaropolk mainly to the Varangian troops. The Varangians were conscious of their important role in the war. From their point of view, they won the war and to them should belong all fruits of victory. Vladimir had to apply all his ingenuity to get rid of his dangerous allies.

According to the chronicler, after the end of the war

the Varangians said to Vladimir: 'This city [Kiev] belongs to us, and we took it; hence we desire ransom from it at the rate of two grivny per man.' Vladimir requested them to wait for one month until the funds be collected. They waited a month and he gave them nothing, so that the Varangians protested that he had deceived them and requested that he let them go to Greece. He said to them: 'Do go there.' He then selected from their number the good, wise and brave men to whom he assigned cities [for 'feeding'], while the rest departed for Tsargrad [Constantinople]. But in advance of them Vladimir sent couriers bearing this message to the emperor: 'Varangians are on their way to your country. Do not keep many of them in your city, or else they will cause you such harm as they have done here. Scatter them in various localities, and do not let a single one return here.'[1]

The boundaries of the Kievan state were expanded by Vladimir both westward and eastward. Towards the west his first move was made in the direction of the Galician triangle at the junctions of Czechia, Poland, and Ukraine, with the object of not letting the Poles interfere with his contacts with the Czechs. In 981 Vladimir marched upon the Poles and took Peremyshl, Cherven, and a number of other west Ukrainian towns, known since as the 'Cherven cities'. Two years later Vladimir undertook a campaign against the Iatviagi, a Lithuanian tribe, and seized their country in the upper basins of the Nieman and the western Bug rivers, his intention being obviously to open for

---

[1] *Povest' Vremennykh Let*, i. 56; Cross and Sherbowitz's translation, p. 93.

Russian trade the Nieman and the Bug-Visla riverways to the Baltic.

East of the Dnieper River Vladimir had first to reconquer the Viatichi who had revolted after Sviatoslav's death. He then attacked the Radimichi and overcame them. Vladimir's next move was against the Volga Bulgars. The campaign ended in victory, but rather an indecisive one. A treaty of friendship and commerce was then concluded with the Volga Bulgars. The treaty ended with a characteristic formula: 'May peace prevail between us till stone floats and straw sinks' (985).[1]

It should be borne in mind that Vladimir was not only the head of the army and administration of the Kievan state but the religious leader of the Russian nation as well. As soon as he felt himself firmly established in Kiev, he attempted to raise the prestige of the Slavic faith by creating an open-air sanctuary of the ancient gods in the centre of Kiev (980).

And he set up idols on the hill outside the princely palace, that with the tower [*terem*]: an idol of Perun, made of wood with a head of silver and moustache of gold, and others of Khors, Dazhbog, Stribog, Simargl, and Mokosh. The people sacrificed to them, calling them gods, and brought their sons and daughters to sacrifice them to these devils. They desecrated the earth with their offerings, and the Russian land and this hill were defiled with blood.[2]

The Slavic deities Vladimir ordered his people to worship had been revered by the Slavs from time immemorial.[3] Each Slavic tribe had its preferred patron god. Now the idols of most of these gods were displayed together in Kiev, forming an impressive pantheon of the expanded Russ nation. The prominent position given to Perun may be explained by his likeness to the Norse Thor. Both Varangians and Slavs worshipped this divinity. Perun was also apparently the tribal god of the Poliane.

Human sacrifices were revived by Vladimir, not invented by him. As has been mentioned, the 'doctors' of the Russ kaganate demanded such sacrifices from time to time.[4] From the 'Life of St. George of Amastris' we know that the Russes sacrificed war prisoners to the gods. When Vladimir returned from his campaign against the Iatviagi (983), he 'made sacrifice

---

[1] *Povest'*, i. 59; translation, p. 96.   [2] *Povest'*, i. 56; translation, p. 93.
[3] See Chapter 4, section 2, above.   [4] See Chapter 5, section 2, above.

to the idols'—apparently of a quota of prisoners. This, however, was not enough for the 'doctors'. To complete the cycle of the blood offerings, they required blood from the local people as well.

According to the chronicler, 'The elders [i.e. "doctors"] and the boyars then proposed that they should cast lots for a youth and a maiden, and sacrifice to the gods whomsoever the lot should fall upon.' The lot fell on the son of a Varangian who had immigrated to Kiev from Greece; this man and his family were Christians. The Varangian refused to surrender his son, saying: 'These are not gods, but only idols of wood. Today it is, and tomorrow it will rot away . . . they are fashioned by hand out of wood. But the God whom the Greeks serve and worship is one; it is he who has made heaven and earth, the stars, the moon, the sun, and man, and has granted him life upon earth.' The people of Kiev then attacked the Varangian and his son in their house and killed them.[1]

This happened in 983. Five or six years later Vladimir himself became a Christian. What were the motives behind his conversion? One of them must have been the steadily growing impact of the Christian faith on the Russ society. The tragedy of 983 must have made a deep impression on both Christians and non-Christians. A number of influential Russes must have been shocked by it and might have questioned the wisdom and validity of the human sacrifices.

It is possible that dissensions started between Christians and non-Christians, and also, among the non-Christians, between the extreme heathen party, which demanded human sacrifices in the name of Perun and the more moderate worshippers of the other Slavic deities. News of religious discussions in Kiev might have spread abroad. This could have been the reason for the appearance of several foreign religious missions in Kiev about this time. According to the chronicler, following Vladimir's peace treaty with the Volga Bulgars, who were Moslems, the latter sent their envoys to Kiev urging Vladimir to accept Islam. (The Moslem mission may have actually come to Kiev from Khorezm, not from Bulgar.) Other neighbours of Russia followed suit and sent their religious missions to Kiev. Thus a Jewish mission from the Khazars and a Roman Catholic mission from the Germans

[1] *Povest'*, i. 58; translation, pp. 95–96.

appeared in Kiev. The Greeks, likewise, sent a 'philosopher' (apparently a professor of philosophy at the University of Constantinople). Vladimir agreed to listen to all of them; he was most impressed by the Greek philosopher but took no immediate decision, saying: 'I shall wait yet a little longer.'[1]

Such is the story in the Chronography. In his Eulogy of Vladimir the Metropolitan Hilarion makes it clear that for Vladimir himself the choice was only between keeping his old faith and accepting Christianity from the Greeks.

And as he [Vladimir] thus lived and shepherded his land with justice, valour and good sense, then there came God's visitation upon him. The gracious God cast his eye on him, and reason radiated in his heart [helping him] to understand the falseness of the heathen faith and to search for One God, the creator of all things visible and invisible. Moreover, he had always heard of the Orthodox Greek land, Christ loving and strong in faith. [He was told] how [the Greeks] venerate the One God in three [hypostases]; what forces [are revealed]; what miracles and signs occur; how the churches are filled with the faithful; how villages and cities are full of true faith and are ready [to fulfil God's will]. And having heard all this, Vladimir desired with his heart and longed in his spirit to become a Christian, he and his nation. This was fulfilled since God so wished in His love of human nature.

Hilarion wrote his Eulogy of Vladimir around 1051, i.e. thirty-six years after Vladimir's death and sixty-two or sixty-three years after his conversion. The date of Hilarion's birth is unknown. He probably was born between 1005 and 1010, which would mean that he was a boy of from five to ten at the time of Vladimir's death. Undoubtedly Hilarion knew well many men of the older generation, both laymen and clergymen, who remembered Vladimir; some of them might have been intimately acquainted with Vladimir and in a position to know the inside story of his conversion. What Hilarion says about Vladimir is thus no mere rhetoric. His statement is certainly of great value.

The three basic factors in Vladimir's conversion, as Hilarion interprets it, are (1) Vladimir's innate reason; (2) the impact of Byzantine culture on Vladimir; and (3) the mystic revelation resulting from 'God's visitation'.

Around 987 Vladimir convoked the Council of the Boyars and the 'city elders' (not to be confused with the Russ 'doctors'

[1] *Povest'*, i. 59–74; translation, pp. 96–110.

called just 'elders') and asked their advice about accepting a new faith. According to the Chronography the council advised sending envoys to peoples of various religions—Jews, Moslems, Roman Catholics (Germans), and Greeks, to observe how each of them worshipped God. The envoys preferred the Greek rite. Of the service in Sancta Sophia in Constantinople they reported: 'We knew not whether we were in heaven or on earth.' The boyars then added one more argument in favour of accepting Christianity from the Greeks: 'If the Greek faith were evil, it would not have been adopted by your grandmother Olga, who was wiser than all other men.'

Accordingly the council decided to accept Christianity from Byzantium. 'Vladimir then inquired where they should all accept baptism, and they replied that the decision rested with him.'[1]

Strange as this may seem, the evidence in Russian sources concerning Vladimir's actual conversion is incomplete, and there is much confusion about it. We do not know precisely when and where Vladimir was baptized. According to the Life of Vladimir, based on the work of the monk Jacob (Iakov), Vladimir was christened in Kiev in 987, two years before his Crimean campaign.[2] According to the so-called 'Korsun Legend', on which the account of Vladimir's baptism in the Chronography is based, Vladimir was baptized in Korsun (Cherson) in the Crimea after his capture of that city in 989. In any case it is certain that a conflict occurred between Vladimir and Byzantium either soon after or just before his baptism. What were the causes of this conflict?[3]

From both Byzantine and Arabic sources it is known that in the years 986 to 989 the young Byzantine emperor Basil II found himself in an almost desperate situation because of the attacks of the Bulgarians and of the rebellion in Asia Minor of two powerful Byzantine generals, one of whom proclaimed himself emperor. Finding himself in a critical position Emperor Basil turned to Vladimir for help. According to the treaty of 971 the Russian great prince was bound to send auxiliary troops

---

[1] *Povest'*, i. 74–75; translation, pp. 110–11.

[2] Iakov, 'Pamiat' i pokhvala kniaziu Vladimiru', Makarius, *Istoriia Russkoi Tserkvi*, i (3rd edn., St. Petersburg, 1888), 249–57; V. A. Rozov, 'Lichnost' Vladimira Sviatogo v Russkoi literature', *Vladimirskii Sbornik* (Belgrade, 1938), p. 167.

[3] For the Byzantine background of Vladimir's conversion see G. Ostrogorsky, 'Vladimir Sviatoy i Vizantiia', *Vladimirskii Sbornik*, pp. 31–40.

to Byzantium if asked to do so. Vladimir honoured the treaty and sent to Basil a brigade of choice Russ troops 6,000 strong. It arrived at Byzantium in the summer of 988 and saved Basil by winning two decisive victories over the rebels.

As a shrewd diplomat Vladimir attempted to extract as many advantages for himself from Emperor Basil's plight as he could. Consequently, as we may infer from the evidence available, he set three conditions on which he was willing to save Basil:

(1) He demanded that Basil's sister Anna be given him in marriage. (As a prerequisite for this, Vladimir had to be baptized, which he promised to do.)

(2) He required that the Russian church he was to organize should enjoy a considerable degree of autonomy.

(3) He insisted that the Russian claims on the eastern part of the Crimea, which had been confirmed by the treaty of 944 but annulled by the treaty of 971, be again recognized by Byzantium.

It seems that Basil's envoys, who according to Ostrogorsky arrived at Kiev in February 988, accepted all three conditions. On this ground Ostrogorsky concludes that Vladimir was baptized in Kiev early in 988.[1] While this is possible, we cannot be sure of it. Vladimir could have decided to postpone his baptism until the ratification of the agreement by Basil, possibly even until the arrival of his fiancée.

From the following events it is obvious that Basil was reluctant to keep his promises, especially since he felt himself much more secure after the arrival of the Russ auxiliary brigade.

When Vladimir understood that he was about to be deceived he decided to apply pressure on Byzantium. Since one of the points of the agreement of 988 must have been the restoration of the Russian control in the eastern part of the Crimea, he led his army there (989). His first objective was the Byzantine stronghold of Korsun (Cherson). According to the Chronography, the Korsunians at first defended themselves valiantly, but then one of them, Anastasius, shot into the Russian camp an arrow with a message written on it, advising Vladimir to dig down and cut off the pipes which supplied the city with water from springs outside. When the water supply was cut off,

[1] *Vladimirskii Sbornik*, p. 39.

the Korsunians surrendered.[1] The story shows that there were pro-Russians in Korsun. In the eastern Crimea which Igor and Sviatoslav had controlled, part of the population was Russian, and the pro-Russian party there must have been stronger than in Korsun.

The fall of Korsun was a serious blow to the Byzantine interests in the Crimea. In fact, to Byzantium the loss of Korsun meant the loss of the whole Crimea. Emperor Basil now hastened to send his sister Anna to Vladimir's camp at Korsun. According to the Chronography Vladimir had not been baptized until Anna's arrival. 'By divine agency, Vladimir was suffering at that moment from a disease of the eyes, and could see nothing, being in great distress.' The empress[2] declared to him that 'if he desired to be cured he should be baptized with all speed.' Vladimir agreed and his sight was restored straightaway. 'Upon experiencing this miraculous cure, Vladimir glorified God.'[3] This might have been the 'God's visitation' Metropolitan Hilarion had in mind.

At his christening Vladimir was given the name of 'Vasili' (Basil)—that of the reigning Byzantine emperor.

After Vladimir's baptism and recovery, his wedding was celebrated in Korsun. Vladimir then returned the city to the emperor as *veno* (the bridegroom's gift). On the other hand, he took possession of the former Russian cities in the eastern Crimea. From the story of Tsaritsa Anna's illness and miraculous healing, which is an appendix to the Life of St. Stephen of Surozh we know that she undertook a voyage from Korsun through Phullae to Kerch.[4] Undoubtedly Vladimir also went to Kerch and we may likewise conjecture that on this occasion he visited Tmutorokan, across the strait. It was then and there that he must have assumed the title of kagan.

The most important task which now faced Vladimir was to make preparations for the organization of the future Russian Church. Vladimir turned to the Crimean bishops to obtain priests, church vestments, and vessels, as well as icons and church books, for Russia. From this point of view, his control

[1] *Povest' Vremennykh Let*, i. 75–76; Cross and Sherbowitz's translation, pp. 111–12.
[2] In most of the Russian sources of the period Anna is called 'empress' (*tsaritsa*), not 'imperial princess' (*tsarevna*).
[3] *Povest' Vremennykh Let*, i. 77; Cross and Sherbowitz's translation, p. 113.
[4] V. G. Vasilievsky, *Trudy*, iii (Petrograd, 1915), 96.

of Tmutorokan was of paramount importance, since that town was (as I believe) the site of the oldest Russian eparchy headed by an archbishop.[1] Vladimir's prestige with the Crimean bishops and priests was greatly enhanced by the presence of his bride Tsaritsa Anna, a 'Porphyrogenete' princess. Through her, Vladimir became a member of the Byzantine imperial family.

Kagan Vladimir and Tsaritsa Anna stayed in the Crimea for almost a year. They set forth for Kiev in the late spring or summer of 990. With them went a number of Crimean priests, including Anastasius of Korsun. They carried the relics of St. Clement, sacred vessels, and icons. Vladimir also ordered to be brought from Korsun to Kiev two bronze 'idols' (statues of Greeks gods?) and four bronze horses. The twelfth-century chronicler remarks that they 'now stand behind the Church of the Mother of God [i.e. the Holy Virgin]', in Kiev.[2]

Following his return to Kiev, Vladimir ordered the statues of the Slavic deities to be thrown down and destroyed. The idol of Perun was bound to a horse's tail and dragged to the Dnieper. The whole population of Kiev was instructed to betake itself to the river to be baptized, rich and poor alike. Similar orders were issued by Vladimir's lieutenants in Novgorod and in the other cities. Pagan sanctuaries were destroyed and replaced by Christian churches. Most of the latter must have been wooden at first but Vladimir lost no time in starting Kiev's first magnificent cathedral of stone, that of the Dormition of the Mother of God.[3] Its construction was begun in 991 and completed in 996.

Once baptized, Vladimir accepted the new faith with all possible sense of responsibility. He continued to consider himself the religious leader of his nation just as he did before his conversion. His programme of Christianization of Russia may be summarized under three headings: the building of churches; education; and charities.[4] In regard to education, Vladimir

---

[1] See Chapter 5, section 5, above.

[2] *Povest' Vremennykh Let*, i. 80; Cross and Sherbowitz's translation, p. 116. 'The Mother of God', in Greek *Meter Theou*, in Church Slavic *Bogomater'*. Also invoked as 'Begetter of God', in Greek *Theotokos*, in Russian *Bogoroditsa*.

[3] The concept of 'Dormition' (in Greek *Koimesis*, in Russian *Uspenie*) of Holy Virgin prevails in the Eastern Church instead of 'Assumption'.

[4] G. Vernadsky, *Kievan Russia*, pp. 71–73.

ordered that children of the best families should be sent to schools for instruction in book learning. 'The mothers of these children wept bitterly over them, for they were not yet strong in faith, and mourned as for the dead.'

Vladimir's extensive charities are vividly described in the Chronography.'

He invited each beggar and poor man to come to the prince's palace and receive whatever he needed, both food and drink, and money from the treasury. With the thought that the weak and the sick could not easily reach his palace, he arranged that wagons should be brought in, and after having them loaded with bread, meat, fish, various vegetables, mead in casks, and kvas, he ordered them driven out through the city. The drivers were under instruction to call out 'Where is there a poor man or a beggar who cannot walk?' To such they distributed according to their necessities.[1]

Another writer adds that this was done not only in Kiev but in other cities as well.[2]

Our information on the organization and status of the Russian Church during Vladimir's reign is scant, and there are many moot problems about the matter. Even the relation of the new Russian Church to the Byzantine patriarchate is not clear. Most of the historians of the Russian Church believe that Vladimir could not obtain from the Byzantine authorities the degree of autonomy for the Russian Church he wanted and therefore refused to accept the patriarch's direct control over Russia. The late E. Honigman is one of the few scholars who deny any rift between Vladimir and Byzantium in church affairs.[3] His argumentation does not seem convincing to me.

Vladimir himself in his 'Church Statute' emphasized the basic importance for Russia of the first baptism of the Russes under the auspices of Emperor Michael and Patriarch Photius.[4] This for him is the historical foundation of his own baptism. He did not mention the names of the emperor and the patriarch in power at the time of his baptism. From my point of view this is

[1] *Povest' Vremennykh Let*, i. 86; Cross and Sherbowitz's translation, pp. 121–2.

[2] Life of Prince Vladimir (ascribed to the monk Iakov), Makarius, *Istoriia Russkoi Tserkvi*, i. 255.

[3] E. Honigman, 'Studies in Slavic Church History', *Byzantion*, xvii (1945), 128–42.

[4] G. Vernadsky, 'The Status of the Russian Church during the First Half-Century following Vladimir's conversion', *SEER*, xx (1941), 308.

a clear indication of his unwillingness to recognize their authority over the Russian Church he organized. Vladimir then says that he 'took the metropolitan Leon to Kiev, who christened the whole Russian land by holy baptism'. Vladimir's 'Church Statute' is known to us in several manuscript copies of which the earliest extant dates from the thirteenth century. There are reasons to believe that in the original manuscript Leon was called 'archbishop', not 'metropolitan'.

In 1913 M. D. Priselkov suggested that Vladimir, unable to come to terms with the Byzantine authorities, addressed himself to Bulgaria and placed the Russian Church under the authority of the Archbishop of Ochrida.[1] The theory seems ingenious, but in my opinion there is not enough direct evidence for it. It is much more likely that the archbishop whom Vladimir 'took to Kiev' was that of Tmutorokan, not that of Ochrida. In the Eastern Church the authority of an autocephalous archbishop is practically equal to that of the patriarch (consider the position of the archbishop of Cyprus). To this class the archbishop of Ochrida belonged, and according to Golubinsky the archbishop of Tmutorokan as well.[2] The see of Tmutorokan is mentioned in some of the Byzantine lists of bishoprics of the tenth century. In the late eleventh century (1078–88) Tmutorokan was one of the Russian eparchies. The only possible time when the eparchy of Tmutorokan could have been transferred to Russia was the period of Vladimir's sojourn in the Crimea after his capture of Korsun (989).

The assumption that the archbishop of Tmutorokan was the primate of the Russian Church during the reign of Vladimir fits well into the general picture of the church of this period as we have it from other evidence. No eparchy of Kiev is mentioned in the contemporary sources. Presumably the archbishop of Tmutorokan visited the capital from time to time and in the intervals the bishop of nearby Belgorod officiated in Kiev whenever need arose. It is characteristic that the prelate John

[1] M. D. Priselkov, *Ocherki po tserkovno-politicheskoi istorii Kievskoi Rusi* (St. Petersburg, 1913); Hans Koch, 'Byzanz, Ochrid und Kiev, 987–1037', *Kyrios*, iii (1938), 272–84. For a more recent review of the problem see also N. Zernov, 'Vladimir and the Origin of the Russian Church', *SEER*, xxviii (1949–50), 123–38 and 425–38.

[2] E. E. Golubinsky, *Istoriia Russkoi Tserkvi*, i, Part 1 (2nd edn., Moscow, 1901), 264–7.

mentioned as the primate of the Russian Church in the period 1008–24, bore the title of archbishop and not of metropolitan. Priselkov for this reason identifies him as the archbishop of Ochrida. In my opinion he must have been of Tmutorokan.

It is clear that Vladimir did not hestitate to take, on his own authority, such measures for the better organization of the young Russian Church as he deemed necessary. In that sense, we may call him the protector of the Russian Church, even though not the actual head of the church administration. Consider from this point of view the 'Church Statute' he issued (some time between 1007 and 1011).[1] The core of it consists of four sections: (1) invocation; (2) declaration of conversion; (3) granting of the tithe for the sustenance of the church; and (4) immunity of the church courts.

The invocation reads: 'In the name of the Father, and the Son, and the Holy Ghost.' The declaration of conversion, as has been already mentioned, emphasizes the role of the first baptism of the Russes by Photius. Next, Vladimir declares that he built the church in the name of the Holy Mother of God and granted it a tithe from all over Russia.

The section on the immunity of the church courts reads as follows:

Then, having opened the Greek *Nomocanon* [manual of canon and civil law], we found in it that neither to the prince, nor to his boyars, nor to his judges is it proper to interfere with these [church] courts and lawsuits. And I, having consulted my princess Anna and my sons, granted [the administration of] these courts to the metropolitan [in the original presumably 'to the archbishop'] and to all bishoprics throughout the Russian land.

It may be seen that Vladimir, while invoking God and remembering Patriarch Photius, made no references to any church authorities contemporary with him. The clause on the church courts he based on the *Nomocanon* which he himself read for this occasion. Besides, he also consulted Tsaritsa Anna and his sons. In this document Vladimir reveals himself as a national leader, conscious of his duties towards the church, not only towards the state.

[1] V. N. Beneshevich, ed., 'Pamiatniki drevne-russkogo kanonicheskogo prava', *Russkaia Istoricheskaia Biblioteka*, xxxvi (Petrograd, 1920). For the history and analysis of the text see S. V. Iushkov, *Ustav Kniazia Vladimira* (Novouzensk, 1926).

During the first years after the christening of the Russes Vladimir's chief assistant in church affairs was the priest Anastasius of Cherson. He was apparently the same Anastasius who, during the siege of Korsun, sent to Vladimir the important message by arrow, which helped Vladimir to take possession of Korsun. After that Vladimir had every reason to trust him and to be sure of his loyalty to Russia. When the church of the Mother of God was finished (996) and Vladimir granted it a tithe from all over Russia, he entrusted to Anastasius the management of the tithe. Presumably Anastasius was appointed archpriest of the new church. The decree on the tithe was later included in the Church Statute.

By the end of Vladimir's reign seven bishoprics were established in Russia not counting Tmutorokan: Novgorod, Chernigov, Vladimir in Volynia, Polotsk, Turov, Belgorod (near Kiev), and Rostov.

The status of the Russian Church was radically changed in the reign of Vladimir's son Iaroslav the Wise. In 1037 an agreement was reached between Iaroslav and Byzantium, according to which the Russian Church became a diocese of the Patriarchate of Constantinople. It was to be headed by the metropolitan of Kiev ordained by the Patriarch of Constantinople. In other Russian cities bishops were to be ordained by the metropolitan, but it was understood that the prince of Kiev would have the right to nominate suitable candidates. Not later than 1039 the first metropolitan of Kiev, Theopemptus, arrived in Russia from Constantinople.[1]

The agreement of 1037 became the foundation of Russia's church administration for four centuries. In 1448 the Russian Church became practically autocephalous and in 1589 the first Patriarch of Russia, Job, was ordained.

Vladimir's foreign policy in the Christian period of his life was not aggressive. As the chronicler has noted, 'he lived in peace with the neighbouring rulers, Boleslav of Poland, Stephen of Hungary, and Udalrich of Czechia, and there was unity and friendship among them'.[2] Except for one expedition against the Galician Khorvats—presumably to quell a revolt—Vladimir

---

[1] *Povest' Vremennykh Let*, i. 103; Cross and Sherbowitz's translation, p. 138. See also Sherbowitz's 'Notes', n. 171, pp. 259–60.
[2] *Povest'*, i. 86; translation, p. 123.

concentrated his attention on the defence of Russia's southern frontier against the Pechenegi, who raided Russia at least three times (in 992, 995, and 997) but were each time repulsed, although with great difficulty.

In order to protect the country from the nomads Vladimir built several lines of forts along the northern banks of the steppe rivers.[1] In this he set a model for generations of Russian rulers to come, and 'fortified lines' as a protection against the nomads were still built by the Russians in south and east Russia as late as the eighteenth and early nineteenth centuries.

Following the example of his father, Vladimir ruled distant cities and lands through his sons as viceroys. In the latter part of his reign his son Iaroslav was viceroy of Novgorod, Sviatopolk of Turov, Boris of Rostov, Gleb of Murom, Sviatoslav of the Drevlianian Land, Iziaslav of Polotsk, and Mstislav of Tmutorokan. Most of these sons were born of different mothers of various nationality. They did not form a closely united family, and most of them were suspicious of others. Towards the end of his life Vladimir favoured Boris, born to Vladimir's Bulgarian wife, and apparently intended to appoint him his successor. This presaged a conflict with the eldest son Sviatopolk. The latter's mother was Iaropolk's widow whom Vladimir married after the murder of Iaropolk; according to the chronicler she was pregnant at that time, so Sviatopolk seems to have been actually Iaropolk's son, not Vladimir's.

In 1014 the viceroy of Novgorod Iaroslav, Vladimir's son by Rogned of Polotsk, refused to send to Kiev the annual quota of the Novgorod tribute. Vladimir was indignant and started preparation for a campaign against Iaroslav. The latter refused to yield and hired a body of Varangians from overseas to defend himself. War between father and son seemed imminent. Vladimir actually set forth against Iaroslav but fell ill in the very beginning of the campaign and had to stop at Berestovo not far from Kiev. He was accompanied by his son Boris. At that juncture the news came that the Pechenegi were on their way to attack Russia, and Vladimir sent Boris with choice troops against the Pechenegi. Meanwhile Sviatopolk arrived at Kiev, apparently getting ready to seize power after Vladimir's death.

[1] See D. A. Rasovsky, 'Rus' i kochevniki v epokhu Sviatogo Vladimira', *Vladimirskii Sbornik*, pp. 149–54.

In this atmosphere of anxiety, suspicion, and intrigue Vladimir died on 15 July 1015. His boyars were in a state of suspense and confusion. They knew that Vladimir preferred Boris as his successor, but Boris was in the land of Pereiaslav, guarding the frontier against the Pechenegi. Sviatopolk was nearby in Kiev, and the boyars were afraid of him. At first they attempted to conceal Vladimir's death from everybody to gain time. However, Vladimir's body was to be given due funeral.

At night they [Vladimir's druzhiniki] took up the flooring between the two rooms, and after wrapping [Vladimir's] body in a rug, they let it down to earth with ropes. After they had placed it upon a sledge, they drove it [to Kiev] and buried it in the church of the Mother of God that he himself had built. When the people heard of this, they assembled in multitudes and mourned him, the boyars as the defender of their country, the poor as their protector and benefactor. They laid him in a marble coffin and buried the body of the blessed prince amid their mourning.[1]

In the middle of the eleventh century a 'Eulogy' of Vladimir was written by the monk Jacob, and a Life of Vladimir compiled on its basis. Metropolitan Hilarion in his famous 'Eulogy' likened Vladimir to Emperor Constantine the Great. It is obvious that a number of Russian church leaders were in favour of canonizing Vladimir at that time. The canonization was postponed, however, apparently because of the opposition to it on the part of the Patriarch of Constantinople. It was only as late as 1263 that Vladimir was canonized by the Russian Church.

5. *The aftermath of the conversion*

Vladimir died, but the main work of the second half of his reign—the Christianization of Russia—did not die with him. In fact, as we know, Christianity had taken roots in Russia even before Vladimir. With the impetus given it by Vladimir and the mighty support of the princes and boyars, its ascendancy was now secured.

By the time of Vladimir's son Iaroslav, the new faith was already firmly entrenched in Russia. Iaroslav put forth every effort to make Kiev the centre of Christian art and learning, taking Constantinople as the pattern. A sumptuous cathedral dedicated to Sancta Sophia (the Divine Wisdom) and several

---

[1] *Povest' Vremennykh Let*, i. 89; Cross and Sherbowitz's translation, p. 124.

other churches were built, mainly by imported Byzantine masters, as well as a new citadel and the so-called Golden Gate, a picture of which centuries later inspired the composer Mussorgsky for a theme in his 'Pictures from an Exibition'. Great attention was paid to learning. According to the chronicler, Iaroslav 'applied himself to books and read them constantly day and night. He assembled many scribes to translate Greek books through which true believers are instructed and enjoy religious education. . . . Iaroslav, as we have said, was a lover of books and, as he had many written, he deposited them in the Church of Sancta Sophia.'[1] Taken together, Iaroslav's ambitious translation and writing project and the library at Sancta Sophia amounted to the establishment at Kiev of an important institution of learning and research. Michael Hrushevsky aptly called it Russia's first learned academy.[2]

Historically speaking, Slavic Christianity was a branch of Byzantine Christianity. However, in each of the Slavic countries as they accepted the new faith, a new educated élite was rapidly formed, which not only supplied the Slavs with translations from the Greek, but prompted Slavic letters as well. The use of the Slavic language in the church greatly facilitated the spread of the new faith among the Slavs. It also gave great impetus to the growth of Slavic literature at large.

The 'Slavic Apostles' themselves fully realized the implications of the use of the native language in the new church they created and were filled with enthusiasm for their cultural mission.

To his translation of the Gospel Constantine the Philosopher (St. Cyril) wrote a remarkable foreword which started with the following inspired lines:

Now hear with the power of your understanding!
Thus hear, Slavic people!
Hear the Word which feeds human souls.
The Word which strengthens the heart and the mind,
This word ready for the cognition of God.

Constantine then emphasized the importance for the Slavic people, as for any people, of hearing the Gospel and having books

[1] *Povest'*, i. 103; translation, pp. 137–8.
[2] M. Hrushevsky (Grushevsky), 'Tri Akademii', *Kyivski Zbirnyky*, i (Kiev, 1930), 1–14.

in their own language. 'And, therefore, Saint Paul has taught: I would rather speak five words with my understanding that I might teach others also, than ten thousand words in an unknown tongue.'[1]

Even though the Slavic rite in Moravia was replaced by the Latin rite after St. Methodius's death, the cause of Slavic letters did not perish. Bulgaria replaced Moravia as the main centre of Slavic learning in the tenth century, and Russia now followed suit. It should be borne in mind that Slavic scholars in both Bulgaria and Russia were not merely translators from the Greek or imitators of the Byzantine writers. Both in Bulgaria and Russia men arose who fully mastered the new learning and the new philosophy.

Russia's greatest Christian luminary of this period was Hilarion (metropolitan of Kiev, 1051–2). His famous *Discourse on Law and Grace* is not only deep in its contents but a masterpiece of literary style as well.[2] While Hilarion towered above all the others, he did not live in a cultural vacuum. A thin but well educated élite fully appreciated Hilarion's sermons and writings. He explicitly addressed some of his sermons to those who were 'saturated with the sweetness of book-learning'.

The approach to Christianity of this Slavic élite, both in Bulgaria and Russia, may be called philosophical and historico-philosophical. Their thought centred around the mystery of the Incarnation of the Word which bridged the gulf between the infinite and the finite man. The spread of this concept through the expansion of Christianity constituted for them the essence of history. In his *Discourse on Law and Grace* Hilarion said: 'Faith of Grace spread over the earth and finally reached the Russian people. . . . The gracious God who cares for all the other countries now does not neglect us; he has desired to save us and to lead us to true reason (*razum istinnyi*).' The mystery of Incarnation is not imposed on men; man's will is free. Hilarion emphasized the antithesis between the formal 'law' (*zakon*) of the Old Testament and the 'Grace' (*blagodat'*) of the Christian faith.

---

[1] See R. Jakobson, 'The Beginnings of National Self-Determination in Europe', *The Review of Politics*, vii (1945), 31.

[2] Hilarion, 'Slovo o Zakone i Blagodati', in A. I. Ponomarev, *Pamiatniki drevnerusskoi tserkovnouchitelnoi literatury*, i (1894), 59–69. See also Dmitrij Tschižewskij (Chyzhevsky), *Altrussische Literaturgeschichte* (Frankfurt-am-Main, 1948), pp. 116–22.

The Incarnation of the Word has many aspects and one of them, in which the early Slavic scholars were especially interested, is the interrelation between reason and language, and reason and letters (*gramota*). It was characteristic of Constantine the Philosopher (St. Cyril) that he started his translation of the Gospels with St. John's opening sentence 'In the beginning was the Word, and the Word was with God, and the Word was God.' As we know, the notion of 'Word' (*Logos*, in Slavic *Slovo*) was one of the basic concepts of the old Slavic culture.[1] It now became one of the main themes of Christian thought of the Slavic élite.

An interesting treatment of this theme is found in an old Russian *Colloquy on Teaching Letters* which has been recently translated into English by Justinia Besharov and which Roman Jakobson aptly calls 'A Treatise on the Divine and Human Word'.[2]

The extant manuscript of this Colloquy belongs to the sixteenth or the seventeenth century, but the original was undoubtedly written much earlier. Roman Jakobson links this work with the south Slavic grammarian tradition, and especially with the first Slavic treatise 'On the Letters', compiled in Bulgaria by the monk Khrabr at the beginning of the tenth century. Khrabr's work undoubtedly was known in Russia in the eleventh century —the earliest known manuscript copy of it is that of the former Synodal library at Moscow, dated 1348.[3]

The Colloquy starts with the question: 'What was formed first: reason (*razum*) through letters (*gramota*) or letters through reason?' The answer is: 'Reason was not formed through letters but letters through reason.' The basic idea of the Treatise is the analogy between the Incarnation of the Logos (*Slovo*) and the emergence of 'our word' from its abode in our soul into a spoken word. 'Imitating the twofold birth of the Son of God, our word, too, has its twofold birth. For first, our word is born in

[1] See Chapter 4, section 5, above.

[2] 'An Old Russian Treatise on the Divine and Human Word.' Text translated by Dr. Justinia Besharov. Preface by Dr. Roman Jakobson. Notes by Dr. Harry A. Wolfson, *St. Vladimir's Seminary Quarterly*, Summer, 1956, pp. 45–50.

[3] On the Monk Khrabr's treatise 'The [Slavic] Characters' see S. G. Vilinsky, *Skazanie Chernoriztsa Khrabra* (Odessa, 1901); P. A. Lavrov, 'Materialy po istorii vozniknoveniia drevneishei Slavianskoi pismennosti', *Trudy Slavianskoi Komissii*, i (Leningrad, 1930), 162–4; J. Vašic, *Mnicha Chrabra Obrana Slovanského Pisma* (Brno, 1941).

the soul, through some incomprehensible birth, and abides unknown near the soul, and then, born again through a second,
fleshly birth, it emerges from the lips and reveals itself by the
voice to the hearing.'

The philosophical aspects of Christianity could have been
fully appreciated by the intellectual élite only. Much wider was
the aesthetic appeal of the new faith. As has been mentioned
(see section 4 above), one of the motives of the acceptance of
Christianity from the Greeks was the splendour of the Byzantine
church service. Every effort was taken by Vladimir and his successors to transplant Christian art into the Russian soil. At first,
Byzantine architects and painters were engaged, but before long
many of the Russians mastered the techniques of the Christian
arts. While no instrumental music was allowed in the Byzantine
and Russian Church, singing was an important part of the church
service and one of the aesthetic attractions for the congregations.

With the Christian Church, Christian monasticism appeared
in Russia. There were two currents in Russian monasticism of
the Kievan period: one best represented by St. Antony, the
founder of the Kievan Crypt Monastery, and his disciples; and
the other by St. Theodosius, an abbot of that monastery. The
monks of the former school were inspired by the ideals of severe
asceticism and seclusion. For St. Theodosius the foundations of
monasticism were prayer, humility, work, and charities. Even
as an abbot he wore shabby clothes and did not shun any manual
work. He was not a strong disciplinarian, preferring to lead
by setting an example to the brethren by his own behaviour.[1]

While Christianity made steady progress in Russia in the
Kievan period, we should not forget that it spread mainly in the
cities. Most of the churches and monasteries of this period were
built in or near towns. Rural population was left with little
spiritual guidance from the clergy, almost none in the remote
districts. The people were ordered to have their children
christened, for which they had to bring them to the nearest town,
or to wait until a priest toured their district. Few marriages
among the rural population were sanctioned by a church
wedding.

A paradoxical situation thus arose in Russia after its official

[1] See G. P. Fedotov, *The Russian Religious Mind: Kievan Christianity* (Cambridge,
Mass., 1946).

conversion to Christianity in the late tenth century. Christianity became the official faith of the Russian people; the old Slavic religion was outlawed and its sanctuaries destroyed. And yet the Christian Church of Russia was able actually to offer its services to the upper classes and the urban population only. The rural populations were left practically to themselves. The result was that while the upper stratum of the old Slavic religion was shattered, the ancient clan cult was preserved almost intact in many a rural community. Centuries, not years, had to pass before it could be eradicated.[1]

We have little information on the fate of the spiritual leaders of the old Slavic religion after its official suppression. According to Vladimir's 'Church Statute' all trials of cases involving magic and soothsaying (*ved'stvo*) were subject to the church courts. Scattered evidence on the volkhvy may be found in the chronicles. Under A.D. 1071 the chronicler noted:

At this time a magus (*volkhv*) appeared inspired by the devil. He came to Kiev and informed the inhabitants that after the lapse of five years the Dnieper would flow backwards, and that the various countries would change their locations, so that Greece would be where Russia was, and Russia where Greece was. . . . The ignorant believed him, but the faithful ridiculed him and told him that the devil was only deluding him to his ruin. This was actually the case, for in the course of the night he disappeared altogether. . . . A magus likewise appeared in Novgorod in the principate of Gleb. He harangued the people, and by representing himself as a god he deceived many of them. For he claimed to know all things, and he blasphemed against the Christian faith, announcing that he would walk across the Volkhov River in the presence of the people. There was finally an uprising in the city, and all believed in him so implicitly that they went so far as to desire to murder their bishop.[2]

Prince Gleb then killed the volkhv with an axe which he had hidden under his garment, and the people dispersed.

We may think that a number of volkhvy fled from Russia in the late tenth and eleventh centuries. Some might have found

---

[1] On the remnants of the old Slavic religion in medieval Russia see E. Anichkov, *Iazychestvo i Kievskaia Rus'* (St. Petersburg, 1914); N. Galkovsky, *Borba Khristianstva s ostatkami iazychestva* (Moscow, 1912–16, 2 vols.); G. Florovsky, *Puti Russkogo Bogosloviia* (Paris, 1937), pp. 2–4.

[2] *Povest' Vremennykh Let*, i. 116–17 and 120–1; Cross and Sherbowitz's translation, pp. 150 and 154.

FIG. 1. The Roukhs letters. Words (1) to (13) of the Life of Vladimir.

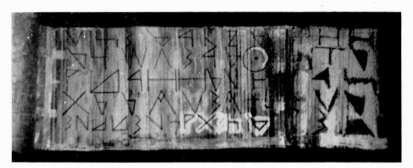

FIG. 2. The Roukhs letters. Words (13) to (27).
[(23) is not a word but the symbol of invocation.]

*Yury Arbatsky's transcription of the initial lines of the 'Life of Vladimir
the Ardent Sun'*

(1) S[e] (2) prst[u]p[i]l: (3) l[e]t (4) dvanad[e]st (5) t[i]s[ja]č (6) i (7) j[e]dn[e]
(8) s (9) p[o]č[e]t, (10) a (11) g[o]da (12) s[e]m[o]g (13) sa (14) z[a]h[o]da
(15) Snca (16) Rhsa, (17) p[o]č[e]š (18) da (19) b[e]l[e]g (20) sl[o]v[e]sa (21) da
(22) j[o]bl[e]k (23) . . . (24) sj[a] (25) u (26) p[i]sja (27) r[u]hsska.

F<small>IG</small>. 3. General view of the initial part of the parchment
containing words (1) to (27).

Translated by George Reavey

H<small>EREBY</small> I enter: In the year twelve thousand, and one
thousand more, after the very beginning, and in the
seventh year after the going down of the Enlightening Sun,
I began to record these words; and let them be garbed in
Rouxsian letters.

refuge among the Baltic Slavs who were still heathen. Others probably went to the Balkans where it would be easier for them to hide from the Christian authorities than in Russia where they were well known. Still others might have remained in Russia, accepting Christianity outwardly but keeping their faith secretly. It should be borne in mind that many of the leaders of Slavic 'heathenism' seem to have been men of high spiritual powers and great intellectual abilities. The description of them given in the Christian sources must have been a distorted one in many cases. Slavic 'heathenism', like that of the Greeks, had its philosophical aspects. It seems that the leaders of the old Slavic religion, who now had to go underground, attempted to meet the challenge of Christianity by formulating anew their own philosophy.

It is, presumably, in these circumstances that the so-called *Books of Deep Wisdom* (literally 'Books of Depth' *Glubinnye Knigi*) were written. Only a distorted fragment of them, adapted to Christian notions, was preserved in Russian oral tradition.[1] There is, however, a definite indication that as late as the thirteenth century, manuscripts of these 'Books' circulated in Russia. From the Life of St. Avraami of Smolensk (thirteenth century) it is known that he was abused by his enemies for reading the 'Books of Depth'.[2] These Books might have been written in the tenth or the eleventh century. The volkhv who appeared in Novgorod in 1071 and 'claimed to know all things' might have drawn his knowledge from them.

The period of the tenth and eleventh centuries was that of intense religious fermentation both in Bulgaria and in Russia. In Bulgaria it was the time of the rapid spread of the so-called Bogomils whose teachings were based on Manichaeism.[3] The philosophy of Manichaeism presents a form of sharp dualism.

From all eternity there exist two opposite and mutually independent principles, God and Matter, represented respectively on the physical plane by two 'natures', Light and Darkness.[4]

The followers of Mani were divided into two main groups: the

---

[1] See Chapter 4, section 1, above.

[2] See S. P. Rozanov, ed., 'Zhitiia prepodobnogo Avraamiia Smolenskogo', *Pamiatniki drevne-russkoi Literatury, I* (St. Petersburg, 1912) pp. 10 and 27.

[3] See D. Obolensky, *The Bogomils* (Cambridge, 1948).

[4] Ibid., p. 5.

elect, or 'Righteous' [also known as 'the Pure', Cathars], bound to
a rigid observance of the ethical principles of Manichaeism, and the
catechumens, or 'hearers', who could make some concessions to the
weakness of the flesh. To the elect, who alone were regarded as true
Manichaens, sexual intercourse, the eating of any animal food, and
the drinking of wine were strictly forbidden; the 'hearers' were
allowed to marry, to eat meat, and to drink wine.[1]

Manichaeism as a philosophical system was strongly influenced
by Gnosticism. In the teaching of different Gnostic sects the idea
that Matter, which is essentially evil, cannot be the creation of
God occupied an important role.

The Bogomil movement threatened the very existence of the
Christian church and state in Bulgaria, and it was but natural
that every effort was made by the Bulgarian Church and state
leaders to refute and suppress it. We know of the Bogomil doc-
trines mostly from the Christian polemic treatises against the
Bogomils. Undoubtedly there were in Bulgaria in that period
other intellectual currents of which no definite evidence has
been preserved, since they did not constitute any mass movement and did not seem dangerous to the authorities. It seems
thus quite possible that the traditions of the old Slavic religion,
perhaps coloured in some cases with Gnosticism, were preserved
from destruction by 'heathen' religious leaders. These latter did
not come out into the open but worked through small groups,
similar to the Rotu 'Concealed Concord' of which we know from
Yury Arbatsky's researches. When discovered by Christian
authorities these groups might have been mistaken for Bogomils
and so called in the official reports.

Among the basic concepts of the philosophy of Rotu, besides that of *ruxs* 'light',[2] are those of the primordial energy,
called *nun* in the esoteric language of Rotu; and of the abyss
of non-being (*nunt*).[3] It should be noted in this connexion that
in Egyptian *Nunu* denotes the Sky-god, and *Nunu-t* the Sky-
goddess.[4]

Among the manuscripts found by Arbatsky in the archives of
the Rotu there is a Life of Vladimir the Ardent Sun (*Slnce*

---

[1] D. Obolensky, *The Bogomils*, p. 6.
[2] See Chapter 4, section 3, above.
[3] See note U, p. 322.
[4] E. A. Budge, *An Egyptian Hieroglyphic Dictionary*, i. 349–50.

Krasno; this corresponds to the Russian *Krasnoe Solntse*).[1] According to the Life, Prince Vladimir became eventually disappointed in Christianity, left Russia, and went to the Balkans where he returned to the 'faith of his fathers' (i.e. the old Slavic religion). He then founded 'the Imperishable Monastery'(*Netleni Monastir*) for the perpetuation of the society of the faithful (of the Old Faith).

According to the Russian chronicles, as we know (see section 4 above), Vladimir died in Berestovo near Kiev in 1015, at the beginning of his campaign against his son, Iaroslav of Novgorod. Owing to the troubled political and dynastic situation, Vladimir's boyars at first tried to conceal his death from the army and the people. When they decided to carry his body to Kiev for the burial, they took it from the house where he had died, at night and in strict secrecy, cutting the flooring between two rooms. While later Vladimir's body was buried publicly in Kiev amid general mourning, the initial delay and secrecy might easily have created rumours that Vladimir did not actually die at that time and that the body buried in Kiev was not his (consider similar rumours which followed the announcement of the death of Emperor Alexander I of Russia in 1825).

In 1051 Metropolitan Hilarion concluded his 'Eulogy' of Vladimir with an appeal to the deceased prince: 'Rise, oh honoured ruler, from thy tomb, shake off thy sleep, since thou art not dead but only sleeping until the general resurrection.' To this Christian concept the Rotu Life of Vladimir opposes a concept of a different nature: Vladimir did not die at the time the Christians announced that he died; and he continued spiritually to live in his 'Imperishable Monastery'. That latter concept also has its counterpart in Hilarion's Eulogy of Vladimir. After mentioning Vladimir's baptism, Hilarion says that through this sacrament Basil (Vladimir's Christian name) 'was inscribed in the Books of Life (*Knigi Zhivotnya*) and [admitted] into the Highest City, the Imperishable Jerusalem' (*Netlennyi Ierusalim*).

Vladimir's 'Imperishable Monastery' is invisible, but there is also a visible monastery bearing Vladimir's name, a Christian monastery, now almost abandoned. It is known as the monastery of St. John (in Albanian *Ion* [*Jon*]) Vladimir and is situated not far from Elbasan, Albania. Prince Ion-Vladimir of Dioclea lived

[1] See note V, p. 322.

at the end of the tenth and in the early eleventh century, being thus a contemporary of Vladimir of Kiev. According to the Life of Ion-Vladimir, he led an ascetic life and did not cohabit with his wife, a sister of the Bulgarian Tsar Samuel. She suspected that her husband neglected her because of his infatuation with another woman and so she complained to her brother. By Samuel's order Ion-Vladimir was murdered. His relic is kept in the monastery dedicated to him.[1] However, there is a popular belief around Elbasan that the relic is actually that of Vladimir the Ardent Sun of Kiev. This belief is not confirmed and not denied by the Rotu.

As regards the name Ion-Vladimir, note that in Rotu *Ion* is an abstract notion corresponding to the Greek *Pneuma* 'Spirit'.[2]

The pre-Christian concept of Vladimir the Ardent Sun (*Krasnoe Solntse*) survived, though in a modified form, in the Russian epic literature. As V. A. Rozov rightly observes,[3] the image of Vladimir as preserved in Russian oral tradition differs considerably from that which we find in written church literature. In the latter, Vladimir's leading role in the Christianization of Russia is emphasized and his Christian virtues after his conversion are praised. In the epos—the *stariny* (byliny)—Vladimir is represented as the benevolent chairman of his druzhina and most of all as the genial host at his lavish banquets. A characteristic story has been recorded by the chronicler under A.D. 996:

On one occasion, after the guests were drunk, they began to grumble against the prince, complaining that they were mistreated because he allowed them to eat with wooden spoons, instead of silver ones. When Vladimir heard of this complaint, he ordered that silver spoons should be moulded for his retinue to eat with, remarking that with silver and gold he could not secure his retinue, but that with a retinue he was in a position to win these treasures.[4]

A characteristic saying ascribed to Vladimir has been recorded by the chronicler: 'Drinking is the joy of the Russes. We cannot exist without that pleasure.'

Vladimir the Ardent Sun of the byliny is not the saintly man of the church literature. But neither is he an active military leader.

---

[1] J. G. von Hahn, *Albanesische Studien* (Jena, 1854), pp. 82–84 (I am indebted to Y. Arbatsky for referring me to this publication). On the Life of St. John-Vladimir see also D. Obolensky, *The Bogomils* (Cambridge, 1948), pp. 93–94 and 149–50 (note).

[2] Y. Arbatsky's communication to me.   [3] *Vladimirskii Sbornik*, pp. 155–63.

[4] *Povest' Vremennykh Let*, i. 86; Cross and Sherbowitz's translation, p. 122.

It is to his valiant knights—the bogatyri— that he appeals for assistance whenever an emergency arises. It is the bogatyri who fight for him and defend the Russian land from the steppe nomads.

While the Church played a role of paramount importance in unifying Russia spiritually and culturally, it is the druzhina which was, in the eleventh and twelfth centuries, the main vehicle for the rising feeling of Russian national unity. At the base of that concept lay the pre-Christian notions of clan cult and Sun-worship. In the *Igor Tale* the Russian people are called sons of Rus (*Rusichi*) and grandsons of Dazhbog (the Sun-god). This means that Rus, the mythical progenitor of the Russes, was considered the son of the Sun-god.

This idea was apparently quite popular in the late twelfth century among the princes of the Chernigovan branch. (The author of the *Igor Tale*, in all probability, belonged to the Chernigovan druzhina.) Under A.D. 1174 and again under A.D. 1195 we find in the Kievan Chronicle an appeal for peace addressed by the princes of the Chernigovan line to the Monomashichi, descendants of Vladimir Monomach of Kiev, which contains a characteristic formula of the basis of Russ unity: 'We are not Hungarians, nor Poles, but are grandsons of the common grandfather.' Now the princes in question had no common physical grandfather.[1] The grandfather they meant was obviously the mythical progenitor of the Russes—Rus, son of Dazhbog, or perhaps Dazhbog himself.

If even among the Russian upper classes pre-Christian notions were strong two centuries after Russia's conversion to Christianity, the lower classes, especially in the rural districts, continued at that period to live spiritually in the pre-Christian traditions, only slightly affected by the outward forms of Christianity. The result was the so-called 'double faith' (*dvoeverie*) about which we find so many complaints in the Russian church literature, especially in the sermons, not only of the Kievan period but of the Mongol and Muscovite periods as well. People were baptized and performed some of the Christian rites, but continued secretly to invoke the old Slavic gods and to sacrifice to Rod and Rozhanitsy. As a matter of fact, in the Kievan period, the people in the rural districts could not even have been

[1] See for details G. Vernadsky, 'The Origin of the Name Rus', *Südost-Forschungen*, xv (1956), 96.

blamed for this since the Church was not able to provide them with enough parish churches and priests. It is only by the sixteenth century that a network of parish churches was established in rural areas, so that the church authorities could at least insist on regular attendance at church services and on a stricter performance of church rites. Church weddings now were considered indispensable.

From a broader point of view it may be said that one of the most important aspects of the Russian cultural history of the Middle Ages and the early modern period was that of the superimposition of a coat of Byzantine civilization over the deeper layer of the old Slavic culture. The result was a certain dualism of medieval Russian culture which was felt not only in religion but in literature, the arts, and music alike. The written literature of medieval Russia was that of the Church, or in any case it was sponsored by the Church. Byzantine patterns of art and music were transplanted into Russia, even though in a modified form. Side by side with the Byzantine sponsored literature, art, and music, the old Slavic forms continued to live among the people, and even the Christianized upper classes continued to enjoy them. While written literature was considered the domain of the Church, the old Slavic concepts were preserved in the oral tradition, extremely rich and varied. 'Oral literature' (folklore) was generated at the bottom in every community, and so were folk-music and folk-arts, such as embroidery and wood carving. Besides, however, works of oral literature, drama, and music were created, recited, and performed by skilful artists—the *skomorokhi* (musicians, actors, singers, and reciters). Their companies were disbanded by the state and church authorities in the course of the sixteenth and seventeenth centuries.

It was but natural that a process of osmosis gradually developed between the Byzantine and the old Slavic cultures in Russia. Christian elements penetrated into the oral tradition and the folk-art, and in their turn old Slavic elements affected the Christian arts and music in many ways. By the sixteenth century a degree of amalgamation between the two cultures in Russia was reached. The cultural equilibrium thus achieved was again upset in the late seventeenth and the eighteenth centuries by the steady and ever increasing impact of Western civilization on Russia and the subsequent Europeanization of Russia.

NOTES

A. Among the numerous works on the early Slavs see P. J. Šafařík, *Slavische Alterthümer* (Leipzig, 1843–4, 2 vols.); Lubor Niederle, *Slovanské Starožitnosti* (Prague, 1906–27, 4 vols.); id., *Život starých Slovanů* (Prague, 1911–34, 3 vols.); id., *Manuel de l'antiquité slave* (Paris, 1923–6, 2 vols.); Russian translation of the Czech edition of the preceding work, *Slavianskie drevnosti*, A. L. Mongait, ed., preface by P. N. Tretiakov (Moscow, 1957); Max Ebert, *Real-lexikon der Vorgeschichte*, xii (1928), 251–92; Iuri V. Gotie, *Zheleznyi Vek v Vostochnoi Evrope* (Moscow, 1930), pp. 5–16, 38–45, 204–47; T. Lehr-Spławiński, *O pochodzeniu i praojczyznie Słowian* (Poznań, 1946); J. Kostrzewski, *Les Origines de la civilization polonaise* (Paris, 1949); Francis Dvornik, *The Making of Central and Eastern Europe* (London, 1949); id., *The Slavs: Their Early History and Civilization* (Boston, 1956); George Vernadsky, 'Das frühe Slawentum. Das Ostslawentum bis zum Mongolensturm', *Historia Mundi*, v (Bern, 1956), 251–300; Witold Hensel, *Słowiańszczyzna wczesnośredniowieczna* (2nd edn., Warsaw, 1956). Sergei Lesnoy has recently published *A Revision of the Bases of the Slavonic History*, i (in Russian, sub-title in English; Melbourne, 1956). His book is an attempt at a new interpretation of the early history of the Slavs. (In my opinion his argument is not convincing.) Of S. Lesnoy's other work, *Istoriia Russov v neizvrashchennom vide* (6 fascicles, Paris, 1953–6), I have seen only fasc. 6 (1956).

B. On the role of the nomads in history see W. Kotwicz, 'O rolę ludow koczowniczych w historii', *Pamietnik IV Zjazdu historyków polskich w Poznaniu* (1925); P. N. Savický (Savitsky), 'O zadachakh kochevnikovedeniia', supplement to N. P. Toll, *Skify i Gunny* (Prague, 1928); R. Grousset, *L'Empire des steppes* (Paris, 1939); A. J. Toynbee, *A Study of History* (2nd edn., Oxford, 1935; 3rd impression, 1945), iii. 393, 395, 399–402, 421, 431; G. Vernadsky, 'The Eurasian Nomads and their Art in the History of Civilization', *Saeculum*, i (1950), 74–85; id., 'Der sarmatische Hintergrund der germanischen Völkerwanderung', ibid. ii (1951), 340–92; M. de Ferdinandy, 'Die nordeurasischen Reitervölker und der Westen', *Historia Mundi*, v (1956), 175–223.

C. Among the works on the Alans (as well as on the Sarmatae) see W. Tomaschek, 'Alani', *PW*, i (1894), cols. 1282–3; Iu. A. Kulakovsky, *Alany po svedeniiam klassicheskikh i vizantiiskikh pisatelei* (Kiev, 1899); K. Kretschmer, 'Sarmatae', *PW*, Part 2 (1920), cols. 2542–2550; id., 'Sarmatia', *PW*, ii (1923), cols. 1–13; M. Rostovtzeff, 'The Sarmatae and the Parthians', *Cambridge Ancient History*, xi (1936), ch. iii; M. A. Miller, *Studii z istorii Prioziv'ia*, viii–ix (mimeographed edn., Geneva, 1947); Dzambulat Dzanty, 'L'Empire des Oss-Alanes', *Oss-Alanes*, 1953, i. 4–20; ii. 13–24; iii–iv. 6–42; 1954, i–ii (Nos. 5–6 of the whole series), 35–47; *Voprosy Skifo-Sarmatskoi arkheologii* (Moscow, 1954); W. Parducz, 'Beiträge zur Geschichte der Sarmaten in Ungarn', *AAAH*, vii (1956), pp. 139–82. On the descendants of the Alans, the Ossetians, see V. F. Miller, 'Osetinskie Etiudy', Part III, *Moscow, Universitet, Uchenve Zapiski, Otdel Istoriko-filologicheskii*, viii

(1887); V. I. Abaev, *Osetinskii iazyk i folklor*, i (Moscow and Leningrad, 1949); H. Field, 'Contributions to the Anthropology of the Caucasus', *Papers of Peabody Museum of American Archaeology and Ethnography*, xlviii, No. 1 (1953).
D. On the art of the Eurasian nomads see E. H. Minns, *Scythians and Greeks* (Cambridge, 1913); M. Rostovtzeff, *Iranians and Greeks in South Russia* (Oxford, 1922); id., *The Animal Style in South Russia and China* (Princeton, 1924); G. Borovka, *Scythian Art* (London, 1926); M. Rostovtzeff, *Le Centre de l'Asie, la Russie, la Chine et le style animal* (Prague, 1929); E. H. Minns, *The Art of the Northern Nomads* (London, 1942); S. I. Rudenko, *Kultura naseleniia Gornogo Altaia v Skifskoe vremia* (Moscow, 1953); T. T. Rice, *The Scythians* (New York, 1957); D. Carter, *The Symbol of the Beast: The Animal-Style Art of Eurasia* (New York, 1957).

E. See S. Feist, *Etymologisches Wörterbuch des gotischen Sprache* (Halle, 1923); S. Feist, *Vergleichendes Wörterbuch der gotischen Sprache* (Leiden, 1936–7); G. Vernadsky, 'Goten and Anten in Südrußland', *Südostdeutsche Forschungen*, iii (1938), 14; Roman Smal-Stocki, *Slavs and Teutons* (Milwaukee, Wisconsin, 1950), pp. 49–70. On the Andian origin of the Gothic and Slavic words for 'sword' see V. Kiparski, *Die gemeinslawischen Lehnwörter aus dem Germanischen* (Helsinki, 1934), p. 134; K. Bouda, 'Ein slawisches Lehnwort aus dem Kaukasischen', *Zeitschrift für Slawische Philologie*, xviii (1942), 36; V. Polak, 'K probleme lexikalnich shod mezi jazyky kavkazskymi a jazyky slovanskymi', *Listy Filologické*, lxx (1946), 23–31. In my opinion the word for 'sword' in Slavic (*meč*) may be originally Slavic.

F. On the Huns and Attila's empire see E. A. Thompson, *History of Attila and the Huns* (Oxford, 1948); Franz Altheim, *Attila und die Hunnen* (Baden-Baden, 1951); G. Vernadsky, 'Der sarmatische Hintergrund der germanischen Völkerwanderung', *Saeculum*, ii (1951), 375–9; M. de Ferdinandy, 'Clariores Genere', i, *Anales de Historia Antigua y Medieval* (1953), pp. 14–30; id., 'Die nordeurasischen Reitervölker und der Westen', *Historia Mundi*, v (1956), 186–98; H. W. Haussig, 'Indogermanische und Altaische Nomadenvölker im Grenzgebiete Irans', ibid., pp. 233–48.

G. On the Khazars see Gyula Moravcsik, *Byzantinoturcica*, i (Budapest, 1942), 44–46; W. Barthold, 'Khazar', *EI*, ii. 935–7; Iu. V. Gotie, *Zheleznyi Vek v Vostochnoi Evrope* (Moscow, 1930), pp. 70–90; J. Marquart (Markwart), *Osteuropäische und ostasiatische Streifzüge* (Leipzig, 1903), pp. 1–27, 270–305, 474–7; M. I. Artamonov, *Ocherki drevneishei istorii Khazar* (Leningrad, 1936); P. K. Kokovtsov, *Evreisko-Khazarskaiia Perepiska v X Veke* (Leningrad, 1932); A. Zajączkowski, *Ze studiów nad zagadnieniem Chazarskim* (Krakow, 1947); S. P. Tolstov, *Po sledam drevnekhorezmiiskoi tsivilizatsii* (Moscow, 1948), pp. 226–31; D. M. Dunlop, *The History of the Jewish Khazars* (Princeton, 1954); T. Lewicki, 'Źrodła Hebrajskie do dziejów środkowiej i wschodniej Europy w okresie wczesnego średniowiecza', *Przegląd Orientalistyczny*, iii (15) (1955), 283–91; id., 'Ze studiów nad trw. Korespondencyą Chazarską', reprint from *Żydowski Institut Historiczny, Bulletin*, 11–12 (n.d.); H. W. Haussig, 'Indogermanische und altaische Nomadenvölker im Grenzgebiete Irans', *Historia Mundi*, v (1956), 245, and map on p. 237; S. Szyszman, 'Le Roi Bulan et le

Notes   319

problème de la conversion des Khazars', *Ephemeridae Theologicae Lovanienses*, xxxiii (1957), 68–76.

H. Tadeusz Lewicki, *Źródła arabskie do dziejów Słowiańszczyzny*, i (Wrocław and Kraków, 1956), 224 (al-Baladhuri, Arabic text), 225 (Polish translation), 239 (commentary); T. Lewicki, 'Osadnictwo słowiańskie i niewolnici słowiańscy w krajach muzułmańskich według średniowiecznych pisarzy arabskich', *Przegląd Historyczny*, xliii, No. 3–4 (1952), 7–9. Lewicki identifies the 'Slavonic River' as the Volga, not as the Don, but according to all archaeological and historical evidence available to us, there were numerous Slavic settlements in the Don area. There is no evidence of Slavic settlements in the lower Volga region at that time. In my opinion the name 'Slavic River' can refer only to the Don. On the 'Slavic River' see also V. F. Minorsky, *Hudud al-'Alam*, pp. 216–17.

I. On the Magyars prior to their migration to present-day Hungary see C. A. Macartney, *The Magyars in the Ninth Century* (Cambridge, 1930); H. Grégoire, 'L'Habitat primitif des Magyars', *Byzantion*, xiii (1938), 267–78; G. Vernadsky, 'Lebedia: Studies on the Magyar Background of Kievan Russia', ibid. xiv (1939), 179–203; Gy. Moravcsik, *Byzantinoturcica*, i (Budapest, 1942), 58–64; L. Ligeti, ed., *A Magyarság Östörténete* (Budapest, 1943); Gy. László, *A honfoglalo Magyar nép élete* (Budapest, 1944); Géza Róheim, *Hungarian and Vogul Mythology* (New York, 1954); M. de Ferdinandy, 'Studie zu den Quellen der ugrischen Mythologie', *Ural-Altaische Jahrbücher*, xxviii (1956), 18–34; M. de Ferdinandy, 'Clariores Genere', ii, *Anales de Historia Antigua y Medieval*, 1954, pp. 5–54; M. de Ferdinandy, 'Die nordeurasischen Reitervölker und der Westen', *Historia Mundi*, v (1956), 204–9; 'Studien zur Ungarischen Frühgeschichte: G. Vernadsky, Lebedia; M. de Ferdinandy, Almos', *Südosteuropäische Arbeiten*, No. 47 (München, 1957).

J. On the early Slavic society and civilization see Lubor Niederle, *Manuel de l'antiquité slave* (2 vols., Paris, 1923–6); Iu. V. Gotie, *Zheleznyi Vek v Vostochnoi Evrope* (Moscow and Leningrad, 1930), pp. 204–47; A. Brückner, *Dzieje kultury Polskej*, i (Krakow, 1930); D. Odinets, *Vozniknovenie gosudarstvennogo stroia u Slavian* (Paris, 1935); Zygmunt Wojciechowski, *L'État Polonais au Moyen Age* (Paris, 1949), pp. 7–27; G. Vernadsky, 'Das frühe Slawentum. Das Ostslawentum bis zum Mongolensturm', *Historia Mundi*, v (1956), 269–74; F. Dvornik, *The Slavs: Their Early History and Civilization* (Boston, 1956), chapter ii; Witold Hensel, *Słowiańszczyzna wczesnośredniowieczna* (2nd edn., Warszawa, 1956).

K. M. Vasmer, *Russisches etymologisches Wörterbuch*, i. p. 209, likens the first part of Vladimir's name (Vlad-) to the Church Slavonic *Vlad* 'Macht' ('power'), and the second part (-mir) to the Gotic *mers* 'gross' ('great'), and the old Germanic *mari* 'berühmt' ('renown'). The connexion of the first part of the name 'Vladimir' with the notion of ruling power (*vlad, vladeti*) is obvious. On the other hand, Vasmer's derivation of the second part of the name from *mers* or *mari* does not seem convincing to me. In view of the existence of the Old Slavic word *mir*, it seems much more natural to base on it the ending -mir of the Slavic princely names.

L. On the Viking expansion and Varangians in Russia see T. D. Kendrick, *A History of the Vikings* (London, 1931); T. J. Arne, *La Suède et l'Orient* (Uppsala, 1914); B. Nerman, 'Die Verbindungen zwischen Skandinavien und dem Ostbaltikum in der jüngeren Eisenzeit', *Vitterhets Historie och Antikvitets Akademiens Handlingar*, *40* (1929); Iu. V. Gotie, *Zheleznyi Vek v Vostochnoi Evrope* (Moscow and Leningrad, 1930), pp. 248–62; M. Vasmer, 'Wikingerspuren in Russland', *Sitzungsberichte der Preußischen Akademie der Wissenschaften*, *Phil.-Hist. Klasse*, 1931, xxiv: Birger Nerman, *Sveriges första storhetstid* (Stockholm, 1942); id., 'Scandinavischer Ausklang des germanischen Heidentums', *Historia Mundi*, v (1956), 25–44.

M. N. A. Aristov, 'Zametki ob etnicheskom sostave tiurkskikh plemen i narodnostei', *Zhivaia Starina*, vi. 3/4 (1896), 414; J. Benzing, *Einführung in das Studium der altaischen Philologie* (Wiesbaden, 1953), p. 94 ('Jomud', which is the plural form). The name 'Yom' may be compared to that of a 'Scythian' tribe Iamae, or Iamoi, on which see M. Vasmer, *Die Iranier in Südrußland*, p. 12. Johannes Rahder kindly let me know, in his letter to me of 16 April 1957, that *yam* in Hebrew and Arabic, *yam*, *yom*, *eiom* in Coptic, and *umi* in Japanese, means 'sea'. In Kuril Ainu *yam* denotes 'lake'. Professor Rahder thinks that all these names derive from the same stem. On that basis it may be supposed that the name 'Yom' denoted 'The Sea People' (cf. the Slavic Pomorane) or 'the Lake People' (cf. the Slavic 'Ezeritae', i.e. Ezeriane).

N. The old Russian text of the Life of St. Stephen of Surozh was published by V. G. Vasilievsky, together with the latter's studies of the Life of St. Stephen, as well as with the Life of St. George of Amastris, in 'Russko-Vizantiiskie issledovaniia', *Letopis zaniatii Arkheograficheskoi Kommissii*, ix (1893); reprinted in V. G. Vasilievsky, *Trudy*, iii (Petrograd, 1915), 77–98. The appendix on the miracle during the attack of the Russes is on pp. 95–96. A. A. Vasiliev used the document in his study *The Goths in the Crimea* (Cambridge, Mass., 1936), pp. 111–12. Mme Germaine da Costa-Louillet denied the authenticity of the Life of St. Stephen (as well as that of the Life of St. George of Amastris) in her article 'Y eut-il des invasions russes dans l'Empire Byzantin avant 860?', *Byzantion*, xv (1940–1), 231–48. A. A. Vasiliev accepted her point of view in his book *The Russian Attack on Constantinople in 860* (Cambridge, Mass., 1946), pp. 78–81. To me her argument does not seem convincing, see G. Vernadsky, 'The Problem of the Early Russian Campaigns in the Black Sea Area', *ASEER*, viii (1949), 1–9.

O. T. Lewicki, *Źródła arabskie do dziejów Słowiańszczyzny*, i. 76 (Ibn-Khurdadhbih's Arabic text) and 77 (Polish translation). It should be noted that it is hard to establish the correct reading of some proper names in old Arabic manuscripts since the latter have no diacritical signs. In this case, the validity of De Goeje's reading of the name of 'the Slavic River', *Tanais* (Don), was questioned by Josef Marquart and, more recently, by A. Z. V. Togan (see Lewicki, *Źródła*, pp. 133–7). Marquart read *Tin*; Togan offered the reading 'Etil'; this name (Itil, Atil) is usually applied to the Volga River. However, *til* means just 'river' in Turkic, see O. Pritsak, 'Der Titel Attila', *Festschrift für Max Vasmer* (Wiesbaden, 1956), pp. 410–15. Consequently *til* (or *etil*) may refer to the Don as well.

P. See S. P. Tolstov, *Drevnii Khorezm* (Moscow, 1948), pp. 184–5; P. N. Tretiakov, 'Anty i Rus', *Sovetskaia Etnografiia*, 1947, No. 4, pp. 71–83; B. A. Rybakov, 'Znaki sobstvennosti v kniazheskom khoziaistve Kievskoi Rusi', *Sovetskaia Arkheologia*, vi (1940); B. A. Rybakov,' Drevnie Rusy', *Sovetskaia Arkheologiia*, xvii (1953), 96; G. Vernadsky, 'The Origin of the Name Rus', *Südost-Forschungen*, xv (1956), 174. On the emblem of the Russian princes of the Kievan period (the Rurikids) see Baron M. de Taube, 'Zagadochnyi rodovoi znak sem'i Vladimira Sviatogo', *Sbornik statei posviashchennykh P. N. Miliukovu* (Prague, 1929), pp. 117–32; id., 'Rodovoi znak sem'i Vladimira Sviatogo', *Vladimirskii Sbornik* (Belgrade, 1938), pp. 89–172.

Q. The literature on S.S. Cyril and Methodius and their work is quite extensive. For good bibliographies of it see G. A. Ilinsky, *Opyt sistematicheskoi Kirillo-Mefodievskoi bibliografii* [down to 1933] (Sophia, 1934) and M. G. Popruzhenko and S. Romanski, *Kirilo-metodievska bibliografiia, 1934–1940* (Sofia, 1942). Among the works bearing on S.S. Cyril and Methodius see F. Dvornik, *The Slavs: Their Early History and Civilization* (Boston, 1956), pp. 82–100; André Vaillant, 'L'Alphabet Vieux-Slave', *RES*, xxxii (1955), 7–31; L. V. Cherepnin, *Russkaia paleografiia* (Moscow, 1956), pp. 83–111.

R. Baron Michael de Taube, although handicapped by blindness, is preparing for publication in the French review *Istina* a study on Oleg and the chronology of his reign, basing it chiefly on Swedish sources. Baron de Taube kindly let me know (through our mutual friend Basile Nikitine) that, as he believes, Oleg set forth to Russia from the Danish islands after the battle of Louvain of 891, in which the armies of the Frankish-German coalition defeated the Vikings based on the Danish islands. Oleg went first to the gulf of Riga and up the western Dvina River to Smolensk (thus by-passing Novgorod), and then to Kiev. I am not in a position to discuss here Baron de Taube's new dating of Oleg's seizure of Kiev without knowing his sources and argument in detail.

S. Ibn-Miskawaih, *The Eclipse of the Abbasid Califate*, ed. and translated by H. F. Amedroz and D. S. Margoliouth (Oxford, 1920–1, 7 vols.), v. 67–74. The excerpt on the Russ invasion of Berdaa, in D. S. Margoliouth's translation, is published by N. K. Chadwick, *The Beginnings of Russian History* (Cambridge, 1948), pp. 138–44. There are two Russian translations of Ibn-Miskawaih's narrative: A. I. Iakubovsky, 'Ibn-Miskaveikh o pokhode russkikh v Berdaa', *Vizantiizkii Vremennik*, xxiv (1926), 63–92; and A. V. Florovsky, 'Izvestiia o drevnei Rusi arabskogo pisatelia Miskaveikhi', *Seminarium Kondakovianum*, i (1927), 175–86.

T. See A. Markov, *Topografiia Kladov vostochnych monet* (St. Petersburg, 1910); P. G. Liubomirov, 'Torgovye sviazi Rusi s Vostokom v viii–ix vekakh', *Uchenye Zapiski Saratovskogo Universiteta*, i (3) (1923), 5–38; B. A. Romanov, 'Dengi i denezhnoe obrashchenie', *Istoriia Kultury Drevnei Rusi*, ii. 381–90; T. Lewicki, 'Z dziejów pieniądza arabskiego w Europie Wschodniej', *Archeologia*, iii (1949), 224–9 (French and Russian resumés, 436–8); V. L. Ianin, *Denezhno-vesovye sistemy Russkogo Srednevekovia* (Moscow, 1956). On the trade and trade routes see B. A. Rybakov, 'Torgovlia i torgovye puti', *Istoriia Kultury Drevnei Rusi*, i. 315–69.

U. The 'Concealed Concord' is briefly mentioned, by Jaap Kunst, 'Cultural Relations between the Balkans and Indonesia', *Koninklijk Instituut voor de Tropen, Mededeling CVII, Afdeling Culturele en Physische Anthropologie*, No. 47 (Amsterdam, 1954), p. 11 and note 42. See also Alexander Myrsky, 'Radiation of Ancient Cultures', *SOF*, xv (1956), 553–8. On the basis of the materials collected by him in the Balkans in the 1930's Yury Arbatsky delineated the basic precepts of the Rotu in his book *The Byzantine Folk Music* (not yet published). Dr. Arbatsky was kind enough to let me read part of the manuscript of this book.

V. The *Life of Vladimir the Ardent Sun* is not yet published. According to Y. Arbatsky's communication to me, the text is written on a parchment in Old Slavic in Ancient Albanian characters. A chemical (and general) analysis of a piece torn off it was made in Prague in the 1940's for the Prague Musicological Institute. According to it, the parchment (and the writing on it) must be referred, approximately, to the seventh century A.D., in any case not later than the ninth century ('Das Waldemarpergament [the Vladimir Parchment] im ca 7.Jh., jedoch nicht später als im 9.Jh., geschrieben wurde'). However, on the basis of the contents of the Life, the manuscript may be referred to the eleventh century. Arbatsky has a copy of the manuscript (which he had made personally) and also has photographs of a part of the manuscript.

BIBLIOGRAPHY

I. SOURCES

AMMIANUS MARCELLINUS, *Res Gestae*, J. C. Rolfe, ed. and transl., 3 vols. (Loeb Classical Library; Harvard University Press).

Antiquités russes d'après les monuments historiques des Islandais, ed. C. C. Rafn, vols. i–ii (Copenhague, 1950).

BAKRI, AL-, *Kitab al-Masalik wa'l Mamalik*. Excerpts in English transl., Macartney, pp. 189–90, 192–208.

BALADHURI, AL-, English transl. by K. Hitti and F. C. Murgotten, *The Origins of the Islamic State* (2 vols., New York, 1916–24). Excerpts in Polish transl., Lewicki, i. 217–27; in Latin transl., Lewicki, i. 370–3.

BARSOV, E. V., *Prichitaniia Severnogo Kraia*, i (Moscow, 1862).

Bertinian Annals. See Prudentius.

BEŠEVLIEV, B., '*Prvobŭlgarski Nadpisi* [Proto-Bulgar Inscriptions]', *GSU*, xx (1935), 1–162.

CHARMOY, F. B., 'Relation de Maçoudy et d'autres auteurs musulmans sur les Anciens Slaves', *MAS*, 6ᵐᵉ série, ii (1834), 297–408.

'Chronography.' See *Povest' Vremennykh Let*.

'Church Statute' of Vladimir the Saint, V. N. Beneshevich, ed., *Pamiatniki drevne-russkogo kanonicheskogo prava*, *RIB*, xxxvi (Petrograd, 1920).

CONSTANTINE PORPHYROGENITUS, *De Administrando Imperio*. Greek text edited by Gy. Moravcsik. English transl. by R. J. H. Jenkins (Budapest, 1949).

—— *De Ceremoniis Aulae Byzantinae*, J. Reiske, ed., reprinted in the Bonn Series (Bonn, 1829–30) and in *PG*, 112. New edition (incomplete): *Le Livre des Cérémonies*. Texte établi et traduit par A. Vogt. (4 vols., Paris, 1935–40).

Fontes Historiae Religionis Slavicae. Collegit C. H. Meyer (Berlin, 1931).

GARDIZI, *Zayn al-Akhbar*. Excerpts in English transl., Macartney, pp. 189–200, 203–215.

GROOT, J. J. M. DE, *Chinesische Urkunden zur Geschichte Asiens* (Berlin and Leipzig, 1921–6).

HARKAVY, A., *Skazaniia musulmanskikh pisatelei o Rossii* (St. Petersburg, 1870).

HERODOTUS, *Historiae*, ed. H. Stein (Berlin, 1884). George Rawlinson's translation, *The History of Herodotus*, 2 vols. (Everyman's Library).

HILARION, METROPOLITAN, 'Discourse on Law and Grace' and 'Eulogy of Kagan Vladimir' (Old Russian text), A. I. Ponomarev, ed., *Pamiatniki drevnerusskoi tserkovnouchitelnoi literatury*, i (St. Petersburg, 1894), 58–76.

Hudud-al-'Alam, transl. and explained by V. Minorsky (London, 1937).

IAKINF (BICHURIN), *Sobranie Svedenii o narodakh obitavshikh v Srednei Azii*, 3 vols. (2nd edn., Moscow, 1950–3).

IAKOV, MONK. See Jakob.

IBN-FADHLAN, *Risala*, ed. and transl. into Russian by I. Krachkovsky (Moscow and Leningrad, 1939); ed. and transl. into German by A. Z. V. Togan, *AKM*, xxiv. 3 (1939).

IBN-HAUQAL, 'Viae et Regna', *BGA*, ii (1873). Excerpts in Russian transl., Harkavy, pp. 218–32.

IBN-KHURDADHBIH, 'Kitab al Masalik wa'l Mamalik', *BGA*, vi, with French transl. Excerpts in Russian transl., Harkavy, pp. 48–49; in Polish transl., Lewicki, i. 67–81; in Latin transl., Lewicki, i. 361–6.

IBN-MISKAWAIH, *The Eclipse of the Abbasid Caliphate*, ed., transl., and elucidated by H. F. Amedroz and D. S. Margoliouth. 7 vols. (Oxford, 1920–1). Excerpt in Chadwick, pp. 138–44.

IBN-RUSTA, 'Kitab-al-Alak an-Nafisa', *BGA*, vii. Excerpts in English transl., Macartney, pp. 191–215.

Igor Tale (Slovo o polku Igoreve). H. GRÉGOIRE, R. JAKOBSON, *et al.*, 'La Geste du prince Igor', *Annuaire*, viii (1948). Old Russian text; French and English transl.

Iry Dada. G. VERNADSKY and D. DZANTY, 'The Ossetian Tale of Iry Dada and Mstislav', *Journal of American Folklore*, lxix (1956), 216–35.

IUSTINUS, M. IUNIANUS. *See* Trogus, Pompeius.

JAKOB, MONK (ascribed to), 'Pamiat' i pokhvala kniaziu Vladimiru', Makarius, Metropolitan, *Istoriia Russkoi tserkvi*, i (1888), 249–57.

—— (ascribed to), Life of St. Vladimir, in Makarius, Metropolitan, *Istoriia russkoi tserkvi*, i (1888), 257–61.

JORDANES, 'Gethica', ed. Mommsen, *MGH, Auctores Antiquissimi*, v (Berlin, 1882).

'Kievan Chronicle.' In the Hypatian Codex, *PSRL*, ii (St. Petersburg, 1843).

KOKOVTSOV, P. K., ed., *Evreisko-Khazarskaia perepiska v X veke* (Leningrad, 1932).

'Königsberg Chronicle.' *See* 'Radziwill Chronicle'.

KUPFER, FRANCISZEK, and TADEUSZ LEWICKI, *Źródła Hebrajskie do dziejów Słowian i niektórych innych ludów środkowej i wschodniej Europy* (Wrocław and Warszawa, 1956).

LATYSHEV, V. V., *Scythica et Caucasica*, 2 vols. (St. Petersburg, 1890–1904).

LEWICKI, T., *Źródła arabskie do dziejów Słowiańszczyzny*, i (Wrocław and Kraków, 1956).

LUCIAN, 'Toxaris, or Friendship', *Lucian*, English transl. by A. M. Harmon (Loeb Classical Library; Harvard University Press), v. 101–207.

MAHLER, E., *Altrussische Volkslieder aus dem Pečoryland* (Basel, 1951).

MANSIKKA, V. J., *Die Religion der Ostslaven*, i, Quellen (Helsinki, 1922).

MARKOV, A., *Topografiia kladov vostochnykh monet* (St. Petersburg, 1910).

MASUDI (MAÇOUDI), *Les Prairies d'or*, texte et traduction par C. Barbier de Meynard et Pavet de Courteille (Paris, 1861–70, 9 vols.), ch. xxxiv, 'Les Slaves' (ii. 61–65); ch. lxvi, 'Des Édifices religieux des Slaves' (iv. 57–58). *See also* Charmoy.

MAURICIUS, 'Strategicon', ed. J. Scheffer, *Arriani Tactica et Mauricii Ars Militaris* (Uppsala, 1664).

MELA, POMPONIUS, *Chronographia*, ed. Frick (Berlin, 1880).

MENANDER PROTECTOR, 'Fragmenta', ed. Dindorf, *Historici Graeci Minores* (Leipzig, 1870–1).

MINORSKY, V., *Marvazi on China, the Turks, and India* (London, 1942).

MORAVSCIK, GY., *Byzantinoturcica*, 2 vols. (Budapest, 1942–3).

MUQADDASI, 'Descriptio Imperii Moslemici', *BGA*, iii. Excerpts in Russian transl., Harkavy, pp. 281–3.

'Nestor's Chronicle.' See *Povest' Vremennykh Let.*

'Nikon Chronicle', *PSRL*, ix (1862).

Novgorodian Chronicle, First, *Novgorodskaia pervaia letopis*, A. N. Nasonov, ed. (Moscow and Leningrad, 1950).

ORLOV, A. S., *Bibliografiia russkikh nadpisei XI–XV vekov* (Moscow and Leningrad, 1936).

PHOTIUS, PATRIARCH, 'Epistolae', *PG*, 102; 'In Rossorum incursionem Homiliae I–II', ed. A. Nauck, *Lexicon Vindobonense* (St. Petersburg, 1867), pp. 201–32.

PLINY, *Naturalis Historia*, ed. Jahn (Leipzig, 1870).

Povest' Vremennykh Let ('Chronography'). Ed. by V. P. Adrianova-Peretts. Text prepared for publication by D. S. Likhachev. 2 vols. (Moscow and Leningrad, 1950). English transl. S. H. Cross and O. P. Sherbowizt-Wetzor, *The Russian Primary Chronicle* (Cambridge, Mass., 1953).

Pravda Russkaia. See *Russkaia Pravda*.

PROCOPIUS OF CAESAREA, *Anecdota*; *Buildings*; *History of the Wars*, H. B. Dewing, ed. and transl. (Loeb Classical Library; Harvard University Press).

PRUDENTIUS, *Annales*, ed. G. Pertz, *MGH, Scriptores*, i. 429–54.

PTOLEMY, *Geographia*, ed. Noble (Leipzig, 1843).

'Radziwill Chronicle', Illustrated. Photomechanical reproduction, *OLDP*. cxviii (1902).

RAVENNAS ANONYMOUS, 'Cosmographia', ed. J. Schnetz, *Itineraria Romana*, ii (Leipzig, 1940).

'Rotu' ('Concealed Concord'). Materials collected by Yury Arbatsky (not yet published).

Russkaia Pravda, ed. by B. D. Grekov, i (Moscow and Leningrad, 1940). German transl., L. K. Goetz, *Das russische Recht*, 4 vols. (Stuttgart, 1910–13). English transl., G. Vernadsky, *Medieval Russian Laws* (New York, 1947).

ST. CYRIL (CONSTANTINE), 'Vita'. Ed. by P. A. Lavrov, *Trudy Slavianskoi Komissii*, *Academy of Sciences*, i (Leningrad, 1930). French transl., Dvornik, *Légendes*, pp. 349–80.

ST. GEORGE OF AMASTRIS, 'Vita'. Greek text and Russian transl., Vasilievsky, *Trudy*, iii. 1–71.

ST. METHODIUS, 'Vita'. Lavrov, pp. 67–68. French transl., Dvornik, pp. 381–93.

ST. STEPHAN OF SUROZH, 'Vita'. Slavic text, Vasilievsky, *Trudy*, iii. 77–98.

SHEIN, P. V., *Velikoruss v svoikh pesniakh, obriadakh, obychaiakh* (St. Petersburg, 1900).
SMIRNOV, IA. I., *Vostochnoe Serebro* (St. Petersburg, 1905) (Album of Plates).
SNORRI STURLUSON, *Heimskringla*, ed. by E. Monsen, transl. with the assistance of A. H. Smith (New York, 1932).
STRABO, *Geographica*, ed. H. L. Jones (Loeb Classical Library).

TACITUS, CORNELIUS, *Germania*, ed. M. Hutton (Loeb Classical Library).
—— *Historiae*, ed. C. Moore (Loeb Classical Library).
TROGUS, POMPEIUS, *M. Iuniani Iustini Epitoma Historiarum P. Trogi*, ed. O. Seel (Leipzig, 1935).

VARENTSOV, V., ed., *Sbornik russkikh dukhovnykh stikhov* (St. Petersburg, 1860).

Zacharias Rhetor. German transl. by K. Ahrens and G. Krüger, *Die sogenannte Kirchengeschichte des Zacharias Rhetor* (Leipzig, 1899).

II. DICTIONARIES

1. Slavic

BERNEKER, E., *Slavisches etymologisches Wörterbuch* (Heidelberg, 1908–13).
MIKLOSICH, F. *Die Fremdwörter in den slavischen Sprachen* (Wien, 1867).
PREOBRAZHENSKY, A. G., *Etymological Dictionary of the Russian Language* (phototypic reproduction of the Russian edition) (New York, 1951).
SREZNEVSKY, I., *Materialy dlia slovaria drevnerusskogo iazyka.* 3 vols. (St. Petersburg, 1893–1912).
VASMER, M. *Russisches etymologisches Wörterbuch*, 2 vols. (Heidelberg, 1950–8).
WANSTRAT, L., *Beiträge zur Charakteristik des Russischen Wortschatzes* (Berlin, 1933).

2. Ossetic, Persian, Sanskrit, and Tokharian

BARTHOLOMÄ, C., *Altiranische Wörterbuch* (Strasburg, 1904).
KASAEV, A. M., *Osetinsko-russkii Slovar'* (Moscow, 1952).
KENT, R. G., *Old Persian* (New Haven, 1950).
MAYRHOFER, M., *Kurzgefaßtes etymologisches Wörterbuch des Altindischen* (Heidelberg, 1953–) (not yet completed).
MILLER, B. V., *Persidsko-russkii Slovar'* (Moscow, 1953).
MILLER, V. F., *Osetinsko-russko-nemetskii Slovar'* 3 vols. (Leningrad, 1927–34).
SIEG, E., W. SIEGLING, and W. SCHULTZE, *Tocharische Grammatik* (Göttingen, 1931).
STEINGASS, F., *A Comprehensive Persian–English Dictionary* (London, 1892; 2nd impression, 1930).
UHLENBECK, C. C., *Kurzgefaßtes etymologisches Wörterbuch der Altindischen Sprache* (Amsterdam, 1898–9).
VAN WINDEKENS, A. J., *Lexique étymologique des dialectes tokhariens* (Louvain, 1941).

3. Magyar and Turkic

Byzonfy's *English-Hungarian and Hungarian-English Dictionary* (Cleveland, Ohio, n.d.).

GABAIN, A., VON, *Alttürkische Grammatik* (2nd edn., Leipzig, 1950).

KAKHANA, M. G., *Vengersko-russkii slovar'* (Moscow, 1946).

KNIEZSA, I., *A Magyar Nyelv Szlav jövevényszavai*, i. 1–2 (Budapest, 1955).

MALOV, S. E., *Pamiatniki drevnetiurkskoi pismennosti* (Moscow and Leningrad, 1951).

RADLOFF, W., *Versuch eines Wörterbuchs der Türkdialekte*, 4 vols. (St. Petersburg, 1893–1911).

REDHOUSE, J. W., *Turkish and English Lexicon* (Constantinople, 1921).

III. GENERAL LITERATURE AND SPECIAL STUDIES

ABAEV, V. I., *Osetinskii iazyk i folklor*, i (Moscow and Leningrad, 1949).

AFANASIEV, A. N., *Poeticheskie Vozzreniia Slavian na prirodu*, 3 vols. (Moscow, 1866–9).

ALFÖLDI, A., 'Theriomorphe Weltbetrachtung in den hoch-asiatischen Kulturen', *Jahrbuch d. Deutschen Archäologischen Instituts*, xlvi (1931), cols. 393–418.

ALLEN, W. E. D., *David Allens: the History of a Family Firm, 1857–1957* (London, 1957), pp. 7–8 and 23–26.

—— 'Ethiopian Highlands', *The Geographical Journal*, ci (1943), 12–13.

—— *A History of the Georgian People* (London, 1932).

—— 'Two Georgian Maps of the First Half of the 18th Century', *Imago Mundi*, x (1953), 104.

ALPATOV, N., and BRUNOV, N., *Geschichte der altrussischen Kunst* (Augsburg, 1932).

ALTHEIM, F., *Attila und die Hunnen* (Baden-Baden, 1951).

—— *Goten und Finnen* (Berlin, 1944).

—— *Niedergang der Alten Welt*, i (Frankfurt-am-Main, 1952).

ANDA, T., 'Recherches archéologiques sur la pratique médicale des Hongrois à l'époque de la conquête du pays', *AAAH*, i (1951).

ARBATSKY, YURY, *Beating the Tupan in the Central Balkans* (Chicago, 1953).

—— *The Byzantine Folk Music* (not yet published).

—— *Etiudy po istorii russkoi muzyki* (New York, 1956).

—— *The Roga, a Balkan Bagpipe, and its Medico-Magical Conjurations* (read at the Annual Meeting of the American Musicological Society) (1953) (mimeographed).

——'Sex and Musical Fornication', *Antiquity and Survival*, iii, No. 1 (forthcoming).

ARISTOV, N. A., 'Zametki ob etnicheskom sostave tiurkskich plemen i narodnostei', *Zhivaia Starina*, vi, 3/4 (1896), 227–456.

ARNE, T. J., *La Suède et l'Orient* (Uppsala, 1914).

ARTAMONOV, M. T., ed., 'Etnogenez Vostochnykh Slavian', *MIAS*, vi (1941).

ARTSIKHOVSKY, A. V., 'Nouvelles découvertes à Novgorod', *Rapports de la délégation Sovietique au Xe Congrès Intern. des Sciences Historiques à Rome* (Moscow, 1955).

BAILEY, H. W., 'Analecta Indoscythica', i, *Journal of the Royal Asiatic Society*, Oct. 1953, pp. 95–116.
—— 'Ariaca', *BSOAS*, xv (1953), 530–40.
—— 'Asica', *TPhS*, 1945, pp. 1–38.
—— 'Recent work in Tokharian', *TPhS*, 1947, pp. 126–55.
—— *Zoroastrian Problems in the Ninth-Century Books* (Oxford, 1943).
BASCHMAKOFF, A., *Cinquante siècles d'évolution ethnique autour de la Mer Noire* (Paris, 1937).
BAUMGARTEN, N., DE, 'Généalogies et mariages occidentaux des Rurikides russes du Xᵉ au XIIIᵉ siècle', *Orientalia Christiana*, xxxv (1937).
BELAIEW, N. T., 'Rorik of Jutland and Rurik of the Russian Chronicles', *Saga-Book*, x (1929); in Russian, 'Rorik Iutlandskii i Riurik Nachalnoi Letopisi', *Seminarium Kondakovianum*, iii (1929), 215–70.
BONFANTE, G., 'Sabadios-Svoboda le libérateur', *Annuaire*, vii. 41–46.
CARTER, D., *The Symbol of the Beast: the Animal Style Art of Eurasia* (New York, 1957).
CHADWICK, N. K., *The Beginnings of Russian History* (Cambridge, 1946).
CHIZHEVSKY (TSCHIZEVSKY), D., *Altrussische Literaturgeschichte* (Frankfurt-am-Main, 1948).
DEGEN-KOVALEVSKY, B. E., 'K istorii zheleznogo proizvodstva Zakavkazia', *IGAIMK*, cxx (1935), 238–418.
DJAPARIDZE, D., *Mediaeval Slavic Manuscripts: A Bibliography of Printed Catalogues* (Cambridge, Mass., 1957).
Drevniaia Rus' (Po sledam drevnikh kultur), (Moscow, 1953).
DUMÉZIL, G., *Légendes sur les Nartes* (Paris, 1930).
DUNLOP, D. M., *The History of the Jewish Khazars* (Princeton, 1954).
DVORNIK, F., *Les Légendes de Constantin et de Méthode* (Prague, 1933).
—— *The Making of Central and Eastern Europe* (London, 1949).
—— *The Slavs: their Early History and Civilization* (Boston, 1956).
DZANTY, D., 'L'Empire des Oss-Alanes', *Oss-Alanes*, 1953, i, 4–20; ii, 13–24; iii–iv, 6–42; 1954, i–ii (Nos. 5–6 of the series), 35–47.
EBERT, M., *Reallexikon der Vorgeschichte*, 15 vols. (Berlin, 1924–32).
—— *Südrußland im Altertum* (Bonn and Leipzig, 1921).
EFIMENKO, P. P., and P. N. TRETIAKOV, 'Drevnerusskie poseleniia na Donu', *MIAS*, viii (1948).
ELIADE, M., *Le Chamanisme* (Paris, 1951).
EVREINOV, N. N., *Istoriia russkogo teatra* (New York, 1955).
FERDINANDY, M., DE, *Ahnen und Schicksal* (München, 1955).
—— 'Almos', *Südosteuropäische Arbeiten*, No. 47 (München, 1957), pp. 35–112.
—— 'Clariores Genere', i–ii, *Anales de Historia Antigua y Medieval*, 1953, pp. 14–30; 1954, pp. 5–54.
—— *A Kettőskirályság* (Budapest, 1941).
—— 'Die nordeurasischen Reitervölker und der Westen bis zum Mongolensturm', *Historia Mundi*, v (1956), 175–223.
—— 'El paisaje mítico', *Anales de Arqueología y Etnología*, Universidad Nacional de Cuyo, ix (1948), 179–279.

FIELD, H., 'Contributions to the Anthropology of the Caucasus', *Papers of Peabody Museum of American Archaeology and Ethnology*, xlviii, No. 1 (1953).

FILOV, B. D., *Starobŭlgarskoto izkustvo* (Sofia, 1924).

FINDEISEN (FINDEIZEN), N., *Ocherki po istorii muzyki v Rossii*, i (Moscow and Leningrad, 1928).

GASTER, M., *Ilchester Lectures on Greco-Slavonic Literature* (London, 1887).

GOLUBINSKY, E. E., *Istoriia Russkoi tserkvi*, i (Moscow, 1903).

GRABAR, I., *Istoriia Russkogo iskusstva*, i (Moscow, n.d. [around 1912]; 2nd edn., Moscow, 1953).

GREKOV, B. D., *Kievskaia Rus'* (4th edn., Moscow and Leningrad, 1944).

—— *The Culture of Kievan Rus'* (Moscow, 1946).

GUDZY, N. K., *History of Early Russian Literature* (New York, 1949).

HAASE, F., *Folksglaube und Brauchtum der Ostslaven* (Breslau, 1939).

HARMATTA, J. 'The Golden Bow of the Huns', *AAAH*, i (1951).

—— 'Le Problème Cimmerien', reprint from *Archaeologiai Értesítö* (*c.* 1948).

—— 'Studies in the Language of the Iranian Tribes in South Russia', *MGT*, xxxi (1952).

—— 'Studies on the History of the Sarmatians', *MGT*, xxx (1950).

—— Das Volk der Sadagaren', *Biblioteca Orientalis Hungarica*, v (1942).

HAUSSIG, H. W., 'Theophylakts Exkurs über die Skythischen Völker' (extrait de *Byzantion*, xxiii) (Bruxelles, 1954).

HENSEL, W., *Słowiańszczyzna Wczesnośredniowieczna* (2nd edn., Warszawa, 1956).

HERZFELD, E., *Zoroaster and his World*, 2 vols. (Princeton, 1947).

HORN, G., *Arca Noae sive Historia imperiorum et regnorum a condito orbe ad nostra tempora* (Lugdunum Batavorum, 1666).

HROZNÝ, B., *Histoire de l'Asie Antérieure, de l'Inde et de la Crète depuis les origines jusqu'au début de second millénaire* (Paris, 1947).

HRUSHEVSKY (GRUSHEVSKY), M., *Istoriia Ukrainy-Rusi*, i (2nd edn., Lvov, 1904).

IAKUBINSKY, L. P., *Istoriia drevnerusskogo iazyka* (Moscow, 1953).

Istoriia Kultury Drevnei Rusi, ed. by B. D. Grekov and M. I. Artamonov, 2 vols. (Moscow and Leningrad, 1948–51).

IUSHKOV, S. V., *Ustav Kniazia Vladimira* (Novouzensk, 1926).

JAKOBSON, R., *Slavic Languages* (New York, 1955).

—— 'Slavic Mythology', *Funk and Wagnells Standard Dictionary of Folklore*, ii (1950), 1025–8.

—— 'Studies in Comparative Slavic Metrics', *OSP*, iii (1952), 21–66.

—— 'Vestiges of the Earliest Russian Vernacular', *Slavic World*, vol. viii, No. v (1952).

—— 'The Vseslav Epos', *Russian Epic Studies* (Philadelphia, 1949), pp. 13–86.

—— J. BESHAROV, and H. A. WOLFSON, 'An Old Russian Treatise on the Divine and Human Word', *St. Vladimir's Seminary Quarterly*, Summer 1956, pp. 45–50.

JUNG, C. G., and C. KERÉNYI, *Essays on a Science of Mythology* (New York, 1946).

KALMYKOV, A. D., 'Iranians and Slavs in South Russia', *JAOS*, xlv (1925), 68–71.

KASTALSKY, A., *Osobennosti narodno-russkoi muzykalnoi sistemy* (Moscow and Petrograd, 1923).

KENDRICK, T. D., *A History of the Vikings* (London, 1930).

KIPARSKY, V., *Die gemeinslawischen Lehnwörter aus dem Germanischen* (Helsinki, 1934).

KOCH, H., 'Byzanz, Ochrid und Kiev, 987–1037', *Kyrios*, iii (Berlin, 1938).

KONDAKOV, N. P., *Ocherki i zametki po istorii srednevekovogo iskusstva i kultury* (Prague, 1929).

—— *Russkie drevnosti. See* Tolstoy and Kondakov.

—— *Russkie Klady*, i (St. Petersburg, 1896).

KOTWICZ, W., 'O rolę ludów koczowniczych w historyi', *Pamiętnik IV Zjazdu historyków polskich* (Poznań, 1925).

KRUSE, F., *Chronicon Nortmannorum* (Hamburg and Gotha, 1851).

KUNIK, E., *Die Berufung der schwedischen Rodsen durch die Finnen und Slaven* (St. Petersburg, 1844).

KUNST, J., 'Cultural Relations between the Balkans and Indonesia', *Royal Tropical Institute, Mededeling CVII, Afdeling Culturele en Physische Anthropologie*, No. 47 (Amsterdam, 1954).

LÉGER, L., *La Mythologie Slave* (Paris, 1901).

LEHR-SPŁAWIŃSKI, T., *O pochodzeniu i praojczyzne Słowian* (Poznań, 1946).

LEWICKI, T., 'Obrzędy pogrzebowe pogańskich Słowian w opisach podroźników i pisarzy arabskich głównie z IX–X w.', *Archaeologia*, v (1952–3) (published in 1955), 122–54; French and Russian resumés, 437–8.

LIKHACHEV, D. S., *Russkie letopisi* (Moscow and Leningrad, 1947).

LINEVA, E., *Velikorusskie pesni v narodnoi garmonizatsii*, i–ii (St. Petersburg, 1904–9).

LOZINSKI, B.Ph., 'Le lieu d'origine des Huns', *Anales de Historia Antigua y Medieval*, 1953, 90–111.

—— 'The Original Homeland of the Parthians' (forthcoming in *Central Asiatic Journal*).

—— 'A Workshop of Medieval Jewelry' (not yet published).

MACARTNEY, C. A., *The Magyars in the Ninth Century* (Cambridge, 1930).

MARQUART (MARKWART), J., *Osteuropäische und Ostasiatische Streifzüge* (Leipzig, 1903).

MAYANI, Z., *Les Hyksos et le monde de la Bible* (Paris, 1956).

MIKUCKI, S., *Études sur la diplomatique russe la plus ancienne* (Cracovie, 1953).

MILLER, O. F., *Opyt istoricheskogo obozreniia Russkoi Slovesnosti*, Part I, fasc. 1 (2nd edn., St. Petersburg, 1865).

MILLER, V. F., 'Osetinskie etiudy, part III', *Moscow, Universitet, Uchenye Zapiski, Otdel Istoriko-Filologicheskii*, viii (1887).

MINNS, E. H., *The Art of the Northern Nomads* (London, 1942).

—— *Scythians and Greeks* (Cambridge, 1913).

MINORSKY, V. F., 'Rus', *EI*, iii (1936), 1181–3.

MORAVCSIK, Gy., 'Zur Geschichte der Onoguren', *Ungarische Jahrbücher*, x (1930), 53–90. *See also* Sources.

MOSZYŃSKI, K., 'Badania nad pochodzeniem i pierwotną kulturą Słowian', *Polska Akademja Umiejętności, Wydzial Filol.*, *Rozprawy*, lxii, No. 2 (1925).

MUTAFČIEV, P., *Istoriia na Bŭlgarskiia narod*, i (Sofia, 1943).

NIEDERLE, L., *Slovanské Starožitnosti*, 4 vols. (Prague, 1906–27).

—— *Život starých Slovenů*, 3 vols. (Prague, 1911–34).

—— *Manuel de l'antiquité Slave*, 2 vols. (Paris, 1923–6).

—— *Slavianskie drevnosti*, A. L. Mongait, ed., preface by P. N. Tretiakov (Moscow, 1957).

NIKITINE, B., *Les Kurdes* (Paris, 1956).

NIKOLSKY, N. K., 'K voprosu o Russkikh pismenach', *Akademiia Nauk, Izvestiia po russkomu iazyku i slovesnosti*, i (1928), 1–37.

NYBERG, H. S., 'Die Religionen des Alten Iran', *MVAG*, xliii (1938).

OBOLENSKY, D., *The Bogomils* (Cambridge, 1948).

Oss-Alanes, D. DZANTY, ed. (Institut d'Ossétologie, Clamart, Seine, France), Nos. 1–6 (1953–4).

OSTROGORSKY, G., *Geschichte des byzantinischen Staates* (München, 1940); English transl., *History of the Byzantine State* (New Brunswick, New Jersey, 1957).

PIGULEVSKAIA, N. V., 'Imia Rus v siriiskom istochnike VI veka', *Sbornik*, in honour of B. D. Grekov (Moscow, 1952), pp. 42–48.

PIOTROVSKY, B. B., 'New Contribution to the Study of Ancient Civilizations in the *USSR*', *Reports of the Soviet Delegation at the X Intern. Congress of Hist. Science in Rome* (Moscow, 1955).

—— P. N. SCHULTZ et V. A. GOLOVKINA, S. P. TOLSTOV, *Ourartou, Neapolis des Scythes, Kharezm* (Paris, n.d.).

POZNANSKY, N., *Zagovory* (Petrograd, 1917).

PRISELKOV, M. D., *Ocherki po tserkovno-politicheskoi istorii Kievskoi Rusi* (St. Petersburg, 1913).

PRITSAK, O., *Die bulgarische Fürstenliste* (Wiesbaden, 1955).

RALSTON, W. R. S., *The Songs of the Russian People, as illustrative of Slavonic Mythology and Russian Social Life* (London, 1872).

RAST, N. A., 'Les Alains dans la littérature, la poésie et la langue Persanes' (not yet published).

—— *Origin of Persian Personal Pronouns* (in Persian) (Tehran, 1955).

—— 'Russians in the Medieval Iranian Epos', *ASEER*, xiv (1955), 260–4.

RICE T., *The Scythians* (New York, 1957).

ROSTOVTZEFF, M., *The Animal Style in South Russia and China* (Princeton, 1924).

—— *Le Centre de l'Asie, la Russie, la Chine et le style animal* (Prague, 1929).

—— *Iranians and Greeks in South Russia* (Oxford, 1922).

RUDENKO, S. I., *Kultura naseleniia Gornogo Altaiia v Skifskoe vremia* (Moscow, 1953).

RYBAKOV, B. A., 'Drevnie Rusy', *Sovetskaia Arkheologiia* (1953).

—— 'La formation de la Russie de Kiev' (*Rapports de la délégation Sovietique au Xe Congrès Intern. des Sciences Historiques à Rome*) (Moscow, 1955).

RYBAKOV, B. A., *Remeslo drevnei Rusi* (Moscow, 1948).

SALMONY, A., *Antler and Tongue* (Ascona, Switzerland, 1954).
SAVICKÝ (SAVITSKY), P. N., 'O zadachakh kochevnikovedeniia', Supplement to N. P. Toll, *Skify i Gunny* (Prague, 1928).
SCHMAUS, ALOIS, 'Zur altslawischen Religionsgeschichte', *Saeculum*, iv (1953), 206–30 [a survey of problems and literature].
SEDOV, V. V., 'Drevnerusskoe iazycheskoe sviatilishche v Peryni', *KS*, l (1953), 92–103.
SHAKHMATOV, A. A., *Drevneishie sudby Russkogo plemeni* (Petrograd, 1919).
—— *Povest' Vremennykh Let* (Petrograd, 1916).
—— *Razyskaniia o sostave drevneishikh letopisnykh svodov* (St. Petersburg, 1908).
SHEVELOV, G. Y., 'On the Slavic names for the Falls of Dnieper', *Slavic Word*, xi (1956), 503–30.
SINOR, D., 'Autour d'une migration des peuples au Vme siècle'. Extrait du *Journal Asiatique*, 1946–7.
SMIRNOV, A. P., 'Ocherki drevnei i srednevekovoi istorii narodov Srednego Povolzhia i Prikamia', *MIAS*, xxviii (1952).
SMIRNOV, P. P., *Volzkyi shliakh i starodavni Rusi* (Kiev, 1928).
STENDER-PETERSON, AD., *Varangica* (Aarhus, 1953).
STRZYGOWSKI, J., *Die altslavische Kunst* (Augsburg, 1929).
SULIMIRSKI, T., 'Scythian Antiquities in Western Asia', *Artibus Asiae*, xvii (1954), 282–318.
SZYSZMAN, S., 'Les Khazars. Problèmes et controverses,' *Revue de l'Histoire des religions*, 152 (1957), 174–221.
ŠAFARIK, P. J., *Slavische Alterthümer*, 2 vols. (Leipzig, 1843–4).

TALLGREN, A. M., *L'Orient et l'Occident dans l'âge du fer finno-ougrien* (Helsinki, 1924).
TAUBE, BARON M. DE, 'Nouvelles recherches sur l'histoire politique et religieuse de l'Europe Orientale à l'époque de la formation de l'État Russe', *Istina*, 1957, No. 1, 9–32 (to be continued).
—— *Rome et la Russie avant l'Invasion des Tatars, I. Le prince Askold, l'origine de l'état de Kiev et la première conversion des Russes* (Paris, 1947).
THIEME, PAUL, 'Mitra and Aryaman', *Transactions of the Connecticut Academy of Arts and Sciences*, xli (1957), pp. 1–96.
TOLL, N. P., *Skify i Gunny* (Prague, 1928).
TOLSTOV, S. P., *Drevnii Khorezm* (Moscow, 1948).
—— *Po sledam drevnekhorezmiiskoi tsivilizatsii* (Moscow, 1948).
TOLSTOY, COUNT I. I., and N. P. KONDAKOV, *Russkie drevnosti*, 6 vols. (St. Petersburg, 1889–99).
THOMSON, V., *The Relations between Ancient Russia and Scandinavia and the Origin of the Russian State* (Oxford and London, 1887).
TRETIAKOV, P. N., 'K istorii plemen verkhnego Povolzhia v pervom tysiacheletii n.e.', *MIAS*, v (1941).
TRUBETSKOY, PRINCE N. S., *K istorii russkogo samopoznaniia* (Prague, 1927). Abridged English transl., *The Common Slavic Element in Russian Culture* (New York, 1951).

Vasiliev, A. A., *The Goths in the Crimea* (Cambridge, Mass., 1936).
—— *History of the Byzantine Empire* (Madison, Wis., 1952).
—— *The Russian Attack on Constantinople in 860* (Cambridge, Mass., 1946).
—— *The Second Russian Attack on Constantinople*, Dumbarton Oaks Papers, 6 (Cambridge, Mass., 1951).
Vasilievsky, V. G., *Trudy*, i–iii (St. Petersburg, 1908–15).
Vasmer, M., *Die Iranier in Südrußland* (Leipzig, 1923).
—— 'Wikingerspuren in Russland', *Sitzungsber. d. Preuß. Akad. d. Wiss., Philos.-hist. Kl.*, xxiv (1931).
Vernadsky, G., *Ancient Russia* (New Haven, 1943).
—— 'Das frühe Slawentum. Das Ostslawentum bis zum Mongolensturm', *Historia Mundi*, v (1956), 251–300.
—— *Kievan Russia* (New Haven, 1948).
—— 'Lebedia', *Südosteuropäische Arbeiten*, No. 47 (München, 1957), pp. 9–31.
—— *Medieval Russian Laws* (New York, 1947).
—— *The Mongols and Russia* (New Haven, 1953).
—— 'The Origin of the name Rus"', *Südost-Forschungen*, xv (1956).
—— 'The Riddle of the Gothi-Tetraxitae', *Südost-Forschungen*, xi (1952), 281–3.
—— 'Der sarmatische Hintergrund der germanischen Völkerwanderung', *Saeculum*, ii (1951), 340–92.
—— 'The Status of the Russian Church during the First Half-Century following Vladimir's Conversion', *SEER*, xx (1941), 294–314.
—— 'Svantovit, dieu des Slaves Baltiques', *Annuaire*, vii (1944), 341–56.
—— 'Toxar, t′ma, T′mutorokan', in *For Roman Jakobson* (The Hague, 1956), pp. 588–91.
Vladimirskii Sbornik (Belgrade, 1938).
Voprosy Skifo-Sarmatskoi Arkheologii (Moscow, 1954).
Vsevolodsky (Gerngross), V., *Istoriia russkogo teatra*, i (Leningrad and Moscow, 1929).
Ward, Grace, F., The English Danegeld in Relation to the Russian Dan", *ASEER*, xiii (3) (1954), 299–318.
—— 'The Jomsvikings, (MS.). Part of it published under the title 'Jomsburg brethren in England', *Scandinavian Studies*, xxviii (1956), 135–41.
Zaehner, R. C., *Zurvan: a Zoroastrian Dilemma* (Oxford, 1955).
Zelenin, D., *Kult ongonov v Sibiri* (Moscow and Leningrad, 1936). French edition, *Le culte des idoles en Sibérie* (Paris, 1952).
—— *Russische (Ostslawische) Volkskunde* (Berlin and Leipzig, 1927).
Zeuss, K., *Die Deutschen und die Nachbarstämme* (München, 1837; reimpression, Heidelberg, 1925).
Zlatarski, V., *Istoriia na Bŭlgarskata Država*, i. 1–2 (Sofia, 1918–27).

INDEX